Food and Friends

Also by Simone Beck

Simca's Cuisine

More Recipes from Simca's Cuisine

Mastering the Art of French Cooking
Volume 1
(with Julia Child and Louisette Bertholle)

Mastering the Art of French Cooking
Volume 2
(with Julia Child)

FOOD

+

AND

+

FRIENDS

*Recipes and Memories
from Simca's Cuisine*

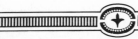

SIMONE "SIMCA" BECK

with

Suzanne Patterson

+ +

Introduction by Julia Child

Illustrations by Paul Grimes

VIKING

$\mathscr{V}$IKING

Published by the Penguin Group
Viking Penguin, a division of Penguin Books USA Inc.,
375 Hudson Street, New York, New York 10014, U.S.A.
Penguin Books Ltd, 27 Wrights Lane, London W8 5TZ, England
Penguin Books Australia Ltd, Ringwood, Victoria, Australia
Penguin Books Canada Ltd, 10 Alcorn Avenue, Suite 300, Toronto, Ontario, Canada M4V 3B2
Penguin Books (N.Z.) Ltd, 182–190 Wairau Road, Auckland 10, New Zealand

Penguin Books Ltd, Registered Offices: Harmondsworth, Middlesex, England

First published in 1991 by Viking Penguin, a division of Penguin Books USA Inc.

1 3 5 7 9 10 8 6 4 2

Copyright © Simone Beck and Suzanne Patterson, 1991
Introduction copyright © Julia Child, 1991
Line illustrations copyright © Paul Grimes, 1991
All rights reserved

Photographs from Ms. Beck's collection

LIBRARY OF CONGRESS CATALOGING IN PUBLICATION DATA
Beck, Simone.
Food and friends : Recipes and Memories from Simca's Cuisine / Simone "Simca" Beck
with Suzanne Patterson.
p. cm.
ISBN 0–670–83934–5
1. Beck, Simone. 2. Cooks—France—Biography. 3. Cookery,
French. I. Patterson, Suzanne. II. Title. III. Title: Food and friends.
TX649.B44S56 1991
641.5944′092—dc20   90-50754 [B]

Printed in the United States of America
Set in Fournier, Antique Solid, and Snell Roundhand
Designed by Amy Hill

To my husband
Jean Victor Fischbacher,
1907–1986

CONTENTS

ACKNOWLEDGMENTS

I WOULD NEVER HAVE DREAMED of writing the story of my life, much less accomplished it, had it not been for the love and encouragement of my dear husband, Jean Fischbacher. The original suggestion came from an American friend, Jane Molard, who found my stories interesting enough to start recording and transcribing them.

The task finally involved digging back into over seventy years of my past to tell my story, including recipes related to the various periods and episodes, with the addition of many new recipes.

There are many people to thank for their help in jogging my memory, not the least of them my dear American "sister," sometime neighbor and partner, always cherished friend, Julia Child. Without her, I might never have had such a successful career in America.

Also, Richard Olney: gourmet, culinary intellectual, and cook par excellence, whose friendship and advice I've valued through the years.

My friend Peter Kump, a booster throughout the book with his advice and good cheer; and who found Jean Kytt Marcus, to whom I am grateful for organizing the testing and editing of my recipes for the American audience. Thanks also to Jean's many testers: Sheron L. Andrews, Dari R. Birnel, Carol H. Black, Flo Bradford, Geraldine Palmer Borell, Margene Brink, Julie Brumlik, Carol Caldwell, Sandra Lee Church, Louise Clement, Stephanie Curtis, Sandy Duch, Bennie Sue Dupy, Steve Frappoli, Joy H. Horstmann, Linda Taylor Howitt, Carmela Ingrao, Harry R. Jacobs, Marjorie Jacobs, Lola Lea, Priscilla Lundin, Barry Marcus, Jean Kytt Marcus, Terry Marcus, Paul D. Mesenheimer, Alice B. Montis, Nancy Neble, Sue Pflugfelder, Diana Pinover, Judy Retensky, Linda Schechter, Alfred M. Serex, Alex Sheerar, Robin Stiebel, Pam Thomas, and Catherine von Lengerke.

I am very grateful to our editors at Viking Penguin: Amanda Vaill, a passionate food lover and new friend at Bramafam, and Beena Kamlani; designer Amy Hill; jacket designer Neil Stuart.

And, of course, my dear friend Paul Grimes, whose inspired sketches illuminate this book.

Also, John Ferrone, for his invaluable editorial suggestions; my bright young friend Susy Davidson and many, many others.

Last but not least, thanks to my coauthor and scribe, Suzy Patterson. She was able to draw out of me a sort of explosion of thoughts and memories and to express them in English better than I could have done myself. By the end, I think she really understood.

—*Simone Beck*

THANKS FIRST TO SIMCA, for her hospitality and patience as we worked (and laughed, and cried, and dined together) in preparing the book. For many years I've loved France and French cooking, and this was a wonderful opportunity to experience Simca's story, as I "climbed into her shoes" to write it.

My warm thanks to those listed by Simca above.

Especially to Julia, whose idea it was to bring me into the project, and who was never too busy to help by phone or letter.

I am also very grateful to Mary Bishop, who gave me excellent editorial suggestions, and to Cynthia Verdow for her help in word processing, typing, and editing.

—*Suzy Patterson*

INTRODUCTION

WHAT A PLEASURE AND AN HONOR to write a few words of introduction to Simca's new book—the very essence of *la bonne cuisine française;* as well as a few words about Simca herself—the very essence of La Belle France. She has been teacher and ambassador of French taste and culture to so many of us in this country, including myself, that it is a delight to have a book that tells about her life and times as well as giving us new recipes and menus for our own kitchens.

Simca is my dear friend and colleague of forty years, my French sister. We met in early 1949, when I was studying at Le Cordon Bleu in Paris, while my husband, Paul, was with the U.S. Information Service at the American Embassy. I had fallen hopelessly in love with French food at, literally, the first bite, and as soon as we were settled I enrolled myself as a student in that famous cookery school. Fortunately, since I wanted to learn as much as I could as fast as I could, I was able to take the professional course with a group of young World War II veterans who were studying under the G.I. Bill of Rights.

We started at seven in the morning and cooked madly, with our wonderful old chef, Max Bugnard, until eleven. Then I rushed home to cook lunch for Paul—those were the lovely days of the French two-hour lunch—and trotted back to attend the afternoon demonstrations, either of pastry, with Chef Claude Thilmond, or of cookery, with Chef Pierre Mangelatte. Days of passionate cooking and learning they were, and utterly absorbing.

None of our American colleagues, however, had the slightest enthusiasm about cooking, and the French friends we were beginning to meet, although knowledgeable indeed about eating, had no interest at all in the kitchen. One evening I was complaining to a well-connected embassy friend about having nobody in my immediate circle with whom to share my enthusiasm; she shortly arranged that Paul and I should meet her marvelous French friend Simca, an accomplished and active cook. It was an immediate take.

Simca was then in her early forties, a tall blonde with a remarkably vivid pink-and-white complexion; she was good-looking and dashing in a most attractive and debonair way, full of vigor, humor, and warmth. She had been fascinated by the art of cuisine since her girlhood in Normandy, had attended classes in Paris with the famous Henri-Paul Pellaprat in the early days of Le Cordon Bleu, and was one of the most active younger members of Le Cercle des Gourmettes, the French ladies' gastronomical club. Her husband, Jean Fischbacher, of Alsatian background, had spent his early years in Paris, had been a captain in the French army during World War II, was captured after the fall of the Maginot Line and remained a prisoner of war for four long years. The Fischbachers lived in Paris but spent time at his family's country home in Chinon, as well as at her mother's homes, both in Normandy and in the south of France. Thus they knew their native country well. What good fortune for Paul and me, foreigners, to meet them and to share their lives as though we were family.

Simca introduced me to Le Cercle des Gourmettes, who met every other Tuesday in the kitchens of Le Gaz de France—the gas company—to prepare themselves a magnificent lunch under the tutelage of a professional chef. The original members of Le Cercle, which had been formed in the late 1920s, were French ladies now in their seventies and eighties, and they came only in time for apéritifs just before lunch. Simca and I, and Louisette Bertholle, who later became our collaborator, arrived promptly at 9:00 A.M. to help out and, of course, to have our own private lesson with the chef. That was the beginning of my really French gastronomical education.

Shortly after joining Les Gourmettes, I was asked by some American friends who knew of my activities to give them cooking lessons. I felt far from adequate, but since both Simca and Louisette had long been active in the kitchen and were indeed at that moment collaborating on a book of French cooking for Americans, I asked their opinion. "Well," said Simca in her forthright way, "why not?" Louisette agreed. Why not, indeed? Two days later we inaugurated l'École des Trois Gourmandes—the school of the three hearty eaters—in the reasonably roomy kitchen of our apartment on the Rue de l'Université.

One of the best ways to learn is to teach, I certainly found, and Simca was a wonderful teacher, not only to our students but to me. My schooling had given me the basics, but Simca gave me the finesse, enlarged my culinary vocabulary, and imbued me with the French attitude about food. Both Simca and Louisette, and the chefs with whom we worked, took their craft with utter seriousness, as a beautiful, marvelous, and creative art form—but an art form with rules. It was that attitude, really, that drew me irresistibly to the profession.

Some months after our school began, I was happy to learn that there was no American collaborator for Louisette and Simca's book, and I was delighted to join the team. *Mastering the Art of French Cooking,* Volume I, slowly evolved over the next ten years, as a result of our joint conceptions of teaching. In the meantime, Paul and I had moved to Marseille, then to Germany and Norway, and finally back to America; the school was held for ten years in Louisette's kitchen on the Boulevard Victor Hugo.

Simca and her husband, as you will learn in these pages, moved from Paris to their property in the south of France, and every summer she has conducted cooking classes there. This is her third book, the first two being *Simca's Cuisine* and *New Menus from Simca's Cuisine.*

Simca's cooking is full of imagination and verve, as well as being backed by the many years in her own kitchen and her years of teaching. What makes her recipes so important for us in this country is that they are thoroughly and genuinely in the French spirit, yet because she knows America and has taught several generations of Americans, they are completely do-able here. Hers is home cooking of the finest sort—*la bonne cuisine bourgeoise,* which is really the basis for all good French food.

Here, then, is Simca's new book, for all of us to enjoy and to cook by.

—*Julia Child*

Part One

A MEMOIR

+

WITH

+

RECIPES

MY FIRST CUISINE

I NEARLY FELL INTO THE SAUCEPAN at seven years old, when I stood up on a stool, stuck my nose well into the pan, and was riveted by what was going on there.

The year was 1911, and this was my first "cooking lesson," taken on the sly, with Zulma, our family cook. In our staffed kitchen in Normandy, children were not meant to be seen, heard, or catered to. They were supposed to be playing proper games or doing lessons with Nanny.

Our English nanny, Frances, was going crazy. I can still hear her: "Simone! Where are you? You must come out of hiding this instant, or I'll put you in the closet."

Zulma and I giggled in our conspiracy. But I was learning one of the basics of cooking, how to make a roux, the first element of so many sauces. The slow transformation of fat and flour simmering together fascinated me. Or maybe it was just the tantalizing smell; I was already quite a *gourmande*. Zulma was explaining that her brown roux would be combined with some stock from yesterday's pot-au-feu, red wine, and, finally, seared pieces of meat—to simmer slowly until the ingredients melded together into a boeuf bourguignon. At least I think that's what she was talking about. Many years later, when I had become a professional cooking teacher, I often conjured up visions of Zulma as I taught that basic, classic roux to others.

Zulma was bustling, small, round, and sturdy—a no-nonsense Norman peasant woman who had grown up near our house in Rainfreville, about ten miles from the English Channel, not far from the city of Dieppe and the beach at Quiberville.

In the background were my mother and father, Madeleine and Maurice Beck, and my older brother, Maurice Eric, my mainstays of love and security. But Zulma was special to me at this precise moment.

As the ardent young pupil, I must have been a sight, the steaming stove making my blond hair damp and curly and my cheeks pink, with a few grease spots spattering my patent-leather Mary Jane shoes.

"Look here, Mademoiselle Simone," she was telling me. "You have to stir this flour and butter for a while to make your brown roux, which will be excellent for cooking the meat."

When Nanny Frances, a young woman with brown hair that tended to come undone in moments of stress, got dangerously close, I ran to hide under the kitchen tablecloth. She later found me in the garden. "You reek of grease, young lady," she scolded. She knew what I had been doing in that forbidden territory, the kitchen, and she propelled me to the bathroom for a proper wash.

Nanny did not punish me, as she had threatened. Our family was proper and strict, but I can remember no physical punishment, except for being shut in my father's wardrobe closet by Nanny. Once I objected violently, stuck my thumb in the door as it was being closed, and tore my nail right off. But Nanny was basically kind; she patiently taught me English very young, and for that I am eternally grateful.

Zulma had a lifelong influence on me that was even more important than knowing English. She was gifted with an almost atavistic sense of how to cook, how to use food, how to prepare it in ways that make it both delicious and healthy.

Under her tutelage, I got a physical grasp of how to deal with food. "Your hands might be too hot," she would observe later, if I was perspiring in summer trying to make a pastry dough. You need cool, cool hands for pastry. These country cooks seem to know it instinctively. The rest of us have to learn it. Zulma had such patience and strength; they just don't make them like her anymore. She used to beat egg whites for soufflés up to great white mounds using two forks. We didn't have any whisks, at least not the solid balloon types I use today.

Our kitchen was undoubtedly technologically advanced for the time. It had a coal-burning oven in the beautiful flat iron-topped stove with a hood that one usually sees only in historical houses these days. Most people then were burning wood, but a coal mine nearby was furnishing my father's factory with fuel, and we used that coal.

As for the boeuf bourguignon Zulma was making that day in 1911, I did not even taste the final result. My brother and I were usually forbidden any dish with wine or spirits.

Faithful and solid Zulma kept giving me cooking hints in spare moments until I was nineteen. From her I gleaned the basics that most people nowadays spend money and time at cooking schools to learn—how to make short pastry, good desserts, sauce bases, and much more.

But of an equal influence on my taste was my family background.

On both sides of the family, the roots were Norman. My mother did not cook, but she was an administrator who knew how to deal with people to get the best of food and service. My father had good taste and a superb eye for what was beautiful.

Born Madeleine Marie Gabrielle Le Grand in 1875 at Fécamp, my mother was the thirteenth in a family of sixteen children, but she was the first child of my grandmother, who was the second wife of Alexandre Le Grand. A widower, he was left with twelve out of fifteen children when he met my grandmother. Infant mortality rates were high, but families were very big, perhaps to compensate.

Marie-Louise Gabrielle Dubosc had been only twenty when she married my widowed grandfather in Fécamp, and his older children were roughly my grandmother's own age. But I don't believe they accepted her as a peer. I think they shunned her politely, or impolitely, and this must have been hard on her.

Originally a wine *négociant,* or wholesale dealer, my grandfather Le Grand started making Bénédictine and thus quite a lot of money, thanks to a chance discovery.

One day he opened an old family trunk he had picked up along with other antiques in a shop some time before. "What's this?" he wondered, ferreting out some ancient, crumbling papers. And he deciphered what was written there—a secret formula for the strong cordial invented by Benedictine monks centuries ago.

Nobody else was making this sweet, strong cordial, so my grandfather, seeing a good business opportunity, started to manufacture and market it, in 1870 launching Bénédictine from his modest factory in Fécamp. But in 1880 (five years after my mother was born), a couple of pyromaniacs set it on fire, and it burned to the ground. My grandfather decided to reconstruct it as a grandiose showplace that looked more like a pompous post-Gothic church—stained-glass windows and all— or perhaps a mad château, than a factory. It still stands today, complete with staircase of honor, museum, etc., as a monument to my grandfather's enthusiasm and his rather flamboyant taste in architecture.

The Le Grand family owned the business, which was passed down to each living eldest son in succession, until 1989, when it was bought by Martini and Rossi, the saddening fate of so many smaller family businesses today. Still, I often use Bénédictine in desserts or as a cordial if a guest wishes to sample it.

A Benedictine nunnery was founded in Fécamp in the year 658, and two centuries later, a monastery was built. It became a venue both royal and noble under Robert the Magnificent and his bastard son, William the Conqueror, who commissioned very grand buildings. Around 1510, a resident monk from Venice, Don Bernardo Vincelli, created an elixir from twenty-seven local and exotic plants and spices. The monks developed a brisk trade with their cordial, but the revolution of 1789 put an end to the monastery, which was reduced to a ruin, and the liqueur and its formula disappeared.

However, my grandfather Alexandre became passionately interested in archae- ology, including the monastic treasures, buying up whatever he could find. And then came the day in 1863 when he opened the trunk and discovered the "recipe." With its heady, sweet qualities, it became perhaps more popular abroad than in France, especially when promoted by Alexandre Le Grand, who had excellent com- mercial sense. Americans were particularly keen on the cordial.

Today over 100,000 visitors a year roam through the Bénédictine factory and museum—appreciating not only the vaulted rooms full of the old copper utensils that were used until 1974 in Bénédictine production, but also the herbs that go into the aromatic recipe; you can really smell the lavender, thyme, cardamom, juniper, vanilla, etc., as displayed in their jute sacks. The same room has several cases that attest to Bénédictine's popularity, displaying about six hundred bottles of imitation stuff from all over the world. And the fabulous medieval art collection, which is still growing, could be "worth the trip," as the Michelin guide would say, for lovers of fifteenth- to eighteenth-century religious art.

The first child of my grandfather's young bride, my mother, Madeleine, was the new and adored baby of this privileged family in the late 1870s—a beautiful little hazel-eyed blonde, who was spoiled by her parents and became headstrong and willful.

She spent many holidays down on the Riviera in a house her father built for her when she was very young: the Villa Saint-Michel on La Croisette, the beachfront promenade of Cannes. Like the properties of others in her set—dare I say class?—hers had a stable, a coach house, and a garden, with all the servants necessary to keep this up. My mother, much as I loved and admired her for her courage later on, was always distant, sometimes imperious, with servants, who she'd been taught were in a world apart from hers. In fact, her small villa had a little tower staircase for servants so that she would not have to see them.

My mother's first marriage, at age eighteen, was tragic, for it ended with the death of her equally young husband six months later in a tuberculosis sanatorium in Switzerland. He knew he was ill, but they went ahead with the marriage anyway.

Maman went into deep mourning and quasi-seclusion. But finally, thanks to a priest's advice a few years later, she took off the widow's veils and began to lead a normal life.

One of her brothers, René, brought home Maurice-Jules Joseph Beck, an army pal and fellow soldier, also from Normandy, and a romance bloomed. In 1900, when Mother was twenty-five, they married, at about the same time selling her villa on La Croisette. It was later torn down and replaced by the first Palais des Festivals, the hub of the annual Cannes Film Festival. They used a large part of this money to build a big house at Rainfreville, on the site of a farm that our Beck family already owned.

Rainfreville

MY PARENTS BUILT THE ROOMY and comfortable family house, called in France a *maison bourgeoise,* a kind of small château. This is where I grew up and later spent months at various times, especially during the German occupation of 1940–45.

It was a handsome ruddy brick structure with towers and ornamental white trim, in the Norman-Edwardian style of the day. The property surrounding it was magnificent, with a large lawn and a rose garden, big beech and pine trees, and vast fields beyond.

My brother Maurice was born in 1901, and I was born July 7, 1904, in Tocqueville-en-Caux, baptized with a very long name, the custom in French families: Simone Suzanne Renée Madeleine. The family always called me Simone, a name I did not like much, though fortunately I was called Nonne or Monette for short. I became Simca much later, thanks to my second husband, Jean.

I was apparently given a few drops of Bénédictine when I was a newborn baby, about one day old. My parents told me that I screamed my head off, rather foolish considering how Bénédictine would help me out in later life, a source of income and even a commodity to barter for food in World War II. That drop of alcohol they gave me as an infant was in line with Norman tradition, usually a rite for baptismal days performed with the fiery Calvados, our Norman brandy made with apple juice.

My father, always the humanitarian, was terribly upset that farm women in Normandy were putting "Calva" drops into babies' bottles as a daily routine. Perhaps it was a kind of tranquilizer to stop the children from screaming while mothers were trying to get their chores done. He went around on a kind of crusade to dissuade people from such unhealthy practices—especially after he became mayor of Tocqueville-en-Caux, in 1910.

My first memories, of course, revolve around the warm nursery with its playroom, but the enormous attic later became an even better place to play, with rings on ropes to swing from and trunks full of old clothes that we weren't supposed to "mess around with" but often did.

Then there were the grown-up rooms: three main sitting rooms included the large salon with its grand piano, Directoire and Empire furnishings, and many other antiques and bibelots; the smaller salon, an array of flowers—flowered *toile de Jouy* fabric on the walls, flowered upholstery on the chairs; a *fumoir,* or smoking room. And my father had his study. The antiques were often chosen by my father, who had impeccable taste. They were paid for at what might be bargain prices today. But at that time it seemed a fortune, especially the ninety francs in gold paid for the fabulous Louis XVI marquetry backgammon table signed "Jacob" or another prestigious cabinetmaker's name. I don't think we ever played on it.

I can still recall the clean, varnished smell of the vast dining room, which could seat forty, with its long mahogany table and its chandelier, the fireplace faced in wood and old faïence, the four buffets for dishes and silver.

There was also a long billiards room, later converted into a comfortable, casual living room. My only vivid memory of that room was, at about age two, clutching one of the fat legs of the billiards table and throwing up! It was a humiliating moment of digestive rebellion—I must have been into some grown-ups' chocolate.

In the roomy upstairs there were eight main bedrooms, one bathroom, and a lavatory for the whole family, plus the servants' quarters.

Outdoors, I used to love to play in the *basse-cour,* the farmyard behind the kitchen, and especially to feed the chickens and rabbits, a little duty that I never minded. Gathering eggs took fierce concentration to avoid breakage. But I wasn't strong enough to milk the cows and knew nothing about how calves were born, as that usually happened in the middle of the night. Anyway, our family was so prudish, I wasn't supposed to know.

We had a greenhouse and an enormous number of rosebushes around the house, some of them quite rare, like one called Le Deuil de Madame Imbert (Mourning for Madame Imbert)—named for an unfortunate lady who lost all her money, I was told.

I remember sitting in the garden and imbibing that sweet, grassy fragrance of summer, with golden sun streaks filtering through the greenery. When I had learned to read, on warm days I'd take a book out there and spend hours reading or dreaming.

"School" was sessions with Nanny, who taught us the three R's. And a priest came to instruct us in Catechism—deadly dull or rather amusing, depending on the lesson.

In some ways I was strictly brought up, with admonitions or orders like: "Simone, time to say your prayers." "Please curtsy nicely to the visitors." "Don't bother Zulma." "Above all, don't *ever* talk about servants when they're within earshot!" But all in all, I had quite an idyllic childhood.

Ever since those golden years at Rainfreville, I've been at heart a country girl, enchanted with the seasons, the smells and colors of flowers, trees, grass. Although I've lived in Paris and enjoyed all the things it offers, I have almost always had a physical need to be far away from concrete, in a beautiful environment where seasonal changes dictate the rhythm of life rather than in a man-made, industrialized city setting.

The stables were also important in our family. My mother and father rode horseback a lot and well, and Maman was a very elegant *amazone,* or sidesaddle rider. But I must have been indifferent to the horsey life, because I didn't learn much about riding until I was nearly thirty.

People went out in carriages in those days and dressed up as for a fashion parade, to see and be seen, but we children were not often included, unless we "went on display."

When the motorcar came in, our family was the first in the area to have one, and how proud I was when Papa said, "Come, *ma petite fille,* and join me for a ride." I don't exactly remember what our first car was, but one can imagine. It was the crank-up style, made a lot of noise, emitted noxious, smoky fumes, and created a great stir. I often wonder if it ended up in a junkyard or made it into a car museum. I think we had two cars early on in the garage—a De Dion-Bouton and a Moto-Bloc. For motoring, my mother always wore a huge hat and a flowing scarf, like the one that strangled Isadora Duncan when it caught in the wheel.

My attractive, distinguished mother dressed with style, for car outings or otherwise. A headstrong, determined person, she encouraged my father to get on in business; so he started a garage in Dieppe and also sometimes organized "rallies" for the Michelin tire company, to encourage the nascent auto trade. Finally, taught by my father, I learned to drive myself.

My father, Maurice Beck, was an idol to me. Well over six feet tall, he was elegant and handsome. He was the child of an English-born mother and an Alsatian father, a brilliant engineer who had made some money by inventing a way of brushing wool that made it suitable for softer new tweeds, popular back in that Victorian era, as indeed they are now.

Papa had a long face with chiseled features and a mustache. He was warm and loving, and in spite of a natural diffidence, he was beloved by everyone from society ladies to children, dogs, and servants. He had learned English from his mother and wanted his own children to grow up bilingual, the reason for our English nanny.

Concerned with the less fortunate in life, Papa went out of his way to help others, whether they were peasants in need of medicine for an ailing child or Americans who could not speak French well enough to order in a French restaurant.

In 1910, encouraged and backed financially by my decisive mother, my father bought what was to become his main business—a factory manufacturing silicate powder for ceramic tiles. It was at Saint-Aubin-sur-Scie, sixteen kilometers (ten miles) from Rainfreville.

To make the powder, they started out with black pebbles from the Normandy beaches. In very high heat, the pebbles were baked and crushed into the white powder used in making tiles and enamel glazes for bathrooms. Even as a little girl, I found this process and the things you could do with heat fascinating.

My mother not only wanted my father to have an interesting job, she expected it to be rewarding, because she really did like things money could buy, from pretty clothes to household goods; and though she had money of her own, she never wanted to have to scrimp and save. My father used to tease her: "Madeleine, when it comes to money, my dear, you're just like a basketful of holes."

Our household at Rainfreville included a staff of about six servants. Cook Zulma had seven children, and one of them, Eugène, was quite bright, though shy and easily embarrassed. Somehow Mother and Zulma persuaded him to train as our butler. Maman followed him around until she could find no trace of dust on any piece of furniture or silver he'd cleaned.

Country boys and girls smelled terrible in those days; they didn't have much in the way of bathing facilities. So Maman taught Eugène not only how to clean but how to *be* clean and properly outfitted at all times.

He was so terrified when he began his first *services à table* that he perspired and shook. We quailed for him. Years later, he served at the genteel Saint-Cloud Golf Club, outside Paris, and was as suave as any waiter at the Ritz. He had learned to dress well, wear gloves, serve from the left, take off from the right. Our dining table always looked beautiful, with crystal, silver, and candles all in place, thanks to my mother's training.

We set our table the French way—with forks and spoons placed bottoms-up, which still astonishes newcomers to France. The reason for this is that the fancy family initials are placed on the underside of silverware. Also, French people find forks faced upward aggressive-looking. Through Eugène, via mother's teaching, I learned a lot about *élégance à table*. About the same time as I learned driving, at age fifteen or so, he did, too, and became our chauffeur.

Lunch was our big meal, for me a festive occasion featuring wickedly mouth-watering Norman specialties and ingredients. We ate healthy food like crudités, green vegetables, and melons out of the garden. Then, as now, apples were Normandy's pride. They went into everything from the world's most delicious and bubbly sweet or hard cider and tongue-burning Calvados to flans, or caramel-topped tarts. Our usual menus at home were well balanced and seasonal. Here is a typical one Zulma might have prepared:

Un bon déjeuner à Rainfreville

(A Hearty Lunch at Rainfreville)

Apéritif: Kir (dry white wine with Cassis)—for the adults

✦ *Le dôme rose*
Beetroot salad with apples and potatoes

✦ *Poulet de Varvannes à l'estragon et à la crème*
Chicken in tarragon cream sauce

Salade verte

Fromages variés

—

Bordeaux, Médoc, ou Cabernet Sauvignon (Napa Valley)

✦ *Le flan normand aux pommes*
Norman flan with apples

Le dôme rose

Beetroot Salad with Apples and Potatoes

—

For 6 to 8

½ lb. boiling potatoes
⅔ lb. red beets
7 oz. raw Golden Delicious apples

For marinade:
4 Tbsp. vegetable oil
1 Tbsp. olive oil
1 tsp. Dijon mustard
8½ Tbsp. red-wine vinegar
Salt and pepper

1 recipe Mock Mayonnaise with herbs
  (page 474)

For garnish:
1 tsp. minced fresh herbs: parsley,
  chives, basil

Special equipment needed:
A 3-cup mixing bowl

The day before serving, boil the unpeeled potatoes in water until tender, and let cool. Cook the beets in water in the oven, let cool, and peel. Cut the potatoes, beets, and apples into medium slices.

Prepare the marinade by placing all ingredients in a mixing bowl and blending thoroughly. Add the vegetables, apples, and seasoning, and mix well, turning the mixture over to ensure that everything is well coated. Let macerate 24 hours.

Prepare my special Mock Mayonnaise with herbs (page 474) and set aside. Stir the vegetable-apple mixture with a wooden spoon until it is uniformly red, then drain in a colander. Discard the marinade. Add enough mayonnaise to the potato mixture so that it sticks together, and mix well to blend. Pack into a round bowl and refrigerate until time to serve. Unmold over a serving dish and sprinkle with minced herbs to decorate.

Wine suggestion: A light red from Bordeaux or Touraine.

Poulet de Varvannes
à l'estragon et à la crème

Chicken in Tarragon Cream Sauce

—

For 5 to 6

8 Tbsp. butter, creamed
Salt and pepper
One 4-lb. capon or chicken
Bunch fresh tarragon plus 1½ Tbsp.,
   minced
2½ cups heavy cream
1½ Tbsp. Dijon mustard

Cream 2 Tbsp. butter with salt and pepper to taste, and spread inside the chicken. Push the tied bunch of tarragon in the cavity as well. Truss with string and smear the skin with more butter. This can be prepared one day ahead and kept in the refrigerator.

Preheat the oven to 350°F. One hour before serving, put the chicken in a shallow oiled roasting pan and roast for 25 minutes. Basting every 10 minutes, turn the chicken to allow it to brown evenly. After 25 minutes, remove from oven and allow to cool slightly, then carve into 7 pieces. The joints will be pink. Set aside.

Pour the cream into the roasting pan to deglaze it, then pour the contents into a skillet and reduce slightly, adding some minced tarragon and the mustard. Finish cooking the chicken pieces in the simmering cream, adding more salt and pepper, since the cream is sweet. Let simmer very slowly until the chicken is done, about 15 minutes, then correct the seasoning.

Serve with the cream sauce in a warmed shallow serving dish, and sprinkle with the rest of the minced tarragon.

Vegetable Suggestion: Tiny string beans (*haricots verts*), sautéed in butter.

Beverage Suggestion: Good fermented cider or a red Bordeaux wine.

Note: If you like the taste of applejack brandy, deglaze the roasting pan with applejack instead of cream. Pour in the applejack, scraping the roasting pan with the back of a fork and letting the mixture boil for 1 minute, then add the cream. Pour into a skillet and let reduce before adding the chicken. Continue as directed above.

Flan Normand aux pommes

Norman Flan with Apples

—

For 8 to 10

For crust:
3 Tbsp. butter
½ cup dry stale cookie crumbs,
    pulverized in a food processor

For filling:
2½ lb. Golden Delicious apples, to yield
    2 lb. ready to be cooked
3–4 eggs, depending on size
½ tsp. cinnamon
¾ cup plus 1–2 Tbsp. sugar, depending
    on tartness of apples

3 cups heavy cream
2 Tbsp. butter, cut into tiny cubes

For glaze:
8 oz. good red currant jelly
2 Tbsp. Kirsch

Special equipment needed:
A 12″ fluted porcelain tart pan
A food processor

*P*repare the tart pan by spreading a heavy layer of butter over the bottom and sides. Sprinkle with the pulverized cookie crumbs and press the crumbs into the butter to make a crust. Place in the refrigerator until needed.

Peel, core, and halve each apple, then thinly slice each half. Place the slices in a single layer on a cookie sheet covered with aluminum foil. Arrange the slices in rows, slightly overlapping each other. Bake in a moderately hot oven (375°–400°F) until golden. Do not let them brown. Remove from oven and allow to cool.

To prepare the flan mixture, beat the eggs with the cinnamon and sugar in a mixing bowl until completely homogenous, then add the cream, mixing thoroughly. Set aside.

Remove the prepared mold from the refrigerator and spread a thin layer of flan mixture in the bottom. Place the apple slices in rows, slightly overlapping each other, making an attractive pattern. Fill the mold with the rest of the flan mixture, dot with the tiny cubes of butter, and bake in a preheated 375°–400°F oven for about 25–30 minutes, or until the center is set and nicely golden.

To prepare the glaze, melt the currant jelly with the Kirsch and 2 Tbsp. water until completely dissolved. Let cool slightly.

Serve the flan in the same dish, nicely glazed with the melted currant jelly.

Beverage suggestion: Sparkling sweet cider.

BACK THEN, NOBODY KNEW about cholesterol, and a lot of our food was loaded with it. I still like dishes made with cream and butter. I shouldn't have them, and I'm told it's unhealthy, but *tant pis*. Once in a while I throw care to the winds.

Dairy products are legendary Norman specialties, so back in my childhood days, gourmands neglected waistlines as they savored fabulous sauces made with Norman butter and the incomparable ivory-colored heavy crème fraîche (page 501).

The veal and meat cuts from Norman cattle (a special breed mixed with Jerseys from across the Channel) were always excellent, as were pork products. They included all kinds of sausages, made from everything the pig could give—from chops, to offal, to blood for black *boudin* sausage.

The great Norman cheeses were served as well: Camembert, Pont l'Évêque, and the stinky Livarot. But my father warned: "Not for Mademoiselle Simone, the strong cheeses." He thought young girls shouldn't be allowed to pollute their mouths with smelly odors.

And of course, we Becks enjoyed bounty from the sea—Channel sole, hake, shrimp, mussels, lobsters, and more. The children in our family ate plentifully of

*With my brother Maurice, before
my cooking career began*

Our house at Rainfreville

The salon at Rainfreville

The dining room

*My father, Maurice Beck,
in his World War I uniform*

healthy food but were not allowed alcohol after that first sip of Bénédictine. None of us were ever keen "drinkers," though we did learn gradually how to appreciate good wines with lunch or dinner.

Sweets were another matter. I was terribly greedy for pastry and candy. Whenever I could sneak into the kitchen, I learned little tricks for making sweets, watching and licking the pan. And this sweet tooth once came in handy.

"The cook is ill," we were told when Zulma failed to appear at work one day in late March 1912. She was actually having a baby but would be away from the kitchen for only a few days, as was customary in those days. We children were kept in the dark. For all we knew a new baby had sprung right out of the cabbage patch. Anything to do with how babies are made was simply not discussed.

But since I was told my father's thirty-sixth birthday was coming up, I decided we should celebrate and wanted to make his favorite dessert, chocolate cake. So with my nanny's help, at age seven I concocted a rich cake made of dark bittersweet chocolate, plenty of sweet butter, and so on. That chocolate cake I made for my father was the basis for some of the many kinds I've made since. Mona's Divine is particularly simple yet rich, and it happens to be one of my current favorites.

I'll never forget the thrilling moment when, with Nanny's help, I presented the cake with all its candles to my father, who at least pretended to be totally surprised. His face lit up like the candles. "I love it, and thank you, my darling girl!" he said, giving me two big kisses. I felt like a grown-up star, dressed up *en famille* at the glowing table. My father was trim and handsome; my mother was sparkling. They looked splendid, and I was so proud. This was a glamorous moment of my childhood, and I imagine Maurice and I enjoyed that rich cake with even more relish than our parents.

L'anniversaire de Papa
Father's Birthday Dinner, 1913

✦ *Soupe aux poireaux*
Leek soup

✦ *Filets de sole en goujonnettes avec moules,*
sauce crème à l'estragon
Goujonnettes of sole fillets with mussels and tarragon cream sauce

—

Cidre brut ou vin blanc sec (hard cider or dry white wine)—Chablis ou Sauvignon

✦ *Pâté de gibier, de jambon et de porc*
Game pâté with ham and pork

Salade verte
Fromages de Normandie — Camembert, Pont l'Évêque

—

Rouge de Bourgogne—Pommard

✦ *Gâteau au chocolat "Mona's Divine"*
Mona's Divine flourless chocolate cake

—

Champagne de Ayala

Soupe aux poireaux

Leek Soup

—

For 6 to 7

1 lb. fresh cleaned, trimmed leeks

2½ Tbsp. butter

1½ Tbsp. vegetable oil

5 Tbsp. flour

3 cups chicken broth (or water and bouillon cubes)

3 cups milk

Salt and pepper

Optional: ½ lb. diced potatoes

2 cups heavy cream

Minced parsley, for garnish

Special equipment needed:
A 2½-qt. heavy-bottomed skillet

Chop the leeks. Heat the butter and oil in a heavy-bottomed skillet, add the leeks, and let cook, stirring constantly, until translucent. Do not allow them to brown. Stirring constantly, sprinkle with the flour and continue cooking for a few minutes to cook the flour thoroughly. Remove from heat and stir in some of the broth or bouillon to dilute the flour. When the mixture is quite smooth, return to the heat and bring to the boil, adding the rest of the broth and the milk, and stirring vigorously to prevent lumping. If you decide to add the diced potatoes, add them now and let simmer, with salt and pepper, for about 30 minutes. Taste and correct the seasoning. The leeks should be tender. If not, let simmer an additional 10 minutes.

Serve as is in a soup tureen, or make a velouté cream soup. For this, put mixture through a food mill and return to the heat. Stir in the cream and let simmer a few minutes, then taste and correct the seasoning.

Sprinkle the minced parsley over the soup just before serving in shallow soup plates or in cups.

Note: For *Soupe au cresson* (Watercress Soup), chop 4 bunches of fresh watercress (only tender stems and leaves) and 6 oz. sliced onions. Follow recipe for leek soup, beginning with the onion, stirring until tender, then adding the watercress and cooking until wilted. Continue as with leeks. The watercress will be done after 20 minutes.

Filets de sole en goujonnettes avec moules, sauce crème à l'estragon

Goujonnettes of Sole Fillets
with Mussels and Tarragon Cream Sauce

—

For 8 to 10

4 large Dover soles to make 16 fillets
  (about 3 lb.)
Salt and pepper
1 lb. fresh mussels, or ½ cup clam juice
4 oz. peeled potato, cut in half
4 Tbsp. butter
1½ cups heavy cream
1 bunch fresh tarragon

Special equipment needed:
A heavy enameled cast-iron casserole
  with lid
A food processor
An oval gratin dish

*R*inse the cleaned fish and pat dry with paper towels, then divide each fillet into narrow strips, about 3″ long and ½″ wide. Season with salt and pepper, cover, and set aside.

If mussels are not available, substitute bottled clam juice for the mussel juice. If using mussels, however, scrub them thoroughly to remove the "beards," and rinse in several changes of cold tap water. Discard any that do not close when tapped. Cook over high heat in a heavy lidded casserole without salt or liquid, only pepper. Shake the casserole frequently while cooking for 5–6 minutes, or until the mussels are wide open. Discard any that do not open. Remove the open ones from the casserole and set aside. Filter the cooking juices through filter paper to remove any sand.

Cook the potato in boiling salted water for about 15–18 minutes. When soft, drain and immediately purée with the butter in the food processor. Do not overprocess.

Pour the mussel (or clam) juice into a well-buttered gratin dish, add the cream and most of the tarragon, roughly chopped. Reserve a few nice tarragon sprigs for garnishing. Let all simmer until reduced to 1½ cups. Add the goujonnettes and let return to the simmer. When just beginning to boil, remove the goujonnettes and keep warm.

To bind the cream sauce, stir in the potato purée by spoonfuls, let the mixture come to the boil, still stirring, then correct the seasoning. Just before serving, add the goujonnettes to reheat for no more than a minute.

Serve in the same dish, and garnish with sprigs of fresh tarragon. Place the mussels, if using them, around the fish as a garnish.

Wine Suggestion: A dry white wine, such as a Chablis, Pouilly, or Sauvignon Blanc.

Pâté de gibier et de jambon et de porc

Game Pâté with Ham and Pork

—

For 10 to 12

Sheets of fresh pork fat to line pâté mold
¾–1 lb. boneless fresh game, such as
    rabbit or pheasant
4 Tbsp. Cognac
½ lb. boiled York ham (or any high-
    quality ham), with the fat
½ lb. boneless pork shoulder or fresh
    loin-end chops (or fresh pork breast
    for the rabbit or boar)
½ lb. fresh lard
½ lb. pork liver, trimmed
3 Tbsp. equal mixture of minced parsley
    and chives
½ oz. salt and fresh pepper

⅔ cup fresh bread crumbs
6 Tbsp. crème fraîche (p. 501)
Cayenne or Tabasco
3 eggs
1½ Tbsp. oil
3 shallots, minced
1 garlic clove, minced
1 bay leaf

Special equipment needed:
An 8-cup oval ceramic pâté mold
    with lid
A food processor
A nonstick skillet

$\mathcal{L}$ine the bottom and sides of the mold with thin sheets of fresh pork fat (*bardes de lard*) reserving one piece for the top of the pâté, and set aside until needed.

Trim the game, removing any gristle, then cut into dice and place in a mixing bowl with Cognac to marinate overnight. Cut the ham, pork, and lard into cubes, and set aside. Roughly chop the meats in the food processor, beginning with the pork and adding the pork liver, ham, and lard. Finally, add the game and macerating liquid, and pulse briefly. The pieces of game should just be roughly chopped, not in purée. Add the herbs and seasoning.

Meanwhile, soak the bread crumbs in crème fraîche, beat in the eggs, and set aside. Heat 1½ Tbsp. oil in a nonstick skillet and stew the shallots and garlic until softened, not browned. Add soaked bread crumbs, shallots, and garlic to the meat mixture in the food processor, and pulse to mix. Test the seasoning of the pâté by frying a small quantity in a nonstick skillet. Add more seasoning if needed.

Pack the pâté mixture tightly into the prepared mold and cover with the last sheet of pork fat. Place the bay leaf on top and cover with the lid. Seal the lid with a thick flour-and-water paste to keep the pâté well closed. Place in a water bath and add enough hot water to reach halfway up the sides of the mold. Bake in a preheated 375° F oven for 1¾ hours, or until the fat rises, which means the pâté is done. Remove the lid and refrigerate for at least 24 hours, with a 4-lb. weight on it to pack it down.

For a buffet party, unmold and serve it cut into even slices, placed on green lettuce leaves. You can also serve it directly from the mold, slicing it when you need it. To keep the unused pâté fresh, spread a layer of lard over the open slice.

Wine Suggestion: A good red Burgundy, such as a Pommard, Côtes de Nuit, or Côtes de Beaune.

Gâteau au chocolat
"Mona's Divine"

Mona's Divine Flourless Chocolate Cake

—

For 8 to 10

For cake:

1 cup sweet butter, diced, plus additional
   for buttering cake pan
7½ oz. dark bittersweet chocolate
3½ Tbsp. water
1½ Tbsp. instant coffee granules
4 jumbo-size eggs
1 cup sugar
½ tsp. vanilla extract

For glaze:
3½ oz. dark bittersweet chocolate

1 tsp. instant coffee
3 Tbsp. water

Special equipment needed:
A 10″ by 2½″ round cake pan (génoise
   pan)
Parchment paper
A heavy-bottomed saucepan or a double
   boiler
A food processor

*P*repare the cake pan by lining the bottom and sides with heavily buttered parchment paper. Keep in the refrigerator until time to fill.

Break the chocolate into small pieces and melt with the water and instant coffee in a heavy-bottomed saucepan over very low heat, in a double-boiler, or in a saucepan placed in simmering water. Stir constantly until the mixture is completely smooth, then stir in the butter, bit by bit, off heat to prevent the butter from melting too fast and forming an oily film on the chocolate. Stir vigorously, if necessary placing briefly over low heat or hot water while adding the butter. When the butter is thoroughly incorporated and the mixture is quite smooth, set aside to cool.

Separate the eggs and place the yolks in a food processor. Blend the yolks with the sugar until the mixture is very pale and forms a "ribbon," then add the egg whites and vanilla and pulse a few more seconds, until all is homogenous. Pour the chocolate mixture into the food processor and blend all for 30 seconds, to obtain a very smooth mixture. Pour into the prepared cake pan, and bang the bottom of the pan against the counter to settle the batter.

Bake in a preheated 350°F oven for about 45–55 minutes, occasionally rotating the pan in the oven while it bakes, to ensure even baking. Test for doneness after 40 minutes. When the cake is done, a toothpick inserted in the center should come out moist, showing a creamy consistency in the center. Let cool before unmolding onto a serving dish.

For the glaze, melt the chocolate and instant coffee with water as before, stirring constantly. When melted, pour the glaze over the cake and use a metal spatula to spread it evenly over the top and sides. If you wish, serve the cake with a Chantilly (heavy cream whipped in a bowl over ice to the "soft peaks" stage), but I prefer to sprinkle the top and sides with finely chopped macadamia nuts.

Wine Suggestion: A good brut Champagne.

NOT ALL MY EARLY COOKING DAYS were so successful. I loved making toffee, and Maurice devoured it just as fast as we could turn out the sticky stuff. Once it failed badly because I used the only butter we had on hand, which was salted. "Mademoiselle Simone, you're making a big mistake," Zulma warned me. But I went right ahead, stubborn as a mule. Just as predicted, it was salty and dreadful, and even Maurice turned up his nose. That was my first lesson in the importance of the right ingredients.

Nobody could have guessed that I'd make a career of cooking, of all things. In my upper-middle-class environment, careers for women were practically unheard-of, much less a profession based on cooking, a métier left to chefs and domestics. My family assumed I would grow up as a proper bourgeoise, marrying the right sort of gentleman, catering to his household needs as *la maîtresse de maison,* being a good mother to several children. Although both my marriages were to "the right sort of chap" from the appropriate milieu, the rest of my life did not unfold as conventionally.

Normandy Beach Days

"COME ON, CHILDREN, we're off to the beach now," Maman would call, and we didn't need to be told twice. Normandy could get very hot in the summer, and trips to the beach before the war of 1914 were happy occasions that excited us no end. We used to take off in a pony cart, Maman driving, all of us stuffed into our little two-wheeled vehicle—Maman, Nanny Frances, Maurice, and I (our baby brother, Bernard, was not born until 1914).

My mother drove the cart as I later drove a car—fast. She liked to make the pony gallop the full distance of eight or nine miles to the beach, but the beast was recalcitrant, probably because of a shoulder problem, and sometimes we had to shove the wheels forward to get him and the cart going. "Push, Maurice and Simone," yelled Maman. We perspired and were annoyed sometimes, but suddenly the pony would leap forward, leaving us in the dust to scramble on as best we could, usually howling with laughter.

We'd finally end up at a small family cabin at the beach, where we met friends from Dieppe and the environs who also had those little beach houses for changing. We swam in the awful woolen tank suits worn back then, and could easily have caught pneumonia in those hideous costumes that took hours to dry and weighted us down. Women and even children, not encouraged to "sunbathe," sheltered under parasols.

Our real fun was not always in swimming or building sand castles but in gathering shrimp or mussels, depending on the tide, and cooking them over a driftwood fire in seawater, into which we plunged red-hot irons to make the water boil faster, then eating them along with wonderful whole-meal bread and butter. Shrimping was done during a certain tide on the sandy part of the beach; mussels were abundant at another time of day, under the rocky cliffs. After the "Great War" (World War I), we made the same trip as teenagers, mostly by bicycle but sometimes by canoe on the river Saâne, which flowed through Rainfreville to the coast.

Best Friends—Big Names

WE WERE A CLOSE FAMILY and only once in a while saw a few neighbors or relatives. My brother Maurice and I were so strictly brought up that as young children we hardly saw anybody except each other. I looked up to Maurice, very clever and good-looking, becoming tall like my father. And I never played with dolls; I preferred to compete with Maurice in whatever sport we tried out—swimming or running, later portaging canoes. You could say I was something of a tomboy.

But I'll never forget my darling first best friend, Marie de Ayala of the Louis de Ayala Champagne family, and her brother, Bunny, whom we met when I was six. Bunny was about a year older than I, Marie about six years older. But, with Maurice, we children became thick as thieves.

My father had introduced himself to M. Louis de Ayala at the local *tabac* in Saint-Aubin-sur-Scie, where the Beck factory turned out its silicate products. The tobacconist's was a simple little country place, with a familiar old-tobacco odor, where men went as a matter of course, while women avoided it.

The two men happened to be buying the same brand of cigarette; Papa struck up a conversation, and they found they had children in approximately the same age group. Wouldn't it be nice, they agreed, if we four children could play together.

My father, who had a great palate, was a true wine connoisseur and already knew the reputation of the Ayala Champagne, produced over near Reims. The winemaker and his wife had decided to spend their summers near the seashore and rented a grand summer "cottage."

At our first meeting, we might have stuck out our tongues at each other, but no . . . we all needed friends. Marie, a tall, dark, curly-haired girl in a simple white dress, took me by the hand like a big sister. "Hello, little one," she said ever so gently, and I immediately decided that she was admirable and sophisticated. Bunny, nearer my age, was like an elf and truly funny.

I think we were all fairly well behaved. Our governesses practically swooned over tea, and we doted on sweets. So while the nannies swilled their tea, we were gorging ourselves on Zulma's fabulous concoctions—things like apple-filled crêpes, apple flans, or frothy whipped hot chocolate—made with delicious *real* chocolate, of course.

One of our favorite games was blindman's buff. We liked to trick our governesses by hiding from them in Le Moulin (The Mill), a big house that was part of the Ayalas' rented property. They'd come in calling our names, frustrated, and we'd be sneaking around in closets, behind curtains, under beds. We had a lot more fun than the nannies did, but they weren't really angry. Other than a few little rebellions, I don't remember ever being really contrary.

After the 1914–18 war, Marie and I went our separate ways. We did not meet again until nearly fifty years later, in the south of France, when Marie had married a famous millionaire. But that is another story.

Growing Up

THE GREAT WAR SEPARATED ME not only from my first best friend, Marie, but from my beloved father, who went off gallantly with his comrades after France's official declaration of war, on August 2. My handsome soldier father towered over most of the others, and I found it both exciting and scary to see him in uniform. The soldiers had boutonnieres in their jackets; they were optimistic, sure the war would be won by Christmas, and there was a certain amount of fanfare.

Alas, the war was to turn out the terrible, indecisive, pitiful affair of mass slaughter in the trenches everyone has read about in the history books.

We spent most of those war years in Rouen. My mother was always worried about my father; she adored him. But she also worried about her children's education, now that we were outgrowing Nanny's tutelage.

So in that summer of 1914, Maman decided to rent a classic and comfortable house in Rouen and place Maurice and me in proper religious boarding schools as day pupils, keeping on a skeleton crew of domestics to mind Rainfreville.

By now we had a new member of the family, baby Bernard, who had been born on February 6, 1914. Of course, we'd had no idea that a baby was coming. Those things were not discussed in front of us. But we were surprised to be taken to the music teacher's house for our lesson instead of her coming to us. While we were out, the midwife had delivered Bernard. "A baby brother!" I exclaimed, when they ushered us into our mother's bedroom to see the little bundle, his red face all screwed into a grimace as he squalled. "He doesn't look like much," I said. Still, I was delighted and surprised, having no clues yet about the facts of life, although I think Maurice was catching on.

Several months later, we all went off to Rouen, after very fastidious packing by Maman, who asked me to help her fold linens to put into the trunks. My friends think I'm exacting, but I'm not a patch on my mother—a true *maniaque*, orderly to the point of obsession. She kept track of every piece of linen, made sure it was impeccably pressed at all times.

The move to Rouen after the September harvest was a rustic enterprise. Mother took an awful lot of furniture from Rainfreville to furnish the rented house. The family went by train, but I'll never forget what a trial it was for Jules, the gardener. He had to pile everything, grand piano, beds, and all, on a huge two-wheeled peasants' cart—the best we could get in the way of a moving van.

Most of the horses were requisitioned for the war, so Jules had to take our one mare, leaving her nursing foal behind with a neighbor's mare. All the way to Rouen, he milked the mare every three hours. It was warm and hazy, and poor Jules was quite a wilted sight when he arrived with the furniture after a two-day trip that should have taken less than a day.

I remember him as a burly country person, courageous and uncomplaining. He was also the lover of little Bernard's nurse, which my mother discovered by accident one day when she went to see how the gardener was recovering from an illness.

"What on earth happened to your bed?" she exclaimed, noticing that his mattress was poised on the bed's sawhorse-style supports and that the main frame and headboard were missing, as were some wooden parts of chairs.

The farm boy blushed and stuttered, "I've made a lovely trunk for Berthe," lowering his eyes. Maman tried to look stern but could hardly suppress a smile at the upstairs-downstairs—or indoor-outdoor—romance between her baby's nurse and the sturdy gardener. Of course, I didn't hear about this until much later.

I don't remember seeing all that much of Rouen as a young girl, but it was surely more of a typical Norman town back in those days, with the historical old quarter and its black-and-white half-timbered houses, the fabulous Gothic cathedral, so tragically bombed during World War II, and the cobblestone streets.

In late September, Maurice and I were on our way to school. Mine, the Pensionnat Sainte-Marie, belied its location on the Rue de Joyeuse, but as day pupils we were able to come home for dinner and spend the night.

I have a vivid memory of "presentation day," when Maman took me to meet the headmistress.

At ten, in my clean and semi-good clothes (certainly not my "Sunday best"), I was tied in knots, very shy, and terrified of my first real school, a cold and forbidding-looking place with stucco walls. The headmistress, Berthe Morue, was a nun who had been a teacher at a similar school in the same neighborhood. Some thirty years before, my mother had attended the first convent school, by now torn down.

As I stuttered *"Bonjour,"* I reflected that this plain, sallow, gray-haired lady looked as old as Methuselah.

"I remember you, Madeleine Le Grand," said the nun, sternly eyeing Maman, who looked discomfited under her best, smiling, say-hello-to-the-schoolmistress manner.

My mother had been a cutup at school. She told me later that Sister Berthe had bawled her out for rustling papers, doodling in her notebook, or tearing out pages when the subject at hand didn't interest her. One day she was chewing on some little sweet. "What are you eating, Madeleine?" the teacher bellowed at her.

"Salt cod, my Sister," said my mother, without missing a beat. That simply broke the class up and meant a few hours of punishment for Mother, since Morue, the sister's name, means cod!

For a while, I lowered my head whenever I ran into the headmistress, but I soon got used to school life, despite my shyness. Discipline was fairly austere, and we looked a pretty sad lot in our heavy, dark lisle stockings, plain blouses and skirts, and unflattering pinafores. We weren't so naughty as my mother must have been, and we worked assiduously at our French literature, recitation, and math. I loathed geometry, with all those dreary theorems to memorize. Maurice, on the other hand, was a whiz and could have become a mathematician or an engineer; but since he was destined to join my father in business, he finished schooling at l'École Central in Paris instead of the Polytechnique, where the crème de la crème of engineers are educated.

I took an age to memorize anything, but if I can reel off recipes today, it's because I learned techniques for remembering things back at the Pensionnat Sainte-Marie, where I spent hours repeating long poems over and over.

Once I had to recite a fairly long essay by Alphonse Daudet, *"Monsieur le Sous-Prefet aux Champs."* It was quite a sweet tale about a local official crossing the fields, and I slaved and perspired to get through my performance. The teaching sister remained impassive, just glancing at her copy of the book now and then. What a surprise when she announced, "Mademoiselle Simone Beck has won the prize for best recitation." I was thrilled, glad I'd put in all that effort.

By 1917, as the war was fizzling out (and the Americans had finally come over to give us a hand), Maman felt she had to move back to Rainfreville, to prepare for Papa's return. So I became a full-time boarder at the school up until early 1918, and life was not very pleasant. We slept in drafty, chilly dormitories, about twelve to a room, and we washed in such tiny bowls, fetching our cold water from spigots at the end of a corridor, that I wondered how on earth I would get clean.

The schedule at school was rigid: wake-up bells at 6:00 A.M. meant we had to wash in our little cold-water basins, be dressed, and have beds made by 6:30, when prayers were said in the little convent chapel. Breakfast at 7:00 was copious in bread and butter, as much as we wanted, so that we did not starve, by any means. But we were allowed one cup only of coffee or tea. Then classes from 9:00 to noon, with a little recreation in the small graveled courtyard before lunch at 12:30. Playtime was not organized sport or even planned games. There were some games like blindman's buff, and a certain amount of fights and hair-pulling.

Classes resumed till 4:30, when the day pupils went home and the fifty-odd boarders returned to a kind of "study hall" in our dormitory to memorize lessons of the day. More prayers in the chapel at 6:30 were followed by dinner and free time until 9:30 P.M., when lights were firmly turned out and the sisters came round to make sure everything was quiet. "Silence, Simone Beck," I remember a sister yelling at times, peering into the darkness. We could not help trying to talk and giggle after our rigid daytime schedule.

Aside from the generous breakfasts of bread, my gastronomic experience that year was about as close to hell as the convent school could show me: what absolutely *not* to do if you want to master the art of French cooking—or eating.

Our diet was largely boiled potatoes, watery soups, and other disgusting un-mentionables. I'll never forget Fridays, the *jours de pénitence,* featuring meals of badly cooked fish. When *la limande* or *le carrelet,* those weak cousins to sole, arrived embedded in bubbly, cooled-off bits of grease, I was nauseated and more than once threatened the sister on duty that I'd be sick on the spot—my illness more gen-uine than faked. I usually got out of having to swallow those horrors. Thanks to the genes of my tall father, as an adolescent of thirteen I was shooting up like the proverbial beanstalk, at a time when the school diet probably did not give me enough calcium and protein. As a result I developed a kind of scoliosis, or curvature of the spine, that would give me minor back problems for the rest of my life. In more ways than one, school was one of my less enjoyable experiences.

BETWEEN THE TWO WARS

SCHOOL WAS OUT EARLY FOR ME in the terrible winter of 1918, when I came down with the Spanish influenza that ravaged Europe. My fever went up to nearly 105 degrees, and I was hallucinating and probably raving by the time I was taken home to recover. My long blond hair fell out in clumps.

After the years of prayers and suffering, the war had finally come to an end, and Rainfreville was unscathed. But it had been a heartbreaking war, with millions dead before the American "doughboys"—who had been exposed to the horrors "over there" via newspapers and the early wireless—came in 1917 to join the legions of courageous French and English soldiers.

Before the Armistice, my father was badly affected by poison gas at Verdun, as he raised his mask to yell orders at the soldiers slogging around the muddy trenches. It burned his throat and lungs and depleted his whole body, leaving him a kind of living shell.

He had to spend six months recovering in a sanatorium near Rouen, but finally one day he appeared back home. At that moment, each of us knew how ill the other had been. I was recovering from my flu, but Papa was wraithlike, and Maman was beside herself trying to comfort us.

I was shocked when I saw him standing by the fire, and I couldn't help blurting out, "Papa, you look terrible!"

He smiled wryly and tweaked his mustache, winking with his blue-gray eyes. *"Ma petite fille,"* he said, "we've both been through our war."

My father did improve over the following months, but we always suspected that the damage done by the gas contributed to his final illness less than twenty years later.

I resumed my studies at home, to qualify for my school's diploma. The months of recovery were like bliss for me after that devastating flu and the trying confinement of school.

Although I was weak for a long time, my brother Maurice started coaching me back to good health, teaching me swimming at the seashore, as I progressed from dog paddling to a pretty decent breast stroke. Like Father, Maurice was over six feet tall, exceptional in a Frenchman, especially back then. My sports sessions with him were like a crash summer-camp course or scouts' outings.

One day we paddled and portaged our heavy wood-and-canvas canoe about twelve miles downriver on the Saâne, which was not much bigger than a stream as it flowed through Rainfreville to the English Channel at Quiberville. In most places it was and still is gentle, pastoral Normandy at its best. Splendid in summer, the banks were decked in all the greens of willows, oaks, and especially the big poplars. When my father started to get better, he taught me fly casting here. "Your wrist, the *flick,* darling," he'd say patiently as I tried to master the art of landing the fly right in front of the fish, no mean feat. Little Bernard was already better at it than I was.

On that day with Maurice, when we came to a place too shallow to paddle in, we had to portage. Some flour mills there had been abandoned because of lack of wheat and labor after the Great War. So we had to lift the canoe and carry it through undergrowth bristling with nettles around the mills. Maurice hoisted the heavy canoe onto his shoulders, and I lugged the gear.

Trudging through those nettles, I started to feel the terrible prickling they caused but was determined to show up as well as my older brother. I bit my tongue so as not to yell out in pain. I was wearing shorts, and that was a big mistake, because I turned out to be allergic to the nettles; my legs were beginning to swell.

Though in long pants, Maurice was grumbling French profanities unknown in my vocabulary. I hadn't the breath or inclination to inquire what words like *bordel* meant (an extended meaning of "bordello"—"what a mess").

We kept on doggedly until at last we came upon the welcome sight of water—the riffled glaze of the English Channel. I ran across the beach to cool my legs in the water, and Maurice went to see about gathering mussels. We had not counted on our difficulties and on getting there so late.

Low tide was shrimping time, but this was high tide—the moment to collect mussels under the low, rocky cliffs where they lodged around pebbles and small rocks. As the tide went out, Maurice was still presumably filling up the canoe with mussels a few hundred yards away. I was trying to set up camp in our cabin on the beach, so that we could have a shellfish dinner before dark. But the tide was already getting low, Maurice was nowhere around, and I was starting to panic, especially as my legs were painful, giving me nervous jitters.

Maurice finally appeared, dragging the canoe, which started to grate on pebbles as the tide lowered, still dozens of yards from our little beach house. "I can't get it any farther," he shouted.

"Well, you've sure filled up the canoe," I replied. "It looks like enough mussels to feed Rainfreville, Tocqueville, and maybe Dieppe! Let's empty the darn thing." But my stubborn brother wanted to keep his catch.

The sun was setting, and I decided things had gone too far. "We can't just leave the canoe here," I wailed. "It will either get scraped on the rocks or float away." Finally, Maurice agreed to part with about half his harvest of mussels, and the episode ended in a friendly draw. It was too late to make a proper fire for our dinner, and we sat disconsolately, waiting for Papa to appear, as arranged, with one of his cars to take us home. At last, we heard the welcome putt-putt of the noisy vehicle laboring up to the end of the road.

"*Ma pauvre fille,* you look exhausted, and your legs are all scratched up," remarked my father. I did hurt so much I was nearly in tears. But we put dozens of mussels into pails brought by Papa, and hefted the canoe onto the car. At home, Maman took one look at me and bundled me straight off to bed.

During the night, my legs swelled up into fat watermelons, knees hardly discernible. I had to rest in bed, taking aspirin, for nearly a week to get over that violent nettle reaction. I think they tried to feed me mussel soup, but I pushed it aside.

The best way to eat the mussels would have been right at the beach, as we had intended. We usually "bearded" them, made a fire with driftwood, put them into a kettle with some pepper (no salt or water needed; the mussels had their own), waited until they opened, and ate with our hands—au naturel. They were small and seemed to taste more delicious than the pillowlike things one sometimes sees in restaurants today.

Back on my feet, I wandered down to the kitchen, lurking around Zulma's domain and reading my mother's black notebooks filled with recipes she had gathered from all over and inscribed with her impeccable fine hand. Her position as chatelaine prevented her from cooking, of course, but she loved having recipes on hand.

One of the wonderful things we ate at home was game in season, and as I liked doing everything "the men" did, I of course demanded to learn shooting. My father gave me a twenty-gauge shotgun, and I became quite good with it, fine at bagging birds, like partridge, or rabbit and hare. As Maurice wasn't keen on hunting, and Bernard was still too young, this was a marvelous opportunity to please my beloved Papa. I loved those crisp autumn days, and felt so grown-up tramping along beside my father, our hounds and Brittany spaniels and beaters getting up the game for us.

I liked the whole ambience of shooting—the precision and balance of a beautifully made gun (my father had his custom made by a gunsmith nearby), the smell of the cleaning oils, the enthusiasm of the dogs: barking, restless, and panting to get on with *la chasse*.

However, my career as a sharpshooter was not very long-lived. I wasn't particularly moved by the game birds with their gimlet eyes. But one day a *chevreuil*, the small French roebuck, looked me in the eye, and that finished me.

We were moving easily along the leaf-strewn ground, partially hardened by an early frost, inhaling the pleasant smell of burning leaves, the trees nearly divested of their gold and rust autumn colors. I was enjoying myself. Suddenly I heard, *"Madame, à vous!"*—and two roebuck darted out of a thicket. Hardly thinking, I raised my gun reflexively, and my father watched as I shot them both. *"Bravo, ma petite fille, c'est un doublé!"* he shouted. One of the animals dropped in its tracks, but I had only wounded the other, and it dragged along until we caught up to it. We were panting, but it was dying, crying like a child, and my father had to finish it off; I couldn't pull the trigger. I'll never forget its haunting, pleading eyes as my father aimed and shot it twice in the head. Sobbing bitterly, I buried my head in Papa's shoulder and swore I would never shoot a living creature again.

However, I blotted out this cruel picture to force myself to eat game again, and I still occasionally like it, provided it's shot by somebody else. In our family, we hung game neither more nor less than forty-eight hours in a cool, drafty place. Hanging game until it is high, the old English style, is definitely not *my* style. The stronger-tasting game, like roebuck and especially boar, should be marinated before cooking—in red wine with a little vinegar and oil, sliced onions, carrots, herbs, and other seasonings.

Lunch or dinner following our Rainfreville *chasse* was always a spirited occasion after we'd warmed up by a roaring fire, the men drinking a snort of something stronger than tea. Here's a typical one featuring *chevreuil,* although it's unlikely I had the stomach for it after the chase in which I gave up shooting animals.

We worked up ravenous appetites during our hunts, and hearty fall dishes included things like roast leg of venison with two purées and of course a tempting dessert.

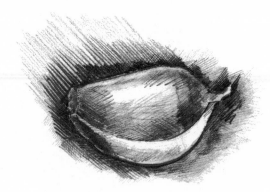

Un dîner après une
partie de chasse en Normandie

Dinner After the Hunt in Normandy

✦ *Les oeufs à la Zulma*

Zulma's stuffed eggs

✦ *Gigue de chevreuil aux deux purées*

Roast leg of venison with chestnut and celery-root purées

Salade de saison

—

Vin rouge léger—Beaujolais

✦ *Gâteau exprès l'arlequin aux fruits*

Special express cake with fruit

—

Vin blanc pétillant (sparkling white wine)—*Vouvray*

Les oeufs à la Zulma

Zulma's Stuffed Eggs

—

For 6

For filling:
6 eggs
½ cup crème fraîche (p. 501) or sour
  cream
1½ cups crumbled stale white bread
2½ oz. grated Gruyère or Parmesan
  cheese
2 Tbsp. minced chives and parsley
  combined
Salt and pepper

1½ cups bread crumbs, toasted
1 egg white, beaten
8 Tbsp. butter, clarified
2 Tbsp. white-wine vinegar
½ cup capers

Special equipment needed:
A food mill or food processor
A large frying pan

Hard-boil the eggs, starting them in tepid water. Eggs weighing 2 oz. require about 10 minutes of simmering. For 3-oz. eggs, 12 minutes is necessary. Break the shells and refresh the eggs under cold water for easy peeling.

Cut each egg in half and remove the hard yolks. Purée the yolks, using a food mill or a food processor. Add the crème fraîche or sour cream, the crumbled bread, half the cheese, and the minced herbs. Taste and correct the seasoning. The mixture will be very thick. Fill the empty white halves, making a dome with the filling. (They should look like balls.) Mix the bread crumbs with the remaining cheese. Roll the eggs in the beaten egg white, remove the excess, and roll in the toasted-bread-crumb-and-cheese mixture. The eggs can be prepared up to this point ahead of time.

Five to 6 minutes before serving, heat the clarified butter in a large frying pan. When hot, add the prepared eggs and roll them in the pan until nicely browned on all sides. Remove the eggs and deglaze the browned butter with the vinegar, then add the capers. Arrange the eggs on a warm serving dish and pour the sauce over.

Wine Suggestion: Serve with a good red wine, such as a Côtes du Rhône.

Gigue de chevreuil aux deux purées

Roast Leg of Venison with Chestnut and Celery-Root Purées

—

For 8 to 12

1 haunch of venison (about 5–7 lb.)

For marinade:
1 bottle dry white wine, such as
   Mondavi Fumé Blanc
7 oz. sliced onions
1 medium carrot, sliced lengthwise
Bouquet garni of celery stalk, parsley
   stems, thyme, and bay leaf
Whole peppercorns, to taste
Peanut oil

For roasting:
Peanut oil

Bouquet garni (see "Aide-Mémoire,"
   p. 503)

For sauce:
Macerating liquid, strained
Salt and pepper
½ cup butter, diced

Special equipment needed:
A large deep pan in which to marinate
   the meat
A roasting pan or skillet large enough to
   hold the meat

*U*se a sharp knife to trim the leg, removing the skin and making it neat. Place the leg in a large, deep, noncorrodible pan for marinating. Pour the bottle of wine over the leg; add all the vegetables, bouquet garni, and peppercorns. If the bone is not covered, tie a piece of aluminum foil around it to keep it from drying out. Cover the pan with foil and let marinate in a cool place 2–4 days, turning the meat twice a day. Drain and wipe carefully with paper towels, reserving the marinade and strained vegetables. Rub the meat with peanut oil, massaging it in lightly.

If you have some venison bones, brown them with the onions in a large skillet or roasting pan, with a thin layer of peanut oil. Let all brown slightly. Add the marinated venison to brown, turning it as soon as one side is nicely browned. When all sides are well browned, pour 1 cup of the macerating liquid over the meat, add the second bouquet garni, and let roast in a preheated 450°F oven for 15–20 minutes per pound. Turn the meat halfway through the cooking. When done, the meat should be pink near the bone. Let the meat rest in the roasting pan, covered, for 30 minutes before carving and serving.

When ready to serve, deglaze the meat juices with the remaining macerating liquid, and strain. Return the strained liquid to the pan and let reduce by half. Correct the seasoning and remove from heat, then stir in the butter, a little at a time, swirling the pan to blend.

Arrange the sliced meat down the middle of a very warm serving platter, and glaze with some of the sauce. Place chestnut purée (below) on one side of the meat and celery-root purée (page 41) on the other side. Serve the remaining sauce in a sauceboat.

Wine Suggestion: A red Burgundy, such as a Pommard or Clos Vougeot.

Purée de marrons

Puréed Chestnuts

—

For about 6

2 lb. fresh chestnuts (1½ lb. cooked, or about 1 lb. if canned)

2–2½ cups chicken broth (or water and bouillon cubes, or 2½ cups hot milk)

3–4 Tbsp. butter

Salt and pepper

1 oz. white part of a celery stalk, minced

1 tsp. sugar

Special equipment needed:

A double boiler

A food processor

*I*n France, good-quality peeled chestnuts are available frozen or canned. If you cannot find them like this, fresh chestnuts can be used. To peel fresh chestnuts, make an incision on the domed side of each with a paring knife and place in a large saucepan covered with cold water. Bring to the simmer and let boil 2–3 minutes, then remove from heat, leaving the chestnuts in the water to keep moist. When the chestnuts have cooled enough to handle, it will be easy to remove the hard outer shell and inner peel together. Simmer the peeled chestnuts in chicken broth for 1 hour. If the purée is to be served as an accompaniment to game, simmer in hot milk instead of the broth, to give a slightly sweeter taste to the purée. If using canned chestnuts, heat them in broth or milk in a double boiler. Drain in a strainer, reserving some of the liquid.

Purée the chestnuts in a food processor, adding a little hot chicken broth or hot milk to make a smoother purée. Pulse in the sugar and a few pieces of butter, then remove from the processor and correct the seasoning, adding more butter and the minced celery stalk. Work vigorously with a wooden spoon, then keep warm until time to serve.

Céleri-rave, en purée, avec pommes de terre

Celery Root Purée with Potatoes

—

For 4 to 6

1½ lb. celery root

½ lb. peeled potatoes, in medium-size slices

6 Tbsp. butter, diced

½ cup hot milk

Salt, pepper, and nutmeg

1 tsp. sugar

½ cup heavy cream

Special equipment needed:

A food processor

A nonstick saucepan

A double boiler

*P*eel the celery root deeply to remove the fibers (which become stringy after cooking), then divide into quarters. Cut each quarter into slices ⅓″ thick and cook in boiling salted water for about 20 minutes or until tender, then add the prepared potatoes and simmer together for 20 more minutes.

Strain through a colander, reserving the vegetable cooking liquid for a soup base, as it has wonderful flavor. Purée the cooked vegetables in a food processor. Then add the diced butter a few pieces at a time, pulsing for a few seconds after each addition until all the butter has been incorporated. Pour in the milk, pulse just until homogenous, season generously with salt, pepper, and nutmeg, then add the sugar and pulse once more to mix.

If the purée is too thin, transfer to a nonstick pan and stir over low heat until sufficiently reduced. Stir in the heavy cream, 1 Tbsp. at a time. Taste and correct the seasoning, then keep warm in a double boiler until ready to serve.

Variation: CELERY ROOT PURÉE IN RAMEKINS
Heavily butter nine small ceramic ramekins and place in the refrigerator until needed. To the well-thickened celery-root-and-potato purée prepared above, beat in 2 whole eggs and ¼ cup crème fraîche. Season to taste with salt, pepper, and nutmeg.

Fill the prepared ramekins ¾ full and set in a bain-marie with hot water. Bake in a preheated 375°F oven for 16–20 minutes, or until puffed and slightly browned. They will deflate somewhat as they cool, but will unmold easily.

Gâteau exprès l'arlequin aux fruits

Special Express Cake with Fruit

—

For 10 to 12

For crust:
10 oz. stale plain cookies
1 ¼ cups butter, creamed

For fruit garnish:
1 cup candied cherries
½ cup green candied fruits

⅓ cup Kirsch, to macerate fruits
1 banana, sliced
½ cup sultana raisins

For filling:
6 eggs
2 cups sugar
1½ tsp. vanilla extract
2 cups heavy cream

For crème anglaise:
8 egg yolks

½ cup sugar
Vanilla extract, to taste
3 cups milk

OR

1 lb. red currant jelly, melted with ¼ cup
    water and 3–4 Tbsp. liqueur

Special equipment needed:
Parchment paper
2 shallow splayed molds made of glass,
    stainless steel, T-fal, or Teflon

*P*reheat oven to 350° F. Place buttered parchment paper in each mold and set in refrigerator until ready to fill.

Using a fork, crumble the cookies in a bowl, then work in the creamed butter until homogenous. Smear the mixture inside the molds in a thick layer, and place in the freezer.

Parboil the candied fruits for 2 minutes, then rinse, dry, and cut into dice. Macerate in the liqueur with the sliced banana and the raisins.

Beat the eggs with the sugar and the vanilla in a mixing bowl, then stir in the cream. Add the fruits and macerating liquid, and mix well.

Remove the molds from the freezer, and fill each with half of the mixture. Bake in the preheated 350°F oven 40–45 minutes, or until the tops are set. Let cool.

Prepare the crème anglaise or red currant jelly sauce. (See method on p. 88, using quantities given above.) When the cake has cooled, unmold carefully over a serving dish. Glaze the top with some of the sauce, and pass the rest in a sauceboat.

BESIDES THE OUTDOOR SPORTS, around this time I was learning so many things, perhaps more than I had at boarding school. By 1920, my father had taught me how to drive our various cars, as he taught just about everybody

Hunting at Rainfreville;
I am standing at left

Walking on the quai at
Cannes with (from left) my
mother, my brother, and
my father

in the neighborhood, and I was proud when he said I was one of his better pupils. I learned a lot about mechanics and how to change tires. In those days you had to do repairs yourself if any mishaps occurred on the roads, and they did fairly often. I was already a demon driver. In fact, I had wanted to fly planes nearly the minute I heard they were in the air.

But those several years at Rainfreville were also filled with more ladylike pursuits, such as piano and singing lessons. I played rather mediocre renditions of Chopin, Liszt, and Beethoven. And I was starting to read novels—anything with a good plot and descriptions, though my reading was restricted to what my parents considered "proper." Nothing with more than a hint of sex would have been permitted on our bookshelves. Flaubert was out; *Madame Bovary* was too racy. I guess Jules Verne was all right. And Dickens was fine. I liked reading about hard times for the likes of David Copperfield. It reminded me of boarding school.

We sometimes gave amateur theatricals at home with friends from Paris and our area, with neighbors and relatives as audiences. We created our "theater" by stringing a curtain on a clothesline, the stage on one side, chairs set up for our audience on the other. Our "director" was Pierre Munier-Jolin, a painter from Paris who came to rehearse us for several days before the big event, coaching us for plays like popular Feydeau comedies. They were supposed to be hilarious, but I never thought I was funny enough. So I overplayed my parts, even changed my lines and ad-libbed, trying to make the role positively side-stitching. My exaggerations and posturing must have been quite a sight, a lesson in how to bend comedy out of shape well beyond farce, to the point of ridicule.

My friends from America and England tell me the French tend to overdo it onstage, even in the best theaters, so maybe I was pretty good by French standards. If I had tried to play French tragedy—something heavy by Racine, for example—then I might have really been funny.

I started learning to dance, and although my mother was a great waltzer, my father wanted to be more daring and learn South American dances, which were coming into fashion. So in 1922, when Papa heard about somebody giving tango lessons in nearby Varengeville, I was his willing partner.

The lessons were given by one Tom Taylor, an Englishman who had found a stark dance hall and an old upright piano for accompaniment by a local amateur. There were other pupils, and we learned standard fox-trots and polkas. But it was the suggestive, outré tango that enchanted Papa and me. We threw ourselves wholeheartedly into its slinky dips and slides, sometimes with deadly serious concentration, more often giggling at our ludicrous poses.

Meanwhile Maman, seated tight-lipped and dubious on the sidelines, perhaps even a bit jealous, furiously stitched at her needlepoint. Unfortunately, I had very little opportunity to use my newfound skills until my second marriage—years later.

The Great Gadsbys

COOKING STILL FASCINATED ME, and I finally got a chance to show off my skills, for some people called Gadsby. My father had started working at the silicate factory again, and one day he phoned Mother from Saint-Aubin, announcing the arrival of an American couple, Bob and Grace Gadsby. Mr. Gadsby was negotiating to buy silicate to use in the enamel coating for washbasins and bathtubs made by the Ideal Standard company, for which he worked, with European headquarters in Dole in the Jura.

Mother was taken aback. "We haven't company food on hand," she complained. "And furthermore, Zulma is off having a baby." I saw an opportunity and leapt into the breach. "I'll do the lunch, Maman. We have enough for a lovely cheese soufflé, cold cuts of meat, and salad, and a fruit mousse for dessert. How about that?"

"Go ahead, *ma petite fille*," said my mother with relief. Helped by a maid, I managed a very good light lunch, and the Gadsbys became my friends for life. They were elegant, seemed so "American," with their polite informality, and I was happy to speak English with them, especially savoring their comments about my cooking skill. Some thirty-seven years later, Grace met me when I disembarked in New York from the *Queen Elizabeth* on my first trip to the United States, the beginning of my adventure with Julia Child to complete and promote *Mastering the Art of French Cooking*.

Grace even mentioned the lunch I had made for her, which included a cheese soufflé, always a good way to gain compliments, and not so hard when done right.

Un déjeuner à l'improviste pour les Gadsby

An Impromptu Lunch for the Gadsbys

✦ *Soufflé normand au Camembert, sauce à la crème*
Norman soufflé, with Camembert cheese

—

Vin rouge—Morgon (Beaujolais)

✦ *"Assiette anglaise" et courgettes sautées*
A platter of cold roast beef and ham slices, sautéed zucchini

Salade verte

Fromages variés

—

Beaujolais

✦ *Mousse à l'orange et au Cointreau*
Orange mousse with Cointreau

Soufflé normand au Camembert, sauce à la crème

Norman Soufflé, with Camembert Cheese

—

For 6 to 9
For a brunch, 18 ramekins of ²/₃ cup capacity

3½–4 oz. stale Camembert, even
    overripened, or 2½ oz. Roquefort or
    Stilton
2 Tbsp. butter
¼ cup stale bread crumbs

For soufflé base:
5 level Tbsp. flour
1 cup cold milk

3 egg yolks
Salt, pepper, and nutmeg
4–5 egg whites, depending on size

Special equipment needed:
A food processor
A 6-cup soufflé mold
A thick-bottomed saucepan
A copper bowl

*I*f the Camembert is stale, crumble it in the food processor. If not stale, cut it into tiny dice. If you are using Roquefort or Stilton instead, crumble with a fork.

Butter the soufflé mold heavily and sprinkle with the crumbs. Place a buttered piece of foil or parchment around the top of the mold to make a collar. Put the mold in the refrigerator while making the soufflé mixture. If you prefer, individual ramekins may be substituted. They should be buttered, crumbed, and refrigerated in the same way, but do not need collars.

To make the soufflé base: The best way to avoid lumps is to put the flour into a thick-bottomed saucepan and, little by little, pour in the cold milk to form a paste, whisking constantly. Add the rest of the milk to thin it, and whisk constantly over medium-high heat until the liquid thickens to a smooth sauce. Stir over heat 1–2 minutes longer to cook the flour slightly, add the cheese, and stir until smooth. Off heat, stir in the egg yolks one at a time. Season to taste with salt, pepper, and grated nutmeg. (Watch the salt, since the cheese contains salt.)

Beat the egg whites in a copper bowl with a pinch of salt until you can see the "tracks" from your whisk. Do not overbeat. Fold a large tablespoon of whites into the cheese mixture to lighten it, then lightly fold the cheese mixture into the egg whites. Fill the mold or individual ramekins, place in a pan of hot water, with the water coming two thirds of the way up the sides of the ramekins, and bake in a preheated 400°F oven 25–35 minutes for the soufflé mold, 12–15 minutes for the ramekins. The top will be a crusty golden brown.

Serve the large mold as it is. (The ramekins can be prepared 24 hours ahead and reheated in the same way; unmold and serve.) Serve with *Sauce à la crème* (below), to which a sprig of tarragon has been added.

Note: If you have leftover egg whites, you can replace the yolks with an equal number of whites, and the results will be about the same.

Sauce à la crème

Tarragon Cream Sauce for Unmolded Soufflé

—

For 6 servings, about 2½ cups

2 Tbsp. butter	Salt, pepper, and nutmeg
2½ Tbsp. flour	1 cup crème fraîche (p. 501)
1½ cups milk	
1 tsp. Dijon mustard	*Special equipment needed:*
Branch of fresh tarragon	A thick-bottomed saucepan

Melt butter in a heavy-bottomed saucepan and stir in flour. Continue stirring over heat for 4–5 minutes, until the flour is thoroughly cooked. Remove from heat and, stirring constantly, add half the milk and mustard. Bring to a simmer, add the branch of tarragon and seasoning to taste, and let cook for 5–6 minutes more. Set aside until needed, with ½ Tbsp. butter melted on the surface to keep the sauce from forming a "skin."

When ready to serve, slowly reheat and stir in crème fraîche, a tablespoon at a time. As soon as the sauce begins to boil, remove from heat and serve with *Soufflé normand au Camembert, sauce à la crème.*

Variation: SAUCE TOMATE À LA CRÈME (TOMATO CREAM SAUCE)
Prepare the *Sauce à la crème,* leaving out the tarragon, then stir in 1 Tbsp. double-concentrated Italian tomato paste.

Mousse à l'orange et au Cointreau

Orange Mousse with Cointreau

—

For 9 to 10

2 large fresh oranges
1 lime
10 eggs, separated
1¼ cup confectioners' sugar
½ cup Cointreau or other good orange
  liqueur, such as Grand Marnier
2½ cups heavy cream
Fresh mint leaves, for garnish

Special equipment required:
A large charlotte mold (6–7 cup
  capacity)
Parchment paper

Using a vegetable peeler, remove the rind of the oranges and the lime, being sure not to remove the pith (white part), which is very bitter. Parboil the rind for 5 minutes, then change the water and repeat, for 10 minutes. Refresh under cold tap water and dry carefully. Mince the rind very fine, and reserve.

Beat the egg yolks vigorously with half the sugar over hot water, to poach them slightly. When the sugar is dissolved, stir in the minced rind and liqueur, and remove from the heat.

Prepare a syrup with the remaining sugar and ½ cup water, boiling until the "thread" stage is reached. At the same time, beat the egg whites with a pinch of salt. When the egg whites reach the Chantilly ("soft peaks") stage, gradually pour the syrup into the whites, continuing to beat vigorously until thick and shiny. Fold in the egg yolk–rind mixture.

Whip the heavy cream over ice cubes to the Chantilly stage, then fold the Chantilly into the other mixture.

Line a charlotte mold with buttered parchment paper and fill with the mousse. Place in the freezer for about 3 hours.

Serve unmolded, garnished with mint leaves.

Travels to the South

IN 1921, I WENT DOWN TO CANNES with my parents in the winter—the fashionable season to be on the Côte d'Azur in those days, a felicitous change from the raw weather up north.

Back then, the drive south was a trek of three days, even with full-throttle speed of forty or fifty miles per hour, quite a contrast to my record a few years ago of seven hours, at about 96 mph.

Stopping to eat and sleep was serious business. My parents were interested in creature comforts, and one of their favorite spots was Saulieu, to this day a gastronomic destination for motorists. The name of the town, derived from Latin, means "stopping place," and those who stop there nowadays still find a quaint small town, though of course the restaurants have changed hands. In 1922, before the days of Alexandre Dumaine and his Côte d'Or restaurant, our family stayed the night at the Hôtel de la Poste, owned by Victor Burtin, who was the restaurant's chef. He had worked for the Kaiser and was a spruce, decisive man—who also served delicious food.

When we pulled up after a long day's drive, we were grateful for what was on hand: all the comforts, in a rather offhand decor, with the added attraction of excellent food and drink. And our stomachs were rumbling. Our dinner fare would be traditional, but we knew what to expect, including fresh lobster *à la nage,* or an asparagus omelet, plus wonderful wines. My father would confer very seriously with Burtin, discussing the merits of this or that wine to go with dinner—a high point of our trip.

This particular evening, we'd just settled in to contemplate the menu and salivate over what was to come, when we heard a terrible row across the room. Burtin was stalking around, muttering that he'd like to throw these two American tourists out.

A born diplomat, my father asked if he could be of assistance, since he spoke fluent English. Gesticulating wildly, the exasperated Burtin explained that the American couple understood no French, knew nothing about French food, and had committed the unforgivable error of asking for Coca-Cola and milk with their main dish of truffled steamed Bresse chicken. "*Mon dieu,* this is sacrilege!" stormed Burtin, with some reason, one has to admit. "Milk is for *babies,*" he hissed. "As for the other thing, I won't even discuss it. This restaurant is not a nursery."

But Papa went to smooth things over, since he liked Americans, as well as promoting French wine and food. He explained gently to the gastronomic tyros that you cannot do justice to a great dish like truffled chicken with anything less than a great French wine. Finally, the American couple was happy to settle for an excellent white Meursault Burgundy for their fish course and a red Château Margaux with the chicken—not a bad introduction to French wine, I might add.

The tourists who were starting to visit France between the two wars were not always sophisticated types like the F. Scott Fitzgeralds and their friends, who grew to like wine so much that sometimes they drank too much of it.

As the Americans enjoyed their dinner, so did we. We always dined well down in Saulieu—unforgettable fish soufflés, perhaps a truffled pâté, and an ice-cream dessert.

Un très bon repas pour les vacances

An Excellent Holiday Dinner

✦ *Amuse-gueules*
Little starters

—

Apéritif: Kir—vin blanc sec et framboise ou Cassis
(dry white wine and raspberry or blackberry liqueur)

✦ *Oeufs brouillés aux asperges, beurre blanc*
Scrambled eggs with asparagus, beurre blanc

—

Vin blanc sec—Sancerre

✦ *Pâté de foies de volaille*
Poultry liver terrine

Salade verte mélangée
Fromages variés

—

Un bon Beaujolais—Morgon, Fleury, ou Julienas

✦ *Crème glacée à la fraise*
Strawberry ice cream

—

Vouvray—vin blanc pétillant (sparkling white wine)

Oeufs brouillés aux asperges, beurre blanc

Scrambled Eggs with Asparagus, Beurre Blanc

—

For 4

4 oz. young green asparagus tips
4 Tbsp. sweet butter
8–10 eggs, depending on size
Salt and pepper

Special equipment needed:
A heavy-bottomed saucepan
A double boiler or a bain-marie (see
    Aide-Mémoire, p. 503)

Parboil the asparagus until barely tender. Refresh under cold water, drain, and let dry on folded kitchen or paper towels.

Generously butter the bottom and sides of a heavy-bottomed saucepan, using all the butter. Break the eggs into the buttered pan, and without beating the eggs, add the asparagus. Cover with plastic wrap (pressed onto the surface of the eggs to keep them from drying out), and let stand for a few hours to let the flavors blend.

When nearly ready to serve, break up the eggs with a wire whisk and mix the eggs and asparagus together. Season with salt and pepper, then place the saucepan over water—using a double boiler or a bain-marie—on very low heat. *Do not let the water boil.* Stir constantly over heat until the eggs thicken and are just set. The eggs should remain creamy and not be cooked to dry curds. Remove from the pan immediately and serve on warmed plates, accompanied by a beurre blanc sauce (see page 473).

Note: The stalks of the tender green asparagus can be used to make a delicious asparagus velouté (page 315).

Pâté de foies de volaille

Poultry Liver Terrine

—

For 8 to 10

½ lb. chicken livers
½ lb. duck livers
Freshly ground pepper
⅓ cup Cognac or bourbon
One 2-lb. roasting chicken
Salt
One 3½-lb. tender duck
1 lb. boiled ham
½ lb. rendered goose fat or lard
½ lb. breast of pork, trimmed and
　roughly chopped
3 eggs plus 1 egg yolk
1 cup crème fraîche (p. 501)

¼ tsp. nutmeg
1 tsp. dried thyme
½ tsp. dried oregano
½ tsp. dried savory
½ tsp. ground coriander
Optional: 2 oz. truffles, in tiny dice
12 pistachios, peeled and sliced
Thin strips of pork fat to cover the pâté

Special equipment needed:
A food processor
A 6-cup pottery terrine with lid
A roasting pan

*C*arefully clean the poultry livers, sprinkle with freshly ground pepper, and macerate in the Cognac or bourbon.

Cut off the wings and legs of the chicken, and set aside. With a sharp knife, slit the skin down the back and carefully remove the skin from the chicken in one piece. The skin will be used to line the terrine, so be careful not to make any holes, except for the areas around the wings and legs. Lightly season the skin with salt and pepper, and set aside.

Bone the chicken, and set the meat aside. Meanwhile, bone the duck, discarding skin and reserving the duck breast meat. Place the chicken meat, duck meat, and boiled ham in the bowl of the food processor. With the metal blade, pulse the meats 4 or 5 times, taking care not to purée the mixture. Add the rendered goose fat or lard, macerated chicken livers, roughly chopped pork breast, eggs and extra yolk, crème fraîche, and all seasonings, and pulse to mix, taking care not to purée the mixture.

Transfer the mixture to a mixing bowl, add the diced truffles and the liver-macerating liquid, reserving the duck livers, and correct the seasoning. Work the mixture thoroughly until it becomes completely homogenous, and set aside. Slice the reserved duck livers and duck breast into thin strips (*aiguillettes*), and set aside.

Line the terrine with the seasoned chicken skin and spread with ⅓ of the meat mixture in an even, tightly packed layer. Place half the duck liver and breast strips and half the pistachios neatly on top. Cover with another layer of the meat mixture, followed by the remaining liver and breast strips and pistachios, and finish with the rest of the meat mixture. Cover with the pork fat (*bardes de lard*) and then the terrine lid, sealed to the terrine with a thick flour-and-water paste.

Place in the roasting pan, add hot water to a depth ⅔ the height of the terrine, and bake in a preheated 375°F oven for about 1½–1¾ hours. When done, remove the lid. The fat will have risen to the top. Replace the lid with a piece of wood covered with foil and press down to close any gaps. Place a heavy weight on the foil-covered wood and compress the pâté in the refrigerator for about 12 hours.

Serve cold, cut in slices, with a highly seasoned green salad.

Wine Suggestion: Red Bordeaux from Haut Médoc.

Crème glacée à la fraise

Strawberry Ice Cream

—

For 8 to 10

For ice cream:
2 pints strawberries
2 Tbsp. lemon juice
1 cup plus 3 Tbsp. sugar

4 eggs, separated
Pinch of salt
1 cup heavy cream
1 tsp. vanilla extract

For strawberry coulis:

1 pint strawberries
6 fresh mint leaves
½ cup sugar
1 tsp. lemon juice

Special equipment needed:

Food processor or food mill
An ice-cream freezer
A double boiler

*C*lean the strawberries. Purée in a food processor or through a food mill, then pass through a strainer to remove the seeds. Mix in the lemon juice and 3 Tbsp. sugar.

In a mixing bowl, mix the egg yolks with ½ cup sugar, stirring over a double boiler until tepid. Remove and stir in the strawberry purée.

Beat the egg whites with a pinch of salt until half beaten. Gradually add ½ cup sugar while beating, to make a meringue. Set aside.

In another bowl, beat the cream with the vanilla to the Chantilly ("soft peaks") stage. Spoon the Chantilly into the meringue, then add the strawberry mixture, folding until homogenous.

Churn and freeze in an ice-cream freezer for 25–30 minutes. This can be packed into an ice-cream mold and unmolded. Decorate with 4 to 6 strawberries, and serve with the strawberry coulis.

To make the coulis, clean the remaining strawberries, purée in a food processor or put through a food mill, then pass the purée through a fine sieve.

Finely mince the mint leaves. Add sugar, lemon juice, and mint leaves to the purée.

Serve the coulis spooned around the unmolded ice cream, with the remaining sauce in a boat.

*R*EACHING OUR DESTINATION IN THE WARM, colorful Midi from the north, subdued under its slate-gray skies, was always an invigorating moment, when we began to relax, laugh, and chat. Cannes was still quite unspoiled and elegant, catering to a moneyed aristocracy and bourgeoisie—an attractive town compared to the aggressive, high-rise haven for vulgarity it has become. But it was already growing fast, and pink, yellow, and cream-colored stucco villas were springing up as profusely as the mimosa in February.

We usually stayed at the Hôtel du Parc or the Continental, both in the near-luxury category. Our view was marvelous, onto the bay of Cannes and the two islands facing it, Sainte-Marguerite and Saint-Honorat. We often took the boat over to look around, and the sights and smells of flowering plants were our excitement, recreation that would look very tame and "retro" now.

Eating was a major occupation and pleasure. Sometimes we had little picnics on the islands—sandwiches packed by the hotel—or occasionally a fish fry by local fishermen who ran a tiny café. Hotel dinners were sedate and organized around dishes like asparagus or mushroom omelets, broiled fish or meat—not very stunning stuff but preferable to eating rich food every day.

I knew little about the sophisticated Riviera vacationers who indulged in some fairly wild carryings-on in those Roaring Twenties days of drinking, dancing, and gambling into the wee hours. I was a young woman chaperoned by my straitlaced parents. If Mother perceived a besotted barfly weaving into a hotel lobby, she steered me firmly up to bed. Our most exciting moments were excursions to picturesque little ports for fish dinners.

Some of the best fish I ever ate was on Port-Cros, a real jewel of an island in those days. It was still almost untouched, carpeted with flowers and bathed in a lovely fragrance of thyme, bay leaf, and other herbs. Although privately owned, it was open to tourists, who were not very numerous. Now it is still "protected," but the public goes over *en masse,* and just by sheer numbers is destroying the beaches and wildlife.

My father went to Port-Cros at dawn to try his luck with the local fishermen, and I came over later with my mother and friends for a fresh fish soup. They would have caught about a kilo or two of fish, mostly small ones such as *rascasse,* or Mediterranean redfish; bluefish; or *cigales de mer*—little crabs shaped like cicadas. The seafood was cooked over a fire in a base of chopped leeks, tomatoes, onion, garlic, and herbs sautéed in olive oil, to which the cleaned fish, seawater, and a large pinch of saffron were added. Everything was simmered for about eight to ten minutes, until the fish was just done; then the soup was transferred to a "serving platter" made out of the hollowed trunk of a cork tree—perhaps for a better taste, I don't know. I was always starved, and when that aromatic "bouillabaisse" was ladled into my soup dish, I knew there was no better way to eat fish—straight out of the sea, prepared as simply and naturally as possible.

Cookbook writers and chefs argue endlessly about what should constitute a bouillabaisse. Do we put in lobster, shrimp, or mussels? Well, we didn't have any of those. We just slurped down that hearty fish stew with tomatoes and plenty of toasted French bread to soak up the juices, and we reveled in our good fortune. Every region has its own version of fish stew and soup, and of course in Paris they add whatever they feel like. Later, I dipped into my memories of many fish stews to elaborate on the big bouillabaisse recipe Julia and I presented in *Mastering* II.

FIRST MARRIAGE:
LA VIE PARISIENNE

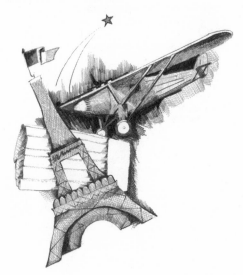

In the fall of 1922, an accident almost sent our home up in smoke. It was a cool evening, and a few of us were enjoying a crackling fire in the billiards room that had been turned into a comfortable "family room." My grandmother Le Grand—by now widowed for several years—had come to stay with us and was resting in her room.

The fire was roaring, flames dancing like a small inferno. It was a masterpiece of a fire. And it made an attractive hearthside scene, a moment we were savoring complacently, satisfied with our creature comforts. Until we noticed that the bricks, coated with residue, were so hot that the chimney was burning merrily away too. Consternation! We all rushed around filling pails with water, which my father started pouring into the fireplace—an ineffective action that just seemed to make the flames leap higher in the chimney and sent smoke billowing into the room. After a half hour of this, it looked as though our house might burn down.

Smelling the smoke, my grandmother marched in and said, "For heaven's sake, smother it. Put a wet sheet in front of the fireplace; that will stop it." So in desperation, we jammed a sheet between the bricks and the mantelpiece, constantly dousing it with water. And sure enough, after ten minutes the fire subsided, because the wet sheet had cut off the oxygen supply. What a close call, we all agreed. And so did the dilatory fire chief, who did not arrive till the next day, when he observed laconically that "Madame Le Grand should be on the fire brigade."

Even though I still enjoyed life traveling or at home with my family, I felt there was a lot missing—maybe the sophistication of Paris, a grown-up's life that seemed to be eluding me. At eighteen, I was becoming bored and restless.

There were often eight or ten extra hunters with Papa during the season. One day after shooting, we ended up in a wonderful small restaurant at Pourville, near Varengeville-sur-Mer, for a supper laid on by a woman restaurateur, Madame Vincent. It was unforgettable, a classic of good country cooking in a rustic setting, with a cheerful fire and checkered tablecloths.

The *potée* was more than just a pot-au-feu; it was very special. We began with the clear, strained bouillon, very *"corsé,"* full of savory taste. Then there were several tender cuts of pork, beef, and chicken in light broth, with the vegetables and some large, soft sausages. Along with this: natural rice in a velvety sauce that was simply a reduction of Norman cream with tarragon, salt, and pepper—a sauce I have used a lot. I'll never forget this fabulous *potée normande,* and Zulma often made an equally exciting Rainfreville version at home. In fact, it was so good that we sometimes served it for New Year's Eve, preceded by smoked salmon or foie gras, preferably both.

Un dîner de réveillon du jour de l'an
A New Year's Eve Dinner

✦ *Foie gras; saumon fumé; toasts*
Foie gras; smoked salmon; toasted brioche slices

—

Apéritif: Champagne brut; with salmon, vodka on the rocks

✦ *La potée de Rainfreville*
Special pot-au-feu (with rice and tarragon cream sauce)

Salade verte
Fromages variés

—

Un bon Bordeaux—Château Margaux

✦ *Sabayon au café*
Coffee ice cream in ramekins

La potée de Rainfreville

Special Pot-au-Feu

—

For about 12

The meats:

3½ lb. bottom round of beef

3½ lb. rolled pork shoulder

1–2 chickens, depending on size

1 tender Polish sausage

The vegetables (not served):

2–3 carrots

2–3 onions, with 2 cloves in each

2 small peeled parsnips

A bouquet garni of celery stalks, thyme, oregano, bay leaf

3 leeks, trimmed

3–4 garlic cloves

Coarse salt

Special equipment needed:

A large soup pot, or *marmite*

This recipe was originally published in *Mastering the Art of French Cooking*, Volume I, to which you can refer for the details, beginning on page 306. In France, this dish is typically served for the Réveillon, or New Year's Eve celebration. It is wonderful for entertaining, since it simmers for hours and is even better when cooked the day before it will be served, especially since fat is easily removed from the cooled dish.

Each of the different pieces of meat should be trimmed and tied with kitchen string to help them keep their shape during the cooking. Ask your butcher for additional bones, as they will improve the flavor of the bouillon.

Place all the vegetables, bones, and beef in the pot and add enough water to cover all by 6″. If you have any leftover stock, add that to the water. Slowly bring to the simmer and add salt. Let the pot continue to simmer for about 1 hour, removing the scum so the final stock is clear. Add the pork and let all simmer 1 hour, removing the scum as it forms. Add the well-trussed chicken(s) and let simmer, skimming as needed. One hour after the chicken goes in the pot, drop in the Polish sausage and let cook for 25 minutes, when all should be ready. Meanwhile, prepare some boiled rice to accompany the *potée*.

Strain and degrease the broth, discard vegetables, and return the meats to the pot to keep warm until needed. To serve, remove any extra fat, and cut meats into slices for serving. Arrange the pieces in groups on a warmed platter with the rice heaped in the middle and sausage slices on top. Serve with a sauceboat of Tarragon Cream Sauce (page 49) poured over the meats and any extra sauce in a sauceboat.

If you wish to have some vegetables with the boiled meats, cook fresh vegetables for 1 hour in another pot with some of the broth. Those cooked with the meats will not have much flavor.

Note: Pot-au-feu is usually cooked with fat on the meat, to add flavor; the fat is removed before serving.

Sabayon au café

Coffee Ice Cream in Ramekins

—

For 6 to 8 generous servings

6–7 egg yolks, depending on size
⅚ cup sugar
2 Tbsp. instant coffee granules
4–5 egg whites, depending on size
Salt
1½ cups heavy cream
½ tsp. vanilla powder or extract

24–36 toasted, slivered almonds, for garnish
Optional: Mint leaves

Special equipment needed:
14 ramekins
Parchment paper

To prepare the sabayon, beat the egg yolks with ⅓ cup sugar over hot (not simmering) water. When beginning to thicken, stir in the granulated coffee and remove from hot water. Beat vigorously until tepid.

Beat the egg whites with a pinch of salt and a drop of water. When half beaten, add ¼ cup sugar and continue beating. Still beating vigorously, add the final ¼ cup sugar in a thin stream to make a meringue. Fold the sabayon into the meringue and allow to cool completely.

Beat the heavy cream into a Chantilly (page 502), add the vanilla, and fold into the completely cold sabayon. Fill the ramekins and place in the freezer for at least 2½–3 hours, or overnight.

To serve, place the ramekins on a warm, wet kitchen towel for a moment and then unmold onto individual plates. Decorate with the toasted, slivered almonds and fresh mint leaves.

Wine Suggestion: Demi-sec Champagne, perhaps Ayala.

L ATER IN THE FALL, one of our shooting guests was Jacques Jarlauld, the son of friends of my parents. He was about ten years older than I and seemed to take an immediate fancy to me.

Although he had a nice profile, he wasn't much to look at. For one thing, I stood several inches taller than he. And he was oddly proportioned: his head seemed to jut right out of his shoulders, without much of a neck. However, I admired him for his exploits during the Great War; he had finally succeeded, on his third try, in escaping the Germans who held him prisoner in eastern Germany.

After just a few days, he asked for my hand, without saying anything to me. His haste was surprising, but it was the custom to ask the father first. Jacques was very insistent, but my father hedged: "Absolutely not before one year. She is still a young girl, must make up her own mind, and needs time to think."

When my father announced abruptly, "This fellow has asked to marry you," I was flattered but also flabbergasted, blushing and wordless. I had never had a beau, much less a serious suitor. I had nobody with whom to compare Jacques and didn't even know my own needs and wishes very well. But I did want to break away from home, warm and secure as it was.

Besides Grandmother Le Grand, we had another guest: my aunt and godmother, Suzanne Beck, who had never married. Their viewpoints from different age levels and sides of the family threw me into confusion.

My grandmother, who had long forgotten what it was to be young and unsure of oneself, had turned into a professional widow since my grandfather Alexandre had died. She always wore black, and when she went out, her mop of white hair was piled neatly under a small, round, tipped "widow's hat," with ruching on the brim, trailing a small black chiffon veil behind. She advised me in no uncertain terms to go ahead with the marriage.

"You're neither very pretty nor rich," she told me bluntly one day, hurting my feelings and pride more than she probably realized. "You ought to seize this opportunity while you have it."

My aunt Suzanne, on the other hand, drew me aside and said, "*Ma petite fille,* you are superior to this man. You deserve far better; don't waste yourself like this." Mother and Father had little advice, and I was too timid to confront them with direct questions. So I was in the dark.

I tried to lose myself in my usual pursuits—gathering more kitchen knowledge from Zulma, practicing shooting clay pigeons, or accompanying my father to the hunt.

I had an unformed thought that I wasn't really "in love" with this man. I knew nothing firsthand about love or sexual attraction, and was naïve in these matters, having lived such a sheltered life, centered in family, sports, travel, and education.

But I wanted to change my life, and the fact that Jacques Jarlauld lived in Paris was the trump that finally won me over to accept his proposal. He seemed to be a clean-cut, decent sort of man, and I could live in Paris, learn something of life in the city, broaden my horizons. A few weeks after the proposal, I finally said yes. Like some wide-eyed fairy-tale princess, I probably hoped that this unprepossessing equivalent of a frog would turn into a prince as he spirited me away.

We formally announced our engagement later in the year, during a *soirée de fiançailles,* a gala private dinner party held at Jacques's parents' Paris flat, near the Gare de Lyon. I remember wearing my first true evening dress—a long green chiffon gown with flared *godet* panels at the hem, inset with sparkling rhinestones and seed pearls.

After dinner, Jacques asked if I'd like to see photographs of him and the other war prisoners in his bedroom. I'd never heard of the expression "Come up and see my etchings, dear." So, deserting guests and family, I followed him, and was genuinely interested as he showed me the pictures and told me stories for about an hour. Amazingly, he didn't lay a hand on me, and all we did was talk. Maybe my reserve put him off.

But as my parents and I were taking a taxi back to my grandmother Le Grand's Paris flat, where we were staying, my father turned to me and exploded with a royal dressing-down. "How on earth could you?" he shouted. "The very idea, spending all that time up in Jacques's room. It's positively disgraceful!" I was aghast, as tears came to my eyes. "I haven't done anything, Papa. I don't understand," I wailed. He just grumbled, explaining nothing. Incredibly, I was still without a clue.

I wintered in Cannes with my parents as usual, and we never spoke of my "indiscretion" again. Back in Normandy, Mother and I ordered a trousseau, to be prepared in Rouen, and I began to feel nervous and excited at being the bride; my wedding would be a real *fête* in the old Norman tradition.

I was just going on nineteen when I married Jacques on June 6, 1923, in Tocqueville-en-Caux, where my father was the mayor.

The civil ceremony was performed a couple of days before the church wedding, the big event that really counted to our families. Preparations were frantic for the reception-dinner for about forty seated guests in our dining room, the food prepared by a caterer from the town of Yvetot. Chef Boquet took pains to lay on a lovely party, even bringing anthracite coal for the ovens, absolutely necessary for turning out the best dishes he knew how to make.

With his brigade of six assistants, Boquet came to Rainfreville a day ahead to work on the wedding feast for the following day, attacking on all fronts—pâtés, pastries, ices. I rarely got near the kitchen, since I had to have final fittings on my gown and help my mother with wedding details. Like any other bride, I was nervous. Next day I would be the star, and I was determined to be up to the occasion.

The night before our wedding, in the stone Norman church near our house, I prayed fervently that I would have a good marriage with Jacques, then tossed and turned most of the night, murmuring, "Please, dear God . . ."

Toward midmorning, my mother and a maid helped me don my bridal gown, a white satin dress to nearly ankle length, cut in the twenties style, with a low waist, the skirt flared below the hip. A coiffeur came to arrange my hairdo in a short wavy style, and my only makeup was a touch of pink on the cheeks, since any more than that would have made me look like a strumpet to our correct, prudish families.

"To the bride and groom," we were toasted at the splendid five-hour lunch after the church wedding. I think our relatives had more fun at this elaborate affair than I did. I don't remember any feeling of expectation or elation—just an impression of merriment, color, and noise. I didn't dwell on the mysterious period that lay ahead with this near stranger I had married.

We celebrated with brut Champagne throughout, and we started with little foie-gras miniature brioches, going on to fresh River Saâne trout *en gelée*, fillet of beef in a puff pastry crust, several vegetables, salad, and a *trou Normand* between two of the courses. This was Calvados, traditionally served as a "digestive," and it was taken seriously; we had to wait half an hour before the next course. There was a rich duck pâté, fabulous Norman cheeses, always best in June, dessert with ices, liqueurs, petits fours, and more. But I could scarcely touch these delicacies. A still, small voice was speaking to me through the pit of my stomach, expressing excitement mingled with cold fear. Yet I kept my gracious young-bride façade, as I made polite conversation with our relatives and sometimes smiled shyly at Jacques.

While the families enjoyed themselves, so did the farm people and gardeners, who looked in from the sidelines, quaffing Champagne along with the guests. And even little brother Bernard, dressed in shorts and lace-collared shirt, had his vinous initiation, though he was only nine.

Before Jacques and I drove off to Paris, I dashed on some lipstick I'd smuggled out of a Rouen store, and was afraid to kiss my parents goodbye. In their eyes, makeup was the stigma of the fallen woman.

From Paris we took a train to Annecy, set in the shadow of the Alps near Geneva, for a short honeymoon. The Pullman car was luxurious enough, with its velvet trim and brass fittings, the varnished smell of a first-class passenger car, the wheels clacking rhythmically. For the sexually awakened, it might have been an exciting setting.

But the overnight trip was a nightmare for me, a disaster. I had heard rumors from cousins and friends that the moment of truth—the virgin's deflowering—might be pretty awful, so I had forebodings. I was still unprepared for the shock, and can only say that from the first night onward, it was obvious that we were a total physical mismatch, and not particularly compatible mentally, either. I would like to give a hilarious French bedroom-farce account of Jacques's clumsy assaults, but to me it was a tragedy. I didn't learn until years later that making love without love is like trying to make a soufflé without egg whites!

However, after we returned to Paris to live together on a day-to-day basis, Jacques agreed to leave me alone as much as possible. While he went off weekdays to his job in the wholesale wine business, I started to get acquainted with Paris, discovering things both cultural and gastronomic.

I was still a country girl, but I knew how to drive, and I set out to educate myself in the ways of the city. Jacques didn't mind. He had his work, and we met in a rather formal way in the evenings. We had a woman to do the household chores for me, and I didn't have to cook, but I did explain what we liked to eat and how to prepare it.

Our first apartment, on the Rue de Lourmel in the Fifteenth Arrondissement, was in an elaborate building with fussy stonework on the façade. But downstairs, just outside our door, was an anachronism—a barn with cows, belonging to the next-door neighbors. Even sixty years ago, this was an oddity in Paris. Naturally, we bought fresh milk there every morning. The decor in our flat had been done by Paul Poiret, who was a decorator as well as a couturier, and it was amusingly Art Deco bordello—in red, black, and gold, with lots of lacquer—ironically fitted out for a *grande cocotte*, or kept woman.

After a year there, we moved to a flat on Rue Lesueur in the Sixteenth Arrondissement, near the Bois de Boulogne, where the only showy touch was a bar we had installed, with a neon sign saying "Sim's Bar." The social things I did then meant little to my life. However, I did learn about giving cocktail parties, making canapés and serving drinks, like sidecars and white ladies, that were fashionable at the time.

I played bridge, went to and gave lunches, met many people in a superficial way. This was the time of my life that I call *la vie oisive*, lightly touching everything like a social butterfly, not particularly happy but picking up information that would always be useful. And I took pride in serving lunches to tempt the fickle Paris ladies, with dishes like eggs poached in Beaujolais and a zucchini ring.

Un déjeuner de dames à Paris

A Parisian "Hen Party"

✦ *Les oeufs pochés au Beaujolais*
Poached eggs with bacon and red wine

✦ *Savarin de courgettes*
Unmolded zucchini ring with tomato sauce

—

Beaujolais

Salade verte
Fromages variés

—

Vin blanc d'Alsace

✦ *Tarte Tatin Simca*
Simca's Upside-Down Apple Tart

Les oeufs pochés au Beaujolais

Poached Eggs with Bacon and Red Wine

—

For 6

7 oz. slightly smoky bacon, diced

4 Tbsp. butter

6 oz. onion, chopped

1 bottle light red wine, such as a
Beaujolais

3 garlic cloves, crushed

Bouquet garni of celery stalk, parsley
stems, thyme, and bay leaf

2 cups chicken broth (or water and
bouillon cubes)

Salt and pepper

12 slices *pain de mie* (page 495) or a

good white home-style bread, crusts
removed

Dash of red-wine vinegar

12 eggs

1 Tbsp. tomato paste

1½ tsp. arrowroot or potato starch

Special equipment needed:

A saucepan

A large flat saucepan

A strainer

*P*arboil the diced bacon to remove excess smoke flavor. Refresh with cold water, then place in cold water and bring again to the boil. Let boil for 3 minutes, refresh, and dry with paper toweling.

Sauté the bacon in a nonstick pan with 1 Tbsp. butter until nicely browned. Remove and let cool. Cook the chopped onion in the same pan, stirring constantly until slightly browned but not burned, then pour in 3 cups of red wine. Bring to the boil, add 2 garlic cloves, bouquet garni, and chicken broth, and salt and pepper to taste. Let simmer uncovered about 15–20 minutes, while poaching the eggs.

Meanwhile, butter each slice of bread and rub with garlic to give a nice garlic flavor. Let dry for a few minutes, without toasting, in a very slow oven.

Place water and a dash of vinegar in a large flat saucepan. Bring to the simmer and poach the eggs, no more than 3 at a time. To poach eggs, break each one, separately, into a coffee cup and slide into barely simmering water. Let cook for 3 minutes, remove with a slotted spoon and dip into cool water to remove the vinegar taste, then drain over dampened kitchen towels. (It is better to delay the cooking of the eggs until the last possible minute, as reheating will result in overcooking.)

When the eggs are ready, reheat the sauce and correct the seasoning, adding tomato paste for added flavor and color. Strain the sauce and return it to the saucepan with the *lardons* (bacon pieces). Bring to the simmer and add the arrowroot or potato starch, dissolved in a little water. Stir with a wire whisk until slightly thickened.

Just before serving, place the toast on a warmed serving platter, top with the poached eggs, and cover all with wine sauce.

Wine Suggestion: Serve the same wine, preferably a tasty Beaujolais.

Savarin de courgettes

Unmolded Zucchini Ring with Tomato Sauce

—

For 6 to 8

2 lb. small, young zucchini
6–8 Tbsp. butter
5 eggs, separated
Salt, pepper, and nutmeg

For white sauce:
4 Tbsp. butter
½ cup flour
1¾–2 cups cold milk

For creamed tomato sauce and garnish:
1 recipe Express Tomato Sauce (page 486)
1 cup crème fraîche (p. 501)
1½ oz. grated Parmesan cheese

Special equipment needed:
A large savarin (ring) mold, preferably nonstick
An ovenproof gratin dish

*I*f a nonstick savarin mold is not available, butter the mold heavily and place in the refrigerator until needed.

Julienne the zucchini, sprinkle with salt, and let set for about 20 minutes to disgorge their water. Rinse in cold tap water to remove excess salt, then drain dry between kitchen towels.

Melt 6 Tbsp. butter in a heavy skillet. When very hot, add the zucchini and cook them, stirring constantly, until they turn slightly golden brown. Set aside while making the white sauce.

Melt the butter for the white sauce, then stir in the flour. Stirring constantly, let boil a few minutes, then remove from heat. Using a whisk, stir in the cold milk, beating until all is completely smooth. Return to the heat and let boil for 5 minutes, stirring frequently. Remove from the heat and stir in the egg yolks, one at a time, stirring until each is completely incorporated. Season highly with salt, pepper, and nutmeg, and mix in the zucchini.

Beat the egg whites with a pinch of salt until stiff, then lightly fold in the zucchini mixture. Taste and correct the seasoning. Pour into the prepared mold and place in a pan of hot water, with water coming ⅔ up the sides of the mold. Bring to the simmer over direct heat, then place in a preheated 375°F oven and bake for 30–35 minutes. When the savarin is done, a toothpick inserted into it will come out clean.

While the savarin is baking, prepare the creamed tomato sauce, following the directions for Express Tomato Sauce (page 486), then stirring in the crème fraîche by tablespoonfuls. As soon as the sauce begins to boil, remove from heat and set aside.

When the savarin is done, remove from oven and let cool 8–10 minutes, then unmold into an ovenproof gratin dish of the same size. Pouring very slowly, coat the top only of the savarin with creamed tomato sauce, sprinkle with grated Parmesan cheese, and return to the oven to *gratiner* and brown nicely (about 15–20 minutes in a preheated 400°F oven). Serve immediately.

Tarte Tatin Simca

Simca's Upside-Down Apple Tart

—

For 6 to 8

For pâte à "croustades":

1 cup pastry flour

12 Tbsp. sweet butter

Pinch of salt

1 egg yolk, beaten with 2 Tbsp. cold
water

1 tsp. sugar

For filling:

4 lb. ripe, but not juicy, apples
(preferably Golden Delicious) or pears

1 lemon, juiced

6½ oz. sugar cubes, preferably, or 1 cup
granulated sugar

2 cups sweet butter

Special equipment needed:

A food processor

A stainless-steel spoon and spatula

A flat cast-iron skillet (9″ diameter by
2½″ deep)

*P*repare the short pastry dough in the food processor: Place the flour, diced butter, and salt in the work bowl, and process for 4–5 seconds. Add the egg yolk with the water and sugar, and pulse 4–5 seconds, or until the dough pulls together. Remove from the processor and shape into a ball, wrap in plastic, and refrigerate until needed. The pastry dough is better if made at least an hour ahead of time, so that it firms up before it is rolled out.

Peel, core, and quarter the apples. Sprinkle them with a little lemon juice, then cut into dice, about ½″ square.

In a heavy-bottomed or enameled cast-iron skillet, melt the butter. Stir in the sugar with a stainless-steel spoon and continue stirring over moderate heat until the mixture turns golden brown, like toffee. Stir in just enough lemon juice to make the mixture smooth, then add half the apples. Stir constantly until the apples are cooked. They should be golden brown and tender. Remove fruit with a slotted spoon and reserve. Cook the rest of the diced fruit the same way and remove with a slotted spoon as before.

Transfer the remaining juices, which will become the glaze for the tart, to a saucepan and return the cooked fruit to the skillet. Smooth the fruit evenly with a spatula, then let cool completely before rolling out the dough.

When the fruit is completely cold, roll out the pastry dough in a circle 1″ larger than the skillet. Set the pastry over the fruit, then push the edges inside and down to make an edge. Bake in a preheated 400°F oven for about 20–25 minutes, or until the top is slightly browned. Remove and let cool.

While the tart is cooling, reduce the fruit cooking juices until thick and caramelized, then remove from heat and let cool until just tepid. When ready to serve, unmold over a shallow dessert dish. Glaze the fruit with the reduced caramelized fruit juice and serve, still slightly warm.

Wine Suggestion: A semi-sweet white sparkling wine, such as a Vouvray from the Loire Valley.

DRIVING AROUND TOWN, I saw many things that excited me. People who missed seeing Paris over sixty years ago do not believe what a paradise it was for drivers back then. Except for the horses and their droppings, and the tramways and trolleys one had to watch out for, it was easy to get around. The streets were nearly empty compared to today's cacophonic chaos. Occasionally I'd be speeding, and I'd hear the high-pitched whistle of a policeman—one of those colorful characters we called *hirondelles,* or swallows, because they looked ready to fly in their big capes, especially the ones on bicycles. "Madame," he would say very solemnly and courteously, "I believe you should not go so fast." But I never got arrested, because speeding tickets didn't come in until cars got to be a real problem, years later.

I felt gloriously free as I tooled down the tree-lined boulevards, always intrigued by the markets. In the Bastille quarter, I investigated and admired butchers' and bakers' shops, with their ceramic Belle Époque decors, and the gaudy displays in caterers' windows. Nearby fishmongers were touting the sole or turbot of the day with reckless abandon and humor, like barkers at a circus.

Paris was my university, and I breathlessly took it all in. I negotiated the curving, confusing roads in the Bois de Boulogne, went to art exhibitions, contemplated the posters, and tried to keep up with whatever was going on.

Fashion was new and amusing back there in the twenties, with those shorter skirts and the freedom of movement permitted to "flappers" liberated from their waist-cinching corsets—thanks to creators like Poiret, Vionnet, and Chanel. I was never a clotheshorse, but clothes were an outlet for my aesthetic sense, indeed for a latent sensuality. I particularly admired a well-dressed woman who had dazzled my father in the Midi and influenced me to become style conscious in my own way. Unable to afford haute couture, I ferreted out little dressmakers who could whip up really excellent couture copies. With friends I snooped around at couture sales, occasionally getting big reductions because I had an easy-to-fit "model's" figure.

Looking back, I realize that those ten years I spent with Jacques were dreary and fruitless but not desperately unhappy. After a couple of years, medical tests indicated that Jacques was sterile, and he finally gave up on bedroom advances. We arrived at a totally platonic relationship, a great relief to me.

We didn't have much "fun," but we did go out to a restaurant once in a while, and I'll never forget an encounter with the incredible Josephine Baker, who had taken Paris by storm. She was not what you would call beautiful, but what absolutely extraordinary sex appeal! You talk about "It," the famous attribute of the silent film star Clara Bow. Well, Josephine had it too; as we say in French, *du chien*. We were in a restaurant, eating an exceptionally good onion soup (which I later made at home, of course), and in sashayed Miss Baker, the coffee-colored exotic, undulating between tables. The men in the room were electrified; the women were gaping, though they feigned indifference. One of the men at our table danced with her, and she sat down briefly, laughing and saying in broken French, "*Mes amis,* pardon my French, but frankly, *La France j'adore.*" And she adopted France later, not to mention all the orphaned children whom she mothered in a château she bought in the Périgord.

Lindbergh and Turning Points

IN THE LATE TWENTIES, a couple of things happened that shook me up, making me yearn for a lot more in life than parties and bridge games.

As I was dressing for a party on May 21, 1927, I heard on my wireless that Charles Lindbergh was due to arrive at Le Bourget airport after his grueling transatlantic flight. Like a journalist who doesn't want to miss a world-shaking event, I felt compelled to see Lindbergh's landing, no matter what. The weather was lowering, but I ran out in my silk party outfit, forgetting my raincoat, to hop in my car and head at full tilt for Le Bourget.

The sky opened in a downpour, and by the time I arrived, the roads and the airport were like a small, raging sea, water and mud swirling in places around car hubs and people's ankles. "Stop! You cannot go any farther," guards kept telling me as I pushed through the crowds to the tarmac. "Rubbish," I replied. "This is urgent business." As a lone woman, in my bedraggled party finery, I cut an odd figure, even in that motley crowd.

While lights flooded the airfield, I waited as I heard and finally saw *The Spirit of St. Louis* drifting onto the end of the runway like a gentle little bird. I was beside myself, along with the others. A roar went up as we screamed, applauded, and cried. I lost a satin shoe in the mud, my coiffure and dress were sodden and lank, but I didn't care. When everyone surged forward en masse to greet this tall and handsome young airman, I turned into an airplane "groupie" of the day, a willing participant in a kind of mass hysteria. I pushed and shoved, getting near enough to touch him. But I couldn't kiss him; my ribs were almost crushed by the mob crowding around as if he were a miracle-maker, and indeed in a way he was. "Out of my way, lady," a photographer or reporter said rudely, roughly grabbing my shoulder. I melted away from Lindbergh, whose luminous blue eyes had for a split second caught mine.

Much later I found out that a kindred spirit was also somewhere in that crowd of 25,000—none other than my future husband, Jean. Without my lost shoe, I limped quickly back to the car and returned to our Paris flat to try to straighten myself up for the party, arriving so late that I'd missed dinner. Jacques, who'd gone on time without me, was furious.

Nobody at the party seemed to notice or care much about what had happened, as I stammered my explanations. "Oh, indeed?" said one man when I announced that I'd actually touched a hero. So I kept it to myself. I'd suddenly been fired up by the idea of learning to fly. But when I suggested it to my parents, they were appalled. Even my indulgent father thought I'd be mad to try such a thing. Shortly thereafter the papers wrote up the first Frenchwoman to get her license, a Mme Jarlaud, and many thought I was the new aviatrix, her name was so similar. How I wished it had been me!

Another crucial event was my near-fatal car accident. When my grandmother

Le Grand died in 1928, Jacques and I attended the funeral, and as we started back to Paris, Jacques had to slam on the brakes to avoid a tipsy pedestrian not far from Rainfreville. We crashed into a telephone pole, and I catapulted right through the windshield and was knocked out. I probably should have died, and I even recall an eerie white light that later I took to mean death. But I was wearing so many dark veils over my big-brimmed funeral hat that they must have saved my life, cushioning the blow somewhat.

I sat up after the shock, gave the whole medical establishment hell as an ambulance hovered nearby, looked with a cold eye at my own blood flowing, and fainted dead away.

As I recovered back home in Paris, I began to think seriously about life, considering my fate. I wanted something more rewarding than the life of a young housewife, which was beginning to pall.

My opportunity to do something worthwhile came when I discovered bookbinding. It does not sound heart-stopping as a profession, but once I got interested, I attacked it with the zeal of a mountain climber going for Everest.

The suggestion came from Charlotte Lebey, the daughter of a trout-fishing friend of my father's. André Lebey was actually more memorable in my life than Charlotte. He was very interested in me, and initiated me into a world of fairly intellectual books and poetry, even dedicating one of his own poems to me. And I think he wanted to be more than avuncular. He even kissed me straight on the mouth once, and I was shocked, pulling away furiously. I was a married woman! But still, it was not totally repulsive, and it made me think.

Deciding, after Charlotte's chance remark about the joys of her hobby, bookbinding, to become an apprentice bookbinder, I was soon devoted to learning this exacting skill. I was the same sort of fanatic perfectionist that I later became about cooking. I shuttled between the teachers in little workshops on the Left Bank and our flat near the Bois de Boulogne, where I took over a maid's room on the sixth floor (we lived on the second), working there days at a time with my leather and tools, coming downstairs only for a quick sandwich at lunch or a late dinner before bedtime.

I kept this up for about four years. I wanted to excel, and as soon as possible. By late 1933, I felt confident enough to enter a competition at the Grand Palais, l'Exposition des Artistes Français, and was stunned to read in the newspaper that my entry of three bound books had won second prize.

Meanwhile, I remained close to my family and loved taking trips with them. There were weekends at Rainfreville and holidays with my parents in the south of France. My husband did not seem to mind. Our favorite overnight stop was always at Saulieu, but in 1932 we pulled up across the street from our customary Poste, which Burtin had left, to visit Alexandre Dumaine, fast becoming one of the most famous chefs of this century at his Côte d'Or hotel-restaurant.

With my father at a society wedding in Paris

Dumaine had trained as a chef, and during the war the officers discovered that he was not only an excellent *canonnier,* or trained artilleryman, but much more important, he was a great cook. So he was asked to prepare lunch for President Georges Clémenceau, visiting the front at Verdun in 1917. As a soldier, Dumaine was awarded a high military honor—but he soon after won equal glory as a chef.

After the war, he spent nine years as chef for the French Line in Algeria, before setting up his hotel-restaurant in Saulieu.

Dumaine was a character, a big, expansive, florid-faced man, very sure of himself. He was perhaps the first of the great chefs to come "out of the kitchen" and meet the customers, consult with them about what kind of dinner they should contemplate, their best choices for wine.

On this holiday in 1932, I was anxious to forget about the ache in my shoulders (from bending over the leather I was tooling) and about my desultory conversations with Jacques. I couldn't have been at a better place, because the food and drink we savored at Dumaine's were nothing short of superb.

We tried the most refined dishes like pike mousseline, *feuilleté* of crayfish, *poularde des ducs de Bourgogne* in a cream sauce made with white Burgundy wine, *la Tour Blanche*—an ice cream dish with wild strawberry and Sauternes garnish.

Although informally rustic, the hotel was an oasis for celebrities, who flocked there in their Citroëns and Rolls-Royces. As I glimpsed it once or twice, the kitchen was already starting to become a scarred battlefield of cracks and grease spots. But it exuded lovely odors of winy sauces, baking pastries and soufflés.

Just over a year later, in 1933, I got a phone call from my father in Cannes. "Come quickly, *ma petite fille,*" he said. "Your mother's in bed with the flu, and I am not well either." I left a note for Jacques, took the overnight Train Bleu to the south, and went to join my parents at the Grand Hôtel du Parc in Cannes, where I stayed for the next two months.

My mother recovered from her influenza, but my father was dying of leukemia. Mother and I gave our blood for the regular transfusions, but it was hopeless, and his life ebbed away, though he did his best to determine that I would have a happier life. We were always close; he had taken so much care to teach me what he knew— the hunting and fishing, the rigors of driving a car when cars were tricky and tough to run—and of course I imbibed his knowledge of wine right along with our meals.

During his weeks of illness, we divulged secrets to each other, talking quietly and alone together as the winter sun streamed into his bedroom. Then his eyes began to hurt, and I gently drew the silk curtains. Papa admitted that he had been only human, not a perfectly faithful husband to my mother, but he hoped she knew nothing. He would not have hurt her for all the world.

"And you, *ma petite fille,*" he said as I held his hand. "You must tell me. I know you're not happy; it sticks out all over you. This marriage is not doing you any good at all, and you deserve better in life." I admitted that Father was right; it was he who persuaded me to leave Jacques, after ten years.

"I'm going to die soon," he sighed in a matter-of-fact way, as if he were discussing the weather. "Please promise me that you will divorce and free yourself to find another man, who can make you happy. I know you can do it—you *must* do it." In spring he returned to Rainfreville, and he died in June, leaving a terrible sadness and void in my life.

Left to my own devices, I'm not sure I would have acted to change my life. But my father's urging gave me the courage to file for a divorce. Before Father's death, I tried to break the news gently to Jacques, but he took it very badly. "It's not true!" he objected when I told him I was going to see a lawyer. "We've had a perfectly good marriage."

Superficially, yes, we seemed like a nice, polite couple. But the essential ingredients were missing, and I knew it. So I decided that even if I had to live alone, I'd be better off separated permanently from Jacques. I knew he would recover.

This was Depression, all around. The Beck side of my family had lost a great deal of money in the stock market, and Jacques had lost not only money but his job as well. I was keeping us afloat, paying rent and the cook's salary at our Paris apartment from my family income, which was still healthy on the Le Grand side.

Pellaprat

ONE DAY IN LATE 1933, driving my white Talbot 10-CV convertible coupé, I pulled up in front of the Cordon Bleu school, then located on the Rue du Faubourg Saint-Honoré. *Tiens!* I thought. I love cooking, and they give courses, so maybe I can refine what I already know, turn out more sophisticated dishes.

The school was run by the Belgian founders, the Distel sisters. I signed up for a short course. Classes were held in an amphitheater, and I soon realized that this method of learning was not for me. The instruction in those days was for domestics, sent by the *maîtresses de maison* to brush up on techniques and ideas for dinner parties. That's not what I minded. It was the fact that we had to watch from afar, without even getting a chance to taste the food. Dishes were made during two-day sessions and then were *sold*, of all things. And many of the dishes in my first few days there were far from exciting; I had learned most of the basics back in Rainfreville.

After one disappointing demonstration, I nevertheless charged down the amphitheater steps to meet the chef-teacher, who was Henri-Paul Pellaprat. He was later to become celebrated in the annals of French cooking as the author of *L'Art culinaire français (French Culinary Art)*, a classic of its kind. He was about sixty-three at the time, a man who obviously loved his métier, and I asked him right away, "Can you help me? I really want to learn new techniques, refined dishes—things I, rather than the cook, can do at home." He agreed to come regularly and help me prepare dinner for friends in my flat on the Rue Lesueur, starting about 5:00 P.M., after his classes. And that is how, during several sessions within a few months, I was able to learn from a great chef.

Pellaprat gave me generous advice from his vast fund of cooking knowledge, and I especially like some words he wrote before his death in 1949, later published in *French Culinary Art*.

> *I have tried to produce a work of lasting value in a field which is overcrowded, though rarely by qualified professionals. I was apprenticed in 1882 and never took off my white coat again. I did pastry-making, confectionery and cookery; I have practical experience of canning, ice-making, chocolate-making, industrial biscuit-making. I therefore believe, without vanity, that I have the right to be called an all-round craftsman and to be qualified to teach the things I know, unlike the many charlatans who pose as professors of a science they have never learned.* *

Voilà! I think all aspiring professional cooks ought to keep those sage words in mind. You can't just take a few lessons, turn out a fancy dish or two, and start teaching others.

* English version, Lugano: Jacques Kramer, 1960.

Pellaprat came several times that winter after his Cordon Bleu classes, and I gave small dinner parties prepared by him, my cook, and me. We all worked together, and I was learning about techniques for producing classic and elegant dishes like *turbot en soufflé,* galantines, and iced soufflé dishes. Everything was presented stylishly, as *haute cuisine*—a different approach from Zulma's down-home dishes.

Pellaprat was a good all-round teacher, as he claimed. But privately he turned up his nose somewhat at pastry-making, which he said required a good oven, a good recipe, and not much more. It was considered an exact discipline rather than an art, and pastry chefs were looked down on as poor cousins to more creative chefs doing meat, game, fish, and sauces.

But of course Pellaprat taught me *trucs* (little tips) about puff pastry, along with the rest. "Don't fuss or work it over," he'd say. "You don't want to produce galvanized rubber. Be cool, go quickly." I learned much from Pellaprat that even my dear Zulma could not teach me, and I must say that his principles were based on those of the great Auguste Escoffier.

A typical dinner I might have made with Pellaprat's help would include dishes like the ones on the following page.

Un dîner en ville
à la façon de Pellaprat

A Parisian Dinner Party, Pellaprat Style

✦ *Paupiettes de sole farcies au saumon*

Rolled sole fillets stuffed with salmon

—

Vin blanc sec—Chablis

✦ *Le canard aux navets et aux olives*

Duck with turnips and green olives

Salade de saison

Fromages variés

—

Bordeaux rouge ou Médoc—Château Margaux

✦ *Soufflé glacé à la Bénédictine*

Frozen soufflé with Bénédictine

—

Sauternes

Paupiettes de sole farcies au saumon

Rolled Sole Fillets Stuffed with Salmon

—

For 10 to 12

A fish *fumet* (stock), already prepared
   (page 363), or a good dry white wine
   with an equal amount of water
12 medium-size sole fillets
Lemon juice
Salt and pepper

For stuffing:
5½ oz. smoked salmon (good quality,
   very light)
3½ oz. sole fillets or lemon sole
Salt and pepper
1 egg white
9 Tbsp. heavy cream, *very cold*

For green sauce:
5–6 oz. watercress or tender leeks
1 shallot, minced
4 Tbsp. butter
3 egg yolks
1 cup crème fraîche (p. 501) or sour
   cream

Special equipment required:
A food processor
An ovenproof gratin dish
Toothpicks

A few days before you plan to serve this dish, make a fish *fumet*. If you do not have time, use only a very good dry white wine, such as a California Fumé Blanc, or any dry white wine from Burgundy or the Loire Valley.

Trim the sole fillets to make them neat, and sprinkle with a little lemon juice. Season with salt and pepper, and roll them around your thumb, keeping them loose in the middle for the stuffing. Place in the refrigerator while preparing the salmon stuffing.

Roughly cut the smoked salmon into small pieces, then purée in a food processor. Add to the salmon 3 oz. sole fillets, salt, and pepper, and process until smooth. Meanwhile, beat an egg white slightly with a fork, then add to the purée. Transfer this mixture to a mixing bowl, beat again thoroughly, then place in the freezer for 20 minutes or in the refrigerator for 1 hour.

Place the bowl over ice and beat again. Add the cream by tablespoonfuls, beating vigorously to make the mixture homogenous. Correct the seasoning, fill the center of each rolled fillet, and secure with toothpicks. (The fillets should be a little overfilled, as the mixture will sink a bit when baked.)

Generously butter a gratin dish and place the paupiettes upright and close to one another. Pour the fish *fumet,* or equal amounts of wine and water, so that it comes halfway up the sides of the dish, and cover with buttered foil. Bake in a preheated 425°F oven for 15–20 minutes.

While the fish is baking, prepare the green sauce. Chop the watercress (leaves and tender stalks) or leeks. Chop the shallot and sauté lightly in the butter for 1 minute, then add the watercress or leeks and stew slowly, stirring, until tender (about 15 minutes). Meanwhile, beat the egg yolks with the crème fraîche, and reserve. Transfer the watercress or leek mixture to a food processor and pulse to purée. Place in a saucepan and add the fish cooking liquid from the baking dish. Leave the paupiettes in the gratin dish, covered with foil, to keep warm. Stir the sauce over low heat and add the crème fraîche–yolk mixture. Stir constantly until slightly thickened, remove from heat, correct the seasoning, and keep warm over hot water until ready to serve.

Serve each paupiette in an individual dish surrounded with green sauce. The dish will be quite attractive, having three colors: the pink-and-white paupiettes with the pale-green sauce.

Serving Suggestion: Serve with a good dry white wine such as Chablis, Sancerre, Pouilly Fumé de la Loire, or a good Fumé Blanc from the Napa Valley.

Le canard aux navets et aux olives

Duck with Turnips and Green Olives

—

For 6

3 cups chicken broth (or water and chicken bouillon cubes)

2 young ducks, about 3 lb. each, not too fatty

Pepper and very little salt

2 Tbsp. dried herbes de Provence (p. 503)

1 Tbsp. olive oil

2 Tbsp. fat, lard, or melted pork

3 Tbsp. flour

Bouquet garni (see Aide-Mémoire, p. 503)

For vegetables:

2½ lb. turnips, peeled

A pinch of sugar

Bouquet garni (see Aide-Mémoire, p. 503)

3–4 dozen large green olives, not too salty, pitted

Minced parsley, for garnish

Special equipment needed:

A large ovenproof skillet with lid

Preheat the oven to 375°F. The broth should be made ahead, or you can use chicken bouillon cubes in 3 cups water.

Remove the necks from the cleaned ducks, leaving the neck skin intact; close the openings with a skewer. Season the insides of the ducks with pepper, a little bit of salt, and the herbs, and truss tightly with kitchen string. Smear olive oil all over the ducks.

Slowly melt the fat with 2 Tbsp. water in a heavy skillet. When the fat begins to smoke, brown one duck on all sides until golden brown. This may take 15–20 minutes. Place on a rack over a platter to collect the juices. Brown the other duck in the same manner.

Remove and strain the fat, clean the skillet, and return 1½ Tbsp. fat to the cleaned skillet. Stir in the flour to make a roux, stirring constantly over heat until it turns a nutty brown. Gradually add some of the chicken broth, stirring until the roux is smooth and thickened. Let simmer a few minutes to cook the flour.

Place the two ducks in the skillet on their sides, add the bouquet garni, the juices from the platter, and more broth to half cover the ducks. Correct the seasoning; cover with parchment paper and the lid. Let come to the simmer, then place in the oven for about 25 minutes. Turn the ducks on their other sides after 15 minutes.

Meanwhile, "turn" the turnips, or, using a paring knife, carve the peeled turnips into football shapes of uniform size. "Turned" turnips should be the same size as the olives. Parboil for 6 minutes with the pinch of sugar and bouquet garni, then drain and dry. When the ducks have baked for 15 minutes, add the turnips to finish cooking with the ducks.

Parboil the olives twice, 2 minutes each time, to remove the excess salt. Add the olives to the duck, and stew for 5 minutes before serving.

Remove the cooked ducks and cut into serving pieces. Place in a warmed shallow serving dish with the olives and turnips. Pour the sauce over and garnish with parsley.

Soufflé glacé à la Bénédictine

Frozen Soufflé with Bénédictine

—

For 8 to 10

Butter and sugar for molds

For crème anglaise:
1 cup milk
½ tsp. vanilla extract
4 egg yolks
½ cup sugar

For garnish:
4 oz. glacéed candied fruits (cherries, apricots, orange segments, etc.)
⅓ cup Bénédictine
Confectioners' sugar

For meringue:
¾ cup sugar
3 Tbsp. water
4 egg whites
Pinch of salt

For Chantilly:
1 cup heavy cream
½ tsp. vanilla extract

Special equipment needed:
2 ceramic soufflé molds (3½–4 cups
    each)

*P*lace an aluminum foil collar around each soufflé mold. The collars should be 3″ taller than the molds. Secure with string or masking tape so the foil fits tightly. Heavily butter the molds and the foil, and sprinkle with sugar to coat. Discard any excess sugar.

Prepare the custard by boiling the milk with the vanilla. Beat the egg yolks with the sugar until thick, so that a "ribbon" forms when poured from a spoon. Beating constantly, gradually pour the boiling milk into the egg yolks, then pour all back into the saucepan. Return to the heat and stir constantly until the custard slightly coats the spoon. Do not let mixture simmer, or it will curdle. Set aside to cool.

Parboil the candied fruits to remove the excess sugar. Drain and dry, then cut in tiny pieces. Macerate in the Bénédictine.

To make the meringue, first prepare a syrup by boiling the sugar with the water until the "thread" stage is reached. While the syrup is boiling, beat the egg whites with the pinch of salt until the beaters or whisk leaves a trace in the egg whites (about half beaten). Immediately pour in the boiling syrup and beat vigorously until the meringue is thick and shiny. Fold in the custard.

To prepare the Chantilly, beat the heavy cream with vanilla over ice cubes (in a bowl) until it is thick and light, then fold into the completely cool custard mixture. (If the custard is warm, the whipped cream will separate.) Add the fruits and macerating liquid.

Fill the molds to ½″ above their ceramic rims. The collars will hold the mixture. Freeze until set (about 3–4 hours).

Serve in the same molds, with foil collars removed and confectioners' sugar sprinkled on top.

Wine Suggestion: A good brut Champagne.

A FEW YEARS AGO, when the fad called *nouvelle cuisine* swept France and then the world, some tried to shrug off Escoffier and Pellaprat as outmoded and old-hat. Today those are the same people who are blowing the whistle on nouvelle cuisine and marching off to proclaim the merits of the traditional cassoulet or *boeuf en daube*—now the fashionable "retro" dishes.

The nouvelle fad was started by two ambitious journalists who coined a clever phrase, later to realize that they had spawned a trend that led to dubious culinary practices like putting tiny fans of food on huge plates.

Escoffier did perhaps advocate food that was not ideal for the health or waistline when eaten in quantity, and everyone nowadays is bombarded with advice on how to avoid cholesterol and calories, to the point of boredom. But you could find everything in Escoffier, and I believe that without the great traditions, French cooking would not exist as we know it today—whether nouvelle, revolutionary, evolutionary, or *minceur*. Nouvelle cuisine was debased when every hash slinger started trotting out pretentious dishes in big plates, and now it's almost a dirty expression.

My gastronomically gala moments by virtue of Pellaprat were going on even as my marriage was breaking up. Civil divorces in this Catholic country were much more difficult then than now, but they were nevertheless possible. I moved away from Rue Lesueur and in with my aunt and uncle Le Grand, who lived in the suburb of Le Vésinet, several miles west of Paris.

I had no special career or other plans then, and my life was almost at a standstill. I had time to breathe and take stock.

In this interim I spent time with my family up in Rainfreville. My mother was still inconsolable about my father's death, going about with a pale, tragic mien, and I was just as sad. But my young brother Bernard often came up for weekends, and having learned riding with the crack Saumur Cadres Noirs, he got me out to the stables. "Come on, Simone," he said. "You can't mope around forever. Riding is in our family. You'll feel a thousand percent better if you have a good gallop now and then." I had ridden some, but Bernard taught me how to deal tactfully with a horse's mouth, how to work in the tack room, how to handle the animal gracefully as we flew over logs (and I sometimes flew over the horse's neck!).

This was recovery time from death and divorce. But a lucky star was up there shining for me, and soon I would have something new to live for.

JEAN

WHAT A BIG CHASSIS, for such a little car!" exclaimed Jean Fischbacher when he saw me, at five foot eight, trying to squirm into the seat
of my small car to zip around Paris. I giggled, and his gentle teasing helped win
my heart, although I didn't know then that he would be my future husband, nor
that "Simca" (the name of the tiny Renault model I was driving) would stick with
me as my nickname for the rest of my life.

That memorable moment was not our first meeting; that had been a more prosaic
occasion, some two months earlier.

By the fall of 1936, my divorce had become final, and for the first time I was a
salaried working woman.

Having sensed that I was restless, my brother Maurice suggested that I start
working for the family company as a saleswoman—literally ringing doorbells to
tell bathroom-supply manufacturers why our product was superior. This was ideal
work for me, as I liked our business and wanted to meet new people. I approached
various companies that might have an interest in silicate, among them L. T. Piver,

which made perfumes and household products such as abrasives for cleaning—one of the uses for silicate.

On November 13, 1936, I drove to the Piver headquarters in central-eastern Paris to see the managing director, the formidably named M. Bouzanquet de Balestrier. The receptionist was a pleasant, clean-cut young man who explained that the boss was out of town, and would I see somebody else? I said, "No, thank you. I only deal with the top person," and I started to leave.

"Please, madame," insisted the receptionist. "You should meet the director's assistant. He is truly efficient and nice."

I reluctantly agreed and was ushered into the office of Jean Fischbacher, who did indeed have a winning smile, and was polite and well dressed, except perhaps for his tie—a drab number that didn't add much distinction to the man. This was no *coup de foudre*—no love at first sight.

Our silicate discussion did not last very long. We were soon comparing notes about mutual friends, and we discovered that Jean, at age thirty, two years younger than I, had spent much of his vacation time up in Normandy, hardly a mile from our house in Rainfreville.

He had been a summer member of the boy scout troop there, and I doubtless saw him then—swimming in the Saâne River or singing around a campfire—for sometimes my father in his role as mayor had taken me along to view the scouts from a distance.

I found this young man attractive, but I was understandably cautious and later did a little research on the Fischbachers through friends. They turned out to be a good old Alsatian Protestant family. Along with the vast majority in France, I was Catholic. I had an idea that the Protestants were successful people, often bankers, rather different from us in a vague upper-class way. I viewed them with some awe, tinged with mistrust. We call a Protestant service a *culte* here in France, and relationships between the Catholics and Protestants have been mutually wary or worse for centuries.

Jean was in no particular hurry to ask me out, and it was not until two months later, in January 1937, that I got a polite note from him, asking if perhaps we could go to a café together. I replied that we could not go to any old café. That was not proper, especially for a recent divorcée like myself. But I did agree to Weber, a smart establishment on the Rue Royale.

I was quite late on purpose—a bit of coquetry on my part, as was my carefully chosen outfit. I was decked out in a silver fox jacket and a little hat with a tall feather standing up on it. And there was Jean, calm as an oyster, his nose buried in a newspaper as he ignored the bustle around him. When he looked up and saw me, he beamed graciously and stood up. I was touched, mentally giving him high marks for being so patient and good-humored to a lady who had kept him waiting.

We ate the house specialty, Welsh rabbit (I prefer that name to Welsh rarebit, because I do think it has to do with some kind of substitution for rabbit, invented by an English cook on the day of an empty game bag). And it was delicious, although I mostly remember that we talked and laughed a lot, not paying too much attention to food and drink.

"How about going horseback riding in the Bois?" he asked, escorting me to my car. And that was when he made his humorous comment and gave me my official nickname. I had always detested Simone, and from then on I told everybody to call me Simca.

I accepted Jean's invitation, but we went a little farther than the Bois de Boulogne, out to the less-manicured Forest of Saint-Germain. Poor Jean; it turned out that he was not much of a rider, and I had learned a lot about horsemanship out in Normandy during the sessions with my brother Bernard.

I knew the minute Jean mounted his rented bay gelding that he'd have a problem. My chestnut filly was lively, but I had no problem galloping all over and jumping small logs, as Jean was doing his best not to look miserable and awkward in the saddle. I found out later that he told his sister that he had suffered the tortures of the damned and gotten blisters on his backside!

But riding turned out to be the only sport at which I could show him up. He was a better shot at clay pigeons (when we tried that much later on; I had given up shooting live game) and a stronger swimmer than I was.

Another rendezvous was more romantic, an evening at Prunier, the fish restaurant, with its splendid Belle Époque faïence decor, on the Avenue Victor Hugo. As Jean didn't yet have his own car, and I lived with my relatives out at Le Vésinet, I didn't mind arriving on my own.

Jean won me over with his good manners—especially the way he handled his mullet, baked and served whole, naturally including the head. He carved the fish with a surgeon's precision, removing the bones as perfectly as any maître d'hôtel could have. These things were and are terribly important to me—the signs of breeding and good manners.

After dinner, we went for a glass of Champagne at Scheherazade, the chic Russian *boîte* on the Rue de Liège, near Pigalle. It was so typically sybaritic and Parisian, as we lounged back on those ornate satin cushions and listened to the balalaikas and violins wailing in our ears. This was heady stuff to me after my previous confined, proper existence.

I could feel that a romance was well on its way, and I was beginning to discover something I guess I could call happiness, even euphoria, emotions I began to feel I'd been cheated out of before.

I had a couple of other beaux at the time, some rather pressing—for example, Xavier Dussac, a rich lawyer with a mansion on the Avenue Marceau near the Étoile. He even gave a ball in my honor, and I was ungratefully bored silly by the whole idea. I only wanted to be with Jean, so I asked him to come and to dance with me at the ball after dinner, toward midnight.

The party was magnificent, in a marble-and-gilt setting lit by candelabra everywhere, with an elaborate buffet for about seventy guests. The list unfortunately included three people I termed "cows," women who were gossipy, jealous, and out for my hide. Two were named Simone . . . a good reason to dislike my real name. I had spent a couple of hours having my hair done, and was wearing my best sun-pleated almond-green silk chiffon evening dress, fluid in the style of the early thirties. And I splashed on some of my favorite perfume, Cuir de Russie, which I hoped would appeal to Jean—who was quite an expert at scents.

When the band struck up, "Du-du," as our host was nicknamed (it doesn't have the same pejorative sound in French as in English, but it's still no winner), asked me to open the ball with him. He was a nice enough man, but his syrupy, unctuous manner reminded me of melting chocolate.

What I did next was not very nice, but as we launched into something jaunty, perhaps an early Gershwin piece, I told Du-du he was looking a little on the peaked side. "So I've invited an extra dancing partner," I informed him. He was quite a good sport about the whole thing and simply looked a little puzzled. Especially as my "dancer," Jean, did not arrive exactly at the hour I expected him. I was getting very impatient and upset, casting distracted glances toward the door all the time.

"Where *have* you been?" I glared at him as he swept in, wearing cape and evening suit. He muttered something, but he looked so handsome, except maybe for his badly tied bow tie, that I had to forgive him. I introduced him to Du-du, who took it in stride, and I started to dance with Jean.

The three "cows" were standing around ruminating, gaping and looking wild with envy, or so I fancied. I'm sure they were dying to know who my new beau was. But I was not going to introduce them to this prize bachelor.

"Let's get out," I murmured in his ear. "I've been here for three hours, and that's enough for me!" He agreed with alacrity, so we collected our coats and sailed out, feeling a little rude but mostly relieved.

I drove us in my sporty little red convertible with its white top, and we ended up at Monseigneur, a nightclub next to the Montmartre cemetery. It was smoky, dark, a rather low dive, but frequented by true Parisian night owls and tourists alike. We danced and talked until 5:00 A.M., noticing nothing much except each other. "How about Le Boeuf sur le Toit?" asked Jean, hopefully suggesting another hot night spot.

In those days, Paris really was the city of light all night long, but I decided that one more club would really do me in, so I offered to drive Jean home before I returned to my uncle's house in Le Vésinet. We stopped on the Pont de la Concorde, facing the National Assembly building; the air in that January predawn was clear and bracing, the sky a luminous indigo. Everything was silent, and the city was still asleep. It was a magical moment, for just us alone. Jean kissed me, ever so gently, and said simply, "You're going to be my wife." We kissed again and again, and I don't think I even had to say "yes."

I drove Jean over to his family's big apartment building, on the corner of Sèvres-Babylone and Boulevard Raspail, across from the Hôtel Lutétia—the first time I had ever seen where he lived.

There happened to be a hearse proceeding out to the boulevard on the Rue de Babylone as we had our last good-night kiss. That lugubrious conveyance could have been a bad omen, but it wasn't. A few months later, Jean would cut out a big sign made from newspapers, on which he'd painted "I love you," and dangle it from the family balcony when I drove up.

But this dawn arrival was certainly not the time to meet the Fischbacher family. And even in acceptable circumstances, I was still a reserved, timid Catholic woman, not knowing much about Protestants except that I thought they might be stuffy.

I drove off, but Jean told me later that as he was sneaking into the apartment at 7:00 A.M., his father was leaving to get the early newspapers. His reaction was hardly stuffy. He merely remarked laconically, "Well, I see you're early, Jean." Frenchmen understand these things.

Exhausted, I somehow made it back to Le Vésinet in my runabout. But I was so ecstatic in my discovery of love that I mustn't have paid much attention to the road. My car practically drove itself, as my mind was reliving the evening with Jean.

Within a few months we would be lovers, and my life would take on a whole new meaning. All of those things that I had viewed coldly as a reader of novels or a cinema spectator were true, and I finally realized they were happening to *me*.

While I was separated and divorcing, I had had no affairs; I was simply not interested, although here I was well over thirty. But how lucky I was! I hear that some people never experience sexual passion, or any passion at all, in their lives, and that is so sad. I was on my way to missing all this when I met Jean.

I went off on a skiing holiday at Arosa in the Swiss Alps, rather an avant-garde thing to do in those days, and I suppose I was also hoping to keep my fiancé anxious and "on the string." This was my fifth year of skiing, and that was real exercise, more cross-country than downhill style.

Those were the good old "planks" days, when we skiers put sealskins on the skis and climbed several hundred meters until we were exhausted, just to ski down in two minutes at breakneck speed. I had no technique, nothing like the racers I see on television today. I always rushed to be the first one down, even though I nearly broke my neck on a few of those falls. Après ski was of course wonderful. I felt so tired and happy, and really savored my tea or chocolate and cakes, then later on something more substantial, like a cheese fondue.

Jean phoned me at the châlet-hotel a few times, whispering his romantic devotion. "Why are you whispering?" I asked. "Speak up." I found out later that Jean's sister, France, could overhear the conversation in their family living room. And sisters can be jealous and make snide remarks.

Jean met me at the Gare de Lyon when I returned to Paris, and in all the hullaballoo of the station, we could see only each other.

"Darling, I've got a wonderful weekend planned for us," said Jean. "You're not returning yet to your uncle's house; I'm abducting you to the Résidence Saint James et d'Albany." Good heavens, what next? I thought, hoping for the best.

We pulled up to the hotel, on the Rue de Rivoli, had the bags taken out by a bellhop, and Jean coolly registered us as an old married couple—while I lurked in the background, pale with anticipation and good Catholic guilt.

When we got to the room, Jean excused himself for a bath. I looked around this veritable "honeymoon suite," with its splendid antique furnishings and fringed silk curtains, and gingerly helped myself to a grape from a table loaded with fruit, little cakes, and the indispensable Champagne in a silver bucket.

As if all this weren't enough, I nearly swooned when my eyes fell upon the ultimate atmospheric touch furnished by Jean—a portable gramophone!

I put on one of my favorite records, Charles Trenet's "*'Y a de la Joie*" ("There's Joy in the Air"). Then, as Jean emerged in his silk dressing gown, angelically sparkling and fresh from his bath, he manfully enfolded me in his arms . . . and keeled over in a dead faint!

My heart sank. What did I have here, a cardiac lover? But he leapt up within seconds. I guess the emotion and the hot, steamy bath had overwhelmed him; the same thing happened a couple of times later in our married life, but meant nothing serious.

After our shaky start, we finally quaffed Champagne, listened to music, and became luxuriant lovers for over forty-eight hours. We played Trenet's song over and over; it became "our song," and throughout my life I have often thought of it to bring back that ecstatic time.

Our engagement became official, and I finally met Jean's family in March, though I was scared to death. His father, Alfred, proved to be a wonderful, kind, and open man. He put down his newspaper, came over, and kissed me warmly, saying, "Welcome to our family." I could feel that Jean's mother was much more reserved about the whole idea. It seemed obvious to me that she was thinking thoughts like: A thirty-three-year-old divorcée, maybe too old to have children, certainly too old for Jean.

I could also sense reservations from the rest of this Protestant family as well. Jean's sister France, a bit my type physically, has always adored him, and sometimes she and I have had our disagreements. Pierre, Jean's younger brother, was always trying to josh me about one thing or another, particularly about the feather I liked to wear on my hat, and at first I found this embarrassing. But I was determined to show my best face to Jean's family.

When I took him up to Rainfreville to meet my mother, she practically fell in love with him herself. He did make an excellent impression, a fairly tall young man with sparkling and humorous eyes and a mouth that turned up at the corners—a model of courtly manners.

Here was a gentleman who really knew the art of kissing a lady's hand and of charming a prospective mother-in-law. We talked and talked, my mother wanting news and gossip of Paris, and we had a very festive lunch. I already knew that Jean was a chocolate-lover, a delicious weakness that persisted throughout his life, so of course our dessert was based on that ingredient.

Le déjeuner de fiançailles
à Rainfreville

Engagement Celebration Lunch for Jean at Rainfreville

✦ *Rissoles au fromage*
Small cheese turnovers

—

Aperitif: Champagne de Ayala

✦ *Côtelettes Prince Igor*
Veal cutlets Prince Igor with cream sauce

✦ *Le rizotto espagnole*
Risotto, Spanish style

✦ *Courgettes sautés, au naturel*
Sautéed sliced zucchini

Salade verte
Fromages normands —
Camembert, Pont l'Évêque, Livarot

—

Un bon vin rouge de Bordeaux

✦ *Gâteau au chocolat et à l'orange, pour Jean*
Orange-flavored chocolate cake, for Jean

—

Champagne brut

Rissoles au fromage

Small Cheese Turnovers

—

For pastry:
About 3¾ cups sifted flour
½ tsp. salt
8 Tbsp. butter (or half butter, half
  margarine)
1 egg yolk, beaten with 2 Tbsp. cold
  water

For Mornay sauce:
1½ Tbsp. butter
2 Tbsp. flour
1 cup milk
Salt, pepper, and nutmeg
¼ cup crème fraîche (p. 501)

⅓ cup Gruyère cheese, cut in small
  dice

Oil, for deep frying (preferably, peanut
  oil)

For the marinade (optional):
2 cups dry white wine
Pepper
2–4 oz. canned truffles, roughly chopped,
  with their liquid

Special equipment needed:
A deep wide pan for deep frying

*M*ake the pastry dough the day before, if possible, or at least 1 hour before needed. It may be necessary to add more water; however, the dough should just barely hold together and not be sticky. Let rest at least 1 hour in the refrigerator.

To prepare the Mornay sauce, melt the butter and stir in the flour. Let cook, stirring constantly, for 2–3 minutes, without letting the roux brown. Remove from heat and stir in the milk all at once, stirring vigorously until smooth. Return to the heat and let boil a few minutes. Season with salt, pepper, and nutmeg, stir in the crème fraîche, and then add the diced cheese. Stir constantly until the cheese melts. (Cheese added in tiny dice will not become stringy when it melts; grated cheese can form strings.) Let cool completely.

Roll out the pastry dough to a thickness of ⅛″. Using the round cookie cutter, cut out 20–24 disks.

Place 1 Tbsp. Mornay sauce on each pastry disk and fold to form a half-moon shape. Using a fork, carefully seal by pressing along the edges on both sides of the pastry. Unless the edges are sealed completely, the filling will leak out during frying. Refrigerate until time to be fried.

Heat the oil in a deep wide pan (fill with about 2″ of oil) until a tiny piece of stale bread dropped into the oil becomes golden in just a few seconds. Fry the rissoles, turning them over so they brown on both sides. Remove with a skimmer and let dry over paper towels. Made ahead, these can be easily reheated in a moderately hot oven for about 10 minutes.

Côtelettes Prince Igor

Veal Cutlets Prince Igor with Cream Sauce

—

For 6

For côtelettes:

4 slices *pain de mie* (page 495)

⅓ cup crème fraîche (page 501)

10 oz. veal scallops

5 oz. boiled ham

3 oz. ham or goose fat

6 Tbsp. butter, creamed

2–3 egg yolks, depending on size

Allspice, dried herbes de Provence (page 503), and salt and pepper

1 cup dry bread crumbs, prepared by rubbing the bread through a sieve

3 Tbsp. butter plus 2 Tbsp. oil

For cream sauce:

2 cups marinade or chicken broth

8 Tbsp. butter

¼ cup lemon juice

⅓ cup crème fraîche (page 501) or heavy cream

Salt and pepper

2 Tbsp. chopped chives

Special equipment needed:

A food processor

A nonstick frying pan

A saucepan

Fireplace matches

If you wish, the meat can be marinated overnight in the refrigerator with the dry white wine, a little pepper, and the truffles. After marinating the meat, strain and reserve the marinade, retaining the chopped truffles as well.

Put the sliced bread in crème fraîche to soak. Cut the veal, ham, and fat into large dice, then chop finely in a food processor. Transfer the meat to a mixing bowl, add the moistened *pain de mie,* and blend until a smooth mixture is obtained. Mix in the creamed butter, egg yolks, chopped truffles if you have used them, and season highly with the herbs and spices. The mixture should be quite thick. If it is not, place in the freezer to firm up. (The recipe may be prepared to this point the day before.)

With slightly wet hands to prevent the mixture from sticking to them, form the mixture into mock veal cutlets (chops), each weighing about 4 oz. Roll the cutlets in stale bread crumbs, patting off any excess, and place in the freezer for 5 minutes to set.

Heat the butter and oil in a nonstick frying pan and cook cutlets 5–6 minutes per side, as many at a time as you can without crowding. When done, remove and drain on paper towels. Cook the others the same way, adding more oil as needed. Place a 3″ piece of fireplace match in each cutlet to simulate the cutlet bone, then keep covered and warm until ready to serve.

If the meat was marinated before cooking, deglaze the pan with the marinade; otherwise use 2 cups of broth. Reduce the deglazing mixture until 6–8 Tbsp. remain, and set aside. In another saucepan, melt the butter for the sauce, beat in the lemon juice, then add the crème fraîche and reduced deglazing liquid. Taste and correct the seasoning.

When ready to serve, place the cutlets in a row on a warmed shallow serving dish. Add the chives to the sauce and pour over the cutlets.

Vegetable Suggestion: Serve with risotto and sautéed zucchini (following recipes), with buttered tender string beans or asparagus tips, or on a bed of puréed spinach.

Wine Suggestion: A fruity white wine from the Loire Valley, such as a Vouvray or a Sancerre.

Le rizotto espagnole

Risotto, Spanish Method

—

For 6 to 8

3½ Tbsp. virgin olive oil

7 oz. red onion, sliced

2 cups long-grain rice (preferably
   Surinam, Le Taureau brand)

5 cups good chicken broth

Salt and freshly ground pepper

1 hot pimiento pepper

2–3 Tbsp. double-concentrated tomato
   paste

1 bay leaf

Special equipment needed:

A heavy ovenproof skillet with lid,
   preferably cast iron

Heat the olive oil in the skillet, add the sliced red onion, and let cook slowly, without browning, until very soft. Remove the onion with a slotted spoon and reserve. Add the rice to the same oil, stirring continuously until the rice grains turn milky and begin to brown. Still stirring, pour in all the broth, and add the cooked onion, salt and freshly ground pepper, hot pimiento, tomato paste, and bay leaf. As soon as the mixture begins to boil, cover and place in a preheated 375° oven for 18–20 minutes, or until the broth has been completely absorbed and the rice is tender and fluffy. Taste and correct the seasoning, adding more salt if needed.

Courgettes sautées, au naturel

Sautéed Sliced Zucchini

—

For 6

2–2½ lb. tiny young zucchini
½ Tbsp. salt.
4 Tbsp. butter
2 Tbsp. olive oil
3 Tbsp. finely chopped shallots or green onions
2 garlic cloves, crushed

Salt and pepper
2 Tbsp. minced chervil or parsley

Special equipment needed:
A food processor with ⅛" slicing disk
A large nonstick skillet

*W*ash and dry the zucchini, but do not peel. Using a food processor equipped with a slicing disk, slice the zucchini ⅛" thick. Place the slices in a mixing bowl, sprinkle with ½ Tbsp. salt, and allow them to disgorge their moisture for about 15 minutes, stirring and shaking the bowl frequently. Rinse with cold tap water to remove all the salt, then spread over paper towels to dry. You should have about 4 cups.

Melt the butter with the oil in a large nonstick skillet. When barely hot enough, add the chopped shallots and the garlic and stir constantly until softened. Add the sliced zucchini to the skillet a handful at a time, without crowding at the beginning, and let cook until tender and slightly browned, about 15–20 minutes. Season to taste with salt and pepper, and keep warm until needed, then sprinkle with minced chervil or parsley and serve.

Gâteau au chocolat et à l'orange, pour Jean

Orange-flavored Chocolate Cake, for Jean

—

For 6 to 8

For filling:

8 oz. bitter chocolate

4 Tbsp. orange juice and the grated peel of 1 orange

1 cup sweet butter

½ cup plus 1½ Tbsp. sugar

½ cup milk with vanilla

1 egg yolk

For Chantilly:

1 cup heavy cream

½ tsp. vanilla extract

Bénédictine liqueur, if needed

36–40 ladyfingers (¾" by 4")

For soaking ladyfingers:

About ½ cup orange juice

¼ cup sugar

Grated peel of 1 or 2 large oranges

3 Tbsp. Bénédictine or Cointreau

Special equipment needed:

A rectangular or square cake pan

Parchment paper or aluminum foil

A pastry bag with a floret tip

ℒine the cake pan with buttered parchment paper or foil, and place in the refrigerator until needed.

Prepare the filling: Melt the chocolate with the orange juice, stirring over hot water until melted and very smooth. Meanwhile, cream the butter with ½ cup sugar. Remove chocolate mixture from heat, let cool completely, then add the creamed butter, the grated orange peel, and the liqueur, and mix vigorously. In a small saucepan, bring the milk to the boil with the vanilla. At the same time, beat the egg yolk with 1½ Tbsp. sugar until the mixture is pale and forms a "ribbon," then slowly pour in the hot milk and place on the heat to thicken, *without boiling*, stirring constantly. When thick, remove from heat and allow to cool before stirring into the chocolate mixture.

Whip the cream with the vanilla and fold half the Chantilly (mixture at "soft peak" stage) into the completely cool chocolate cream.

To assemble the cake, soak the ladyfingers in the orange juice, sugar, grated orange peel, and liqueur. Place a layer of ladyfingers in the pan, tops down and close together, and spread over them a thick layer of the chocolate cream. Continue building in the same way until all the ladyfingers are used, retaining enough of the chocolate cream to spread over the entire cake. Place in the refrigerator for several hours or until completely chilled. Unmold and coat with the remaining chocolate cream, smoothing with a wet metal spatula, then chill again. Fill the pastry bag with the remaining Chantilly and pipe rosettes along the sides and top to decorate. Serve cold.

Optional decorations: 12 tiny strips of candied angelica for the top, or chopped pistachios and candied orange peel, dipped in Bénédictine. Candles may be placed between the rosettes.

Wine Suggestion: A good bottle of brut Champagne.

I MARRIED JEAN VICTOR FISCHBACHER on Friday, April 30, 1937, in a low-keyed but dignified civil ceremony at the Town Hall in Paris's Seventh Arrondissement, with a reception at the Fischbachers' afterward. We had an excellent buffet, with shrimp, foie gras, a bit of caviar, Champagne de rigueur.

My mother's chauffeur drove the three of us back to Rainfreville, where Jean and I were to spend about a week's honeymoon.

That spring still seems a dream time to me. Like all people in love, we were totally self-absorbed, smug at our good fortune—a cut above the rest of the mundane world.

We felt like the world's *only* lovers during our long walks along the paths and roads we knew so well—Jean from his scouting days. We drifted through flowering apple- and pear-tree orchards, climbing over low stone barriers, looking at ruined towers, sometimes getting scratched by nettles, but this time I was too happy (not to mention better clothed) to feel discomfort.

We often went to the beaches, but it was much too cold to swim yet, so we took off our shoes and ran barefoot along the sand, picking up pebbles or driftwood, making jokes and teasing one another. Then we'd return home for a family lunch, welcome to our fresh-air appetites.

Our Norman weather was typically finicky, so on one of the rainy days we had a delicious lunch featuring cheese and pork—both harking back to eastern France and Jean's Alsatian family background.

Un déjeuner pendant
notre lune de miel en Normandie

Luncheon for a Cool Day During
Our Honeymoon in Normandy

✦ *Tartelettes du Jura*
Individual cheese tarts, Jura style

✦ *Casserole de porc Cocher de Fiacre*
Pork stew with vegetables and beer

Salade verte

Fromages variés

—

Vin blanc sec d'Alsace ou bière blonde légère
(dry white Alsatian wine or light blond Alsatian beer)

✦ *Tarte aux pruneaux et aux amandes, flambée*
Flamed prune and almond tart

Tartelettes du Jura

Individual Cheese Tarts, Jura Style

—

The best Gruyère cheese in France is made in the Jura province, in the eastern part of the country.

24 tartlets

2 lb. short pastry dough (see page 488)

1½ oz. grated Parmesan cheese

For filling:
1 cup diced Gruyère cheese
3 eggs
2 cups thick crème fraîche (p. 501) or
   sour cream
Salt, pepper, and grated nutmeg
1 cup grated Gruyère cheese

Special equipment needed:
A rolling pin
A 3″ round cutter
20 small tartlet molds
A mixing bowl

*P*reheat the oven to 375°F. Roll out the pastry dough on a floured surface to ⅛″ thickness. Using the cutter, cut 20 rounds of pastry and line each tartlet mold with a pastry round. Immediately press into the pastry a layer of diced Gruyère, and chill in the refrigerator.

In a mixing bowl, beat the eggs with the crème fraîche or sour cream, salt, pepper, and nutmeg, and mix in the grated Gruyère.

Fill each tartlet ⅔ full and sprinkle with Parmesan cheese, then bake immediately in the preheated oven for 16–18 minutes, or until the tops are puffed and nicely brown. The tartlets will deflate in cooling but will still be delicious.

Note: The tartlets can be made the day before and reheated in the oven.

Casserole de porc
Cocher de Fiacre

Pork Stew with Vegetables and Beer

—

For 6 to 8

3 lb. boneless pork shoulder

Salt and pepper

½ cup flour

2½ Tbsp. melted lard

1 large onion, sliced

1 carrot, quartered

2 stalks of celery, diced

1 small, tender green cabbage, sliced into
 ¾"–1" wedges

2½–3 cups light-colored (blond) beer

Bouquet garni (p. 503)

4 Tbsp. canned tomato paste

Optional: Tabasco

Special equipment needed:

A large ovenproof skillet or cast-iron pot
 with lid

Parchment paper

A shallow heated serving dish

Trim the pork to remove fat and gristle, and cut into 4-oz. pieces. Sprinkle with salt and pepper, and roll in flour, shaking off the excess.

Heat the lard in the skillet, and when hot, brown the pieces of meat, turning them on all sides to brown evenly. Remove the meat and strain the fat to remove any burned particles, then return to the heat, adding more fat and the onion, carrot, and celery. Let stew slowly until the outsides of the vegetables are tender, then add the cabbage and brown the leaves very slightly. Pour the beer over the vegetables and let simmer a few minutes. Then return the meat to the pan, adding additional seasoning, the bouquet garni, and, if needed, water or light broth to just cover. Add the tomato paste, diluted slightly with liquid from the pan, and cover with parchment paper and the lid of the pan. When beginning to simmer, place in a preheated 375°F oven and bake for 40–45 minutes, or until tender. Check the tenderness of the meat halfway through the cooking time, stirring to turn the pieces over.

Note: The dish can be made ahead of time and reheated just before serving.

Vegetable Suggestion: 2 lb. cut-up boiled potatoes, served with 2 Tbsp. melted butter and garnished with minced parsley.

Beverage Suggestion: The same beer or cider.

Tarte aux pruneaux et aux amandes, flambée

Flamed Prune and Almond Tart

—

For about 6

For pastry:
1½ cups pastry flour
¼ cup sugar
Pinch of salt
3½ oz. (or ¾ cup) pulverized almonds
1 egg or 2 egg yolks
4 Tbsp. dark rum
10 Tbsp. sweet butter, cut up and
    softened

For filling:
10 oz. pitted prunes

4 Tbsp. sugar
2 large or 3 medium eggs
½ cup crème fraîche (page 501) or heavy
    cream
¼ cup pulverized almonds
2 Tbsp. sweet butter, melted

To flame:
2 Tbsp. dark rum

Special equipment needed:
An 8″–8½″ tart pan

*P*repare the pastry. Mix together the flour, sugar, salt, and pulverized almonds, then make a well. Pour into it a beaten egg (or the egg yolks) and rum, and blend. Add the softened butter and mix only until you can form a ball. Do not overwork. Place in a plastic bag and chill in the refrigerator at least 30 minutes, or, better, prepare in the morning for use that night.

When the pastry is firm, press it into the tart pan, using only your hands and starting in the bottom center and working outward and up. Form the border with a double thickness of pastry. Prick the pastry and chill for 20 minutes, then bake in a preheated 400°F oven for about 15 minutes.

While the tart shell is baking, prepare the filling. You can buy pitted prunes or steep regular prunes for a few minutes in strong, boiling-hot tea, then cut in half to remove the stones easily. If using pitted prunes, soften them slightly in the same manner and cut in half.

Ribbon the sugar with the eggs; add the crème fraîche, the pulverized almonds, and the melted butter. Arrange the prunes in a single layer in the half-baked tart shell, and cover with the egg mixture. Bake in a preheated 375°F oven until the cream is set, about 15–20 minutes.

To serve, heat the rum, set aflame, and pour over the tart.

OUR MAJOR HONEYMOON OUTING was down to Mont-Saint-Michel, in Brittany. We started out at dawn, having borrowed our most powerful family car.

Several hours later, we stopped to gape at the awesome sight of the monastery on its rock, looming up from the damp sandy flats that fill with water at high tide to make the Mont an island. We were very moved by this glorious monument and made the reverent noises, but our most pressing need after the long drive was to have a good lunch.

After negotiating the narrow cobblestone roads around the Mont and its village, we were happy to stumble out of a windy bastion and into the warmth of La Mère Poulard. As every tourist knows, the restaurant is an institution nearly as famous as Mont-Saint-Michel itself. I imagine the decor is much the same today as what we saw back then—gleaming with copper utensils, commanding vast views from small windows, a fire burning cheerily in the beamed dining room.

I had been there in 1920 with my parents, when the famous Mère Poulard herself was beating and cooking her omelets, which had made her reputation all over

Riding—one of my favorite sports—was also the only one at which I could outdo Jean

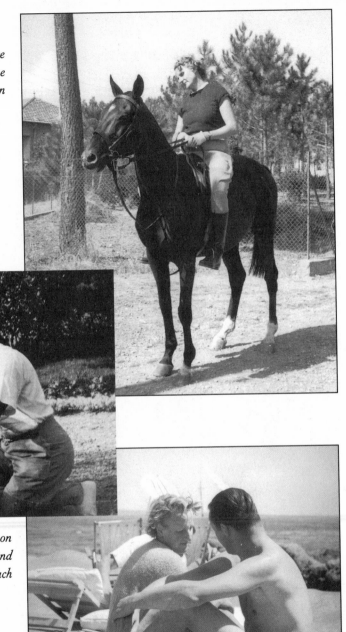

With Jean (above) on our honeymoon and (right) on the beach

Europe. When Jean and I were there, a nephew had taken over, and I'm afraid the puffy omelet was just not the same, not as rich.

They did beat the eggs in clean copper bowls, but they cheated on the butter, not putting as much as they once had into the copper pan to cook the omelet over the wood-burning fire. The whisking time took exactly the prescribed six minutes and sounded like a tin drum—tac, tac, tac. Jean and I ate heartily, including fish dishes and crêpes for dessert, and made it back to Rainfreville for a light supper that night.

Returning to Paris, we settled into the flat we'd chosen for ourselves out at Boulevard d'Argenson in Neuilly, where we lived for the next forty years. It was in an undistinguished nine-story "modern" building that provided a comfortable dwelling with little else to recommend it for either function or beauty.

We had one and a half *salons* (a large drawing room), furnished with some antiques from both families, but the kitchen was minuscule, so I had to make do; when I gave lessons many years later, I often had to use a card table in the living room for such things as overnight marinating of fresh foie gras (in brandy, port, a bit of pepper, hardly any salt), to cook gently the next day.

Jean and I were living a routine but happy existence. Contentedly, I cooked and cooked to please Jean, and in more ways than one he was pleasing me, too. We loved music and often had quiet evenings at home listening to Mozart or Beethoven on the gramophone. But we also occasionally saw friends or family for dinner, or took in a cinema, followed by a restaurant dinner.

I liked having just a few friends over and took pride in dinners that were not too difficult to make but still impressive once on the table.

Un dîner des jeunes mariés pour six amis

Dinner for Six Given by the Newlyweds

✦ *Asperges, sauce gribiche*
Cold asparagus with gribiche sauce

—

Vin rosé de Provence

✦ *Pâté de poisson en croûte, sauce hollandaise*
Fish pâté in a crust, with Hollandaise sauce

Salade verte mélangée

—

Vin rosé

✦ *Tarte duchesse aux poires*
Duchess pear tart

—

Champagne demi-sec

Asperges, sauce gribiche

Cold Asparagus with Gribiche Sauce

—

For 6

3–4 lb. asparagus (the amount depends
    on how much you have to trim the stalks)
Salted boiling water

*W*ash and peel the asparagus, removing all scales and the tough part of the stalk. Tie together in bundles with the tips aligned and drop into rapidly boiling salted water. Cook for about 20 minutes, or until done. (Perfectly cooked asparagus stalks will be bright green and tender, not limp. The stalks will bend a bit, but not droop, if held horizontally.) Drain on kitchen towels, and serve with *Sauce gribiche.*

Sauce gribiche

—

For 1 cup

3 hard-boiled egg yolks
1 generous Tbsp. Dijon mustard
¾ cup vegetable oil
1½ Tbsp. wine vinegar
3 hard-boiled egg whites, sieved or
    finely chopped

2 Tbsp. gherkin pickles, finely
    chopped
2 Tbsp. capers, chopped
2 Tbsp. chopped aromatic herbs, such as
    chives, chervil, and parsley
Salt and pepper

*M*ash the egg yolks with the mustard. Add the oil, drop by drop, whisking constantly, as for a classic mayonnaise. When all the oil is incorporated, slowly mix in the vinegar, and then stir in the rest of the ingredients. Serve on cold asparagus.

Pâté de poisson en croûte, sauce Hollandaise

Fish Pâté in a Crust, with Hollandaise sauce

—

For 10 to 12 (see Note)

For pastry dough:
8½ cups pastry flour
Salt
1½ cups cold butter, diced
2 Tbsp. oil
2 egg yolks, beaten with
    ¼ cup cold water

For fish:
2½ lb. striped bass, salmon, pike, or
    halibut
6 Tbsp. butter
3 shallots, minced

For mushroom filling:
2½ lb. white mushrooms

6 oz. evaporated milk
3 egg yolks
1 Tbsp. dried herbes de Provence
    (see Aide-Mémoire, page 503)
Salt and pepper

For glaze:
2 egg yolks, beaten with
    2½ Tbsp. cold water

Special equipment needed:
A food processor
A nonstick sauté pan
An 11″ by 14″ baking tray
Aluminum foil
A pastry brush

The pastry is better if made the day before it will be baked. Put the flour, salt, and diced cold butter in a food processor. Pulse just a few seconds to mix the flour and butter, then add the beaten egg yolks and water. Pulse until the dough is just blended and pulls together into a ball, but do not overwork. Remove to a pastry board and work very briefly with your hands until smooth, then wrap in a plastic bag and refrigerate overnight, or for several hours at least.

Clean the fish, removing the skin and any bones, then cut into slices ⅔″ thick. Heat the butter and half the oil in a nonstick pan, stir in the minced shallots, and let cook 3 minutes, stirring, without browning. Remove and reserve. In the same fat, sauté all but ½ lb. of the fish slices, reserving the rest for the filling. When nicely sautéed on both sides, remove and reserve. Cut the uncooked fish into small pieces and sauté in the same pan, adding oil and more butter if needed.

Clean and dry the mushrooms. Remove and discard the stems, then slice the caps and sauté in the nonstick pan with nothing else. Stir constantly until the natural moisture from the mushrooms has evaporated, then add the evaporated milk and continue cooking until the mushrooms have absorbed all the milk (about 10 minutes) or until they turn beige.

Remove from heat and purée in a food processor. Add the sautéed fish pieces and shallots and process until homogenous (10 seconds). Mix in the egg yolks and seasonings, then transfer to a nonstick pan and stir over low heat to cook the egg yolks and thicken the filling. Do not let it boil. When nicely thickened, remove from heat and let cool.

To assemble the fish pâté, line an ovenproof baking tray with buttered aluminum foil. Roll out ⅓ of the dough in an oval and place diagonally in the tray. (The dough should cover ⅔ of the tray's area.) Spread ⅓ of the mushroom-fish mixture evenly over the dough and cover with a layer of half the fish slices. As you are building the pâté, try to shape it like a whole fish from head to tail. Spread a second layer of the mushroom-fish mixture over the fish, follow with the last of the fish slices, and finish with mushroom filling.

Roll out the remaining pastry dough and cover all, tightly tucking the top layer of pastry under the first layer. Draw the outlines of a fish head and tail, marking the "eye" with a large caper. Paint the surface with egg yolk glaze, then make a fish-scale pattern on the body and brush again with glaze. Refrigerate for at least 1 hour before baking.

Bake in a preheated 400°F oven for 20 minutes, then reduce the temperature to 375°F and let cook for 25 more minutes. Meanwhile, make a Hollandaise sauce (page 479) to accompany the pâté. When dish is done and crust is golden brown, present it. Then slice for serving and serve with Hollandaise sauce.

Note: This is a dish hard to make in a smaller quantity. But leftovers the next day, without the crust, are delicious—for example, served cold with mayonnaise for lunch.

Tarte duchesse aux poires

Duchess Pear Tart

—

For 6 to 7

Butter
⅔ cup stale cookie or bread crumbs
3–4 pears, depending on size
Lemon juice
3 cups heavy cream
4–5 eggs, depending on size
½ cup sugar

1 tsp. vanilla extract
Confectioners' sugar

Special equipment needed:
A food processor or an electric mixer
A 10″ round, fluted porcelain tart mold
Aluminum foil

*H*eavily butter the tart mold and sprinkle over it a layer of crumbled stale cookies or bread crumbs. The layer should be thick and evenly distributed. Place in the refrigerator until needed.

Preheat the oven to 400°F. Peel the pears and cut into ¼″ slices. Sprinkle with a little lemon juice to keep the slices from turning brown. Place the slices, slightly fanned and close together, on a sheet of aluminum foil and bake until tender, approximately 10–15 minutes. The slices should be very tender but not brown.

While the fruit is baking, blend the cream, eggs, sugar, and vanilla in a food processor or an electric mixer until the mixture is homogenous.

To assemble the tart, arrange the sliced fruit in rows, slightly overlapping the slices. Ladle the cream mixture over the fruit, and bake in a preheated 375°F oven for about 30 minutes or until it is set and the top is slightly golden brown.

Serve warm, in the same tart mold, sprinkled with confectioners' sugar.

Wine Suggestion: A nice dry, sparkling white wine, perhaps a Vouvray.

JEAN WAS GRADUALLY TEACHING ME how to be relaxed and happy, how to have confidence in myself and in what I could do. After fifteen years of being constrained, fairly miserable, and unsure of myself—in spite of my activities with bookbinding and cooking—I really began to think I was somebody. Through Jean's devotion and good humor, I found happiness and "felt good in my skin," as we say here.

He used to delight me with little surprises, like the latest bottle of perfume from his factory, and I began to love scents, learning to identify the "notes" of vetiver or amber, or floral tones.

This simple daily existence does not sound exciting, but with Jean I was really coming into my own. However, as we read the papers and listened to the nightly news, we began to feel uneasy. "This can come to no good," said Jean, as everybody with any sense was saying then. War clouds were in the offing.

I tried to put pessimism aside and please Jean with a good *daube de boeuf* or a *tarte aux pommes*. But I began to feel qualms about the future. We did not have the urgency of today's television images, but what we did have was in some ways more gripping. Those voices on the radio could inflame the imagination in a way that no flickering screen can.

By the time Hitler marched on Poland, in 1939, we knew that things would move fast and in unhappy ways. It was probably lucky that we did not know exactly how awful life would become for us in the next months and years, with occupation, near starvation, and despair blotting our lives and our country. I had learned joie de vivre with Jean. But then the war began. It would be years before I could even begin to recover that feeling.

WORLD WAR II

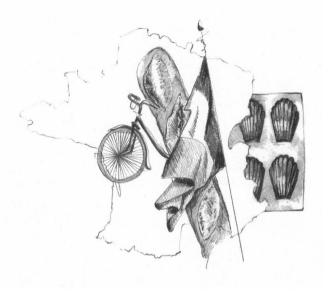

France has lost a battle, but she has not lost the war.

— *Charles de Gaulle,*
London, June 18, 1941

FOR A WHILE IT WAS CALLED THE *drôle de guerre,* or the phony war, but it was no comedy.

When the war began, Jean joined the army, as a second lieutenant with the Colonial Infantry Division, and was stationed at the eastern front, the Maginot line, where German and French troops were at a standoff for several months, with no fighting going on. This, then, was the *drôle de guerre.* For seven months, young German and French troops eyed each other warily, not knowing what to do.

Through a cousin of Jean's, Jacques Fischbacher, and his wife, Vanah-Yami, a very pretty dancer who worked up in Pigalle at the Moulin Rouge, I was able to get permission to go see Jean at the front. Although Vanah-Yami's profession was not exactly high-society style, she nevertheless came from a notary's family, and notaries in France enjoy a cachet of respectability and power. Besides, she was good fun, and I saw her often.

One day in October 1939, as I was having a drink with her, she suggested that perhaps her indirect connections with General Hering, the chief commanding officer for Paris, would enable me to see Jean. I responded with alacrity, went to see the general, and procured a *laissez-passer* to get me to the Maginot line.

I couldn't wait to see my husband and was soon on my way, starting about 5:00 A.M. in my gray front-wheel-drive Citroën, taking along Simone Signorino, my first real friend from my teens, who wanted to see her husband as well. In the village of Frankaltroff, on the eastern border of France, we were stopped, and a courteous officer said, "Go no farther. Leave your car here, in a farmyard, and you'll see your husband. Trust me."

I did that, staying at the farm overnight, and the officer was as good as his word. The next day, a small truck appeared to pick me up, and after hiding me under a blanket, the driver took me to Jean at his headquarters in Forbach. I'd stashed away several good bottles of wine and liqueurs, and these were welcome gifts to all the officers. I left Simone behind, as she was expecting Signorino to come greet her with open arms. Poor Simone. It turned out that Signorino was already involved with a homely Belgian woman, who would become his next wife.

I stayed a couple of days, close to Jean, and just before leaving I went to Mass in Forbach. I had qualms when I looked around the church, realizing that I was the only woman there, which is very rare—women are known to be more devoted to Mass than men. Apparently, the Mass was supposed to be for military men only. As I left, the gendarmes asked for my papers, probably suspecting something fishy on my part. But the *laissez-passer* from General Hering instantly reassured them.

Another time, I was able to meet Jean for a short rendezvous, holing up in a tiny village called Gendreville, near Commercy, between Nancy and Metz. "Hold your nose," warned Jean, his tongue in his cheek as usual. "I've got lodgings for us in a farmhouse."

But he was not joking. This was the real thing, a farmhouse such as I had never experienced, even in Normandy, where we were always near farmers raising chickens and cows. Our accommodation was a room just above a stable. The style of the farmhouse was to keep animals below the family, which warmed the house and made it easier to look after the livestock.

This farmhouse "inn" did reek, with that peculiar mixture of straw and animal dung, but though it was hardly the Ritz, we were happy to be together. While Jean was away on duty, I spent time reading, lying on a lumpy mattress and inhaling the smells of the stable. But there were also tempting odors of baking.

I learned from the farmer's wife, Mme Aubertin, how to make the village specialty, so famous they were called *les madeleines de Commercy*. I later added chocolate to make my own version of these famous little cakes, and years afterward I showed it off during a cooking demonstration with Julia in San Francisco, to promote *Mastering*.

As a gustatory footnote to those few days I spent near Commercy, I recall the platoon's mess cook, a man named Charrier. He made the men and officers quite happy, because everything he turned his hand to—from fish or meat to vegetables— was beautifully and deliciously prepared and served. That is rare in the military services, even in France, where one might hear of mutiny over a failed hollandaise sauce. I was able to eat a meal with Jean and his fellow officers, and we all raved about how excellent the lamb, beans, and gratinéed potatoes *dauphinoises* were. Alas, the food situation for the soldiers and for all of France was soon to deteriorate, as the occupation brought France to the brink of starvation.

The French and Germans began actual fighting in May 1940, which put an end to a short furlough Jean had spent with us down in Cannes. He had been there just a few hours when he heard that he would have to return to the front. This is it, I thought, the time I've dreaded.

A few days later, Jean's brother, Pierre, was shot dead before Jean's eyes during the fighting on the Maginot line. By June, the situation had become a rout, though Jean, I was proud to hear later, was awarded the Croix de Guerre with two stars for valor. Before the Vichy pact and the German occupation that began on June 10, 1940, many of us had started to flee in panic from the occupying forces.

Exodus

ON JUNE 4, I HEARD THROUGH A FRIEND with connections that within days the Seine Maritime *département,* where my brother Maurice and his family lived near Dieppe, would be invaded. Rouen would be taken, the bridges cut off, and escape to the south would become impossible.

Maurice was exempted from military service because he had seven children (by his three marriages). I decided to take off in the Citroën to warn him, and leaving at 5:00 A.M. from Paris, I arrived in Saint-Aubin two hours later. At first my brother and sister-in-law were skeptical, but then they began preparing the family to get away.

I rushed over to the house at Rainfreville, sixteen kilometers away, and with my sister-in-law Françoise, stowed about two hundred pounds of my mother's most beautiful linens in an immense trunk to send for storage down to Jean's family in Chinon. Maman was already in the south of France, and I had told her to stay there for the time being. Françoise and I struggled and sweated, heaving that trunk downstairs and into the truck we'd commandeered from the silicate factory at Saint-Aubin.

In cars and the truck, we all started our escape south. We managed to cross the Seine just a few hours before several bridges were blown up around Rouen, destroyed by the French to stop the Germans—to no avail. The Germans simply went around the main cities and made their advance anyway.

I kept traveling until I reached Jean's family's house in Chinon. Then, on June 15, 1940, we all decided to leave Chinon, because we were afraid the *Boches,* as we called them, were advancing too far and too fast. The roads were already crowded with refugees, people who were afraid to stay at home and face the occupying forces.

My two sisters-in-law and their children took one car, and I drove my mother-in-law in mine, packing in all the valuables we could, plus essentials to living away from home—a bottle of butane gas, a small stove, a sewing machine.

All the refugees' vehicles were similarly loaded down. They were carrying mattresses, beds, clothes, silverware, anything that would go inside or on top of an automobile, and often members of families walked along beside the car heaped with their possessions.

We started out at dawn on June 16, headed southwest, where a family we knew had a house and could shelter us in a little town called Lesparre, north of Bordeaux. We were saddened and horrified by the exodus we were joining. People complain of traffic jams on the autoroutes today as they travel bumper to bumper during weekends or holidays. These are minor annoyances compared to our desperate panic.

The ragtag procession looked like people headed home from a flea market, and might almost have been funny in a Chaplinesque way. But this was heartrendingly real. People were driving, riding bicycles, pushing carts, wheelbarrows, and baby carriages—anything with wheels—transporting whatever could be lugged along.

We were all trying to save our skins and our worldly goods, no matter how humble. Some had valuable antiques, others had just bed linens and a few pots. The air was thick with noxious exhaust fumes.

It was a stifling, sunny day as we crept along through the château country toward Bordeaux.

Suddenly people were jumping off the road and into the ditches. "*Mère,* we're in trouble," I warned my mother-in-law, Jaby, as planes began flying low and strafing the refugees. We leapt out of the car and joined the others in the ditch, watching the planes on their short, murderous mission. Later we found out that these were Italian fighters, and that at least a few refugees had been injured, maybe killed. We couldn't wait around to verify it.

We had no sleep, keeping on at our snail's pace throughout the night, and finally arrived at Lesparre on June 17. I stayed at a farm with one of my sisters-in-law, Jeannine. We all knew that the Germans were advancing quickly behind us, and the farm people instinctively effected a blackout, closing their shutters, extinguishing lights, and waiting in silence to see what would happen.

My mother-in-law and Jean's other sister stayed at a larger country house, and all of us tried to sleep, restless with worries. The farmers were solicitous, giving us vegetable soup and an omelet and as much courage as they could muster to help us relax.

Jeannine had a little radio with her, and at 5:00 A.M. on June 18, we heard de Gaulle's unforgettable words broadcast from London: "France has lost a battle, but she has not lost the war." He was trying to convince the French to quit panicking and go back to protect their homes.

Jeannine and I looked at each other and sighed, realizing de Gaulle had indeed given us the best possible advice. We should be occupying our homes ourselves, rather than leaving them to be overrun by the enemy or even our own countrymen. So that very day, the eighteenth of June, we turned right around to return to Chinon.

Progress was slow, but we made it back late the same day. Many times we were stopped by German troops and guards, but fortunately my mother-in-law spoke fluent German, remembered from her Alsatian background, and handled the questions firmly and with aplomb. "We are going home, where we belong," she said. And they waved us on.

We arrived at my in-laws' house, l'Echo, to discover it was occupied by French refugees, who had found it a haven in their desperation. L'Echo faced the ruined château of Chinon and was named for the echo that rebounded across the gully from the castle walls. (Jean once jokingly said "*Merde*" as an experiment, and the expletive kept on and on . . . about fifteen times!)

We were terribly tired, but the poor "occupiers" were so discouraged that we didn't have the heart to turn them out. We shared a meal with them, and they realized they could stay no longer and dragged off their carts and goods within the next couple of days.

A page was turned, and we waited, the Fischbacher family and I, for news from the front.

Sitting on the porch steps at Blonville, near Deauville

I got through by phone to my mother in Menton, and she was naturally distressed. "Have you any news of Jean?" she asked me.

"Not yet," I told her. "You can imagine the state I'm in. And what about Bernard?" She'd had no word from my younger brother.

A career officer, he had been through a frantic time at Dunkirk, when the English sent over dozens of small vessels—sailboats and motorboats, anything that would float—to pick up a French army division that was surrounded by the Germans. The French officers and men were taken safely to England; but alas, a few days later, they all returned to France and were taken prisoner by the Germans—the men as well as the officers, like Bernard, who were responsible for them.

So Bernard was a prisoner in Germany, and my mother didn't hear anything for several months. It was an agonizing time for her.

I was somewhat luckier. I heard from Jean about a month later. On July 14, our national holiday, somebody threw a letter over the stone fence at l'Echo. The note was from Jean, addressed merely "Simca."

"I've been taken prisoner, am at Bosserville-lès-Nancy. Come if you can." Beside myself, I could hardly wait to get to him.

Trains were hardly moving, but forty-eight hours later, encouraged by Jean's father, I was off to Nancy via Paris, where I stopped overnight in our Neuilly flat to load a knapsack as full as possible of things to eat for Jean, a few necessities for myself. Very early, around 6:00 A.M., I biked across Paris to the Gare de l'Est, starting off even before the métros were running.

At the station, I found swarms of people, no room on any train headed for Nancy. I waited in lines, harangued and pleaded my cause as the wife of a prisoner of war. Finally, a French army doctor took pity on me and made room. "Let her on; she has urgent business," he said. People seemed to be glaring at both of us for this collusion, though we did not even know each other.

The train was sidetracked at least three times, and we had to get off and change repeatedly. The journey seemed to take forever—eighteen hours to cover the three hundred kilometers to Nancy, usually a three-hour trip. The crowd in the train was smelly, impatient, hungry. But I gripped my knapsack full of food for Jean the whole time, opening it only to share a sandwich with the medical officer who had helped me get on the train.

We pulled into Nancy at midnight and were informed by loudspeaker: "Nobody is allowed off the train until morning." This will not do, I told myself, worn out and exasperated by my struggle to reach the city.

We French don't really believe in regulations when we're in urgent situations; I'm always for being *débrouillarde*, making the best of a bad situation. I found an unlocked gate out of the Nancy station, and the army doctor followed me, before anybody could catch us.

It was still dark in the streets, very chilly for July. I saw a blue light like a beacon and headed for it, dragging my loaded knapsack. Behind me, the medical officer was puffing along like a caboose. When we arrived at the source of the eerie light, it turned out to be the city's largest hotel, the Grand.

The doctor hung back, but I was undeterred, barging right in and confronting a crowd of German officers, who were struck speechless, or rather songless. They stopped their beer-inspired revels when they saw me, a feisty blond French-woman, a strange character who had dropped out of the night into their midst. Germanic jaws dropped under the close-cropped heads, and I felt a bit queasy. But I was determined. As I didn't speak a word of German, I turned to the desk clerk for advice. He suggested that I leave immediately and try a small hotel nearby.

Trailed by the French officer, I made my way there, but they had only one room left, with a double bed, an awkward situation. That doctor could have offered me the bed and even the whole room if he had been a gentleman, but I finally bargained with the concierge to have an extra mattress put on the floor for me, leaving the bed to the doctor.

He was looking at me with an unmistakable glint of lechery in his eye, but I glared at him, and we settled down in the makeshift digs. At dawn, he was still snoring peacefully when I picked up my knapsack and crept out to find my way to the convent-prison at Bosserville-lès-Nancy. It was nearly four miles away, but I tried not to think about that. I walked at a steady gait, bent over by the heavy knapsack all the way, plowing through the alien early-morning mist like an errant shade.

Murmuring exhortations to myself as I labored on, asking directions, praying to God and talking to Jean under my breath, I finally made it. I unslung the back-pack and asked the guard on duty to let me see an officer who spoke French or English. One appeared, sleepy and buttoning up his uniform. When I asked to see my husband, this crisp German officer leered at me and said he presumed that I also had a beau or boyfriend back in Paris. I was enraged and tired, and shot back at him, "Maybe they do that sort of thing in your country, but not in mine!"

Luckily, he was not offended by my remark and escorted me to Jean through the corridors of the convent. My husband and I embraced tearfully in a little room. I was allowed only ten minutes with him, the guard looking on. But I was able to deliver the ham-and-cheese and pâté sandwiches, and tell him I would look after him as much as I could during his captivity, no matter what. As we kissed goodbye, Jean slipped packets of letters into my pockets and sack, to people back home from his fellow officers.

On my way out, the Germans searched me and confiscated a few letters, but I got at least ten of them out.

I kissed Jean goodbye with sadness and great love, but I was also determined that he and his fellow prisoners would have as much in the way of provisions as I could get to them. I made the same journey, more quickly, about two weeks later, but after that Jean was removed with the others to Münster, Germany, so I had to send the food.

For months, for years, I shuttled between Paris, Chinon, and Rainfreville, searching for food, becoming a fanatic one-woman provider for these prisoners. Most of the packages miraculously arrived there.

Desperate to have Jean home with me again, I prayed doubly hard at church. Though not usually superstitious, I even resorted to a fortune-teller for reassurance. One day in 1940, depressed and out of sorts, I accompanied my sister-in-law France Fischbacher, by now married to Michel Thibault, to an expensive astrologer's in the Sixteenth Arrondissement.

"Your husband will live and come back from the war," said this woman, who looked very ordinary, the opposite of the cliché of an exotic gypsy sporting bangle bracelets and gazing into a crystal ball. But then she added: "He will die before you do."

I get a chill to this day when I think about her accuracy. She said I would have leg problems, and sure enough I did, enduring an operation that went wrong and a broken ankle with complications that caused permanent swelling. As she announced, France's husband would return from the war by escaping prison camp; they would travel, live abroad, and have a child. That all came true later, as they went to live in Algeria. Their eldest child, Jean-François Thibault, is now one of my favorite nephews, though he lives far away—in Washington, D.C., where he is a professor and Chairman of the Romance Languages Department at George Washington University.

Rainfreville,
Occupied and Reoccupied — by Becks

IN 1940, MY SIXTY-FIVE-YEAR-OLD MOTHER was staying with friends down in Menton, then moved over to her usual rented house near Cannes. But by late summer, when most of the French were moving back to their homes after de Gaulle's exhortation from London, my mother was trying to find transportation north, back home to Rainfreville.

She was a fervent patriot and kept a detailed diary then and later, writing in an elegant, meticulous hand and not mincing words over the invaders, using such dramatic expressions as "dirty *Boches*" and "those pigs."

"Poor Maman!" I exclaimed when I read one of her diaries recently. I cried to think of what she was going through. At one point she wrote that she was sorry about the valuables we'd missed saving in our rush to escape the Germans in June. She added, "This whole moment is an exodus from the Barbarians. Each day I grow weaker, having lost weight, my dresses floating around me."

Passes were necessary for any fairly long journey during the occupation, and finally, on August 9, Mother's pass came through. And the trip she described was a nightmare for a woman accustomed to being tended to by servants.

She traveled in smelly, crowded third-class cars, carrying her little Shih Tzu dog, struggling with luggage, enduring crowds and delays. At one point she was in despair, finding that most of her luggage had disappeared (she finally recovered it). In Paris, she stopped briefly for a short rest, and then had to walk several miles, followed by a porter, to catch the train out. After an epic trip of six days, she made it up to Normandy, nearly home. I still admire my mother for all her pluck.

Her last train was rerouted from Rouen, where the bridge had been blown up two months before. After a circuitous route, it finally reached Mother's destination, Saint-Aubin-sur-Scie, where my brother Maurice lived with his third wife, Françoise, and five of his seven children. There was nobody around to help with luggage, so she walked the half mile to the family factory and engaged a man with a cart to pick up her belongings. Exhausted, she then proceeded to Rainfreville, where she had already sensed the trouble awaiting her.

She was greeted at our family house by a big red Nazi flag fluttering its swastika on the lawn. A German officer with a monocle told her she would have to go all the way back to Saint-Aubin, to stay with Maurice and his family—who had all returned home from the exodus by then. "We are occupying your house, madame," the officer told her.

"Hmph," she said. "We'll just see about that." My stubborn mother asked to see her belongings and the state of the house. The officer acquiesced before this bristling, determined French grande dame.

"I took away a framed photograph of my husband, who was lucky not to see this desecration," wrote my mother in her diary. "I asked for soap from the attic, and the officer gave me half the supply there. What a calvary it was to see our house this way! I felt I couldn't take much more."

Maman went back to Saint-Aubin, but she had murder in her heart, or at least an unflinching determination to reoccupy our house. We kept in close touch, and early in the winter, Mother informed me that Françoise, who was very moody, had gone to stay with her mother and sister in Rouen, leaving my mother in charge of Maurice's children. So I went up to help out. We both began to worry when Maurice's three-month-old baby, Jacques, developed a very high fever. I feared he was dying.

I remember walking nearly two miles to fetch the doctor in the frigid winter weather. The doctor confirmed my fears, pronouncing the child hopelessly ill with meningitis. I held little Jacques in my arms as he died.

We decided to bury him in the family plot at Rainfreville, traveling by mule-drawn cart in the cruel subzero cold. We carried a small butane heater to keep our blood circulating, but after nearly three hours of bone-chilling torture before we reached Rainfreville, we were frozen almost as stiff as the poor little body in its casket.

My mother's former butler, Albert, who now ran a modest bistro with his wife, Louise, told us that they thought the Germans had vacated the "château," as our house was known to the country people, and Mother and I rushed over. The good news proved to be false. A couple of Nazi guards were lounging at the door, under the porte cochère. Proprietary fury welled up in Maman, and she exploded in a burst of energy, pushing the men aside as she charged in.

"This is my house, and you cannot, you will not, stop me." I think she was lashing out at them in both French and whatever German she knew. Inspired by her dramatic posture, I stood tall and marched in behind her as a fully supportive, indignant daughter. The young soldiers fell back in surprise at this unexpected *"Anschluss."*

At a loss for words, they stood there, annoyed and sheepish, as my mother and I made a reconnaissance of the house. We were obviously more in charge than the callow soldiers. "I am staying until the end of the war," my mother announced. The soldiers finally agreed to let us inhabit two rooms upstairs, probably thinking that my mother would not be so tenacious as to remain in the big, chilly house more than a few days. But she settled in for the duration, and I came and went between my Paris apartment and the "château."

Our first night of occupying our own home again was memorable. We had two tiny gas heaters and placed them in the bedrooms we took for ourselves. As I was surveying the cold, drafty, and dusty room I would stay in, Maman appeared at the door. "I want to save as many of our belongings as I can," she announced. I agreed. If I have a stubborn streak in getting just about anything done that I want to, I surely inherited it from my mother. She had already snooped around and found her jewel box—empty. I felt chagrined that I'd forgotten it during the earlier evacuation. "Too bad my daughter forgot the jewel box," I read later in her diary.

It grew dark early, and we pretended to settle down in our chilly house for the night. Eventually, I went out on a landing and heard loud snoring from the young guards. We took a kerosene lamp and crept downstairs to bring up as many furnishings as we could to the rooms we had taken over. We were like furtive midnight marauders, "stealing" our own objects from the living room to have them safe with us.

Most of that night, in the eerie light and penetrating cold, we hauled things like the delicate marquetry backgammon table, the Louis XV and XVI chairs, a few paintings, china and silver—just about everything except the piano. Although she didn't complain, Mother must have felt pain all over the next day; at nearly thirty years younger, I know I did. But we somehow managed to get a lot of our valuables upstairs, moving rather cheaper stuff downstairs to make the salons look furnished.

The next morning, we had a surprise. There was a hesitant knock at my door and a voice asking in broken French if we wanted breakfast. Of course we did! Soon one of the young guards appeared with hot chocolate in porcelain cups, on one of our best silver trays. The chocolate was a wonderful treat, as we hadn't eaten anything except a sandwich for twenty-four hours. But the porcelain service and silver tray were a bonus. "Thank you for the kind thought," Mother said graciously. "We'll just keep all of this, as it's ours anyway." She was always coldly polite to the *"Boches,"* but she never let them intimidate her.

In the bitter cold of that winter, there were agonizing times of illness, as we caught colds and bronchitis and sometimes ran a high fever. When I became well enough, I would carry on my own war, dreaming up ways to send food to Jean. I devised a barter system up in Normandy, spiriting off bottles of Bénédictine from the family factory, then tearing around on my bicycle to trade with farmers for butter, ham, pâté, anything I could get my hands on to make up packets for Jean.

I used to pedal up to sixty miles a day to do my trading, enlisting my niece, Monique, who was ten or twelve: "Come on, dear, we're going on a little mission." She was delighted to help me filch from the Bénédictine factory by bribing the French watchman—with charm and money—to look the other way. The factory had been requisitioned by the Germans, who liked our liqueur though the wartime product was vastly inferior to the real thing, made from Cognac as a base; they had to substitute alcohol distilled from potatoes. Neither the Nazis nor the peasants we traded with seemed to mind the low-grade quality. They all just wanted something fiery in their insides.

I also used the Bénédictine as a sweetener for chocolate truffles to send to the prisoners, now and then putting it into a cake as well, since sugar was a rarity.

The Fischbachers contributed Chinon wine. Once we stuffed Loire Valley goat cheese and a bottle of red Chinon into a tin cylinder that had contained charcoal sold in pharmacies as a remedy for intestinal problems. It made a pretty unorthodox "picnic basket," but it kept the food and wine intact.

My war effort also included being an indirect *résistant.* I was cajoled by a certain Roland Farjon, scion of a family that had made a fortune in the pencil-manufacturing business, into lending my Neuilly apartment as an occasional meeting place for resistance people. They used it, too, as a drop-off point for letters. I also discovered that they must have been printing false passports and identity papers there as well.

One evening as I was returning home, the concierge hissed at me, "Madame, don't go upstairs. They're having a big meeting up there, and this neighborhood is thick with Nazis searching for people like that."

So I took off quickly on my bicycle to stay with Uncle René in Le Vésinet, ten miles away, puffing along in a panic. I barely made it there before the 11:00 P.M. curfew. I got a real bicycle workout every day, because the little available fuel then was for the Germans and a few bigwig collaborators. I don't know what I would have done without my trusty bike, which I cared for like a mother hen, every night hefting it up seven long flights of stairs to lock it in the apartment.

When I finally dragged the bike upstairs after the scare and three nights spent with Uncle René, I was sick to find my apartment a shambles. It was a frightful mess, with papers all over the floor, furniture knocked over and scattered about, a litter of dirty dishes and glasses—even a stray bra on the bedroom floor. The *résistants* had obviously left in a panic. Farjon was later arrested, then released, and he was finally found drowned in the Seine under mysterious circumstances.

As these war years dragged on, I often came back to Rainfreville, and my mother's diary notes how "My darling Simone is so good about taking care of the chickens, goats, and rabbits." That was an old habit ever since my childhood, when it had been an amusing little task; now it had become vital work.

Up in Rainfreville I could cook modest dinners for my mother and myself, but if I was away, Mother usually dined at the bistro where Albert and Louise served the best they could get in the way of food. Eventually, my mother hired a live-in servant to help her out. The Germans had no objections, as this was not one of their major headquarters.

Mother retained an icy disdain for "those bastards." When the Germans wanted to take over our salon as a meeting place in the latter part of the war, she objected strongly. "You haven't won the war yet," she snapped at an officer, shaking her fist at him.

Her description of their meeting is colorful: "It was quite awful. It smelled like wild animals, with the stink of all those boots, the din of all those clinking bottles. We could hardly sleep at night."

Mother also recalled the time that I brusquely refused an officer's invitation to play tennis. I don't even remember what he looked like, but apparently I was appropriately rude. "She really told him off royally," my mother wrote with pride.

All those war years, we at Rainfreville were relatively privileged, with our farm sources of fresh vegetables. People who were Paris-based and had strict rationing and little or no access to farm produce through relatives and friends were obliged to wait in endless lines at shops or scrounge around with black marketeers just to get a little orange juice or milk for their children. I was thankful that we were far from starving, but I remember that all the food we were able to get was still a blessing. And if I still keep my refrigerator nowadays stocked with leftovers until they nearly go off, it is because of that specter of hunger that hung over us during the war. Very few people in France now who were alive then ever waste food or throw away leftovers. We were all obsessed with food, as people on a strict diet are.

Through my sporadic correspondence with Jean, carried on in a kind of secret code we'd devised, he signaled to me that he was optimistic for an Allied victory. Later he told me that, with another officer, he was running a grapevine news service for the ten thousand prisoners in the camp out of his cell block, where a radio was hidden under the floorboards.

When some of the twenty-five men in Jean's block started to carry on about how they were convinced the Germans would win, Jean took it upon himself to inspire some optimism. "You'll see," he said. "The Germans will invade Russia, and that will do them in. Remember Napoleon! Winter is coming, and the Russians can cope with snow and cold. They'll turn the tide. *Tiens!* I'll let my beard grow, something I hate to do, but I'll shave it off when we hear of a German defeat." His beard did not grow very long; he shaved it off shortly afterward, when the exhausted German troops began their retreat from the gates of Moscow after the terrible winter of 1943.

Throughout the war, and especially toward the end, everyone in France was listening to clandestine radio announcements, hoping for news of the impending invasion that we hoped, prayed, and knew would come.

The Invasion

ON THE HOME FRONT, TENSION WAS BUILDING. In the spring of 1944, the English began to bomb Normandy. Mother noted in her diary that many farms and villages were being surrounded by trenches, "as if we were in fortresses," she wrote. Maurice had dug a very big tunnel as a shelter under the beech grove behind our house.

I was constantly worried about Jean, since he and his fellow officers had been imprisoned in southern Germany for years, and news was ever scarcer. Bernard was still in prison camp too, another reason for anxiety.

In Normandy, mail was cut off periodically, and there were blackouts every night. A neighbor's house was surrounded by several V-2 rockets installed by Germans. We lived in suspense, but at last the great day came, the "longest day," June 6, 1944—that unforgettable first wave of the Normandy invasion. We listened to our crackling radio set, and this time the broadcast, preceded by the usual first four notes of Beethoven's Fifth Symphony as the clue to news from England, brought the triumphant announcement: the Norman coast was being assaulted by platoons of American, Canadian, British, and French troops—the latter having been in England with de Gaulle, waiting for this moment.

My mother wrote: "Finally, the moment we've awaited so long! We've heard of 4,000 ships off our coast. We are weeping with joy." Of course, there were not quite four thousand ships, but we held our breath, waiting for the arrival of Allied troops inland.

The invasion had just begun, and the ordeal was far from over. The Germans were hanging on, and there was fierce ground fighting to come.

The few troops occupying our house pulled out at last with polite goodbyes, and we felt like celebrating. When a resistance fighter named Jean Valognes was brought to us, we agreed to shelter him in the attic.

One day, a truck carrying a V-2 rocket—probably powerful enough to destroy most of London—rolled right up our driveway and into the porte cochère. I was beside myself, yelling, "*Halte! Schluss!* Stop!"—anything I could think of to keep it away.

Apart from the rocket itself, I was panicked about Jean Valognes. I pleaded, threatened, and palavered with the Nazis, until finally they drove away.

Come the end of June, around the twenty-eighth, the German threat was over in our district as they retreated in the face of the Allies. We were ready to relax, and Jean descended from the attic, a young man who looked pale but happy to be freed from his friendly "prison." Maurice came to see us from Saint-Aubin for the day, we filled the house with bouquets of roses, and as Mother wrote in her diary, "Simone made an exquisite chocolate-mocha cake."

That summer, Maurice's three eldest children were staying with us during their holidays. When, recently, I mentioned the liberation to my nephew Maurice, who was eighteen at the time, his eyes lit up. "I remember it well, Aunt Simca," he said. "How excited we all were to see the first arrivals, the Canadians. Remember how we made flags—French, English, Canadian, and American—to fly from Rainfreville's balconies? And then of course we kids got lovely little presents from the soldiers—chocolate and chewing gum; I especially liked the cigarettes."

The summer passed fairly quickly for us. We were filled with hope, as the occupiers were beaten back on all fronts around France. On August 15, French and American troops took the Mediterranean coast, moved up the Rhône Valley, and joined troops from the western front in Burgundy. Slowly but surely, France was coming into her own again, and when in late August the Allied troops headed by General Leclerc's division rumbled into Paris in their tanks, the enemy capitulated, and the capital erupted in joy.

But fighting continued throughout the winter as Germany was invaded. Peace would not be official until the following spring, with the unconditional surrender on May 8, 1945.

Nevertheless, during that summer of 1944, our lives in Normandy picked up considerably, and in September, Mother noted in her diary that "We really begin to live again. Young Canadian and American officers are arriving, and sometimes we give little parties at the house."

As I felt like being attractive for all these saviors, I bicycled off one day to the hairdresser—fording a stream where I found a bridge out. It was worth the effort, as I felt a lot better with my hair done. A few days later, my mother was horrified to discover she had lice. "Are you sure you didn't pick them up from a towel at the coiffeur's?" she asked me, but she finally decided it was an unwelcome leftover from the "dirty *Boches*."

Her diary notes that around September 6, a jeepful of nice young Canadian officers from Victoria pulled up to the house. I made dinner for them, which Mother recalled as being absolutely marvelous. I think our menu must have been simple yet hearty, and we celebrated with some of my father's Champagne from the cellar, which had miraculously been left behind by the German soldiers.

Petite fête pour les Canadiens, à la Libération

Dinner to celebrate the arrival of Canadian soldiers at Rainfreville, 1944

Apéritif: Champagne de Ayala (or sparkling hard cider)

✦ *Soupe au cresson*
Watercress soup (see "Note" for *Soupe aux poireaux*, page 20)

✦ *Coq au vin*
Chicken with red wine

Salade verte

Fromages normands —
Camembert, Pont l'Évêque, Livarot

—

Bordeaux rouge (same red wine as used for cooking chicken)

✦ *Les crêpes soufflées*
Crêpes filled with almond meringue

Coq au vin

Chicken with Red Wine

—

For 4 to 6

One 4-oz. chunk of lean bacon with rind
  removed

5 Tbsp. peanut oil

8 Tbsp. butter

18–24 small white onions

½ lb. fresh white mushrooms

One 3½-lb. frying chicken, cut up

Salt and pepper

¼ cup Cognac

3–4 cups full-bodied red wine, such as a
  Côtes du Rhône

2 cups chicken broth (or water and
  bouillon cubes)

½ Tbsp. tomato paste

3 garlic cloves, mashed

1 tsp. dried herbes de Provence (see
  Aide-Mémoire, page 503)

1½ Tbsp. potato starch or arrowroot

Minced parsley, for garnish

Special equipment needed:

A heavy 10″ flameproof casserole

A shallow serving dish

*C*ut the bacon into small rectangles (*lardons*). If using French bacon, which has a stronger flavor than American varieties, place in simmering water and let simmer for 10 minutes, then rinse in cold tap water and drain dry. Sauté the *lardons* in 1½ Tbsp. peanut oil and 2 Tbsp. butter until lightly browned. Remove and set aside.

Peel the onions, and clean and dry the mushrooms, quartering any large ones. Sauté the onions in 1½ Tbsp. oil and 2 Tbsp. butter, rolling them around in the pan for about 10 minutes, or until nicely browned. Set aside while sautéing the mushrooms in the same manner, using 2 Tbsp. butter and 1 Tbsp. oil.

Heat 1½ Tbsp. oil with 2 Tbsp. butter in a flameproof casserole. When hot, brown the chicken pieces, beginning with the dark meat. Season with salt and pepper, add the sautéed bacon, cover, and let stew slowly for a few minutes, shaking the casserole and turning the pieces so they brown evenly on all sides.

Uncover, pour in the Cognac, and ignite, shaking the casserole back and forth until the flames subside, then pour in the wine. Slowly bring to the simmer and continue to simmer a few more minutes to evaporate the alcohol. Add the sautéed onions and just enough chicken broth to cover the chicken, then stir in the tomato paste, garlic, and herbs, and return to the simmer.

Cover with parchment paper and the lid and let simmer slowly for about 20 minutes, or until the chicken is tender. Ten minutes before the chicken is done, add the sautéed mushrooms to finish cooking. The chicken is done when the juices that run out when the meat is pricked with a knife are clear yellow. When done, remove the chicken and vegetables, and keep warm until ready to serve.

Strain and thoroughly degrease the chicken cooking juices, then reduce until only 2½ cups remain. Taste and correct the seasoning. Dissolve the starch in 2½ Tbsp. cold water, and stir into the boiling liquid. Cook a few minutes, until thickened. The sauce should be thick enough to lightly coat a wooden spoon.

Return the chicken to the casserole, add the bacon, onions, and mushrooms, and baste with the sauce. Set aside, uncovered, until time to be served. Shortly before serving, slowly bring to the simmer and baste the chicken again with the sauce. Serve on a warmed serving dish with mushrooms and onions around the chicken, sprinkled with minced parsley.

Vegetable Suggestion: New potatoes au gratin, p. 420, or buttered green peas.

Wine Suggestion: The same wine used in the recipe.

Les crêpes soufflées

Crêpes Filled with Almond Meringue

—

For 6 to 8

For crêpe batter (15–20 crêpes):
1 cup sifted flour
½ cup water, mixed with ½ cup milk
Pinch of salt
3 medium eggs (if small, add 1 more
  yolk)
¼ cup vegetable oil

For meringue filling:
5–6 egg whites
Pinch of salt
¾ cup sugar
1 tsp. vanilla extract

2 Tbsp. pulverized fresh almonds, plus 1
  tsp. for garnish

Butter, for gratin dish
Confectioners' sugar

Special equipment needed:
A mixing bowl and a wire whisk
A heavy iron crêpe pan
An oval baking dish
A basin, preferably copper, to beat the
  egg whites

The crêpe batter is best prepared several hours before cooking. Put the flour in a mixing bowl and stir in some of the liquid, a little at a time, to make a smooth paste. When the mixture is completely smooth and without lumps, pour in the remaining liquid all at once, and whisk until nice and smooth. Add the salt, then the eggs, one at a time, mixing thoroughly after each addition.

If the batter was prepared ahead, stir in 3–4 Tbsp. water to thin it, so the crêpes will be nice and thin. Heat 1 Tbsp. oil in the crêpe pan, ladle in 3–4 Tbsp. batter, and tilt the pan to spread the batter evenly over the bottom. Shaking the pan, leave it for about 1 minute at high heat, then turn the crêpe over, either flipping the pan with your wrist or using a spatula. Cook the other crêpes the same way. Crêpes can be prepared 2–3 hours ahead of time and kept at room temperature until needed.

Twenty minutes before serving, preheat the oven to 425°F. Place the egg whites in a clean copper basin with a pinch of salt and a teaspoon of water. Beat until white and frothy. Slowly add the sugar, beating constantly, to obtain a meringue, then beat in the vanilla and almonds, continuing to beat until the mixture is stiff and shiny.

Place a large spoonful of meringue in the center of each crêpe, then fold in half and arrange in a heavily buttered oval baking dish, slightly overlapping. Do not crush the filling. Sprinkle with almonds and confectioners' sugar, and brown in the oven for about 8–10 minutes. The crêpes soufflées will puff up and become slightly golden. When done, remove from the oven and sprinkle with more confectioners' sugar just before serving.

Wine Suggestion: Serve with a semisweet sparkling white wine.

SIMONE FORGOT TO FEED the chickens," my mother remarked in her diary. I remember there was a full moon just then, and after a rather shy beginning to the evening, we were lifting our glasses in joy, reveling for the first time since the war had begun. We even turned on the gramophone and danced with the young officers. Our festive party made me miss Jean more than ever, and I ached for him to be with us, even as I was trotting around filling glasses.

Shuttling between Rainfreville and the Neuilly apartment, I waited for news. Finally, I got the long-awaited telegram in Neuilly: "I'll be home, arriving at Le Bourget soon. Try to meet me."

I was delirious with excitement, and my main concern was how to get out to the airport. We still owned a car, the Citroën, but I had lent it to Jean's cousin Jacques, whose wife had helped me get the *laissez-passer* to go see Jean at the beginning of the war—a time that seemed more like a century than five years before. Jacques and Vanah-Yami had separated, since she was on the side of Vichy and its collaborationist government and he was a *résistant;* he had worked for de Gaulle in England, then Canada, and had come back to Paris with an important job as a press attaché and needed a car. My faithful Neuilly concierge had already staunchly kept some *"résistants"* from appropriating the car. The ranks of the resistance miraculously swelled at the war's end, by those wishing to look courageous and share in the perks.

I was happy to let Jacques use the car, although it was virtually a wreck. Through his job, he was able to get tires and repairs and procure gasoline.

When I told him I needed to meet Jean, he willingly relinquished it. This was in mid-April 1945, and I drove out to Le Bourget every day, hoping to see Jean, not knowing which group he would turn up in; the prisoners came in successive waves of alphabetical groups chosen by lottery. Finally, on April 22, there he was in a group of officers, his eyes and cheeks sunken, his clothes in tatters—but he was my husband and still alive. We were frantic with happiness, crying and smiling, both shy and garrulous by turns—interrupting each other with news as we drove back to our apartment to get reacquainted with each other.

I could sense that his readaptation to civilian life would take a little time, as he described the nightmare he'd been through in the previous months. "When the Canadians started bombing Holland, then Brussels, and approaching Münster, where we were interned, the Germans sent the French officers farther south, to Söest," he told me. "That was back in December, and we had a terrible time, marching miles every day with hardly any food or drink, only what we could dig up from farms along the way. Some of the men didn't make it, and we had to bury them as best we could en route." His voice broke, and tears welled in my own eyes.

At Söest, a group of Americans came upon the camp and, instead of the Germans they were expecting, found these French officers. Jean more or less took charge of the group since he spoke English, exclaiming right away, "Tell the liberators we're on their side—they mustn't drop a bomb on us!" At one point he spoke to the American officer in charge, General George Patton himself. For his cool head and exemplary conduct throughout his whole imprisonment ordeal, Jean was later awarded the Legion of Honor.

After our reunion and a few days in Neuilly, we went up to Rainfreville in time to celebrate our anniversary on April 30. Mother gave Jean a hero's welcome, and of course tried to restore his health by ordering good food, which I often helped the cook to prepare.

On May 8, the war in Europe was officially declared finished, and we went mad. Mother wrote: "The whole village was out dancing in the road. And Simone was even kissing the unshaven town drunk!" That doesn't sound much like me, especially with Jean looking on, but I guess I myself had indulged in some rare tippling and was carried away like everybody else. I imagine even Jean embraced the drunk.

Two months later, my younger brother, Bernard, was freed from his own detention in a southern German prison camp, "smelling like straw when he walked in," wrote my mother, ecstatic to see her favorite again.

Handsome, dashing career officer Bernard had been scarred by his five years in the prison camp. Thin and dour, he had lost his high spirits and gaiety, and seemed almost another man than the carefree boy who had left home.

At home in Neuilly or at Rainfreville, I worked on nourishing Jean back to good health. I gave him dishes like eggnogs laced with port, easing into a high-protein regimen of tempting dishes like *blanquette de veau* with rice or potatoes. "This is delicious," said Jean one day, gingerly savoring some lamb. "Thanks to you, I'm getting back to my old eating habits."

He was so unaccustomed to substantial food that it almost made him ill at first. He weighed not much more than one hundred pounds when he arrived home, but at Rainfreville, we gradually built him up again. Most of our time there was spent walking in the sun, swimming, enjoying a well-deserved lazy summer.

Of course, we also visited his family in Chinon, who were overjoyed to have Jean home again. He was quickly tucking into delicious Loire Valley specialties, which he certainly hadn't forgotten in prison camp; on the contrary. Loire Valley eel stew was one of our favorite dishes, tasting much like pike, and you can make it with any firm fish.

Un déjeuner de famille à Chinon

Lunch with Jean's Family, Loire Valley Style

✦ *Oeufs brouillés aux courgettes*
Scrambled eggs with zucchini

—

Vin blanc sec—Vouvray

✦ *Matelote d'anguilles*
Eel stew with red wine

Salade de saison

Fromage de l'Indre-et-Loire: Sainte-Maure
Goat cheese

—

Vin rouge de la Loire (full-bodied Loire Valley red)—
Chinon ou Bourgueil

✦ *Clafoutis aux prunes*
Greengage plum clafoutis

Oeufs brouillés aux courgettes

Scrambled Eggs with Zucchini

—

For 20 to 24

5 lb. (about 15–16) small zucchini
8 Tbsp. butter
2½ Tbsp. extra-virgin olive oil
8 shallots, minced
4 garlic cloves, minced
Salt, pepper, and Tabasco
4 Tbsp. minced chives
4 Tbsp. minced parsley

12–15 eggs, depending on size
¾ cup crème fraîche (page 501)

Special equipment needed:
A food processor equipped with a
 "french fry" disk
1 or 2 large nonstick frying pans

*W*ash and dry the zucchini and cut in strips, using the small "french fry" disk on the food processor. Sprinkle with salt, and let drain for about 15 minutes, then rinse with cold tap water and dry between kitchen towels.

Meanwhile, heat half the butter with the oil in a nonstick frying pan. Add the shallots and cook slowly, stirring constantly until tender, not burned. Add the garlic and let stew a few more minutes, then add half the zucchini and continue to stir slowly. If necessary, add more butter. When beginning to get tender, add the rest of the zucchini and continue stirring. Cook slowly for about 5 minutes, or until tender, adding salt, pepper, and fresh herbs at the end. (This first cooking can be done ahead of time.)

Ten minutes before serving, reheat the zucchini, adding more butter if needed. Meanwhile, beat the eggs with the crème fraîche, adding salt and pepper to taste. When the zucchini is hot, pour in the seasoned egg mixture and stir with a fork to scramble (about 3 minutes). Do not overcook. Remove from the heat, taste, and correct the seasoning. If necessary, keep warm over hot water, then serve on warmed plates with toasted bread.

Wine Suggestion: A red Sancerre or a rosé from Provence.

Matelote d'anguilles

Eel Stew with Red Wine

—

This classic Loire Valley dish is usually made with eel. But if you're squeamish about eel (or can't get it, which is quite probable), any kind of firm fish will do just as well.

For about 6

5 oz. medium salted breast of pork, half fat, half lean

12 small onions

4½ Tbsp. butter

3 Tbsp. flour

1½–2 cups chicken broth

2 cups light red wine, such as a Chinon

2 bouquets garni of celery stalks, parsley, and thyme

Pepper and salt

1 tsp. sugar

7 oz. cleaned white mushrooms, quartered

4–5 lb. skinned, ready-to-cook eel, monkfish, or halibut, cut into 2″ sections

1 cup vegetable oil to fry the bread

6–12 slices *pain de mie* (page 495) or good homemade-style bread, crusts removed

1 Tbsp. minced parsley, for garnish

Special equipment needed:

2 large nonstick skillets

*P*repare the base in which the fish will be cooked: Blanch the salted pork breast by placing in a saucepan and covering with cold water. Bring to the boil and boil for 3 minutes. Drain and repeat the process. Pat dry and cut up into ½″ sections. Sauté in oil in a nonstick pan to melt the fat, shaking until nicely browned. Remove the pork *lardons* and reserve. Cook the onions in the same pan until browned, then remove and reserve. Add butter to pan and allow to melt, then sprinkle with flour, stirring constantly until the roux becomes nicely browned and thick. Dilute with half the broth (or water) and the wine, and bring to the boil, stirring with a wire whisk until smooth.

Add all the seasonings, one of the bouquets garnis, salt and pepper, sugar, and the reserved *lardons*. Bring slowly to the boil, adding the remaining broth, if needed, then add the quartered mushrooms. Let simmer 15 minutes, stirring frequently. Correct the seasoning and remove the bouquet garni.

Twenty minutes before serving, bring to the simmer and add the fish, the onions, and a fresh bouquet garni, and let simmer 15–20 minutes, or until the fish is done. Correct the seasoning.

Heat the oil in a nonstick pan and fry the slices of bread. Drain on paper towels and cut each slice into triangles. Place on fresh paper towels and pat dry.

In a warmed shallow serving dish, arrange the fish in the middle, with the *lardons* on one side, the mushrooms on the other side, and the bread triangles around the dish, standing up. Sprinkle with parsley to garnish.

Wine Suggestion: A red or rosé Chinon.

Clafoutis aux prunes

Greengage Plum Clafoutis

—

For 6

½ lb. greengage plums or dried prunes

Hot tea (if using dried prunes)

4 eggs separated

⅔ cup granulated sugar

3 Tbsp. flour

1¼ cups milk

½ tsp. vanilla extract

1 cup heavy cream

4 Tbsp. butter, cut in small pieces

Optional: Confectioners' sugar

Special equipment needed:

A heavy cast-iron gratin dish, buttered

If using fresh greengage plums, remove the skin and stones, and cut in half. If using dried prunes, steep in hot tea (or water), remove the stones, and quarter.

In a mixing bowl, whisk the egg yolks with half the sugar to the "ribbon" stage, add the flour, and mix until homogenous. Meanwhile, heat the milk and vanilla to the boiling point and, stirring vigorously, pour into the egg yolk mixture. Pour all back into the saucepan and return over heat, stirring constantly. When the custard has thickened, remove from heat and mix in the cream and butter; set aside while beating the egg whites.

Beat the egg whites until they begin to form soft peaks. Add the remaining sugar, and beat vigorously until a thick, shiny meringue is obtained. Lightly fold the custard into the egg whites, continuing to fold until the mixture is homogenous.

Pour a layer of this preparation into a gratin dish, distribute the fruit in one layer, then cover with the remaining custard, smoothing the surface with a metal spatula. Bake in a preheated 375°F oven for 25–30 minutes, or until the top is slightly golden brown. The top will rise over the dish and then deflate with cooling, but will have a delicious taste. Serve warm as is or with confectioners' sugar sprinkled over the top.

Wine Suggestion: A sweet sparkling white wine or a Vouvray.

UP IN RAINFREVILLE, it was soon clear that Bernard was unhappy and restless. Apparently, he wanted to get married more than anything in the world. Just a few days after returning home, he said, "Simone, don't you know any suitable women?" I was stunned. I'd never fancied myself a matchmaker, and I thought it was premature for Bernard to contemplate marriage so soon after the dark years he'd endured in prison camp. But I dredged up an idea. I knew that some neighbors of mine in Neuilly named de Francolini had a daughter named Marie-José. We invited her for a weekend, not expecting much to come of it. But when she arrived to be presented to the eligible young bachelor, the way those two visibly fell for each other was almost embarrassing. They were affianced within days and married barely a week after that. I think my mother, who had waited so long to be close to her beloved youngest child again, was stupefied.

As a professional officer, Bernard soon had to return to his army job. In the following years he was posted at various places around the world, but finally he and Marie-José settled not far from me in the Midi, where they live now.

My elder brother, Maurice, was fully occupied with reestablishing the family silicate factory, having run it on a minimal basis during the war.

And Jean eventually returned to his job at L. T. Piver. We were all learning to live normally again, and that agonizing page of our lives was turned forever.

TOWARD THE LANDMARK YEARS

Postwar: The Aftermath

JEAN AND I WERE PRACTICALLY starting our life together all over again after those five years apart. We had both changed, matured, and in particular, Jean was more sensitive after all his suffering. Still in love, we were in many ways almost strangers. But this period of rediscovery was a joy, and my devotion to Jean both sharpened and deepened as I realized how dear he was to me, how terrible the separation had been.

Our daily existence was mostly routine, and there were hardships, because in a material sense France was a very poor country after the occupation. But I thanked my lucky stars that Jean was back in my life. In fact, through little things he did and said, always with humor, I often felt I was living just for him.

I foraged around Paris looking for fresh produce, as food was still scarce. Jean was happy to be working again for the L. T. Piver perfume company in his job as a chemical engineer, and I was still thanking them mentally for having sent the

equivalent of his salary to me throughout the war—making it possible for me to support my mother.

It was like a second honeymoon as Jean and I reveled in our dinners together. We spent hours listening to music. The following year, we took a trip to Bayreuth to hear Wagner's *Parsifal* and *Tristan und Isolde*—which Jean, a romantic at heart, adored.

We had our private jokes, among them Jean's nickname, Sing. Learning from Jean's cousin, who had traveled widely and wisely in the Far East, that *singh* means "strength and wisdom" in Hindi, I adopted the sobriquet immediately as my private pet name for Jean. He was of a more intellectual turn of mind than I, producing clever jokes as well as presents. For my birthday he once gave me a record of Bach's B-Minor Mass, which he loved, and as B is called in France by its solfège name, *si*, he wrote on the record sleeve a dedication based on a play of words involving *si*, Simca, and Sing.

Because of war privation and our mutual *gourmandise,* food had become ever more important to us. One day Jean returned from the factory and announced that he was practically salivating at the description given by a colleague, Pierre Armingeat, of a dinner given by the Club des Cent. Limited to one hundred members, this was France's most prestigious gastronomic club.

"I've never eaten so well," M. Armingeat had told Jean, describing an elaborate five-course dinner that included delicacies like oysters, foie gras, lobster, game, elaborate desserts, and perfect wines. Apparently, no postwar shortages existed for the club.

Jean would probably have been eligible to join, since he had the necessary qualifications as a professional man with a very good palate, but there were no vacancies at the time. As with the Académie Française, a member of the Club des Cent had to die (even if from overindulgence!) before a new candidate could be admitted.

I was vigorously whipping up a soufflé for our dinner, but as Jean stood behind me describing the food, my mouth watered.

"Stop!" I smiled at Jean as I stopped whisking. "You're making me hungry."

Jean had a gleam in his eye. "Good news," he said. "There's a sort of sister club for women, called the Cercle des Gourmettes, and Mme Armingeat is a member. I'll bet she would sponsor you."

I was keen to join, was invited to a luncheon by Mme Armingeat, and was looked over closely by the Gourmettes. I knew it was what we would call a *mondain* assemblage of women from a certain social class, to the manner born. They had to know the finer points of food, but more important, they had to come from the right family background. The family tree mattered more than table manners. Everybody got dressed up for the lunches, so I wore my best suit and hat and gloves, and was only mildly nervous about the whole thing. I had no complexes about my breeding and manners, and I knew more about cuisine than many of the members, whose names I knew by the time I went to the lunch.

The elegant meal was held at one of the members' houses, a huge place fit for a grand reception. There I heard the history of the Gourmettes, which still exists today, much on the same lines.

This superexclusive club was started in 1929, the brainchild of an American woman whose husband was a prominent member of the Club des Cent. Once a year (only), wives were allowed to attend a dinner, which always took place at a top restaurant, such as the Café de Paris, Le Grand Véfour, or—more rarely—at a place out of town, such as the Côte d'Or in Saulieu.

At one such feast, a postprandial speech by the Cent's president, Louis Fourest, included the somewhat tactless, facetiously intended remark that "Unfortunately, women would not be able to create such a club or such great eating events." Paulette Etlinger was incensed by this male chauvinist remark. She rose, bristling with offended dignity, and announced, "I'm sorry, but you'll see we can do it. We shall start our own club tomorrow!"

The outspoken American was roundly applauded, and the wives of the Club des Cent members were gleeful at the prospect. Most joined Mrs. Etlinger's band immediately, and they voted to call it the Cercle des Gourmettes.

By the time I joined, women whose husbands were not members of the Club des Cent were admitted. Our lunches or dinners took place in various kitchens lent by the EDF, Électricité et Gaz de France, and our annual "event," with outside guests, was held in the sumptuous salon of our president.

Unlike the Cent, where men simply gather to savor a great dinner at a plush restaurant, our Gourmettes were encouraged to take part in the preparation—in the EDF's starkly efficient kitchens. We peered into the pots, asked questions of the professional chef on duty, and once in a while even did some scullery jobs. I'll never forget peeling and seeding several kilos of grapes for a quail sauce.

I learned a lot from the chefs at the Cercle des Gourmettes, especially one Aimée Cassiot—a wizard of a cook, who was a professional caterer. When she'd call and ask if I wanted to help make a *ballottine de canard* or whatever, I'd drop everything and go, to watch and assist this friendly, competent woman who had more than one cooking *truc* up her sleeve.

"Anybody can make an ordinary pâté," she said. "But you go to a lot of trouble for a ballottine" (p. 156). So we carved the duck, made the stuffing, arranged it ever so carefully. By the time it emerged from the bain-marie and then was cooled and glazed, it was a work of art.

Those primitive pre-processor days meant lots of manual labor. For fish quenelles, for instance, we started by filleting the fish, then grinding it up with a heavy pestle. Then we went through all the other laborious steps, including forcing it through the tamis sieve and beating in cream in tiny amounts over a bowl of ice. Meanwhile, I was frantically jotting down notes in a food-spotted little notebook.

Most of the Gourmettes were content to stand around gossiping and watching, but they were happy enough to eat the cloud-light little quenelles. Today I might do fish mousseline instead of quenelles, and in any case I'd use modern equipment for some of the work involved, whenever possible.

Un déjeuner Cercle des Gourmettes

Lunch with Members of the Cercle des Gourmettes, Paris

✦ *Mousseline de sole*
Sole mousseline

—

Vin blanc sec—Chablis

✦ *Canards en ballottine aux foies de volaille*
Duck ballottine with a duck liver stuffing

Légumes verts — petits pois
Sweet fresh garden peas

Salade mixte

Fromages variés

—

Beaujolais rouge (Morgan ou Julienas) ou Bourgogne

✦ *Charlotte brésilienne*
Brazilian mocha charlotte

—

Champagne brut

Mousseline de sole

Sole Mousseline

—

For 8 to 10

2½ Tbsp. butter, softened

For mousseline:
10 oz. skinned and boned sole fillets (see note)
Grated nutmeg, salt, and pepper
2 eggs
1½ cups light cream

For beurre blanc sauce:
1 cup dry white wine
4 Tbsp. white-wine vinegar

1½ oz. finely minced shallots
1 tsp. freshly ground pepper
2½ Tbsp. light cream
1–1½ cups cold butter, diced

Special equipment needed:
A rectangular Pyrex loaf pan with lid (or individual ramekins), plus a larger bin to hold water and mold
Parchment paper
A food processor
An enameled cast-iron saucepan

*H*eavily butter a Pyrex loaf pan or individual ramekins and line with parchment paper. Set in the refrigerator until needed.

Purée the fish fillets in a food processor until the mixture is completely smooth. Add salt, freshly grated nutmeg, and pepper, to taste, and pulse until well mixed. Add the eggs, one by one, and pulse after each addition. Transfer to a mixing bowl and set in the freezer for about 20 minutes, or until the mixture is chilled and very firm. Add the cream, a tablespoon at a time, and mix with a wooden spoon until completely incorporated before adding more.

Fill the mold with the mixture and set in a pan of hot water, to reach no higher than ⅓ the height of the loaf pan (or ramekins), then bake in a preheated 375°F oven for 20–25 minutes or until the mousseline begins to pull away from the sides of the mold.

Just before serving, prepare the sauce. Bring the wine, vinegar, and minced shallots and pepper to a boil in an enameled saucepan. Let reduce until 2 Tbsp.

liquid remain. Strain, and return the liquid to the saucepan over heat. Stir in the cream, and bring the mixture to a boil. Over low heat, vigorously whisk in half the diced cold butter, then remove from heat and whisk in the remaining butter.

Wrap the covered saucepan completely in newspapers to keep the sauce warm up to a half hour, or pour into a wide-mouth thermos to keep warm for up to 2 hours. (Do not reheat sauce, or it will break.) Serve the mousseline, with the beurre blanc in a sauceboat.

Note: Other fish, such as sea bass or monkfish, may be substituted for the sole.

Canards en ballottine aux foies de volaille

Duck Ballottine with a Duck Liver Stuffing

—

For 8 to 12

Two 3-lb. ducks

For stock (to be made the day before):

2 quarts water

Necks, wingtips, and gizzards from the ducks

3 lb. veal bones, cut up

1 large onion, sliced

1 large carrot, sliced

Bouquet garni of celery stalk, parsley stems, bay leaf, and thyme

Salt

For stuffing:

1 lb. duck and chicken livers

Pepper

⅓ cup Cognac, brandy, or bourbon

½ lb. turkey breast, cut into cubes

½ lb. breast of pork, half lean and half fat, cut into cubes

½ lb. rendered goose fat or lard, melted

Dried herbes de Provence, to taste (see Aide-Mémoire, page 503)

Salt, to taste

Optional: 2 oz. truffles, half julienned and half diced

2 Tbsp. mixed fresh minced tarragon, thyme, oregano, and coriander leaves

½ lb. boiled ham, cut into strips

Special equipment needed:

A stockpot

A food processor

Cheesecloth and string

A fish poacher or large covered pot

*P*repare, strain, and degrease the stock the day before assembling the ballottine: Simmer the duck trimmings, veal bones, vegetables, and herbs in water until you have a nicely flavored stock. Strain and salt to taste. Skim the fat and refrigerate until needed, removing additional accumulated fat from the surface.

Trim the livers to remove any sinews and discolored portions. Season with pepper to taste and place in a bowl with Cognac, brandy, or bourbon, cover, and let macerate overnight in the refrigerator.

The next day, remove the livers from the macerating liquid and let drain on paper towels, reserving the liquid. Cutting along each side of the breastbone, remove the duck breasts, and reserve. Remove the rest of the meat from the bones (discarding the fatty skin), cut into chunks, and place in a food processor. Pulse to chop roughly. Cut half the livers into strips, and reserve. Place the remaining livers in the food processor with the duck, turkey, and pork breast meats, and roughly chop. Transfer to a mixing bowl, add the melted goose fat or lard, and season highly. Mix the diced truffle into the meats, stir in the macerating liquid, and correct the seasoning, adding fresh herbs.

Remove and discard the skin from the duck breasts, cut meat into strips, and reserve. Spread a piece of moistened cheesecloth over a cutting board. To build up the ballottine: Use a metal spatula to spread ⅓ of the meat mixture evenly in a rectangle about 5″ by 10″ in the middle of the cloth. Make a design, arranging half the reserved livers, duck breasts, ham, and julienned truffles close together and lengthwise along the top of the first layer. Repeat with another third of the meat mixture, spreading evenly. Cover with the remaining livers, truffles, duck, and ham strips, arranged in the same design as before, and finish with the rest of the meat mixture. Roll into a large sausage shape and wrap tightly with the cheesecloth. Tie securely at each end and several places in between to help the sausage retain its shape.

To cook, place the ballottine in a fish poacher or covered pot large enough to hold it without bending. Cover with cold stock and slowly bring to the simmer. Cover and simmer 1½–1¾ hours, then remove from heat. Let cool in the stock, then drain over a rack. When cool, remove the cheesecloth and roll the ballottine in plastic wrap. Place in refrigerator for at least 12 hours before serving.

Serve cold in slices, with a mixed green salad.

Wine suggestion: A good fruity red wine, such as a Sancerre from the Loire Valley.

Charlotte Brésilienne

Brazilian Mocha Charlotte

—

For 9 to 10

Butter, for mold

For filling:
½ lb. bittersweet chocolate (such as
   Lindt or Ghirardelli)
¼ cup strong coffee
1¼ cups sweet butter
2 oz. cocoa powder, unsweetened
10 egg yolks
1 cup granulated sugar

For Chantilly:
3 cups heavy cream
Optional: ¼ cup confectioners'
   sugar

24 ladyfingers
1 cup sweetened strong coffee (to
   moisten ladyfingers)

For coffee custard sauce:
2½ cups milk
2–2½ Tbsp. instant espresso granules
6–7 egg yolks, depending on size
⅔ cup granulated sugar

Special equipment needed:
One 8-cup charlotte mold, or two
   smaller molds
A food processor
An electric mixer or a whisk

Heavily butter the charlotte mold and place in the refrigerator until needed.

Melt the chocolate with ¼ cup strong coffee, stirring until completely smooth. Set aside to cool.

Cream the butter, then fold in the cocoa powder, working the mixture until homogenous. Set aside.

Using a food processor, pulse the egg yolks with the sugar until creamy. Add melted chocolate and creamed butter and cocoa mixtures, and pulse for about 10 seconds to mix. Do not overwork.

In a large mixing bowl set over ice, beat the heavy cream to a soft, not too firm, Chantilly. Turn the chocolate mixture into the Chantilly, and fold to mix. Considerable folding may be required, but *do not beat*. Taste, and if the mixture is not sweet enough, add confectioners' sugar by tablespoons, to taste.

To fill the mold, moisten each ladyfinger for a few seconds only in the sweetened coffee. Do not overmoisten the ladyfingers, or the charlotte will be soggy when unmolded. Pack them, tightly pressed together, first on the bottom of the mold and then on the sides. Fill halfway with the filling and then add a layer of ladyfinger pieces that have been slightly moistened in the coffee, followed by the rest of the filling. Top with another layer of barely moistened ladyfinger pieces. Cover with foil and refrigerate until set, at least 3–4 hours.

For the custard sauce, boil the milk with the coffee. Using a food processor, mix the egg yolks with the sugar for about 6–8 seconds, or until pale. While the processor is running, add half of the boiling milk and coffee, then pour all into the remaining hot milk mixture. Over heat, stir slowly with a wooden spoon until the custard coats the spoon. Immediately remove from heat and stir until cool. Alternatively, "ribbon" the egg yolks and sugar, using a whisk or an electric mixer, then proceed as directed above.

To serve, unmold the charlotte onto a shallow serving dish, and coat with a little of the coffee custard sauce. Serve the remaining sauce in a sauceboat.

Wine Suggestion: A very good Sauternes, such as Château d'Yquem, Château La Tour Blanche, or Château Clime.

I WAS A DEVOTED MEMBER OF THE CERCLE. After a while I was appointed a kind of super-*brigadière,* overseeing the person working with our current chef to plan exquisite and balanced menus. Occasionally, a little squabble on style erupted between the women, and apparently I had the knowledge and authority to make the final decision. My appetite was being whetted by this work, both by the food and for the responsibilities involved.

Without consciously realizing it, I was working up to a career in cooking. Here's how it happened, as I see it: The seed for the idea of a cookbook for Americans came from Louisette Bertholle, or rather from America via Louisette.

Around 1948, social life was picking up again. The worst war memories and shortages were fading, and the French had a tremendous desire to immerse themselves in all life's possible pleasures.

At a cocktail party, Jean was talking to Louisette, whom we'd both met before the war. She and her husband had been in Grosse Pointe, Michigan, and visited Lucille Tyree (whom I later met, was immediately drawn to, and eventually visited). After a good dinner of *boeuf à la mode* that Louisette had helped prepare, Lucille remarked, "You'd be doing Americans a favor if you'd write a cookbook telling them about French cooking." Louisette mentioned this to Jean, who then passed it on to me.

"Why don't you start doing something like that?" he said. "You're a wonderful cook; it would give you something worthwhile to do, and I'm sure you could be successful."

And *voilà!* Like a light bulb popping on in my head, I felt a compelling inspiration and motivation, backed by Jean, who always gave me confidence in myself. It's said that people excel at what they really like to do, so I was already well on my way.

The first thing I did was learn to type. I'm still not a great typist, and friends tell me some of my manuscripts look like a smudged, crowded bible text. Louisette and I collaborated with high hopes and managed to turn out a small book of recipes for America, *What's Cooking in France*. It was brought out by Putnam but was given no promotion, and it made not a ripple in the publishing world. I found a moth-eaten copy along with other ancient papers in my attic recently and am ashamed to say it's a pretty paltry cooking book—full of mistakes, maybe owing to a faulty translation.

About that time I also wrote my only work published in French—*Le pruneau devant le fourneau*—a modest brochure about prunes and prune liqueurs, requested by a group of prune-boosters.

These efforts were far from satisfying my ambition to do something really worthwhile with cooking. Louisette was busy raising her two little girls, so I forged ahead on my own. I went wild, becoming a workaholic as I frantically wrote down recipe after recipe to create a valid cookbook for Americans. I wrote in French, with the expectation that any book published would be translated into English.

I worked rather the way I had at bookbinding, only this time my obsession was to garner and write down recipes, methods, and ideas from every source I could muster—my mother's black recipe notebooks, memories of Zulma's cuisine, tips from chefs in restaurants, and of course Mme Cassiot at the Gourmettes.

After a year, I sent more than a hundred recipes off to Mrs. Dorothy Canfield

Fisher, who was on the editorial board of the Book-of-the-Month Club and a friend of the Fischbacher family.

Mrs. Canfield Fisher kept my group of recipes for quite a while, and I was dying to know what had happened. Her reply was American style, right to the point. "It won't do," was the idea. I was disappointed at first, but also encouraged, since I still yearned to write this cookbook and she had given me ideas about the American mentality.

"This is just a dry bunch of recipes, with not much background on French food attitudes and ways of doing things," she said. She wrote that Americans were so used to processed foods and simply barbecued or roasted meats that French cooking was a mystery. "You've got to preface the recipes and tell little anecdotes—something that explains the whole way the French do things in the kitchen," she said.

I looked a little down when I showed the letter to Jean. "Don't be discouraged," he said. "She's right; you've just got to keep plugging along." And her greatest idea was this: "Get an American who is crazy about French cooking to collaborate with you; somebody who both knows French food and can still see and explain things with an American viewpoint in mind. This is the angle you need."

Right. But where was this paragon who knew all the finer points of French cooking? Certainly not among our present acquaintances.

Enter Julia Child

I N LATE 1949, JEAN AND I WERE CHATTING with Jacqueline Grédy, a good friend from way back, who was intrigued by my project: "I think I can help you find the right American through George Artamonoff, a director of the Marshall Plan. He knows loads of Americans and could introduce you to a few of them."

Artamonoff, a Russian-born American—who was the first president of Sears International, Inc.—was mainly connected with the Far Eastern branches of the Marshall Plan but also had a temporary post in Paris. He had rented a big house in the suburb of Saint-Germain-en-Laye.

With Julia Child (left) and Curnonsky, "Prince of Gastronomes," in Paris

"I'm inviting a hundred people to a cocktail party," Artamonoff told Jacqueline. "With all those guests, I can't look after introducing Mme Fischbacher to the American who might be interested, Mrs. Paul Child, but I think she will be fairly easy to spot. She's over six feet tall."

The party was elegant, but also very noisy and crowded, so I went cruising, looking for a tall American woman. I saw one possibility, but she was sitting down, in deep conversation with somebody. I positioned myself behind her chair and thought I overheard some talk of food. Then Julia stood up, and I knew I'd found my quarry in this handsome, curly-headed woman. "Mrs. Child?" I said. "I've been looking for you. My name is Simone Fischbacher, but please call me Simca."

"Delighted," said Julia in her warm soprano-contralto voice, fairly exuding warmth and sunny charm. The spark was instant; we immediately hit it off and introduced our husbands to each other. Julia and Paul had met during the war while serving in the OSS (Office of Strategic Services), and by now Paul was in the United States Information Service, attached to the American Embassy in Paris. We were soon engrossed in a favorite topic for all of us—food, and how to make a valid professional project out of it.

Julia was taking lessons at the Cordon Bleu and was mad about French food, as was Paul. He had lived in France before the war, teaching at an American boys' prep school in Pau, and he spoke fluent French.

Thus began our lifelong friendship, as Julia and I became more like sisters than just friends working together. Julia has always been close to me, and has even helped right up to and including this very book.

I told her about the idea of teaching French cooking to Americans through a cookbook and perhaps giving lessons in Paris, and with her usual enthusiasm, she said, "A terrific idea. Why don't we meet at our apartment tomorrow, on the Rue de l'Université?" I didn't hesitate, drove over from Neuilly, and we talked almost exclusively about food for hours. We were excited by how to tell American cooks all about French techniques and cooking bases, the intricacies of pastry or sauces, the differences in American and French tastes and produce.

Julia wanted to meet Louisette, who had planted her germ of an idea from America, and after I introduced them to each other, we soon became a kind of triumvirate of cooking.

Louisette became a member of the Gourmettes, and Julia was dying to join as well. Not only because Mrs. Etlinger was American and Julia wanted a compatriot friend in Paris, but because she loved the idea of a gastronomic club where people could exchange their ideas on food. She was readily accepted into the Cercle and was thrilled by the opportunity to have her first experience in an all-French environment.

Then we all three made an interesting gastronomic acquaintance—Curnonsky, "Prince of Gastronomes."

He was a celebrated character of the French culinary scene, a great and witty writer and editor of the only true French cooking magazine back then, *Cuisine et vins de France*. His true name was Maurice-Edmond Sailland, and he was born in 1871, the son of a pastel painter in the Anjou. His piquant writing intrigued *le tout Paris* of gastronomy, and he was later known as the ultimate critic of gastronomic quality, a poet for the food world.

A writer named Alphonse Allais commented early on that Sailland was a dull nom de plume. Things Russian were *très à la mode* back in the early part of the century—with Stravinsky, Diaghilev, Lifar, and the Ballets Russes all the rage—so Allais suggested a name ending in "sky." Sailland—who liked to show off a certain erudition—replied with a Latin combination: *cur non* sky (why not *sky?*).

Although the name Curnonsky was soon to be revered all over France, its adoption caused the gastronome some problems at the outbreak of World War I. The French gendarmerie, understandably a bit paranoid, decided he must be a suspicious character and in 1914 arrested him as a Bulgarian spy!

Happily, his incarceration was only temporary, and after his initial discomfiture, he was considerably amused by the gendarmerie's gaffe and loved telling stories about it.

Urbane, mustachioed, and well dressed, Curnonsky regaled us with his charm and skill as a raconteur. We were a little nervous about cooking for this great expert, but he was always good-humored and tactful.

He had an obsession with food being fresh, especially shellfish. So if I planned to serve him fish, I marketed just a couple of hours before lunch, getting the fishmonger to choose perfect specimens, then poking and examining them myself, taking only those that seemed practically alive. Of course, serving things like lobsters or crayfish, I took them alive and active from the tray or tank—always a golden rule.

Un dîner de fête pour Curnonsky

A Festive Dinner for Curnonsky

Apéritif: Champagne

✦ *Les diablotins*

"Little Devil" *bouchées* (bite-size tidbits) with cheese

✦ *Poulet aux écrevisses*

Chicken fricassee with crayfish

—

Vin blanc de Bourgogne—Meursault

Salade verte

Fromages variés

—

Bordeaux (Château Margaux)—
or another excellent red wine for the cheeses

✦ *Chantilly glacé aux fruits frais*

Frozen Chantilly mousse with fresh fruit

—

Champagne

Les diablotins

"Little Devil" Bouchées with Cheese

—

For 6 (18 to 24 "devil crackers")

For choux paste:
1¼ cups water
5 Tbsp. butter
1 large cup sifted flour
4 eggs
Salt, pepper, and nutmeg
Cayenne or Tabasco

For garnish:
3 oz. Roquefort or Stilton cheese (or any cheese of good flavor), well crumbled
Optional: 12 tiny Niçoise olives, pitted and roughly chopped

Special equipment required:
A deep frying pan containing 1 qt. peanut oil

Place water, a pinch of salt, and the butter in a thick-bottomed saucepan, and bring slowly to a boil. The butter should just be melted as the boil is reached. Remove from the heat and add flour all at once, stirring until a smooth paste results. Return to the heat to dry the paste, stirring constantly with a wooden spoon and spreading it until a sandy glaze covers the bottom of the pan. Remove from the heat and add the eggs, one at a time, stirring thoroughly after each addition. Season to taste with pepper, cayenne, and nutmeg. Add the finely crumbled cheese and mix well. (Adding the chopped black olives will impart a special flavor.)

Heat the oil in the frying pan until hot. (Test for proper temperature by throwing little cubes of stale bread crust into the oil. Small bubbles will form on the crust when oil is ready.) With a large spoon, drop small (1¼") balls into the hot oil, turning them until slightly browned (about 2 minutes). Remove with a skimmer or slotted spoon, and drain over paper towels. Keep wrapped in foil until needed.

Note: Fried ahead, these crackers can easily be reheated over foil in a moderately hot oven (375°F) for about 10–15 minutes, and are very good for cocktail parties.

Poulet aux écrevisses

Chicken Fricassee with Crayfish

—

For 6 to 8

Two 3½-lb. chickens

3 Tbsp. butter

1½ Tbsp. olive oil

12–16 fresh crayfish (or shrimp)

¼ cup Cognac

1½ cups dry white wine

Salt and pepper

1 lb. ripe tomatoes, peeled and
  seeded

1 medium onion, sliced

2 Tbsp. tomato paste

Bouquet garni (see page 503)

2–3 garlic cloves, not peeled

2 Tbsp. dried herbes de Provence
  (see Aide-Mémoire, page 503)

1½ cups chicken broth

1–1½ cups heavy cream

Optional: 1 tsp. arrowroot or potato
  starch

Parsley, for garnish

Special equipment needed:

A heavy-bottomed casserole, preferably
  enameled cast iron

A food processor or food mill

Parchment paper to cover

*C*ut each chicken into 7 serving pieces. Heat the butter and oil in a heavy-bottomed casserole and, beginning with the dark meat, brown the chicken on all sides, then remove and brown the white meat. Do not crowd the pan. When all the chicken has been browned, remove from the pan and set aside while cooking the crayfish.

Add the crayfish to the same hot fat, and cook until they turn a ruddy orange color. Pour in the Cognac, ignite, and let flame briefly to evaporate the alcohol. When the flame dies, add the white wine and cook the crayfish for 10 more minutes, then season and remove from the pan with a slotted spoon. When cool enough to touch, remove the crayfish meat from the shells, and reserve. Retain a few of the crayfish heads for decoration, and place the rest of the shells in a food processor. Pulse very briefly to roughly chop. Remove and set aside.

Purée the peeled and seeded tomatoes in a food mill or food processor. Return the chicken pieces to the pan, add the onion, tomato paste, a bouquet garni, garlic cloves, the herbs, crushed crayfish shells, and enough chicken broth to cover. Place parchment paper on top, followed by the lid of the casserole, and bring to the simmer over direct heat. Place in a preheated 375°F oven and allow to simmer gently for about 20 minutes, then test the white meat for doneness. If done, remove all the white meat, leaving the dark meat to continue cooking for 4–5 more minutes. Remove and keep warm with the white meat. Taste and correct the seasoning.

Strain the cooking juices, pressing hard on the solids to get all the flavor and juice out of them. Degrease the sauce, return it to the pan, and let reduce over high heat to concentrate the flavors. Add the cream and let the sauce continue reducing until it has thickened to a nice consistency, then correct the seasoning. (If the sauce does not thicken, add a teaspoon of arrowroot or potato starch and stir constantly while the sauce is simmering.) The dish may now wait for up to 30 minutes, if desired.

A few minutes before serving, place the chicken and the crayfish meat in the sauce to reheat slowly, without boiling. To serve, arrange the chicken on a warm platter, surrounded by the crayfish meat, and place the crayfish heads here and there to decorate. Sprinkle with parsley, and serve the remaining sauce on the side.

Vegetable Suggestion: Serve with risotto (page 390).

Wine Suggestion: A Sancerre or California Sauvignon Blanc.

Chantilly glacé aux fruits frais

Frozen Chantilly Mousse with Fresh Fruit

—

For about 10

1 generous lb. fresh raspberries and/or strawberries, or 10 oz. each frozen raspberries and strawberries (thawed)
½ cup confectioners' sugar
¾ cup granulated sugar
4 Tbsp. water

3 large egg whites
Pinch of salt
2 cups heavy cream
1 tsp. vanilla extract (or pinch vanilla powder)
3–4 Tbsp. Kirsch

Fresh mint leaves, for garnish
Fresh raspberries, for garnish

Special equipment needed:
A food mill or food processor
A strainer

A large savarin (ring) mold, lined with
    parchment paper
Two mixing bowls (the larger containing
    ice and water, the smaller—preferably
    copper—sitting on the ice)

*R*inse and hull the fruit, as needed. Sprinkle with the confectioners' sugar, then put through a food mill (or pulse briefly in a food processor), and strain. Refrigerate the juice until needed.

Line the bottom of a savarin mold with parchment paper, and set aside. Prepare a syrup by boiling the granulated sugar with 4 Tbsp. water until the "thread" stage is reached.

Meanwhile, beat the egg whites in a copper basin with a pinch of salt until half beaten. Continuing to beat vigorously, pour the boiling syrup in a thin stream into the egg whites, and beat until thick and shiny. Place the meringue over ice, and continue to beat until cool. Set aside.

Beat the whipping cream over ice to a Chantilly ("soft peaks") stage. Stir in the vanilla, the prepared fruit juice, and the Kirsch, then fold this mixture into the cold meringue. (If the meringue is still warm, the mixture will collapse.)

Fill the savarin mold, cover with parchment paper, and freeze for about 3 hours. Just before serving, unmold over a serving dish and garnish the center with a bunch of fresh mint leaves and fresh raspberries.

*C*URNONSKY'S FAMOUS DICTUM WAS *"Laissez aux choses le goût de ce qu'elles sont."* In other words, all foods should be cooked to show off their natural flavors, not masked with overly strong sauces and spices. Curnonsky was such a star that the best restaurants put brass plaques with his name behind his favorite table.

But few of his friends knew that Curnonsky was in trouble. I found out later that he was so poor that he took turns using the bed with his cleaning lady. When he was working, she would sleep; when she was out or working in his flat, he'd lie down.

And he was in poor health as well. Sometime in the mid-fifties, he had a bad fall on the polished floor of a château he was visiting—apparently the beginning of a serious illness, which was complicated by an excess of albumin in his system. He was put on a dreary diet and could drink only milk. Anyone would be depressed by that, but imagine its effect on a renowned gourmet like Curnonsky. In 1956, in his mid-eighties, he committed suicide by jumping out a window. What a sad, sordid end for this discerning bon vivant.

Shortly thereafter, a society of Friends of Curnonsky was founded, and food writers make an annual pilgrimage to his grave outside Paris, commemorating him afterward with a jovial and good lunch.

We do tend to revere things gastronomic in France. Where else would you have, as we do, an encyclopedic volume to list the hundreds of food and wine organizations? America, of course, now has the American Institute of Wine and Food—a serious and even scholarly organization endorsed by Julia, a founder and board member, and other American food authorities.

Some of our organizations are fairly serious, others less so. There's even the A.A.A.A.—l'Association des Amateurs de l'Andouillette Authentique—for people who prepare and appreciate authentic tripe sausage. (I wouldn't make any detours for it; especially as some versions have a knockout barnyard smell and taste, which means the tripe haven't been cleaned very well.)

The wine-producing regions all have their *confréries* to promote the local tipple— and so many people are now clamoring to join one of the oldest (the Chevaliers du Tastevin de Bourgogne), which I belong to, that not all candidates can be taken in. They now admit only celebrities or wine and food professionals.

Julia and I were committed to our project to take French cooking to America via a book, while giving lessons to other Americans. With her impressive stature and personality, Julia was a natural for teaching, but she rather terrified me at first. I felt intimidated, kind of "small in my shoes," as we'd say in France, although I'm sure Julia had no idea of this. Her cheerful, generous nature soon put me at ease.

The Childs' rented apartment was impressive too, with a view onto the gardens of the French war ministry. It was decorated with some ponderous ersatz Louis something-or-other furnishings and other bibelots, which Julia found to be in dubious "landlady's taste."

I was particularly interested in Paul Child's paintings. He is an inspired and talented figurative painter, evoking scenes and atmosphere with a very special lyrical quality, as well as being a top-notch photographer.

By 1951, we had decided to launch ourselves into giving cooking lessons, using Julia's apartment, which was more centrally located than mine. As Julia pointed out, at the Cordon Bleu you absolutely had to understand French to get much out of the lessons, and many Americans would probably love to learn French cooking with teachers who spoke English. We could explain everything to small groups, who could also "get their hands on the dough" (*mettre la main à la pâte*). Ours would be a practical cooking course, of the kind now so popular in the United States, Australia, and other countries.

With Louisette, we soon called ourselves l'École des Trois Gourmandes, and once we began, the school kept on at various periods until the late 1970s, in the latter years held at Louisette's beautiful apartment on Avenue Victor Hugo. I still have good friends from among our many pupils, people like Carol Cutler, an avid learner, whose husband, B.J., was then editor of the Paris *Herald Tribune*. Now she's known as a cookbook author on her own, working in Washington, D.C.

Our first pupils were signed up in very small groups of five or six from the American Embassy, for a couple of lessons a month, and we had great backup advice from chef Max Bugnard. He was a favorite teacher not only at the Cordon Bleu when Julia was a student (her fellow students mainly being men on the G.I. Bill who wanted to learn French cooking) but also with our Cercle des Gourmettes. In his Gourmette sessions in a crowded room on Rue de Naples near the Gare Saint-Lazare, Bugnard never failed to impart fine professional techniques and special hints—or *tours de main*—for everything from pastry to boning fish and meats.

I can't remember what Julia said to introduce our first lesson, nor my words either, but I'm sure we must have somehow hidden our initial shyness. I was afraid that nobody would understand my English, which was more British than American, and I also had tinges of a French accent. "We've got to plunge right in, Simca!" said Julia, who has always done just that, even during her difficult early TV days much later. And I guess I have always done the same. Naturally, we didn't agree on everything, and sometimes we even disagreed with our chef-adviser, as is wont to happen among strong personalities, but we always managed to reach a compromise.

"American ingredients are often totally different from yours here," Julia pointed out, and I concurred wholeheartedly that we ought to perfect every recipe using what would be available in the United States. Fortunately, Paul had access to the PX through his government job, so Julia and I went on regular suburban treks (the biggest branch was west of Paris) to pick up staples like flour. I think one of the reasons *Mastering* was such a hit was that we explained how to substitute American ingredients for French and get an excellent result. Crème fraîche, butter, everything was quite different, though Americans would become accustomed to using their own ingredients in preparing French recipes; many specialty stores now sell French products, and some supermarkets do as well.

The fun of our lessons with the Americans was always the relaxing lunch or dinner afterward. There would be something like *potage Germiny, fricassée de poulet,* or whatever, in the Childs' dining room, wine served by Paul. He poured with a flourish and talked with eloquence, as if the wine were nectar. He is quite erudite in oenology and knows how to point out the best qualities in wine.

During that period while Julia and I were working hard on food affairs, I had a rich life with Jean, especially on weekends, as we often took long walks with the Grédys and George Artamonoff and other friends in the Fontainebleau forest. There were wonderful moments in those hilly woods of pines with their ruddy, scaly trunks among the gray rocks—just like the Cézanne paintings. We'd often go in big groups of twelve or fifteen, walking at least fifteen kilometers during a day, working up big appetites for the midday picnic break.

We walked in nearly every kind of weather, cold or hot. Weather permitting, we'd gather firewood, I'd whip out my trusty frying pan, and we'd often have a hot omelet as part of the meal. We'd bring meat pâtés, bread and cheese, fruit in season, *gâteaux* or tarts I'd made the day before. If it was rainy, we'd have our picnic in the rustic cabin of the forest guard. We'd always continue on after lunch, making a circle to end up at our original meeting place, where we'd left the cars. Whether in Fontainebleau, Chantilly, or another forest, Jean, with his expertise in compasses and maps, always knew how to get us back to home base.

Another diversion for Jean was shooting game in season, a sport he adored. With a group of friends, we sometimes traveled down to Saint-Cyr-en-Val, not far from Orléans, south of the Loire. The countryside was always lovely, in woods or fields, so I went along for the outing, since I'd given up shooting on that terrible day so long before when I shot two deer with my father up in Normandy and realized I couldn't kill animals.

Thanks to friends who organized the weekends, we rented a rustic, unheated gamekeeper's cottage on the property of a Belle Époque–style château. It was owned by a rarely seen maiden lady, who sometimes drifted around like a white-haired spirit and said little beyond a vague greeting.

Besides fresh air, my main interest here was in watching the cook during our weekends, a certain Mme Lantoine, who prepared our Saturday night feasts and two meals on Sunday. She was officially retired, but was a very cheerful old woman and had lots of class as a cook. I never failed to learn little hints from her.

However, it wasn't possible to teach her anything, though I occasionally found a fault with some of her recipes. On Saturday nights, she always served us a tempting dessert, such as a *bavarois* or a charlotte based on fruits. I thought she put in too many eggs, making the charlotte both too heavy and too "stiff" for my taste. "Mme Lantoine," I observed timidly one day, "why don't you try using a few less eggs, to make it lighter?"

"This is the way I've always done it," said the old lady, unruffled and smiling, stubbornly keeping on in her habitual way. At that age, she didn't want to change. But I enjoyed every minute in that simple kitchen, working on the wooden table and ancient stove with her, and I can still nearly taste the delicious food we enjoyed on those weekends.

Un dîner de chasse en Sologne

A Hunt Dinner in Sologne

✦ *Croquettes au fromage*
Cheese croquettes

—

Pouilly Fumé ou Mondavi Fumé Blanc

✦ *Le canard à la Duchambais*
Duck cooked in browned flour

Salade

Fromages variés

—

Bordeaux rouge, Médoc ou Macon rouge, ou Cabernet Sauvignon (Californie)

✦ *Bavarois royale de Mme Lantoine*
Mme Lantoine's Royal Bavarian

—

Vin blanc pétillant—Vouvray

Croquettes au fromage

Cheese Croquettes

—

About 25 croquettes, or bouchées

3½ Tbsp. butter
1 cup sifted flour
1 cup milk
2 egg yolks
4 oz. Gruyère cheese, finely diced
Pepper

To shape the croquettes:
½ cup flour, spread on a plate

1 egg white, slightly beaten with a fork
⅔ cup stale bread crumbs, spread on a
    plate

Fried parsley, for garnish (see note)

Special equipment needed:
An oiled baking pan
A deep frying pan with 1″ vegetable oil

Heat the butter in a thick-bottomed saucepan. When melted, stir in the flour and let cook, stirring constantly, for about 2–3 minutes, then remove from heat and pour in the milk, whisking until absolutely smooth. Return to heat and bring to the boil, still stirring, then let cool slightly before whisking in the egg yolks and the cheese. Add pepper. When smooth, spread in an oiled baking pan and refrigerate for 12–24 hours. The mixture should be very thick.

One hour before serving the croquettes, use your hands to shape the mixture like small eggs. (For cocktail parties, form the croquettes into walnut-size shapes.) Roll them in the flour, shaking off any excess, then in the beaten egg white, and finish with the bread crumbs.

Heat the frying oil until just beginning to be hot. (Test with a piece of bread.) Fry the croquettes in small batches, turning them over as they become golden brown. When done, remove and let drain over paper towels, keeping them warm until serving time. Serve on a heated platter decorated with fried parsley.

Note: To fry the parsley, wash and carefully dry some fresh parsley, then drop into hot oil. Remove after just a few seconds, and drain on paper towels.

Le canard à la Duchambais

Duck Cooked in Browned Flour

—

For 5 to 6

3 oz. pork lard

1 lean duck, about 4–5 lb., cut into
   8 pieces

4–5 shallots, roughly chopped

⅓ cup red-wine vinegar

1½ Tbsp. flour

2 cups light red wine

2–3 cups rich chicken broth

Salt and pepper

Bouquet garni of celery, bay leaf, thyme,
   and parsley

3 slices *pain de mie* (page 495) for
   croutons

2 Tbsp. butter

1 Tbsp. oil

1 cup heavy cream

Special equipment needed:

A large skillet with lid, or a Dutch
   oven

A shallow ovenproof pan, such as a
   cookie sheet or jelly roll pan

Parchment paper

A shallow serving dish

*M*elt the lard in a skillet, with 1 tablespoon of water, over low heat. Stir frequently and do not allow the fat to brown. Beginning with the dark meat, add the duck pieces in one layer, without crowding them. Lightly brown the duck pieces on all sides, adding the chopped shallots near the end so they become tender but do not burn. When all is golden brown, remove duck meat and shallots, pour off and discard all the fat. Deglaze the pan with the vinegar, stirring over medium heat and scraping up the browned bits, until liquid is almost gone.

Meanwhile, spread the flour on an ovenproof pan and brown for a few minutes under the broiler, shaking frequently. The flour should brown evenly without burning. (Alternately, place the flour in a preheated 400°F oven for 30 minutes, shaking pan about every 10 minutes.)

Return all the duck pieces to the skillet and sprinkle with the browned flour, turning the pieces to coat them evenly with flour. Let cook and, when quite hot, pour in the wine, stirring to dissolve the flour. Bring to the boil and let boil a few minutes to cook the flour and evaporate the alcohol from the wine, then add enough broth to completely cover the duck. Season highly with salt and pepper, place a bouquet garni in the middle, and bring to the simmer. Cover with a piece of parchment paper and the skillet lid, and bake in a preheated 350°F oven for 1 hour.

Cut the crusts from the *pain de mie* and cut each slice into four triangles. Melt some butter with a tablespoon of oil and fry the croutons until golden. When nicely golden brown on both sides, remove and drain on paper towels. Keep warm until ready to serve.

Remove the duck meat from the cooking juices, and keep warm. Correct the seasoning of the juices, then strain and degrease thoroughly. Return the cooking liquid to the pan, stir in the cream, and heat, without letting the mixture come to the boil. Return the duck pieces to the slightly thickened sauce to reheat.

To serve, place the duck, together with its sauce, in a warmed shallow serving dish and set the croutons around the edge of the dish. Serve with tiny green peas, fresh from the garden, heated with butter.

Wine Suggestion: The same light red wine.

Bavarois royale de Mme Lantoine

Mme Lantoine's Royal Bavarian

—

For 10

12 ladyfingers

For syrup:
1 cup water
3 Tbsp. sugar
3 Tbsp. Kirsch or framboise
   liqueur

For Bavarian base:
2¼ cups sweet white wine, such
   as Sauternes, or a sweet
   Champagne
2¼ cups milk
½ tsp. vanilla extract
7 egg yolks (8, if small)
⅔ cup sugar
3 envelopes unflavored gelatin

For sabayon sauce:
3 egg yolks
½ cup sugar
2 cups sweet white wine (Sauternes)
¾ cup heavy cream
1 tsp. vanilla extract

For garnish:
Chocolate rolls (made by shaving a
   chocolate bar with a knife) or candied
   mint leaves

Special equipment needed:
Parchment paper
A glass or nonstick charlotte mold (7–8
   cup capacity), or 2 smaller molds
Two stainless-steel saucepans

Slightly moisten one side only of the parchment paper and place it on the bottom of the mold, damp side down. Refrigerate until needed.

Cut the ladyfingers into 1″ cubes and set aside. Meanwhile, prepare a syrup by boiling the water with the sugar. Remove from heat, let cool completely, and then stir into the liqueur. Set aside.

Moisten the powdered gelatin in a little of the wine. Set aside while preparing the bavarois base.

To make the bavarois base, bring the wine to a boil in a stainless-steel saucepan. Let boil a few minutes to evaporate the alcohol. In a second stainless-steel pan, heat the milk with the vanilla. Meanwhile, beat the egg yolks with the sugar to the "ribbon" stage. Beating constantly, slowly pour in the boiling milk and then the boiled wine. Return to the heat, stirring constantly with a wooden spoon, until the mixture coats the back of the spoon. Remove immediately, add the gelatin, and stir until the gelatin is completely dissolved and the mixture is cool. Do not allow to set.

Moisten the cubed ladyfingers in the syrup for 2 seconds only, and mix into the cooled, but still unset, custard. Fill the mold and chill in the freezer for about 2 hours, or longer in the refrigerator. Do not let the bavarois freeze.

To prepare the sabayon sauce, beat the egg yolks with the sugar until pale and "ribboned." Boil the wine in a stainless-steel saucepan to evaporate the alcohol. Whisking constantly, pour the boiling wine into the egg yolk mixture, then pour all back into the saucepan and place over heat to thicken, stirring constantly with a wooden spoon. As soon as the sauce coats the spoon, remove from heat and keep stirring, over ice, until completely cool.

Beat the cream with the vanilla to the Chantilly ("soft peaks") stage and fold into it the chilled sabayon custard. If the custard is warm, it will cause the whipped cream to separate. Place in refrigerator until serving time.

To serve, unmold the bavarois on a chilled shallow serving dish and decorate with chocolate rolls or candied mint leaves. Serve the sabayon on the side.

Wine Suggestion: Serve with the same sweet white wine or a demi-sec Champagne.

WE USUALLY TOOK ALONG VICKY, our poodle, on our hunting weekends. The little dog was bright and affectionate, and without any training at all retrieved game from the marshes and ponds—an atavistic gesture, as she "remembered" that poodles were essentially hunting dogs. Some of the dogs brought by our friends just ignored their hunting duties. Vicky gave us five little black puppies, and when she died, at age twelve, I cried as if she'd been our baby.

All our outdoor activities on these weekends made for ravenous appetites, and it was a joy to come back to the irresistible scents of roasting meat or game, or the sweet, fruity smell of a deep-dish *tarte tatin* cooking in the oven. Most American cooks by now know about *les soeurs Tatin,* who carved their place in gastronomic history with the legendary upside-down deep-dish apple pie they served in their Sologne restaurant.

Louisette told me that it was the elder sister, Fanny, who created the celebrated pie. She died in 1917, but it was our friend Curnonsky who, thrilled with his discovery of the *Tarte Tatin* at its source, took the recipe to Paris in 1926. Now it turns up in every little café and bistro—often a soggy travesty of the real thing, a sodden lump that may not even be warm, of all things! It's usually best made fresh at home. (My version appears on page 74.)

Julia and I were working together whenever we could, and we both kept learning about food from whatever came up, even in our leisure time. As Paris got back to normal supplies of food in the early fifties, we often went out to restaurants together or separately, with our husbands. Restaurants in Les Halles were especially fun, since this was in the old days when it was the main Paris market—before they moved it out to the new buildings at Rungis because of the traffic chaos the trade created in central Paris.

Now Les Halles has been replaced by the Pompidou Center and what's called Le Forum des Halles—peppered with slick clothes boutiques and fast-food places that seem to change daily. It may be lively, and food shops still exist, but it's not quite up to the living theater scene of forty-odd years ago, when the bustling streets were filled with butchers' trucks, and great crates of fruits and vegetables were piled everywhere. The air was redolent with the smell of food, giving a sharp edge to our appetites—from the inimitable yeasty odor of baking bread to whiffs of garlic from a restaurant specializing in snails. Snail butter, by the way, should not really bubble; it should just be piping hot.

Each little bistro had its chummy aura, with the small marble tables, the faïence walls, the zinc bars. It was terribly *authentic.* In the wee hours, the dressy after-theater crowd used to mingle and rub elbows with burly meat porters in their bloody aprons, all quaffing beer or *ballons* of red wine and downing onion soup. We would visit places like Le Grand Comptoir, l'Escargot, and Le Pied de Cochon, which specialized in breaded calves' feet and *tête de veau* with *sauce gribiche.* I still appreciate this gelatinous, rustic dish when the sauce is right, made with eggs, vinegar and oil, chopped pickles, capers, herbs. The food at Les Halles was always hearty, no nouvelle cuisine frou-frou yet.

FORGING AHEAD

Spain

IN 1952, JEAN'S COMPANY wanted to resume its perfume-lotion business in Spain, but the factory there lacked "essential oils" necessary for the products. So Jean was detailed to smuggle cans of the oils down to Barcelona, and I was delighted to go along. It was June, the weather already warm, as we crossed over the French Pyrenees into Catalonia, overlooking the spectacular cliffs and the sea.

"Well, here we go," said Jean as we pulled up to the customs barrier. "We'll just play it very easy and calm." He was always unperturbed, never lost his head or his nerve. The Spaniards, dressed in their military-looking green customs uniforms with those peculiar square-fronted black hats, started checking our passports and papers. And I started passing out bars of soap—still very scarce in that poor country—to the customs men, who wanted to search our car's luggage compartment (we'd stashed the cans under our bags and coats). We didn't feel guilty: this was not like hauling drugs or weapons. They finally waved us on our way without incident, and we heaved sighs of relief, free to enjoy the winding, roller-coaster drive down to Barcelona via the sleepy little fishing villages, the mountains rising green on our right, the sun bearing down with dazzling light and heat as we got farther south.

In Barcelona, we were greeted warmly by Señor Nistal, the L. T. Piver representative, who lodged us at his house. I remember the wonderful time he showed us and the food we ate there, prepared by his cook, Sagrario.

We were touched by the Spaniards, a courageous, dignified people who had almost nothing then. Rice, flour, all other staples were in short supply. But morale was high, and I discovered the excitement of flamenco, in smoky little *boîtes* right out of *Carmen,* where we sipped sherry and clapped along with the compelling music.

In Sagrario's kitchen, I made a great foreign food discovery—paella. It was a special treat, since all the food necessary for that opulent dish was scarce. Of course, there were many versions, but what fascinated me about Sagrario's was the perfect marriage of shellfish and meat, the texture of the saffron rice, the hint of tomato flavor. Sagrario wanted to teach me the language, but I learned more about cooking. My version of the recipe I learned in Spain is *Paella escondido* (which means "hidden"), from Murcia, and is covered with an omelet to keep it warm for a period while serving. She also gave us *biscocchio,* an ice-cream dessert in a rectangular mold lined with ladyfingers, but when I went home and duplicated the Spanish paella, I followed it up with a typically French dessert.

Eating a granita *on holiday*

Un dîner en souvenir de l'Espagne

A Dinner Inspired by Spain, 1952

Apéritif: Rioja rouge

✦ *La tapenade*
Olive spread for canapés

✦ *Paella escondido*

Salade verte
Fromages variés

—

Rioja rouge, ou rosé espagnol ou français

✦ *Charlotte aux fraises*
Strawberry charlotte

—

Vin blanc doux ou rosé

La tapenade

Olive Spread for Canapés

—

About 20 to 24 canapés

For filling:
3 eggs
Vinegar
7 oz. tiny Niçoise olives, pitted and
  chopped
2½ oz. peel, from 2 oranges
2½ oz. capers, well drained on paper
  towels
Freshly ground pepper
Cayenne or Tabasco

8 Tbsp. butter, creamed
2½ Tbsp. Cognac

For canapés:
6 thin slices *pain de mie* (page 495) or
  rye bread or melba toast, buttered and
  cut into quarters
2 Tbsp. finely minced chervil or parsley

Special equipment needed:
A food processor

Boil the eggs for 12 minutes in water acidulated with a little vinegar. Refresh in cold water, first breaking the shells, to be able to remove them easily.

Put the hard egg yolks in the food processor, add the pitted, chopped olives, and process a few seconds. Mince the orange peel and add to the food processor. Add the capers and pulse briefly again. Add the seasoning and creamed butter, process again, and taste. (The mixture should be quite peppery.) Add the Cognac, pulse, and taste again for seasoning. Pulse the mixture until very homogenous, then place in a jar and refrigerate until firm. Refrigerated, the tapenade will keep for many weeks.

When ready to serve, spread over buttered slices of bread, and sprinkle with minced chervil or parsley.

Paella escondido

—

For 10 to 12

⅓ cup olive oil

Two 4-lb. chickens, cut up

4–5 garlic cloves

1 red bell pepper, cut in strips

2½ cups reduced fresh or canned tomato
   sauce

Salt and pepper

1 hot pepper, or Tabasco

1 tsp. dried herbes de Provence (see
   Aide-Mémoire, page 503)

2 cups short-grain rice

2 medium onions, sliced

5 cups good chicken broth

1 bay leaf

Saffron

24 fresh mussels (well scrubbed)

12–18 large shrimp

1 cup sweet green peas (freshly cooked,
   frozen, or canned)

Optional: 3–4 artichoke bottoms, freshly
   cooked or canned, sliced

For garnish:

½ lb. boiled ham or smoked lard, diced

½ lb. chorizo (a spicy Spanish sausage,
   usually available in Spanish grocery
   stores)

3 Tbsp. olive oil

Special equipment needed:

A large cast-iron skillet

Parchment paper

A smaller skillet

*H*eat ⅓ cup olive oil in a large cast-iron skillet. When hot, add chicken pieces in a single layer and brown them, turning until they are evenly browned on all sides. Remove and brown the rest of the chicken in the same manner, adding more oil if needed. Remove the last pieces of chicken, and add the garlic and bell pepper strips. When softened, moisten with the tomato sauce, add the seasonings, and return the browned chicken pieces to the pot.

Cover with parchment paper and the lid, and cook in a preheated 375°F oven for 30–40 minutes, adding more tomato sauce, if needed, to cover the chicken pieces. After 20 minutes of cooking, turn the chicken pieces over, correct the seasoning, add the ham (or lard) and chorizo, and return all to the oven for the remaining 10–20 minutes of cooking time.

Heat 3 Tbsp. oil in a smaller skillet, add the rice, and stir constantly until it turns slightly golden. Add the sliced onions and stir to mix. When the onions have softened, add the chicken broth, the bay leaf, and a generous pinch of crushed saffron. Cover and let cook for about 18 minutes, or until the rice has soaked up the broth. Then, without disturbing the rice, place the mussels and shrimp on the surface of the rice, and cover. The shellfish will poach in just a few minutes from the steam of the rice and broth. Keep warm.

When ready to serve, remove the mussels and shrimp from the top of the rice. Stir the cooked green peas and the artichoke bottoms into the rice, and correct the seasoning. Reheat the chicken in its tomato sauce, then mix the rice into the chicken preparation, heating all together. While dish is reheating, make the omelet for the "cover."

To serve, place paella in a large shallow heated dish, garnished around the sides and on top with shrimp and mussels in their shells. Cover with the omelet and a sprinkling of herbs. The covered paella can thus be kept warm for several minutes before serving, or even left up to 30 minutes in a warming (very low) oven.

Wine Suggestion: A Spanish Rioja red or rosé, or a French Côtes du Rhône rosé or red.

Omelet for *Paella escondido*

—

2 Tbsp. olive oil	*Special equipment needed:*
5–6 eggs	Omelet pan the same size as the paella
Fresh chopped herbs (mixture of parsley, thyme, savory, basil)	serving dish
Salt, to taste	
Pinch of cayenne	

Heat oil until quite hot in omelet pan. Whisk eggs, stirring in herbs, salt, and cayenne. Add egg mixture to the pan, turning the pan to spread the eggs around evenly. Cook until omelet is just firm, and turn it onto the paella to cover the paella entirely, producing the hidden effect for the Escondido.

Charlotte aux fraises

Strawberry Charlotte

—

For 8 to 10

¼ cup Kirsch
¼ cup water
20 ladyfingers, separated in half
    lengthwise
1 lb. strawberries

For meringue:
¾ cup granulated sugar
½ cup water

3 egg whites
1 cup heavy cream

Granulated sugar for berries

Special equipment needed:
A 4-cup Pyrex brioche mold, jagged form
    and splayed, measuring 7″ across the
    top, 3¼″ deep, and 4″ across the base

*B*utter the brioche mold and set aside. Mix the Kirsch and water in a soup bowl. Arrange some of the ladyfingers into a star-shaped design by cutting wedges to fit the bottom of the mold exactly. Dip the pieces for 1 second only in the diluted liqueur, and place them in the mold, rounded side down. Next, line the sides of the mold with more liqueur-moistened ladyfingers, placing them rounded side out and close together. Refrigerate until time to fill.

Prepare the strawberries by hulling them and cutting in quarters. Put a layer of fruit in the prepared mold.

Bring the sugar and water to a boil in a small saucepan. Continue boiling until it becomes a thick syrup. Meanwhile, clean a copper basin with vinegar and salt, rinse well with cold water, and dry with paper toweling. Beat the egg whites lightly in the copper basin until half whipped. Pour the thickened syrup slowly into the whites, beating vigorously over ice until thick, shiny, and cool.

Beat the cream to the Chantilly ("soft peaks") stage, and when the meringue is completely cold, fold the cream into the meringue until the two mixtures are completely homogenous. Add the remaining fruit to the creamed meringue and fill the mold halfway. Then place a layer of moistened ladyfingers over the mixture, and continue filling with the remaining fruit mixture. Top the mold with another layer of moistened ladyfingers, placed tightly together.

Cover with aluminum foil and place in the refrigerator for about 3 hours, or in the freezer for 1 hour. To serve, unmold over a serving dish, decorate with more sliced strawberries, and sprinkle with confectioners' sugar. Serve as is, or with Crème Anglaise Sauce (page 88).

Notes: If you prefer, an equal amount of raspberries can be substituted for the strawberries. This recipe is based on ripe berries in season. If your berries are a little tart, sweeten to taste before using.

Wine Suggestion: A good still or sparkling white, such as Crémant de la Loire.

OUR TRIP CONTINUED DOWN TO GRANADA and over to Portugal. We were bitten by the travel bug. Over the years, Jean and I were to see a good deal more of the world, adding richness to our full life.

As Julia and I kept on in our mutual and personal research in 1952, I met an old friend of Julia's who would become a key person in helping us with our still-unformed book.

"Come meet Avis DeVoto up in Normandy. She's arriving from the States via England." Julia knew my Norman knowledge was solid and I loved any excuse to go back out there. Paul and Julia picked up Avis, the wife of the eminent historian Bernard DeVoto and an editor in her own right, when she came in at Le Havre.

We didn't talk too much business that day, but we did enjoy a fabulous lunch when we all met up at the Hôtel de Dieppe in Rouen. The famous specialty *canard au sang,* made by the chef Marcel Guéret, was unforgettable for all of us. The duck was cooked to perfection, the sauce as savory and beautifully flavored as any I've ever tasted. Avis and the Childs were dazzled, proclaiming it the best and most authentic duck in its blood sauce they had ever tasted.

This is a dish native to Rouen, which the French don't make at home as a rule. The ducks are very special little half-wild birds, bred and raised in farms bordering the Seine all around Duclair, near Rouen. The tame females are staked out and "covered" by wild male ducks. Their offspring, still young but grown and ready for eating, are smothered in order to preserve their blood, essential to the sauce.

After a quick roasting of about 18–20 minutes, the duck is carved, the breasts are removed, skinned, and cut into thin strips (*aiguillettes*), and the legs are breaded to be cooked separately. The wings are not used.

The carcass goes into a special silver or stainless steel duck press and is squeezed with the crank until all the blood has been removed and saved. Then the blood is mixed with very good red wine and the puréed liver in a shallow silver tray (the wine would turn black if the tray were not silver), highly seasoned with freshly ground pepper, and simmered very slowly without boiling. The wine does not have to be an old vintage but should be of excellent quality, say a Gevrey-Chambertin, which brings out the duck blood flavor. This sauce simmers gently, and the bloody-rare *aiguillettes* are poached until pink. The first service is of duck slices with sauce; the breaded legs are put in the oven to crisp up for a second serving. The classic accompaniment is freshly fried potato chips, dried on a towel and salted.

After that impressive Rouen feast, Avis became a good friend of mine, thanks to the Childs, and would one day play an important role in our professional lives.

A couple of years later, to our great regret, Paul was transferred in his governmental post down to Marseille, and I think Julia was just as sad to leave as I was to see her go. For a while the cooking school had to be discontinued, until we started up the Trois Gourmandes later with Louisette in her large apartment with its good kitchen—mine was impossible for any "group" larger than two people. At that time, my mother had a house at Mandelieu near Cannes, and I went down at various times, often joining Julia for more discussions.

"How about French bread? Could we teach that to Americans?" Julia wondered. So in her Marseille kitchen we used about fifty pounds of all-purpose American flour to experiment. A real disaster! Try as we might, we couldn't get the thing quite right. We also tried puff pastry, but neither seemed quite right for *Mastering* I, still a formless embryonic collection of recipes and ideas without a name.

When Julia and Paul were later transferred up to Bad Godesburg, where I visited once, we maintained our correspondence, our friendship, our single-minded purpose of bringing good French cooking into American homes.

By 1957, Paul and Julia had been transferred back to Washington. I was invited to visit and do something about getting our manuscript to a publisher. We now had a raft of recipes, perfected by us together or separately, mostly based on poultry and sauces. Julia thought we could present our book to Houghton Mifflin in Boston.

I had long been dying to go to America. "Shall I?" I asked Jean anxiously.

"Absolutely!" he exclaimed. "This is your golden opportunity."

America, Here I Come

IN JANUARY 1958, I SAW JEAN OFF AT ORLY on a business trip to South America. I was distracted and excited about my own voyage, just over a week later, on the *Queen Elizabeth I.* It was hard to pack light, since I planned on spending at least a couple of months in America, and I'd heard about the cold winters. I didn't have money to throw around, but I scraped together a suitable wardrobe, squeezed in my piles of notes and my part of the manuscript.

I was as excited as a teenager when I boarded the enormous liner in Le Havre. I'd seen these traveling resorts from a distance, but I couldn't believe the space and luxury on board—it was like a frantic village, with friends seeing people off, Champagne corks popping, porters scurrying around, pursers greeting us and assigning cabins.

I was in tourist class, next down from first, and delighted with my stateroom— not large, but all to myself. What an adventure! I thought as I sat gingerly on my

Our little poodle, Vicky, learned how to retrieve game with no training at all

bunk for a few seconds, eyeing my luggage, which I decided to leave to go on deck. I stood by the rails in the crowd of other passengers, shivering with the chilly air and the excitement, and didn't even mind that nobody was there to see me off. When I heard "All ashore who's going ashore," I knew this was a big moment. America, here I come!

I wasn't totally alone for very long, since a young man had introduced himself to me as we were leaving the Gare Saint-Lazare on the boat train. "Madame," he had said, "if you're traveling alone, I'd be happy if you could help me, as I speak no English." He came from Aubusson, where both he and his father were in the tapestry business and were teachers of the petit-point technique. He was on his way to Mexico to take some tapestries and set up a school in Mexico City, and the poor man couldn't speak Spanish, either.

He soon searched me out, we explored the ship together, and I had a nice companion for tea or cocktails.

He told me his father had made a big tapestry for the *Queen Elizabeth*'s first-class dining room, but he was too shy to go up there. "Don't be silly," I said, pushing him along. The steward eyed us suspiciously, but he graciously let us view the tapestry when I explained. It looked beautiful in this vast and opulent Art Deco room, and we went up close to admire the intricate, flowered Aubusson design, all fifteen by eighteen feet of it, backing the captain's table. "You realize," he told me, "that it takes eight hours just to make each little two-inch area," and he pointed out his father's signature on the underside corner. Then the steward brought out a kind of register of the room's decorators, and the tapestry was attributed to some South Africans. This poor man cried out, "But that's not true. My father's signature is on it." Apparently, the tapestry had to be credited to somebody in the British Empire. In his consternation, my shipboard pal didn't come to dinner that night.

I was so interested in shipboard life and my great adventure ahead that I did not take much notice of the *Queen Elizabeth*'s food. Others may have gotten seasick, but I never had an ill moment. I usually enjoyed a rather copious English-style breakfast in my cabin. Unfortunately, the custom was to serve the heavier meal for dinner, and I've always liked eating light in the evening. The emphasis was on classic English food: plenty of good red meat and Yorkshire pudding as well as fish that was edible if not memorable. There was some resilient green gelatin with vegetables in it as a salad; I took a mental note that nothing like that should go into our cookbook. The midmorning clear broth was welcome, if boring.

As the liner was finally towed by its tugs past the Battery into New York Harbor on one slate-gray winter day, it all seemed cinematic, almost unreal. I'd seen photographs and films, of course, but nothing could compare to the exultation I felt with the wind whipping my cheeks and nose until they were red, the sight of Miss Liberty and those skyscrapers looming up. Like millions of others before, I was stunned by the real thing. How can people live and work in such big buildings? I wondered.

As we waited for our passport checks before disembarking, I looked far below at the throbbing port life. It was a little scary, what with all those truckers and porters scurrying around in what appeared to be total confusion.

What if Grace Gadsby, who was supposed to meet me there, hadn't made it? What if I couldn't find her? I felt like a lost puppy dog, eager for a familiar presence, not knowing what was next. Pull yourself together, I told myself. You're fifty-four years old, and you can handle this.

But as I lurched down the gangplank in my warm polo coat and hat, there she was, waving in the crowd—the delightful, warm woman I'd made lunch for so many years before, back in Rainfreville. My first American friend. We hugged with tears in our eyes.

As we were having my bags inspected by customs officials, behind me trailed the Frenchman from Aubusson with all his tapestries, on his way to Mexico. He was desperate, knowing no English, and chic, gray-haired Grace stepped in with confidence to save him; they wanted to confiscate his tapestries, which he needed to set up the school in Mexico City.

"Here, here!" said Grace with authority, understanding the problem immediately as I quickly whispered to her. "This young man is honest; he is going to leave for Mexico on the next plane; he is only in transit and needs everything he has." She saved the day, and he thanked us effusively as he climbed into a yellow cab, perspiring from nerves and his efforts.

We hopped into the next taxi, and I was off on one of the most exciting periods of my life. We had little time for sightseeing, and I simply marveled at the canyons of concrete as we drove—somewhere uptown, I believe—to have lunch in the apartment of a friend of Grace's. I was in a daze.

Right after lunch, we took another taxi back down to Penn Station, to catch the train for Allentown, where Grace lived. Another overwhelming sight—that cavernous, monstrous building with its huge square columns and mosaic floors, echoing with the din of a thousand voices, throbbing with humanity that ranged from beggars in tatters to well-dressed matrons and businessmen headed single-mindedly for the

Main Line, oblivious of the chaos. France never had any *gares* like this, I reflected, even the crowded stations during the war.

As I was to discover, Penn Station was very representative of America—it was made on a grand scale. Americans' cars, houses, markets—everything looked bigger. Their hearts seemed bigger too, to stretch the metaphor. French people are often so suspicious of newcomers, even of people of their own nationality and class. I immediately learned how casual, generous, and outgoing Americans are.

"Take your bags, ladies?" asked a scrawny black porter with a cart. He had a huge smile and looked as though he ought to be doing a tap dance, he was so brisk and rhythmic in his movements. "You ladies got a right nice day to travel," he said. "No snow yet."

He seemed to know a lot about the weather; we got the snow during the weekend I spent in Allentown with Grace before meeting up with Julia. The evening we arrived at Grace's house, the snowfall began, turning into a monumental blizzard that blanketed most of the Eastern Seaboard. I'd never seen such snow, even in the Alps. We were cozy in her house, and when I looked out the next morning, the drifts loomed up about ten feet high. I decided not to let mere snow keep me from my regular and necessary Mass.

I asked Grace to lend me a shovel and started digging out the driveway. A neighbor named John Yoder produced a little French flag and cheered me on. *"Vive la France!"* Many years later, he turned up to stay with Jean and me in the south of France and asked if he could play a few holes of golf somewhere, so I suggested the eighteen-hole course at Valbonne. There was a tournament on that day, and when John returned, he said, somewhat stupefied, "I won!"

I made it to Mass that Sunday, and the next day John drove me on the barely cleared roads from Allentown to Bethlehem, where I was to meet Julia and go on via New York to Boston, to present our manuscript to Houghton Mifflin. Avis DeVoto had managed to procure a $250 advance for us. "We'll reach our rendezvous with Julia, of course?" I queried John somewhat nervously.

"Well, you made it to church yesterday, didn't you?" He winked, driving along cautiously, with the car sometimes skidding or even tipped up as we hit drifts on the roadside.

There was Julia, waiting at the station with her bags. We were both raring to go, the weather be damned.

We arrived in New York, to find a messy madhouse. "No trains," we were told. "The tracks are still under snow." So we got ourselves to the Greyhound station and boarded the bus. It seemed to take forever, but we finally arrived in rather limp shape after midnight, going on to stay with Avis DeVoto in her house in Cambridge. The next day, we went to show editors at Houghton Mifflin the big manuscript we'd compiled on poultry and sauces.

But the editors did not even see us. They left us up in a little attic room with a kind of clerk. So we just left the manuscript and went down to Julia's house in Georgetown to wait for news. There was another snowfall, so we mostly stayed indoors and exchanged ideas and hoped for the best from the publishers.

At one point, Jean arrived for a couple of days on his way back to Paris from Mexico, and he and I explored Washington's monuments and museums.

For diversion, Grace and I had decided to travel for about a week or so to New Orleans by Greyhound. In the midst of a cocktail party she was giving, Julia hooted, "This silly girl wants to go by bus to New Orleans." But somebody who had connections with Greyhound said, "Oh no, you're right. Best way to see America! I'll get you a special pass, and you'll be taken care of."

Grace was fearless and so was I, and we flashed our pass and stayed near the driver. We always got VIP treatment: "Honey, how about a pillow? Now, you just take off your shoes when you feel like it. I'll show you America like you oughta see it." We giggled and enjoyed the sights our drivers pointed out.

The restaurant stops shocked me a bit. I had expected what Americans call "greasy spoon" joints, like our simple *routier* stops for truckers. But I was surprised and saddened to see the strict segregation back then, as the blacks were relegated to a separate part of the diner, or sometimes not allowed in at all. France has racist tendencies these days, but there has never been a color bar in public places.

A few days after we'd set out from Washington, we reached New Orleans, and I have to admit it was not the picturesque French-style city I had expected. The Vieux Quartier looked run-down, with peeling walls, a disappointment, even though I'd come from a country still showing the effects of the occupation ten years before.

But I discovered mint juleps! This sweet Southern specialty with its bourbon, crushed ice, and fresh mint leaves made a filling meal, or nearly so. Although Bourbon is the name of a French royal dynasty, it was virtually unknown as a type of whiskey in France then. I sipped it in a modest hotel restaurant romantically named the Court of the Two Sisters, where the drinks were more intriguing than the food. However, that didn't turn me into a big drinker. I really appreciate good wine, and sometimes a tot of Scotch or bourbon, but I've never come close to being a barfly or even a regular cocktail consumer.

I think I must have missed the best Creole cooking on that trip, though when Jean and I visited years later, we did have some wonderful gumbos and giant crayfish ("crawdads," they call them there).

About six weeks after we had left our manuscript in Boston, we got a letter at Julia's, telling us it was unpublishable, which in a way it was. There were nine hundred pages on poultry and sauces; it was quite academic and technical. Houghton Mifflin wanted a more readable, practical book. We had worked so hard all those years! Julia, crushed, said, "Well, at least it will be useful to me." And she claims she has indeed used all the information that was never published as reference material.

I shrugged my shoulders and said, "Let's fight back. Let's do another book." Julia agreed. We decided to go the whole hog, work like Trojans to take French cooking from A to Z and sell it.

Of course, we did not throw out our poultry sauce recipes, many of which Louisette had been working on as well, during our Trois Gourmandes period.

After nearly three months in the U.S.A., I returned to Paris, to work as I never had before in my life—often twelve hours at a stretch, with no social life to speak of. I was rushing around to the PX, using Julia's old card to buy American goods for my own testing.

For two years, Julia and I corresponded madly—between Paris and Washington and then Norway, where Paul was assigned for a tour of duty. We pounded off letters about things like the quality of French butter versus American, with its higher water content, differences in the way flour works in each country, how to choose the right cut for something like a *daube de boeuf*. We realized that we had to get the practical advice right, or not do a cookbook at all. It had to work. Julia did in-depth research, consulting everyone from butchers and fishmongers to the United States Department of Agriculture.

We had quite a to-do by mail about cassoulet, because Julia said *confit d'oie* should not be included, as it could not be found in America, and that we should give the recipe with lamb and pork. People from Toulouse are adamant about including the preserved goose meat. We volleyed letters back and forth on this one, and finally decided on our version, using pork loin, lamb, and sausage.

Our voluminous correspondence piled up; it is now in an air-conditioned vault in the Schlesinger Library at Radcliffe College—an informal food "dialogue" for posterity.

By late 1959, with Julia still in Norway, the book was finally finished. Avis

DeVoto agreed to help again, and we dumped the manuscript in her lap, so to speak. Avis was a free-lance editor then, and did some work with Alfred A. Knopf, so when the book was rejected by Houghton Mifflin, she sent it in to Knopf, where it landed on the desk of a young editor named Judith Jones.

Judith had lived in France with her husband and had just started out with that formidable couple Alfred and Blanche Knopf. They'd already published a cookbook by a famous American cook but, having never heard of us, were naturally skeptical. But Judith and William A. Koshland, vice president at Knopf, liked our book and pushed it through.

Bill and Judith were good cooks, and Avis told me that he and a couple of other enthusiasts at Knopf tried out the recipes, cooking their way right through our manuscript, as "all of us bit our nails and lay awake nights and worried," according to a recent letter from Avis to me. She had been such a help in getting the book this far. I didn't know much about this at the time, as Julia was in closer contact with them.

Finally, in 1960, I got a letter from Julia with the exciting news that the book was at last accepted and would be published in 1961. There was a contract, which I signed immediately, but I don't remember the exact terms. Jean and I celebrated with a special bottle of good wine that night, toasting our first evidence of success.

After a long search, Judith Jones and her Knopf colleagues came up with the title *Mastering the Art of French Cooking*. What's in a name? Obviously you can't sell a book on its name alone. But you can attract attention. Our title was appropriate; it worked. It would be signed in alphabetical order: Simone Beck, Louisette Bertholle, and Julia Child. I used my maiden name as a simple and striking nom de plume.

Mastering the Art of French Cooking came out in 1961, and while it was not an immediate blockbuster, it did turn out to be the first book for the home cook to cover the basics of French cuisine. Avis told me that it took Alfred Knopf several years to admit that he had a winner on his hands.

But this was just the beginning. As Julia has pointed out, and I agree, our success was largely due to lucky timing. We came into our own with our recipes at the right time and in the right place.

With the jet age, Americans were on the move, open to new ideas and tastes, ready to learn the art of French cooking, and the book we'd taken so much care over offered what amounted to a step-by-step, do-it-yourself cooking school.

A POSSIBLE DREAM:
SUCCESS IN THE SIXTIES

WHEN KNOPF BROUGHT it out in 1961, *Mastering the Art of French Cooking* got some terrific reviews, with high praise from Craig Claiborne in *The New York Times*—a welcome accolade. Another great bonus, one year later, was from Carol Cutler, wife of the Paris *Herald Tribune*'s editor, B. J. Cutler. An enthusiastic cook and a former pupil, Carol succeeded in getting a series of our recipes run in the newspaper, thus boosting our fame and credibility.

We also made a mini-tour in 1961 to promote the book in the United States; it was mainly my idea, but Julia went along enthusiastically. In those days, splashy book promotions were rare, for cookbooks even nonexistent. We were again breaking new ground.

I was overjoyed to return to America, and the Childs and I went to see Judith Jones at Knopf, to consider influential cooking people who might help us. We didn't know anybody—only names like Clementine Paddleford, Craig Claiborne, and so on. "How about Dionne Lucas, or Jim Beard?" suggested Judith. I had friends in France who knew Dionne, and I especially wanted to meet her; Julia was keen to meet Jim; and we finally met both of them.

We were staying in a little West Side apartment that belonged to a niece of Julia's, and one day we took the subway downtown to meet Jim in his Greenwich Village brownstone, where he was conducting a class.

"Welcome, ladies," said the inimitable, good-humored James Beard, who instantly radiated magnetic good cheer. "You have written a wonderful book," he added, putting us totally at ease.

He had a well-designed kitchen, and we felt privileged to meet one of America's great cooks and authors, whose heart was as big as his enormous girth. Our day there was memorable. The demonstration dish was a cheese soufflé, and I nearly passed out when I saw Jim folding the egg whites into the cheese base with his hands. Julia didn't flinch.

Jim explained to me, "But that's the only good way to fold in the whites. You've got to feel it with your fingers." I'm afraid I was not converted by his hands-on approach, and I still teach my favorite method, cutting down into the mixture with a spatula and scraping the white over the rest with a flick of the wrist.

Jim was darling to us, inviting us to The Four Seasons, introducing us to other cooks, generally "mothering" us, thus beginning the close friendship that would last over twenty years, until his death in 1985.

As the French had set up a yearly homage to the great gourmet Curnonsky, so the Americans have organized a way to revere Jim's memory. The James Beard Foundation managed to buy his house in Greenwich Village. To it, on a regular basis, renowned chefs make a pilgrimage and serve meals they've prepared in his stainless-steel kitchen. Many of the foundation members and guests are old friends of Jim's, and I imagine there are as many anecdotes told as there is discussion of the cuisine served. Someone is sure to mention his famous reply when asked what he would do if he were ever forced to become a cannibal: "I might manage if there were enough tarragon around."

Dionne Lucas was a different kettle of fish—charming but quirky. Our first meeting was in her little omelet bar–restaurant, The Egg Basket, on East Fifty-ninth Street, where we duly convened along with Paul Child at two o'clock one day. As she was still whipping up omelets, she kept us waiting for a while in a room beside her restaurant, but finally she appeared. "You've turned out an excellent book," she said. "So I'd like to give you a party." We thought that sounded pretty ambitious, since we knew hardly anybody to ask, but agreed willingly.

We fixed a date for sometime in December, and the way Dionne was planning things, the party would truly be ours, including most of the work. "You'll do the invitations, of course, some of the dishes, and so on." We were a little nervous, but asked Judith Jones and Jim Beard for advice and had invitations printed up. We finally sent them to just about anybody in the food establishment at that time whose name we could dredge up.

Meanwhile, we went off on our do-it-yourself tour out West, mainly seeing friends and their friends, stopping in Detroit, where we were introduced around by Lucille Tyree, and in Chicago, where the food editor of the *Tribune* interviewed us. The article looked fine, featuring a photo of us as we made our Reine de Saba cake in their test kitchen.

Then we went on to California, all introductions courtesy of Julia, who had grown up in Pasadena. At our first big demonstration—arranged by Julia's sister and brother-in-law, Ivan Cousins—we were "flying by the seat of our pants," as we put on our show in a department store that no longer exists, the City of Paris. We started at 10:30 A.M. and continued nonstop all day, doing the same menu several times: Roquefort quiche, sole in white wine, and my version (in chocolate) of those little madeleines I'd learned to make twenty-one years before in the farmhouse where I'd lodged with Jean during the war, before he was taken prisoner.

We attracted a motley audience; sometimes friends would drop in along with curious store customers, and a few old bums lurked around, waiting for free food.

The chocolate madeleines elicited a lot of attention, since at that point in America few cooks knew about madeleines. It was apparently a bonanza for the wife of the store's owner, who had a lot of madeleine tins gathering dust in the stockroom. "Now that people know what they're for, we can sell them," she said delightedly.

This first introduction to California was dazzling to me. I was crazy about it, and I've continued to love it during my various trips out there. Lucky Californians must have the best year-round food resources in the United States, if not the whole world—excepting France, of course, which can offer everything in the largest markets. In California I saw a huge array of vegetables and fresh fish, but there were very few native wines—which later became so admirable as the winemaking business progressed out there.

Like many visitors from Europe, I found San Francisco not only exciting but, oddly enough, the most "European" of American cities. Perhaps that is because it is picturesque—not because of its age, which is relatively youthful, but because of its dimensions, which are geared to the human body. The sight of all those pastel town houses climbing up the hills, with the trolleys shuttling by, made me feel right at home.

In the kitchen at L'École des Trois Gourmandes with Julia

We took a trip down to Julia's hometown of Pasadena and spent a few days in her father's big and beautiful California-style house. Mr. McWilliams was a toweringly tall man, a gracious host and humorous raconteur. He fascinated me, and it was obvious where Julia's impressive stature and charm came from.

In Pasadena, we gave two big demonstrations at a kind of public hall or "club," which, although it had a stage, was not geared to cooking shows. The atmosphere was informal, as Julia's friends kept piping up with quips and questions. But the bad part was cleaning up, as there were no facilities for it. Paul Child, who was with us, staunchly took on the dirty work, and as usual found a way to improvise. He ended up using a sink in the ladies' room, tirelessly scraping off bits of quiche and fish, and chocolate from the madeleine molds, washing with soap from a dispenser and cold water! He was a stoic about the whole thing, and wonderfully good-humored, considering the inconvenience.

Meanwhile, Dionne Lucas had told us to telephone on November 29 to discuss the menu for the big party we were to give in New York. On that day we happened to be in Disneyland, where our California friends had arranged for us to be driven in a big limo by a chauffeur, whose nasty cigar smoke polluted our car air unpleasantly. We called Dionne from a pay phone, for which Paul ran off to gather up hundreds of quarters. (He was by now our indispensable factotum and troubleshooter.)

That was quite a coast-to-coast phone call. Dionne wanted to do something like veal Pojarski, but I told Julia that such a Russian-style dish would never do. We finally fixed on a menu of fillet of sole with white-wine sauce (such a success in our demonstrations), which Dionne volunteered to do, along with a dessert. We were to produce the main meat course, as yet undecided, and somehow procure the wine.

Back in New York, we decided on our dish: rolled shoulder of lamb Viroflay with spinach stuffing. But we were going to have to make it in Paul's niece's little apartment. Then, a couple of days before the big event, Paul went over to The Egg Basket, where we intended to hold the party, and was perplexed to find that nothing had been done. The room for the party was devoid of chairs and tables, and no wine was in sight.

We were growing apprehensive; what if all those strangers we'd invited should show up? Paul had to start flying around to rent basic furniture. And through an acquaintance of mine, Julius Wile, we were at last provided with wine. His family had been in the wine-promotion business a long time, the first importers of my grandfather's Bénédictine, and he was kindly disposed toward our project. So thanks to his generosity, good wine appeared as if by a wave of the wand.

The big day arrived. While we made the stuffed lamb, Paul went to the restaurant. Throughout this trial, he was being porter, diplomat, and "gofer," doing whatever was necessary, including seeing to the printing of the menu and the seating arrangements—although he knew next to nobody on the guest list.

He had placed Dionne at the head table with Jim Beard, but when Dionne came out of the kitchen, she looked at the list and said, "No, that will never do. My place is behind the scenes." He had to juggle other seating arrangements as well. A deaf man had been seated next to a woman with a throat impairment, so he had to change that all around so they could communicate with others. And then he opened dozens of bottles of wine.

After our initial panic, the dinner finally came off in grand style. Everybody who was invited came. Jim Beard introduced us to all the guests—a resplendent company—and the evening was a huge success.

After dinner, Dionne fluttered out and took a bow, looking flustered with her hair all awry, and then she rushed back up the stairs, which seemed rather odd, as we very much wanted to talk to her. We finally got to know and like her. She was a talented cook and writer, but somehow she didn't run her life very well; she should have had plenty of money, but it just seemed to run through her fingers. She was soon to undergo a double mastectomy, after which she went back to England, where she would die—a real loss to our cooking world.

While in New York, we appeared on the *Today* show. John Chancellor, the anchorman, was most cooperative and jovial throughout the show. This was an exciting moment, as neither of us had ever been on television before.

I was to do an omelet and was getting pretty nervous. So back in Paul's niece's apartment, they coached me along as I did the same omelet over and over: "With *panache,* Simca! Toss that omelet! Ham it up, and make it visual fun for the audience." When the camera and the sweltering lights were at last upon me in the studio, I nearly froze with fear, but my crash course brought me through, though I didn't want to see another omelet for a while.

My First Thanksgiving

O N   T H E   L A S T   T H U R S D A Y of that November, I celebrated Thanksgiving for the first time—with the Childs at Paul's twin brother Charlie's house.

I knew that Thanksgiving was America's main big eating fest—*la grande bouffe,* so to speak—and looked forward to the occasion. It was to be laid on by Charlie's wife, Freddie, at their home in Lumberville, Pennsylvania—a name I found delightfully frontierlike.

They received us generously, along with other family members and friends in their white frame house, and the dinner was indeed unforgettable.

Freddie amazed me with a forty-pound fresh turkey she had procured from a farm near New Hope. It had been parked in the oven to roast contentedly all day long, to be served at 8:00 P.M. I knew Americans liked to think big, but this was a staggering proposition for a home-cooked meal. I was interested to see how the leviathan would turn out.

We finally enjoyed it, with gravy and all the "trimmings"—which seemed exotic to me, even the bread-crumb-herb-sage stuffing. At home in France, we usually have sausage- or chestnut-based stuffings, or none at all. I was also intrigued by the cranberry sauce, corn, yams, and other side dishes overflowing our plates. I was pleased to discover pumpkin pie, something still unknown in France today, except to people with American friends.

I realize that those seventeenth-century pilgrims who started the tradition were celebrating a harvest after a long year of hardships, and they used what was on hand—including pumpkins. Unfortunately, that member of the squash family is not highly esteemed here, though pumpkin soup is a delicious peasant specialty.

About this time, there was a brewing interest in French food, with the Kennedys giving excellent White House dinners masterminded by their chef, René Verdon. And what with transatlantic air travel constantly increasing, Americans were coming home fired up by French gastronomy.

Although the British seemed cool to us at first (they were still immersed in Mrs. Beeton in those "pre-foodie" days), our book, published by Cassell in 1963, nevertheless started to sell well. Julia and I met briefly in London around that time, and that's when she first told me she would like to do a television show, which would be the best promotion our book could get.

And indeed, it was TV that brought our big breakthrough in the United States. By 1962, Julia and Paul had moved back up to Cambridge, where Julia was asked to do a review of our book and then a small cooking series for educational station WGBH in Boston.

She tells the story better than anybody else, but here it is anyway: The WGBH studio had burned down, so the Boston Gas Company loaned premises for filming. Julia brought her own equipment and supplies, and despite the problems she faced, she and the producers went ahead stubbornly, brooking all odds.

The rest is history. Her show, which began in 1964 as a kind of "amateur half hour of cuisine," finally took off as *The French Chef* and made a hit in the States. With her offhand manner and patter, she won the hearts not only of cooks but of people who had never heard of cassoulet or *poule au pot* and couldn't care less. Many watched her simply for the entertainment.

Here I quote Julia, who summed up her philosophy in her *French Chef* cookbook (Alfred A. Knopf, 1968), the first one she wrote on her own after *Mastering*: "I would prefer to have things happen as they naturally do, such as the mousse refusing to leave the mold, the potatoes sticking to the skillet, the apple charlotte slowly collapsing. One of the secrets of cooking is to learn to correct something if you can, and bear with it if you cannot."

Julia filmed her recipes straight through, accidents and all, and the sometimes hilarious results were part of the magic of her shows. People laughed hysterically, recognizing themselves in her casual approach or outright slips. "We just let the gaffes lie where they fell," she said. American TV viewers, even those who didn't know a roux from a béchamel, appreciated this—and they became Julia's fans.

She is a natural film star, has what I call great class and outright *culot,* or nerve when on camera. I saw her doing the program on how to cook a whole suckling pig. And there she was, whipping out a toothbrush to clean the pig's ears and teeth! What an amusing and sanitary American idea, I thought.

Thanks to all this indirect TV publicity, the book was beginning to sell, though we were hardly a best-seller yet.

What clinched our success was Julia's appearance on the cover of *Time* magazine in 1965. Jean and I had been listening to de Gaulle's speech saying that Quebec ought to be *libre,* or free—a breathtakingly chauvinistic French approach, which provoked an uproar on both sides of the Atlantic—when the phone rang. Fortunately, it had nothing to do with Franco-American squabbles. It was Julia, who breathlessly announced that her portrait by Alexander Chaliapin, the artist son of the great basso Fyodor Chaliapin, was going to grace *Time*'s cover—of course, to illustrate a big story on her and our book.

This was a great boost to sales of *Mastering,* which shot up to 100,000 or so in the month following the story, and we were soon hard at work on Volume II of our magnum opus, this time working with confidence, going into detailed explanations of more sophisticated procedures, such as how to make puff pastry without fear. This one Julia and I produced alone, for Louisette Bertholle was working up her own book—later translated into English as *Secrets of the Great French Restaurants.*

I must say that Volume II was fun to do, especially since we had a lot more confidence. But again we became willing slaves to our task, and this time we had an even more voluminous transatlantic correspondence. But Julia was often my next-door neighbor, since she and Paul now had their own part-time base in France, La Pitchoune.

Bramafam

BY THE TIME *Mastering the Art of French Cooking* was making real money, Bramafam, Jean's property in the south of France, had become part of our lives, and of the Childs' as well.

During our first visit to Mother in the south of France, Jean and I had gone to call on Marcelle Challiol, a cousin of his who lived near Grasse. Little did I know that this pastoral stretch of hill and valley would later become our country refuge, then our main base and the site of many cooking lessons.

A maiden lady and an artist, Marcelle lived on a property that she had bought some time before World War II. Called Bramafam, it consisted of an old farmhouse and about twelve acres on a rise facing a valley and the village of Plascassier, perched astride a small but steep hill smack between Cannes and Grasse. Here Marcelle painted and lived in a kind of pastoral-bohemian splendor with another woman painter. The tumbledown farmhouse looked suitably picturesque in a flowered landscape that was pure poetry.

Although their greeting was cordial, I don't think the two aging female landscape painters took much to me at first, or to my little poodle, Vicky. On the other hand, I was soon fascinated with the cook, who brought in the tea and offered to show me her primitive kitchen, while musing on the gourmandise of dogs and cats. (My current pet was panting for a cookie handout and got one.) This cheery little individual with her crimped hair knotted at the nape of the neck was later to become my trusted and faithful cook Jeannette, who is still pouring tea for me.

On our several visits to Marcelle, Jean and I were enthralled by Bramafam. The riot of flowers in summer, the startlingly sensual smells of wild thyme and rosemary, the sheer contentment I felt here, were magical.

Bramafam means something like "the donkey is braying with hunger" in the Provençal dialect, though I cannot imagine starvation in such a richly vegetated region.

When Marcelle died, in 1958, Jean's sisters inherited the property, although they found it would be financially difficult to maintain. Jean had apparently been cut out of the will because he was childless.

Nevertheless, Jean loved the place, and he reached an agreement with his sisters whereby he would renovate Bramafam and become its owner for life, with the

Our house, "Le Mas Vieux," at Bramafam

Relaxing on the terrace at Bramafam with Julia

property reverting to the sisters or their heirs after our deaths. The sisters were also to take over the house every year for a month's holiday.

Now, frantically busy with the cookbook, I knew I had to stay in touch with Bramafam. The cool, beamed dwelling was aptly named Le Mas Vieux—"the old house" in Provençal. And yes, indeed, it was truly ancient, even more ramshackle than when we had first seen it. And we knew we wanted comfort—more rooms, more light and heat, new bathrooms, a proper-size living room. We decided to do it right, and countless times I went down with Jean in the following years to get things shipshape for civilized living.

Fortunately, Jeannette—a farm lady who can neither read nor write but has good country sense—stayed on as "part of the property," to become our chief caretaker and cook, and now simply my friend. She has her own little house next to my garage. I think she was horrified when we first started fixing the place up in late 1958. I've recently overheard her telling visitors: "Oh, Lord, you should have seen Madame carrying on! She wanted walls ripped down, pipes put in, new floors and ceilings. She was a taskmaster, a perfectionist." Indeed, both Jean and I were *exigeants,* as we say in French. If we hadn't been, the house would have tumbled down right around us.

During the early sixties, Julia and Paul came down to visit, and they, too, fell under the spell of this gentle corner of Provence. "I wonder if we couldn't try to buy our own house," mused Julia after one of our idyllic sunny afternoons. So the next day, we all set out to view properties for sale in the area. There was always something not quite right about each of the houses we saw.

Finally, Jean said, "Look, maybe you could build a house not far from ours, on the property. I can arrange that." And thus, in 1962, we started building a Provençal house for the Childs just fifty yards away from ours, as their pied-à-terre for holidays in France. It is not large, but it's comfortable, with a great view. The Childs paid for the building, and we agreed to lease them the property it stands on.

This arrangement was convenient for all of us. Julia had her efficient holiday kitchen within shouting distance of mine, and we could run back and forth during the Childs' visits as we launched into Volume II of *Mastering,* which would come out in 1970. Paul fixed up a room as a studio for painting; he has always been very fond of Provençal colors and light.

We decided to call their house La Pitchoune, which means "a little thing" in Provençal, and over the years we've enjoyed innumerable lunches or dinners on their stone terrace overlooking the valley and hill of Plascassier. And, naturally, I give my own terrace lunches, for the Childs or my other friends.

We usually begin with our own tomatoes when they're in season, the most delectable treat I can conjure up. There really is nothing to compare with sweet red slices of perfectly ripe tomato. I serve them with a little vinaigrette, some tiny black olives from our own trees, and a tray of radishes. But I may also include pâté, a special omelet, or a fish mousse. Typical of my terrace menus would be one like this:

Un déjeuner à la terrasse de Bramafam pour Julia et Paul

Luncheon on the Terrace at Bramafam
for Julia and Paul

✦ *Soufflé de poisson, sauce sabayon*
A special fish soufflé with sabayon sauce

—

Vin blanc sec de Bourgogne—Meursault

✦ *Filets de dinde au poivre vert sur purée de laitue*
Turkey fingers with green peppercorns on lettuce purée

Salade verte

Fromages variés

—

Vin rouge de Bourgogne—Pomerol

✦ *Tarte aux citrons de Menton*
French lime tart

Soufflé de poisson, sauce sabayon

A Special Fish Soufflé with Sabayon Sauce

—

For 4 to 6

1 lb. fish fillets, such as Dover sole,
  lemon sole, flounder, or sea bass
4½ Tbsp. butter
1 Tbsp. vegetable oil
2 shallots, finely minced
Salt and pepper
2–3 cups dry white wine

For soufflé base:
½ cup flour
1½ cups cold milk
Salt, pepper, and nutmeg

4 egg yolks
1½ oz. grated Parmesan cheese
6 egg whites
Pinch of salt

Special equipment needed:
A heavy 4-cup oval or round soufflé
  mold, 7½″ diameter × 3½″ high
A flat flameproof baking dish
Parchment paper
A small enameled cast-iron saucepan
A larger pan to contain soufflé mold

*T*he soufflé will be served in the soufflé mold. Butter the mold heavily and refrigerate until needed. Preheat the oven to 375°F.

Split the fish fillets in half to make 6–8 pieces, and sprinkle lightly with salt.

Melt 2½ Tbsp. butter with the oil, add the minced shallots, and cook until soft but not browned, stirring frequently.

Arrange the fish fillets in a buttered baking dish and cover with the cooked shallots. Season lightly with salt and pepper, dot with the remaining butter, and pour wine over the fillets to just barely cover them. Top with buttered parchment paper and bring slowly to a simmer over direct heat for 3–4 minutes.

Carefully remove the fish from the wine mixture, then strain and reserve for the sauce.

To prepare the soufflé base, place the flour in an enameled cast-iron saucepan and slowly add the cold milk, stirring until smooth. Place over heat and stir with a wire whisk until smooth and quite thick, letting the mixture simmer a few minutes to cook the flour and the milk. Season highly, then remove from heat and stir in the egg yolks and half the cheese.

Beat the egg whites with a pinch of salt until stiff but not dry. Stir a ladle of the whites into the soufflé base to lighten it, then turn all of the egg whites into the base mixture and fold lightly.

Fill the soufflé mold, then insert the fish fillets vertically into the soufflé base in rows, like soldiers. Sprinkle with the remaining cheese, place in a bain-marie, then in the oven to bake for 25–30 minutes, before serving in the same mold.

Serve with *Sauce sabayon*.

Sauce sabayon

(flavored with fish *fumet* or clam juice)

—

For 1½ cups sauce

1 cup water
1 small onion, sliced
2 shallots, halved
½ carrot, sliced
½ leek, green portion only
1 bouquet garni of celery stalk, thyme, bay leaf, and parsley stalks
1 lb. fish bones (preferably from Dover sole, halibut, trout, or salmon), cut up, or an equal weight of small fresh mussels, well cleaned and not open

Salt and pepper
1 cup dry white wine
Pinch of saffron
1–2 egg yolks
Optional: ½ cup butter, in small pieces
Optional: 2–3 Tbsp. lemon juice

Special equipment needed:
A large skillet
A heavy-bottomed saucepan

*T*o prepare the *fumet*: Bring the water to a boil in a large skillet, then add the vegetables, bouquet garni, the cut-up fish bones, and a little salt. Let simmer 15 minutes, removing the scum as it builds. Add the white wine. and let boil 5 more minutes. Remove from heat, and strain to remove the bones and vegetables.

If you prefer to use mussels, as I do, instead of fish bones, scrub well and remove "beards." Place in a dry skillet with nothing else. Cover with lid, shaking over heat until all mussels open, about 6 minutes. Pour through a fine-mesh strainer lined with dampened cheesecloth to remove sand and grit from the mussel base. Meanwhile, boil water and vegetables together (without salt, since the mussel *fumet* is very salty) for 15 minutes, add wine, and let boil 5 more minutes. Stir mussel base into the vegetable-wine mixture.

Or, if you want to make it very easily, use the equivalent amount of clam juice, flavored with pepper (no salt).

Add saffron to the fish or mussel *fumet,* and set aside. Once prepared, this *fumet* can be stored in the freezer until needed. If using it immediately, reduce until 1 cup remains, adding more pepper if necessary. Remove from heat and let cool a little.

Beat the egg yolks in a heavy-bottomed saucepan. Over very low heat, whisk in the *fumet,* a little at a time. Beat vigorously until all is added and the sabayon is foaming and thickening. Taste and correct the seasoning, and serve as is.

If you prefer a thicker and richer sauce, set over another pan with hot water, or a double boiler, and beat in the butter bit by bit, continuing to beat for 1 minute after all the butter has been added. Taste for seasoning, and add the lemon juice if you like a more acid sabayon.

You can also serve this sauce with steamed vegetables, fish, shellfish, and eggs. Leave out the saffron if the sauce will be served with vegetables or eggs.

Filets de dinde au poivre vert sur purée de laitue

Turkey fingers with green peppercorns on lettuce purée

—

For 4 to 6

For turkey:

1 lb. turkey breast

Salt and pepper, to taste

1 small can green peppercorns, drained dry and crushed

½ cup flour

1 cup crème fraîche (page 501)

4–5 Tbsp. vegetable oil

8 tablespoons butter

For lettuce purée:

4 large heads of lettuce, or a mix of spinach and lettuce, to obtain about 4 cups of green purée

4½ Tbsp. butter

Salt, pepper, and nutmeg

1½–1¾ cups crème fraîche (page 501)

Butter, to grease the gratin dish

Special equipment needed:

A large oval gratin dish, preferably enameled cast-iron

A nonstick frying pan

A food processor

The day before you plan to serve this recipe, remove the skin and trim the turkey breast as needed, before cutting it into finger shapes, about ¾″ by ¾″ and about 3″–4″ long. Season with salt, pepper, and crushed peppercorns, then dredge in flour, shaking off any excess. Dip into the crème fraîche, cover with plastic wrap, and place in the refrigerator overnight.

For the lettuce purée, carefully wash the lettuce (or the spinach and lettuce) leaves, removing all stems. Parboil the lettuce in salted water for 7 minutes (4–5 minutes for the spinach and lettuce). Refresh under cold tap water, then drain in a colander and dry between kitchen towels.

Cream the butter and reserve. Purée the greens in a food processor, adding the seasoning, half the crème fraîche, and the creamed butter. Transfer to a saucepan and stir over heat until smooth and homogenous, then pour into a buttered gratin dish and keep warm until time to serve with the meat.

To cook the turkey fingers, heat half the butter with half the oil in a nonstick frying pan. When hot, sauté the turkey fingers without crowding, turning them as soon as one side is lightly browned. When all sides are nicely golden, arrange in an elegant design over the lettuce purée. Sprinkle with a little crème fraîche, then push the meat into the purée so it is still visible. Scatter with dots of butter and gratiné in a hot oven (425°F) for a few minutes, just before serving.

This is an easy dish to prepare ahead of time, even the day before you will serve it.

Wine Suggestion: A light Bordeaux or Côtes du Rhône red.

Tarte aux citrons de Menton

French Lime Tart

—

For 5 to 6

For pastry dough:
1½ cups pastry flour
½ tsp. salt
10 Tbsp. cold butter, diced
2 egg yolks beaten with 2 Tbsp. cold
   water

For filling:
3 egg yolks
1 cup granulated sugar
⅓ cup fresh lime juice (about 2–3 limes)
Grated peel from 2 limes (green part
   only)

1½ cups heavy cream
¼ cup strained apricot preserves
2 egg whites

For garnish:
Confectioners' sugar (from a shaker)

Special equipment needed:
A food processor, or a mixing bowl and
   large fork
A 9"–10" tin tart mold, with sides
   1" high

To prepare the pastry dough, blend the flour, salt, and diced butter in a food processor, or in a mixing bowl with a large fork. When the mixture looks like oatmeal, add the egg yolks and water, and mix together. Do not overwork. Press the mixture together to make a ball, wrap in plastic, and place in the refrigerator while making the filling.

Grate the peel of 2 limes and juice enough limes to get ⅓ cup juice. In a mixing bowl, blend the egg yolks with half the sugar, adding the sugar gradually and mixing until the "ribbon" stage is reached. Add the lime juice, grated peel, and cream, and stir until the mixture is homogenous. Set aside while baking the tart shell.

Roll the pastry dough to a thickness ⅛" thick. Line the tart shell, with a double thickness on the sides. Brush the bottom with the apricot preserves, prick with a fork, and bake in a preheated 375°F oven for 10–12 minutes. While baking, remove once from oven and prick again to let the steam escape. When done, remove from oven and let cool.

Immediately beat the egg whites with a pinch of salt and a drop of water. When half beaten, add the remaining sugar, pouring slowly and beating constantly until all is added and the egg whites are stiff and shiny. Stir a ladle of the whites into the egg-lime mixture to lighten it, then fold into the egg whites, working lightly with a large spatula.

Fill the tart shell, smooth the top, and bake in a preheated 375°F oven 15–18 minutes, or until slightly puffed and golden. When done, remove and sprinkle with a little confectioners' sugar. Return to a 425°F oven to caramelize (about 3–4 minutes), then remove and let cool on a rack. Unmold and serve warm or cold.

ON OCTOBER 31, 1962 (Memorial Day in France), around the time La Pitchoune was being built and Bramafam was still being renovated, I went up to the little cemetery of Châteauneuf-de-Grasse on the Bramafam hill to lay flowers on Cousin Marcelle's grave. I almost dropped dead myself when I looked around at the gravestones and noticed a handsome new marble inscribed "Marie de Ayala Gulbenkian." I looked again, and there was no death date, so I knew that my first childhood friend up in Normandy must be living nearby and had staked out a beautiful resting place for herself.

Through the telephone information service, it was not too hard to find Marie—with her second husband, she was often seen at Riviera parties. This was not the "Mr. Five Percent" Armenian-born Gulbenkian, Calouste, but his fun-loving son, Nubar. The Gulbenkian family later left a fortune in art to the museum they endowed on the outskirts of Lisbon.

I called Marie and learned she was indeed a neighbor, as their holiday villa was perched nearby on the Bramafam hill, above our house. When Nubar's Rolls pulled up to Bramafam, Marie and I were so happy to see each other again after fifty years that we literally fell into each other's arms. The afternoon flew by as we talked and talked, unraveling our separate pasts and putting them together again. She recalled the time in 1912 (we were playmates when I knew her) that her uncle in the Champagne country had predicted a dark future for her after a setback in the Ayala factory, saying she'd never be able to marry well. "I was stricken at the time, but look at me now," and she winked. Marie led a privileged life and went everywhere, thanks to her multimillionaire husband and also to her own good nature, since she was a charmer.

I remember Nubar as a debonair clown who used to drop contrived witticisms to the press, such as "I'm the last of the Rastas," referring to his hirsute, bearded appearance, akin to the dreadlocks of the Caribbean Rastafarians. After Nubar died, in 1972, Marie and I used to call on each other for tea and a good gossip. She died in 1982 and now is buried in that pretty plot she'd picked out for herself some twenty years earlier. I've been up there several times to place flowers on her grave as well as on Cousin Marcelle's.

THE FRUITFUL YEARS

KNEAD THAT DOUGH! Beat it around, let it rise. Yeast is a living thing!" This litany and others like it wove through my life in the sixties, as I worked with bakers to learn the finer points. In fact, I felt there was more to learn about everything.

As *Mastering* was getting off the ground, I was edging up to sixty but not slowing down. I've never been able to lie back and savor the fruits of my labor.

Jean encouraged me to keep on, but he never got directly involved in my work. He was preoccupied with his own problems. His company had "put him on the shelf," with a gentle kick into a less dynamic job, in 1961. He decided to found a company to manufacture facial creams—and called the business Sederma, a name loosely based on *société dermatologique*—and in 1963 was helped by a generous loan from Paul and Julia Child. I think this proved to be a good investment, since Jean was a good manager (he loved scents and people, and he knew his business well), and all debts and interest were paid off.

Meanwhile, Julia and I were already tackling recipes for *Mastering* II—concentrating heavily on things like pastry and bread, which Julia thought were absolutely essential to producing authentic French food in America. We'd already made our more or less disastrous attempts at fabricating bakery fare down in Marseille back in the fifties. I've got to find a way to learn from real bakers, I thought. The opportunity that came up was a natural.

By 1958, I had a hip problem that is medically known as arthrosis; the disease causes deterioration of the joints and accompanying crippling pain. My doctor recommended that I try the mineral baths at Bourbonne-les-Bains, a spa in the Haute Marne area of eastern France. As everyone has heard, the "waters" in France are considered beneficial, and we French reckon that taking cures can help everything from liver and digestive troubles to calcium deficiency and skin, heart, or lung diseases.

So the minerals at Bourbonne, to be soaked in rather than drunk, are prescribed for bone and joint problems. Patients take short mineral baths daily for at least three weeks.

For my first cure, I stayed at the town's best hotel, the Jeanne d'Arc, where I decided during my very first breakfast that their buttery croissants were so good I had to meet the chef. I didn't want to loll around, as some *curistes* did, gossiping and complaining of their aches and pains between baths. I wanted to learn something. So I approached the hotel manager.

"Madame, if you're courageous enough to get up very early in the morning, I'm sure our chef would be delighted to let you watch him prepare the croissants," he said.

So I set the alarm for 5:30 A.M., rubbed the sleep from my eyes, and by 6:00 or so was down in the kitchen, learning how to cut and roll croissants. I immediately understood the necessary speed, the ways the elastic dough acts and reacts in your hands as you fashion the little triangles.

I went back day after day to practice, to get the routine so fixed in my head and hands that it would become automatic. Dressed in my bathrobe, ready to take the waters, I joined the kitchen staff for the work and usually rushed in late and breathless for my cure session.

We must have turned out 350 croissants before every breakfast, and by the time I was finished with my first bath of the day I was ravenous. I'd sit there soaking in the hot water and feel I'd truly earned my breakfast!

I graduated from mere folding to learning the *détrempe*—the butter-flour croissant dough, which most every cook knows is really a type of *pâte feuilletée,* with yeast added to make it rise.

Those Bourbonne waters that bubble from the earth at an infernal 65°C (149°F) are cooled down to just over body temperature, which means they still seem scaldingly hot on the skin. After several baths lasting twenty minutes each, the patient usually feels enervated and logy. This is no Maine Chance beauty cure. But the results can pay off over the years. Bourbonne has helped me, and I've returned faithfully for the annual cure. As a result, I never had to have the famous hip operation invented by a doctor in England that so many sufferers have undergone. My doctor also told me that X-rays showed I had "transparent" bones—a very serious case of osteoporosis. And apparently the mineral water treatments have helped make my bones more solid—though I run around so heedlessly that I still have bone-breakage tendencies.

Cooking made my cure sessions bearable, as I constantly hung around kitchens and bakeries to learn the chefs' secrets. One reason I know all about French bread is that I met a baker in Bourbonne-les-Bains recommended by a clothes boutique owner around the corner from his shop.

Amused, I went to see M. Boulanger the *boulanger*—his name actually meant "baker"—who said, "Fine, come around eleven P.M. or midnight if you want to learn how to make bread." That was a chore, as the cure is fatiguing in itself and I was used to falling asleep well before midnight. But I stuck to my guns, knocked back a strong coffee after dinner, and went almost nightly for a while to put my hands into M. Boulanger's *pâte.* It was no picnic. Boulanger was a rustic type— *brave,* as we'd say here, or well-meaning, though he never even thought to offer me a chair during the three-hour-plus nightly sessions.

I stayed up till around 2:00 A.M., doing a yeoman's job with the bakers. All the kneading was done by hand, and it was tough work. I don't see how a baker could ever have gotten fat. We pulled the dough, twisted it, threw it down on the table time after time, kneaded it. Started again. It smelled delicious, that incomparable live yeast odor. When I catch its scent today, even during a lesson, my thoughts sometimes stray back to Boulanger's bakery.

By the time we had put the dough into straw baskets for the final rising and I heaved myself into bed, I felt as if I were a candidate for an Olympic weight-lifting contest, or maybe for a rest home, if not an asylum. But learning what goes into making a *baguette* made it all worthwhile, I told myself.

Mornings came much too quickly. I could barely pick up the delicious bread and rolls M. Boulanger provided to our hotel; in fact, I took to simply drinking cocoa for breakfast. But my efforts paid off in the end. I've used his methods for breadmaking in my books and classes ever since. My pupils are always amused at my "circus number" with the dough as I throw it around with abandon and make them do the same thing. "Don't be afraid," I've always told them. "You've got to knock the daylights out of this stuff to make it supple and light-rising."

Later on, in Paris, I learned even more about bread from Professor Calvel, head of the French bakers' school. Julia and I had been trying once again to work out how to do French bread for Volume II of *Mastering,* but even with Boulanger's instructions in my head, it wouldn't come out right. What was lacking for our perfect loaves—according to the way we saw Professor Calvel make bread—was the right heat-and-steam combination. Paul Child's ingenuity finally helped us come up with the gimmick—to drop a hot brick in a pan of water in the oven!

Around 1961, I switched to the Hôtel d'Orfeuil in Bourbonne, a simple but cheery place, where I still go. The chef-owner there is Paul Tröisgros, a distant cousin of the famed Troisgros family in Roanne—who also became my friends during various stopovers there.

I was one of the many Troisgros fans who were given generous time and advice by Jean and Pierre in their kitchen. Jean once said, "The most important ingredient in cooking is *taste,* your own taste. And how do you acquire that? Why, by tasting!" Like me, he believed that cookbooks aren't worth much if you can't improvise at times and add your own touch according to taste.

Jean spent much of his kitchen time as a specialist in quick-sautéed meats, but he constantly had a finger in the sauce. And that's something every good cook does—a dish can't just *look* good!

Paul Troisgros is not of the three-star Roanne style, but he still knows plenty about traditional French cuisine. I have always learned something in his kitchen, including my favorite *croustade* pastry for little hors d'oeuvre tartlets, sauces of all kinds, and much else. Just recently he showed me his version of quiche Lorraine, with an original twist that gives good results.

Un dîner sympathique
à l'Hôtel d'Orfeuil

A Dinner Inspired by l'Hôtel d'Orfeuil
in Bourbonne-les-Bains

✦ *La quiche Lorraine de Paul Troisgros*
Paul Troisgros's quiche Lorraine

✦ *Pintade aux poivrons tricolores avec risotto*
Guinea hens with tricolored bell peppers and saffron-flavored risotto

Salade

Fromages de chèvre

—

Un bon vin rosé de Provence ou Tavel

✦ *Charlotte aux pommes caramélisées*
Caramelized apple charlotte

—

Bordeaux blanc, Graves

La quiche Lorraine de Paul Troisgros

Paul Troisgros's Quiche Lorraine

—

For 4 to 6

For crust:
1 lb. Short Pastry (see Basics, page 488; use half the quantity given in that recipe)

For filling:
2 oz. slab bacon, slightly smoky in flavor
2 cups heavy cream

1 Tbsp. sifted flour
4 eggs
Salt, pepper, and nutmeg

Special equipment needed:
An 8″ fluted quiche pan
A nonstick skillet
A food processor

*P*repare the short pastry. Allow the pastry to chill at least 1 hour before using, preferably overnight. Roll the pastry to a thickness of ⅛″ and fit into the quiche pan, making the sides double in thickness.

Meanwhile, cut the bacon into ¼″ dice, and sauté in a nonstick pan over medium heat until slightly browned. (If using French bacon, which has a stronger flavor than American brands, parboil for 5 minutes, rinse in cold water, and pat dry before cutting into dice.) Remove and drain on paper towels, then randomly press some of the bacon into the prepared pastry shell. Place in the refrigerator to become firm while preparing the filling, pricking all over with a fork.

Pour half the cream into the work bowl of a food processor. Sprinkle the flour over the cream, and process for 5 seconds to mix. Add the eggs, one at a time and pulsing after each addition, the remaining cream, and the seasonings. Process for 20 seconds to mix thoroughly, and set aside.

Bake the chilled tart shell in a preheated 400°F oven for 12–15 minutes, or until opaque. Do not allow the pastry to brown. Remove from oven when done, and let cool slightly.

Pulse the egg-cream mixture once more, then transfer to a mixing bowl and stir in the remaining bacon. Do not use the food processor for this step, as it will mince the bacon, which should remain in ¼″ dice. Ladle the filling into the prepared quiche pan, and bake in a preheated 375°F oven for 45–50 minutes, or until the center is set and the top is nicely browned.

Wine Suggestion: A light red Bordeaux or a rosé de Provence.

Pintade aux poivrons tricolores avec risotto

Cornish Hens with Tricolored Bell Peppers and Saffron-Flavored Risotto

—

For 5 to 6

Two 2½-lb. Cornish hens
2 lb. red, green, and yellow bell peppers
5 garlic cloves, minced
3–4 medium onions
2½ lb. fresh, ripe tomatoes
4 Tbsp. olive oil
2 cups dry white wine
Large bouquet garni of celery stalks, parsley, thyme, and bay leaf
1 Tbsp. dried herbes de Provence (see Aide-Mémoire, page 503)
2 cups chicken broth (or water and bouillon cubes)
Salt and pepper

For risotto:
2 cups raw rice
2½ Tbsp. olive oil
5 cups chicken broth (or water and bouillon cubes)
¼ tsp. powdered saffron
Salt and pepper

Special equipment needed:
A heavy covered skillet

$\mathcal{R}$emove the skins from the hens, then cut into 6 serving pieces and set aside. Cut the bell peppers in half, remove their seeds and membranes, and slice into ½″ strips. Mince the garlic and chop the onions. Blanch tomatoes for exactly 10 seconds in boiling water; immediately refresh in ice water, core, and peel. Cut peeled tomatoes in half crosswise, then turn cut sides down and squeeze gently to remove the seeds and extra juice.

Heat 4 Tbsp. oil in the skillet. When hot, add the hen pieces and let brown slowly, turning the pieces until they are evenly browned; remove and reserve. Add the onions and garlic to the same hot oil. Let cook, stirring constantly until softened, then add the tomatoes and bell pepper strips. When the mixture begins to boil, add the wine and let boil 3 minutes to evaporate the alcohol, then return the meat to the pan, place the bouquet garni in the center, and add the seasoning. Cover the skillet contents with hot chicken broth and stir in a little salt and pepper. (If you are using bouillon cubes, remember that they contain salt.)

When the skillet contents return to the simmer, top with a piece of parchment, cover with the lid, and place in a preheated 375°F oven for 40–45 minutes. Turn the Cornish hen pieces after 20 minutes. Before removing from the oven, check to be sure the meat is tender, and correct the seasoning.

When done, remove the hen pieces and reduce the cooking liquids to concentrate their flavors, then again correct the seasoning. When the cooking liquids have reduced to 3 cups, remove from heat and set aside until time to reheat the meat.

Meanwhile, prepare the risotto. First, heat 2½ Tbsp. oil in a skillet. Then add the rice and stir constantly until it has browned slightly. Stir in 5 cups chicken broth all at once, then add the saffron, salt, and pepper. When the mixture comes to the boil, reduce the heat, cover, and let simmer for 18–20 minutes, or until the rice is tender and has absorbed all the liquid. Keep warm until ready to serve.

When time to serve, reheat the meat in the sauce, taking care not to overcook. Serve in a large heated serving dish, with the hen in its sauce and the risotto on the side.

Wine Suggestion: A full-bodied red wine from Provence or a Tavel rosé.

Charlotte aux pommes caramélisées

Caramelized Apple Charlotte

—

For 5 to 6

2 Tbsp. butter
2 lb. Golden Delicious apples
1½–2 Tbsp. freshly squeezed lemon
   juice

For caramel:
¾ cup sugar
1 Tbsp. lemon juice
3 Tbsp. butter

For batter:
4 eggs
⅓ cup sugar
1 tsp. potato starch or arrowroot

3 Tbsp. pulverized almonds
2 Tbsp. Kirsch, or rum or Calvados

For optional raspberry sauce:
2 cups raspberry or red currant jelly
2 Tbsp. water
2 Tbsp. Kirsch or rum

Special equipment needed:
A 6-cup charlotte mold
Parchment paper
A heavy stainless-steel saucepan
A food processor
A bain-marie (see page 503)

*B*utter the charlotte mold, line the bottom only with parchment paper, and place in the refrigerator until needed. Peel and core the apples and cut into cubes about 1½″ square. Sprinkle with lemon juice to keep fresh.

Meanwhile, prepare the caramel: Put the sugar, lemon juice, and butter in a heavy-bottomed saucepan and cook until the mixture turns a nice golden brown, then add the cubed apples and cook until quite tender. Strain out the apples, reserving the juice, and keep warm. Return the juice over heat and let reduce until 1 cup remains. Keep warm.

Pulse the eggs, sugar, starch, and pulverized almonds in a food processor until well mixed. Add the liqueur and reduced caramelized sugar syrup to the egg mixture, and pulse a few seconds more.

Fill the prepared charlotte mold, beginning with a layer of half the cooked apples, followed by half the egg mixture and the rest of the apple mixture, and top with the remaining egg mixture. Cover with buttered parchment paper and place in a bain-marie or large pan. Add moderately hot water to a depth of 1″ and bake in a preheated 375°F oven for 30 minutes, or until the sides come away from the mold and the center is set, not runny. If using a mold without handles, wear oven mitts before touching mold. When done, a knife stuck into the center of the charlotte will come out clean.

While baking, prepare the sauce. If the charlotte is to be served tepid, serve it with Crème Anglaise Sauce (page 88). If served cold, serve with raspberry (or red currant) sauce made by melting jelly with water and Kirsch or rum. When ready to serve, unmold the charlotte over a shallow serving dish, glaze the top with sauce, and serve the remaining sauce in a sauceboat.

Note: If you cannot find pulverized almonds, place whole or slivered almonds in a food processor or blender with 1–2 Tbsp. of the sugar called for in the recipe, and process until a fine powder results. Do not overprocess.

Wine Suggestion: A fine French demi-sec dessert Champagne.

I FEEL AN EXALTED PEACE IN THE DEEP, cool, pine-scented forests of the Vosges, millennial and majestic, cut through with silvery streams in the valleys. It is reverent, almost solemn, compared with my flowery, decorative Provence.

Here and nearby they're producing some excellent cheeses that I got to know and like: Comté, Carré de l'Est, and Münster. From Burgundy I savored things like smelly Époisses (with shades of my father chiding me in the background), or Citeaux, a pressed, uncooked cheese made by monks, which has an incomparable hint of fruit in the flavor.

During my various stays in the hotel, I've also found time to knit five colorful afghan blankets and embroider four bedcovers, to use at Bramafam. Even relaxing in Bourbonne, I can't get away from my persistent need to make my hands do something useful.

Lessons——
Giving and Taking

JUST AS *Mastering* was on its way to publication, and with Julia in America, I realized that our Trois Gourmandes school—now on the back shelf—had been the only American-aimed school in Paris. And what with many Americans tasting French restaurant cuisine and interest sparked by articles in the *Herald Tribune* based on our first book, Americans would probably want some practical training. So Louisette and I revived the school.

We expanded the number of pupils to about fifteen, who could be accommodated in Louisette's Avenue Victor Hugo kitchen. We had no trouble finding pupils. At first, they were recruited from the ranks of wives of NATO personnel and the military establishment. Then some Japanese came; they have always been interested in things French, and nowadays are cutting a swath through the couture world and reveling in French cooking here and in Tokyo.

I greatly enjoyed my Japanese students, in them spotting fellow workaholics. I remember one incident in particular with a budding Japanese cook. She had shown especial interest in my meat sauces, and one day—most hesitantly and politely— she asked me if I could show her once more just how one cooked a *"loup."* Of course, I recommended grilling the fish and perhaps concocting a beurre blanc. The girl said, "No, not fish!" Maybe she meant a wolf. I confess to total ignorance in the preparation or cooking of that beast. Was there an exotic Japanese dish to which she wished to add the French touch? Did she want to open a French restaurant in Transylvania?

Finally, after much gesturing and questioning in our differently accented English, I realized she simply wanted to master a basic roux.

When Julia had spare time between filming, she flew to France to work with me on *Mastering* II, which I consider to be more her book than mine. For the first book, I feel I was the prime mover, more of an authority on French food, more of a "boss." For Volume II, Julia had gained confidence and authority, especially as she was the one living in America, with instant access to the American food mentality and knowledge of products available there.

At the school, we were usually guided by professional chefs. There was Claude

Thilmont, an excellent *pâtissier*, who ruled with an iron whisk, never mincing words in criticism of what we were doing wrong. But he knew what he was talking about and taught us a lot. We also appreciated the help of Max Bugnard, our wonderful chef friend, who came regularly for final tests and awarding of diplomas.

The poor man was crippled and could not walk, and I had the taxing job of getting up before 6:00 A.M. to drive out to the suburb he lived in and pick him up, in both senses, helping to heave his paralyzed legs into the car.

But he surely taught us—teachers and pupils alike—a lot about techniques. Julia, Louisette, and I were all floored by his omelet technique, even though demonstrated from a sitting position. He simply swirled the egg around in the pan, which was perfectly heated ("you know it's ready when the butter stops foaming"), and flipped it over to produce the perfect omelet. The same swirling wrist movement works with crêpes, which I've always had great fun making with students. It's theatrical but fun—and like any stunt or sport, takes nerve at first and then practice.

The pupils all wanted to show enough skill to receive our diploma, but for some of them it wasn't easy, and they often suffered a case of nerves, looking frazzled and hesitant, some even shaking a little, crying if they made a mistake or had to start over. Most got through creditably.

Few were as brassy as the young American who had idled through the course without even trying to understand the points we were trying to make. We decided to withhold her diploma. But she made such an unpleasant fuss—actually threatening to spread lies about our school—that we gave in to her blackmail and sent the diploma without a comment. We were too easily cowed.

In 1967, we had what I call an epic visit by Michael Field and Mary Frances Kennedy Fisher to Bramafam. Michael was general editor of the Time-Life Foods of the World cookbook series, and Mary Frances was a famous food writer in her own right, better known as M.F.K. Fisher. They were working on *Cooking in the Provinces of France* when Julia invited them to stay and work at La Pitchoune. I was delighted when they and Michael's wife arrived.

I think three was sometimes a crowd there, and Michael would often run over to consort with me on the side. He was a talented writer and clever in many ways, but he'd never had any formal cooking instruction. When he dropped in looking for hints, I was glad to give them. But I was flabbergasted when one day he asked, "Could you show me how to make a brown roux?" That's sort of like a science writer asking, What's the composition of water? So I bit back my smile, stirring up a roux for his sauce—gently, gently, until the clarified butter and flour had turned that lovely brown color. "That's all there is to it!" I said, and he was as happy as a boy who had learned to swim.

Zulma surely had no idea what she was starting that day long ago when she showed a curious child the most basic of French cooking *trucs,* the famous roux.

Cooking for these discriminating food professionals presented no problems, since both Mary Frances and Michael liked my use of the available raw materials, including salad and herbs from my garden.

Un déjeuner pour M.F.K. Fisher et M. et Mme Field

Bramafam Lunch for M.F.K. Fisher and the Michael Fields

✦ *Beurre de saumon fumé sur canapés*
Smoked salmon butter canapés

—

Vodka, sangría, vin blanc de Bourgogne—Meursault

✦ *Le gibier en aspic*
Game in aspic

Roquefort

—

Vin rosé—Tavel

✦ *Soufflé aux poires Comice*
Sweet Comice pear soufflé

Beurre de saumon fumé sur canapés

Smoked Salmon Butter Canapés

—

For 3 cups

½ lb. can salmon
6–7-oz. slice smoked salmon of the
   highest quality, cut in small pieces
1 cup sweet butter, creamed
Fresh dill, minced
Salt, pepper, and Tabasco
3–4 Tbsp. vodka

Handful of tiny Niçoise olives, pitted and
   chopped, or fresh dill sprigs, for
   garnish

Special equipment required:
A food processor

Trim the canned salmon, removing the skin and bones. Drain and dry, then purée in a food processor with the pieces of smoked salmon. Pulse until a smooth purée is obtained. Add the creamed butter and all the seasoning. Carefully check the flavor of the salmon butter, adding a little salt and more pepper if needed. Pour in the vodka, pulse, and taste again.

Keep in a glass bowl or a jar with a lid, or it may be molded in small ramekins if served at a brunch.

For canapés, spread on thin slices of rye bread, cut in triangles, crusts removed. Decorate each canapé with tiny bits of Niçoise olives or with tiny sprigs of fresh dill. Keep covered with plastic wrap in the refrigerator until ready to serve.

Beverage Suggestion: Vodka on the rocks, white wine, or sangria (p. 468).

Le gibier en aspic

Game in Aspic

—

For 12 to 15

5½ Tbsp. olive oil
1 cup sliced celery root
1 cup sliced onions
¾ cup sliced carrots
One 3½–4 lb. chicken
1 Cornish hen, or pheasant, partridge,
    domestic rabbit, or wild duck
4 large lemons, or 5–6 limes
10 garlic cloves, not peeled
Thyme, oregano, marjoram, bay leaf,
    salt, and pepper
1 large bouquet garni of celery stalk,
    parsley stems, thyme, and bay leaf

3 Tbsp. wine vinegar
2 cups dry white wine
3 cups chicken stock
2 envelopes unflavored gelatin, softened
    in a little white wine
1 red bell pepper, cut in strips
1 green bell pepper, cut in strips
Fresh parsley

Special equipment needed:
A large heavy-bottomed saucepan or
    skillet, preferably cast iron
A large, shallow oval serving dish

*H*eat 3½ Tbsp. oil in a heavy saucepan or skillet. When hot, add the celery root, onions, and carrots and let stew slowly, stirring. Cut the poultry and game into medium-size pieces, leaving the skin on and not removing the bones. Thinly slice the lemons or limes, keeping aside a few slices for a design.

When the vegetables are just tender, remove ⅔ of the mixture, leaving ⅓ in the pan. Place half the meat on the remaining vegetables, spread with half the garlic cloves and lemon slices, and sprinkle with half of the dry herbs, salt, and pepper, and drops of olive oil. Cover with a second third of the stewed vegetables, the remaining meat, another layer of garlic, lemon slices, and dry herbs, salt, pepper, and drops of olive oil. Top with the remaining vegetables, lemon slices, and oil. Place the bouquet garni in the center, pushing it into the meat and vegetable layers. Pour over the vinegar and white wine and slowly bring to the boil over medium heat. Let boil for a few minutes to evaporate the alcohol, then add the chicken stock. Cover with parchment paper and the lid, and bake in a preheated 375°F oven for about 1½ hours, or until the meat is tender.

When done, uncover and discard the paper. Strain out the meat and vegetables, and put the garlic through a food mill. Degrease the stock, stir in the garlic purée, and reduce the liquid to 4 cups. When the meat has cooled enough to touch, remove and discard the skin and bones. Taste and correct the seasoning of the stock, then stir in the softened gelatin and place over ice to cool.

Using the reserved sliced lemon, red and green bell peppers, and fresh parsley, fashion an elegant design in the bottom of a shallow oval serving dish. Place enough alternating layers of meat and vegetables over the design to fill the dish, being sure to keep the top neat. Pour in enough stock-gelatin mixture to barely cover the top layer, and place in the refrigerator until set, about 2 hours. If in a hurry, place in the freezer just long enough to set, as freezing will hydrolyze the gelatin, making it watery upon thawing.

Serve unmolded, with a good mixed green salad.

Wine Suggestion: The same wine used in the recipe, or a good rosé.

Soufflé aux poires Comice

Sweet Comice Pear Soufflé

—

For 5 or 6

2 ripe pears, preferably Comice
3 Tbsp. Poire William brandy
1 lemon
2 Tbsp. butter
½ cup flour
1 cup milk
4 egg yolks
5 egg whites
Pinch of salt

½ cup granulated sugar
Confectioners' sugar to sprinkle over
    soufflé

Special equipment needed:
A nonstick saucepan
A 1-qt. thick-bottomed saucepan
A 6-cup soufflé mold

*T*he Comice pear is very smooth and tasty, and is recommended for use in this recipe.

Peel the pears. Cut one pear into quarters, then cut each quarter into slices approximately ¼″ thick. Sprinkle with a little of the Poire William and refrigerate. Cut the other pear into dice and sprinkle with lemon juice to keep it white.

Melt the butter in a nonstick saucepan. When hot, add the diced pear and sauté, shaking frequently, until the pear juice is absorbed and the pears are slightly browned and caramelized. Remove and set aside.

Place the flour in a heavy-bottomed saucepan and gradually add the milk, stirring until a smooth paste is formed. Cook over medium heat, stirring constantly, until the mixture has thickened, then let boil until the flour is completely cooked. Remove from the heat and stir in the egg yolks, one at a time, and the remaining Poire William. The soufflé base may be made to this point and held for 2–3 hours if covered with plastic wrap, pressed firmly onto its surface to prevent a skin from forming.

Beat the egg whites vigorously with a pinch of salt and 2 drops of cold water until they begin to form soft peaks. Sprinkle the sugar over them, and continue beating until the mixture is firm and shiny. If the base is cold, rewarm slightly, then stir in a ladle of the meringue to lighten it. Turn the base into the meringue and lightly fold together with the caramelized diced pears and their juices.

Fill the soufflé mold ⅔ high. Pat the sliced pears dry with paper toweling and insert each pear slice into the soufflé, standing them up like soldiers and making a ring. Push each slice to the bottom of the mold. The tops of the pear slices should be visible.

Bake in a preheated 400°F oven for 25–30 minutes. If you like a soufflé with a slightly firmer center, the pear should be cooked ahead. Sprinkle with confectioners' sugar and serve immediately.

Note: The soufflé will rise higher and hold its shape longer if you place a buttered collar of aluminum foil around the mold, extending it 1½″ above the mold and tying with a string.

Wine Suggestion: A good sweet white wine, such as a Sauternes.

ONE EVENING WE ALL DECIDED to drive up to Eze-Village— the quaint medieval town perched on the high corniche road to Monte Carlo—to dine at the Chèvre d'Or. This was considered a gem of a restaurant then, and its spectacular site with a view far below over the Mediterranean, shimmering in the moonlight, was breathtaking on that summer night.

Things started off rather badly, as the place was crowded with tourists and service dragged. We were all getting itchy, and finally Michael, noticing that a small "combo" was taking a break from the music, asked if he could play the piano. I thought he was being facetious, meaning to distract us with a rendition of "Chopsticks." But he launched into a veritable concert of Bach fugues, which had the whole restaurant absolutely spellbound. He told me later that he had once played professionally, so it was no wonder that not a glass clinked or a fork clattered during his recital. It was a truly magical moment that I'll never forget. And of course, I used ideas from some of the dishes we ate that evening for a dinner at home.

Un dîner pour toutes les saisons dans le Midi

A Dinner for All Seasons, in the South of France

✦ *Terrine de poisson en gelée*
Fish terrine in aspic

—

Vin blanc—Sancerre

✦ *Jambon Lucullus*
Succulent ham slices with tomato cream sauce

✦ *Rouleau de verdure*
Green vegetable roll

Salade

Fromages variés

—

Côtes du Rhône, Châteauneuf-du-Pape (full-bodied red)

✦ *Crème glacée au caramel*
Frozen caramel mousse

Terrine de poisson en gelée

Fish Terrine in Aspic

—

For 10 to 12

For the court bouillon:
2 lb. fresh mussels, cleaned
Pepper
1 bottle good dry white wine, such as
    Chablis or Fumé Blanc
4 shallots, minced
Pinch of saffron
Bouquet garni (celery stalk tied together
    with thyme, parsley, bay leaf)
4–5 garlic cloves, peeled and minced
Strip of orange peel, stale and dry

*For clarification of about 4–5 cups
liquid (if needed):*
2 egg whites with eggshells
2 envelopes unflavored gelatin (for 4–5
    cups liquid)

Salt, pepper, and cayenne
Minced fresh dill
3 lb. fish fillets (such as salmon, Dover
    sole, lemon sole, halibut, or monkfish,
    with no skin or bones)
1 large or 2 small red bell peppers,
    cooked and cut in strips

For garnish:
Bunch of parsley or watercress

Special equipment needed:
A cheesecloth-lined strainer or colander
Two 4–5 cup rectangular Pyrex molds,
    or one 7–8 cup Pyrex mold

Fill sink with cold water, add the mussels, and thoroughly clean them with a brush, rinsing in several changes of cold water. Place mussels in a skillet with several grinds of fresh pepper, and shaking the pan constantly, cook over high heat for 4–5 minutes, or until all the mussels are wide open. Do not overcook and discard any that do not open. Remove from heat, discard shells, and strain the pan juices between a double thickness of cheesecloth. You should have approximately ½ cup liquid. Set aside.

Next, prepare the court bouillon. Pour 2½ cups of the white wine into the same skillet used for the mussels, and add the minced shallots, saffron, bouquet garni, garlic, orange peel, a little cayenne pepper, and the mussels and their juices. Bring to the boil, then allow to simmer for a few minutes. Remove the mussels.

Soften the gelatin in the remaining wine (¾ cup), and set aside. Cook the fish fillets in the court bouillon, without boiling and just below simmering, for 7–8 minutes, depending on the thickness of the fillets. Remove the fish, and strain the cooking liquid. If the court bouillon is not clear and sparkling, it should be clarified: Beat the egg whites until foamy; crush the eggshells. Add the egg whites and the eggshells to the court bouillon, whisking to incorporate them. Heat the mixture slowly, whisking all the time, until the egg whites rise to the surface, bringing any scum with them. Allow to simmer for 2 minutes. Gently pour the mixture through a strainer lined with rinsed cheesecloth into a bowl. Add to the wine-gelatin mixture and stir until the gelatin is completely dissolved. Let cool slightly, then stir in minced dill.

To begin building the layers of the terrine, pour a layer of gelatin mixture into the mold to a depth of ⅓" and place in the refrigerator until half set. Make a design, placing some of the red pepper strips crosswise on the half-set gelatin, then cover with a thin layer of jelly. Place in refrigerator again until half set (about 15–20 minutes). Continue building the terrine in the same way, alternating layers of fish fillets, mussels, and strips of red bell pepper, and finishing with jelly and more red bell pepper. Let set in the refrigerator. When ready to be served, unmold onto a platter garnished with parsley or watercress. Serve with Mock Mayonnaise with herbs (page 474).

Wine Suggestion: The same wine that was used in the court bouillon—a very tasty dry white wine.

Jambon Lucullus

Succulent Ham Slices with Tomato Cream Sauce

—

For 10 to 12

For veal stock:

4 lb. veal bones, cut into manageable lengths

3 whole onions, each studded with 2 cloves

3 medium carrots, quartered

Large bouquet garni of 3 small leeks, 3–4 celery stalks, 1 bunch parsley stems, thyme, and bay leaf

Salt and pepper

10–12 ¼″-thick slices of good boiled ham, about 7 oz. each

1 cup port wine

2½ Tbsp. olive oil

For tomato cream sauce:

4 Tbsp. butter

6 Tbsp. flour

About 3–3½ cups veal stock, from above

2 cups crème fraîche (page 501)

1½ Tbsp. tomato paste

Freshly ground pepper

Paprika

Salt, if needed

2 Tbsp. freshly grated Parmesan

Special equipment needed:

A stockpot

A nonstick frying pan

A heavy-bottomed enameled saucepan

1 or 2 enameled cast-iron gratin serving dishes

*P*repare the veal stock the day, or even several days, before needed. It can even be frozen until you are ready for it. Place the bones in a stockpot with sufficient cold water to cover them by 2″. Let come to a simmer, and skim the scum. When clear, add all the vegetables and the bouquet garni, and bring to a boil. Add a little coarse salt, reduce the heat, and simmer 3–4 hours, adding more water as needed to keep ingredients covered. Strain, let cool, and refrigerate. The next day, remove the solidified fat and reduce to 3½ cups.

Trim fat from the ham slices and reserve. Dice the fat and melt in a nonstick frying pan with 2–3 Tbsp. water and the olive oil. (Adding water to the fat will help the melting.) Remove the unmelted fat and sauté the ham slices, without crowding, on both sides until nicely browned. Remove to a warmed ovenproof gratin dish and immediately pour a little port wine over the slices. Keep warm while sautéing the rest of the ham. All the ham slices should be browned in the same way and placed with the others, overlapping, and sprinkled with port. Dribble the remaining port evenly over the arranged ham slices. (The dish should be quite warm, so that it evaporates the port.)

To prepare the tomato cream sauce, heat the butter, and when melted, add the flour and cook over medium heat 4–5 minutes, stirring constantly. Off heat, gradually stir in the veal stock until quite smooth. Bring to a simmer, stirring constantly, then fold in the crème fraîche, the tomato paste, and all the seasonings. (The sauce may be done ahead of time, covered, and set aside.) Before serving, bring to the simmer, correct the seasoning, and keep warm.

Pour the sauce over the ham slices to make a thick coating. Reheat the ham together with the sauce for just a few minutes, and serve in the same dish, with Parmesan sprinkled on top, browning briefly under broiler.

Wine Suggestion: A tasty white wine, such as a Meursault from Burgundy.

Rouleau de verdure

Green Vegetable Roll

—

For about 9 to 10

¾ cup stale bread crumbs

1 lb. spinach, fresh or frozen, or 1 lb.
 Swiss chard leaves

5 Tbsp. butter

1½ Tbsp. oil

4 shallots, minced

2 garlic cloves, minced

2 Tbsp. flour

3 eggs

2½ Tbsp. crème fraîche (page 501)

Salt, pepper, and nutmeg

Cayenne

7 oz. thinly sliced prosciutto, finely
 minced

3 Tbsp. finely grated Parmesan cheese

Special equipment needed:

A 16″ by 12″ jelly roll pan

A large nonstick saucepan

Line the jelly roll pan with aluminum foil, and butter foil heavily. The edges of the foil should be raised all around to contain the mixture. Sprinkle with bread crumbs and refrigerate while preparing the green mixture.

Clean and remove all stems from the spinach, and parboil for 5 minutes. If using Swiss chard, it should be parboiled for 10 minutes. Drain, refresh under cold tap water, drain again, then squeeze out all moisture between kitchen towels. It should be very dry. Chop roughly with a large knife.

Heat half the butter with the oil in a nonstick pan. When hot, add the shallots and garlic, and cook, stirring constantly, for 2–3 minutes, or until tender but not browned. Add the green vegetable, stirring to mix, and the rest of the butter. Sprinkle the flour over this mixture and cook for 3 minutes, stirring constantly. Remove from heat and add the eggs one at a time, stirring vigorously. Place over medium heat and add the crème fraîche by spoonfuls. The mixture should not be runny. Add the seasoning and spread the mixture in an even layer in the prepared pan. Cover with buttered aluminum foil and bake in a preheated 350°F oven for 15–20 minutes, or just until set. Let cool a few minutes before removing the top foil.

Spread the vegetable mixture with an even layer of the minced prosciutto and

Parmesan cheese, and roll the green mixture, detaching from the foil with a spatula. To keep, wrap the roll in the same foil and place in a slow oven until time to serve.

To serve, slice and use as a garnish for roasted meats. If you wish, this is also excellent made without the prosciutto.

Wine Suggestion: A good full-bodied red wine from Provence.

Crème glacée au caramel

Frozen Caramel Mousse

—

For 6

This dessert is best when made a day in advance; it must be made at least 3 hours ahead.

4 egg yolks
½ cup plus 2 Tbsp. water
3½–4⅓ oz. sugar cubes (preferred), or
  ½–⅓ cups granulated sugar
1½ cups heavy cream
½ tsp. vanilla extract
Crystallized violets, for garnish
  (optional)

Special equipment needed:
A mixing bowl and whisk, or an electric
  mixer
A small heavy-bottomed or copper
  saucepan
A stainless-steel bowl

*B*eat the egg yolks until they are a pale, creamy yellow, and set aside. Bring ½ cup water to the boil, then reduce to a simmer. At the same time, put the sugar and 2 Tbsp. water in a small heavy-bottomed or unlined copper saucepan, and let boil. As soon as the sugar syrup turns to a golden-brown caramel, remove from heat and carefully pour in the boiling water, taking care to avoid spattering. Stir and return to a boil to dissolve the caramel, scraping the bottom of the pan.

Gradually beat the boiling caramel into the egg yolks, whipping vigorously until the mixture is creamy and the caramel well dissolved, then set over a bowl of ice cubes and continue to whip while the mixture thickens and cools. Set aside.

Whip the heavy cream and vanilla over ice. Reserve ¼ of the whipped cream to decorate the frozen mousse, and fold the rest into the cooled egg yolk–caramel mixture. Scrape the mousse into a stainless-steel splayed bowl and freeze for at least 2½–3 hours, or until set.

To serve, unmold the mousse onto a serving dish. Decorate with the reserved whipped cream (whipped to stiff peaks) and/or crystallized violets.

ICHAEL AND MARY FRANCES both became good friends of mine. Mary Frances and I still correspond; but Michael, despite his fit and healthy appearance, was stressed by a heavy work load he'd taken on at Time-Life. He also drank and smoked excessively, and finally his body got the better of him. He died of a massive brain hemorrhage in 1972, at barely fifty years old.

Mary Frances, who continued to reside in her native California, visited often. Now she is in her late seventies and traveling less, but we still correspond.

Her food ideas are often subtle and amusing, as shown in such essays as "A Recipe for Happy Hens"—all about eggs. I was astonished when once she made up a menu comprising soups only. But from somebody who claimed he knew why, I heard the sweet logic of it—she'd composed the meal for a friend of hers, an Italian count who had lost all his teeth!

During a U.S. visit in 1973, I was invited with Julia to visit M.F.K.'s ranch in the Sonoma Valley. I knew she liked artichokes, because she'd mentioned them several different times within a few pages in one of her books, writing extensively and ecstatically on the subject. So I was not too surprised to see how she presented them as a dish—the leaves alone, plucked from the heart and arranged in wreaths on the plates, elegant and maybe an oblique homage to the artichoke.

Mary Frances is a true original, a totally devoted Francophile, who has always pursued things French (especially food) with intensity. "I love your book *Simca's Cuisine*," she told me once, candidly adding, "except for the cheesecloth." Julia and I knew that Americans would find it difficult if not impossible to procure caul to wrap things like pâté or white *boudin* in, so we decided that cheesecloth imbibed with a little pork fat could do the job. But Mary Frances insisted on the old French authenticity, even if one had to befriend a pig farmer to get the caul.

Launching Mastering II

DURING THOSE SIXTIES YEARS, my cherished mother was getting on—and growing feeble, though fortunately her mind still functioned perfectly. She stayed for long periods with us in the south at Bramafam; when finally she died peacefully in 1964, at age eighty-nine, we buried her in her own beloved countryside at the Rainfreville cemetery.

I grieved for my mother, but fortunately I had a lot to keep me busy. Finally, our second big volume, *Mastering the Art of French Cooking* II, came out in 1970. Again, I went to America to be present at the launching, but this would be different from the Egg Basket launching we'd struggled so hard over nearly ten years previously.

Knopf now laid on a big party in New York at a mansion on the Upper East Side, an impressive exercise in the grand style. I recall a majestic staircase to an upper balcony and about 250 members of *Le tout New York* (cuisine branch) circulating to taste the Champagne and the elaborate buffet. Julia was a celebrity, and I had my American admirers too. I felt quite proud in my black silk dress with red chiffon scarf that I bought specially for the occasion.

We took another tour out west, and on our way down to Pasadena, we stopped in Santa Barbara, where Julia's aunt was in the hospital. I stayed in her apartment, and I remember being delighted to see a bottle of Bénédictine on her night table —she obviously considered it a soothing bedside "restorative," or tranquilizer.

In 1970 and during later trips in 1971–72, I helped Jim Beard give demonstrations at afternoon and evening classes in his Greenwich Village brownstone.

At one class, I was supposed to demonstrate frogs' legs *à la poulette,* with a lemon-flavored mushroom-cream sauce. "Here are the frogs' legs," said Clay, Jim's assistant, presenting me with monstrous appendages that looked as if they'd come from chickens. Good night, I thought, Americans really do have a taste for the grandiose. Jim wasn't there, so I tackled the legs fearlessly, though I was having a terrible time. Finally, Clay took pity on me and with strong hands and a deft knife got the batrachians' legs down to reasonably presentable proportions. I explained to the pupils that our frogs' legs in France were much smaller, and probably tastier—even though we import so many of them from Yugoslavia!

Through Jim I met Peter Kump, a devoted cooking enthusiast who became my pupil and very good friend. He had started out as a teacher of speed reading, but he soon realized that his real passion was for food. Both bright and talented, Peter was soon giving lessons on his own. In 1974 he founded Peter Kump's New York Cooking School, which he still runs; and in 1984 he founded and was the first president of the James Beard Foundation. He says that "developing a palate is just as important as technique in forming young professional cooks"; I totally agree. His son, Chris, came by cooking naturally and is now an accomplished chef. And the school's pupils have been an invaluable help in taking on the American testing of my latest recipes.

During that same 1970 visit to America, I resumed a friendship with Malvina Kinard, known to so many American cooks for her books, her food knowledge, and her franchised shops, the Cooks' Corners, all over the States.

I'd first met Malvina in 1966, when she rang me up in the south of France and said she'd like to come stay at Bramafam for a few days and take some cooking lessons. I said fine, and we agreed on a time to meet in Nice. I drove over to the

With my "American sister," Julia

airport, a couple of miles from Nice—about 35 minutes from Bramafam—and waited, looking in vain for an American who was also presumably looking for me. Assuming a missed plane, I drove home; the phone rang, and Malvina said, "But I've been here all the time!" We'd had a big misunderstanding, and she was waiting in the center of Nice—where I finally found her looking jet-lagged and distraught, sitting forlornly on the curb of the Square Albert I.

We got along fine, and I was glad to see her again at her cozy home in Westport, Connecticut. Her slick, modern basement kitchen was well appointed, and naturally I offered to help with a lesson, something to do with thin-slicing leeks.

I'm red-faced to admit that I was not used to such rapier-sharp knives, and as I sliced merrily away—glancing up a lot at the bright faces in the class—I looked down and there sat part of the end of my index finger, like a morsel of steak on the plate! I was bleeding like a pig. "Sorry, Malvina," I said with chagrin. "Can't we just paste it back on with a Band-Aid and go on?"

"No," she said grimly. "You have to get to a hospital." She rushed me to the nearest clinic, where they threw out my fingertip and grafted on some flesh from my arm. Nevertheless, we resumed our show the next day, and I helped as best I could during Malvina's demonstration of a fancy lobster and other dishes. My photo with bandaged hand looked quite impressive in the local paper next day.

Later, I took off for Michigan to see my friend Lucille Tyree, the woman who had planted the first idea for *Mastering* in Louisette's head so many years before. Lucille had a very comfortable house near the golf club in Grosse Pointe, and during the four days I spent there, I gave demonstrations in her kitchen.

I was seconded by Lucille's gem of a cook, a round black woman who scurried around to get the cream or butter out of the fridge when I needed it, cleaned up the bowls and cutlery, and smiled broadly most of the time, maybe enjoying my French approach. I showed *poulet à la crème* and an apple tart, answering all the pupils' questions about things like differences between French and American cream.

"Your heavy cream will do just fine," I said, explaining that it looks thinner than our Norman *crème fraîche* and has a slightly less acid taste, which for cooking chicken would be different but just as good. "Delicious" was the consensus when we sat down to sample the results.

For this little piece of work, Lucille was able to pay me the grand sum of fifty dollars. I was skeptical when she suggested I might be able to buy a fur coat with it. "Come on," she said, with a glint in her eye, heading for the car.

The thrift shop she drove me to was a Spartan box of a place, crammed with fur coats sold for a pittance after the rich owners had tired of them. Similar second-hand outlets exist in France now, but back then the equivalent bargains were moth-eaten models sold at the flea market.

"Try this one, Simca," Lucille said, pulling out a medium-length brown beaver coat in quite good condition. To be a good sport I tried it on, and it looked fine. I paid little more than my fifty-dollar fee for it, and wore it proudly in America and back in France. I still drag it out of my closet with pleasure when we have one of those unusual cold snaps down on the Côte d'Azur.

And I was of course royally entertained—in customary American style. People came straight up and asked me all about myself (French bourgeois women in similar circumstances often hang back reticently, creating glacial silences).

But that finger was acting up, and obviously it had to be looked at again. So off to a Michigan clinic, where a doctor undid the bandage and shook his head. "Sorry, but this is a mess. That so-called graft did not take." He cleaned it up, sewed it closed again, and this time I grew the end of my finger back.

Simca's Own Cuisine

MANY OF THE RECIPES I had proposed for *Mastering* II were not used, so after the book came out, Judith Jones of Knopf suggested that I write my own cookbook, and this was the germ for *Simca's Cuisine*.

About that time, back at Bramafam, the journalist Patricia Simon came to interview me for *McCall's* magazine, which was to feature a big article about *Mastering* II. She was enchanted with Provençal life, and I got along well with her, so in accord with Knopf, we decided she would write the book with me, couching it in perfectly written English, which I was not able to do.

She came back and stayed a month or so, gathering all her information on tape after tape of recorded interviews. With these "fireside" or "gardenside" chats, we decided to make a personal book. Patricia would quiz me, and I'd come up with the anecdotes that readers of *Simca's Cuisine* know—about the places where I'd lived and about seasonal cooking—to go with the recipes.

On tour in America for
Simca's Cuisine

Patricia's suitcase was so heavy with tapes that she had trouble lifting it. When she got back to New York, the editors—who wanted the book as soon as possible—almost literally locked her into an office for several weeks so that she'd produce a manuscript. We worked over it by correspondence, with help again from Judith Jones, while my artist nephew, Michel Beck, created charming drawings.

I was very happy with the way the book looked, felt, and read by the time it came out in 1972. Julia and I had now completely split off on our own tacks, and that was all to the good. *Mastering* had given us our big chance, gotten us off the ground, and now each of us could do her own thing.

FACES AND PLACES

ONE DAY IN 1970, the doorbell of my Neuilly apartment was rung timidly—just a "ding"—and I opened the door to a string bean of a young man, a nineteen-year-old American named Michael James, who had telephoned for an appointment. His dark-brown hair was an inch or two too long to suit me, but otherwise he looked presentable. "Mme Beck, I would like to learn cooking," he said shyly but in good French. I had no suspicion that Michael was to play a very big role in my professional and personal life.

It was a surprise to have a male culinary candidate; as nearly all my pupils had been women, as was my current assistant. Michael and I were instantly chatting about food, and I realized that his passion for it would probably carry him a long way. I couldn't help taking to the boy, and he worked assiduously with me—later sharpening his skills in the kitchens of chefs like Jean Troisgros.

By the time my assistant had left, after her marriage, Michael was ready to take over. He became not only my right arm in the kitchen, but a coauthor, travel agent, and invaluable friend.

In 1976, when Jean sold his beauty products business and retired, we made

Bramafam our sole residence. The property was flourishing, with the addition of a new house—La Campanette, completed in 1974—which we built partly to accommodate furniture I had inherited from Mother. I had not planned for it to be a "cooking school" house, but that's how things evolved. It's also a regular summer retreat for Jean's sister France and her family—and for other relatives and friends.

My first group of cooking pupils to "inaugurate" La Campanette, in September 1974, were Suzy Patterson, her mother, and two friends, Ginny Larsen and Winnie Stuart, professional cooks who both taught cooking in the States.

Here is Suzy's description of the visit:

Arriving a day ahead of the others, I was enchanted by the hillside Provençal house Simca and Jean had built, with its view over the Plascassier, the neatly trimmed garden bordered with roses and lilies, the sheer peacefulness of the place.

Next day at the Nice airport, I found a group of dazed and wilted travelers after their trying charter flight and a night shuttling between London's Gatwick and Heathrow airports.

"I hope Simca's English is good," said Ginny, speaking for all of them. They felt secure in a kitchen but quite lost in French. It was nearly sunset by the time I'd collected them, and as their "expert on France and French driving," I missed all the right turns to get to Plascassier and La Campanette; we nearly had to spend the night in Antibes.

When we rolled in, night had fallen, but we were greeted by Simca and Jean, both beaming and affable. We fueled the general merriment by fortifying ourselves with a hearty Scotch. "We're wrecks," I explained to Simca, embarrassed that I was still mystified by Provençal roads.

"We hope you'll like the kitchen." Jean smiled, proudly showing off the new decor and equipment. He would often be back to deal with the ornery dishwasher.

Simca, looking tall, efficient, and sure of herself, was trying to be reassuring. "Of course, we'll be starting with some basics," she said, taking little note of our group's crumpled miens. "Even if you know them, it never hurts to brush up. Would you like afternoon lessons too?" Somebody suppressed a giggle. We were punch-drunk, if not quite euphoric from the Scotch.

"How old did you say she is?" asked my mother, truly impressed when I replied, "All of seventy." In fact, our whole little group was struck by Simca's regal and elegant bearing.

We went off to Valbonne for a simple dinner in a semi-tacky bistro, fortunately our only mediocre gastronomic experience the whole time we were there.

Next morning, we were awakened by some energetic plant-watering outside our windows, and we drew the curtains back to see a gnarled, leathery lady wrestling with the hose and sprinklers. "Bonjour, Mesdames," she said cheerfully, introducing herself as Thérèse, the gardener. She would also be a faithful fill-in helper to us—emptying garbage, scraping dishes, making beds.

We had not even had time to down a cup of coffee when a group appeared—Simca and her assistant, escorted by the two dogs: Phano, the big brindle wire-haired mutt, and Iota, the young black miniature poodle. "Feeling courageous?" Simca beamed, obviously in brighter shape than our jet-lagged gang. "We'll start right in today with short pastry, milk bread, a new kind of pizza, and a few other recipes."

She and her assistant were bustling about as we watched in a kind of daze. Plump little Jeannette, Simca's cook, appeared to join the throng. She spoke no English but won everybody immediately with her twinkling smile, grandmotherly crimped hair under a sun hat, and jogging shoes. She was chewing on an herb.

We started to pitch in, everybody setting to different chores of gathering herbs, chopping onions, mixing dough. The kitchen was soon filled with the tempting smells of cooking onions, tomatoes, pastry, and herbs. Simca's use of herbs was prodigal. "They're right from the garden," she said, dumping a handful into the frying pan. "You can hardly use enough of them."

"Something's burning!" I said, removing the onions from the stove. "Non, non, non, mon petit! Don't do that yet," cautioned Simca. "The onions have to cook till they're totally fatigued!" Jeannette laughingly threw up her hands and explained that the odor we'd noticed was burning leaves.

At first leery of her new gadget, the food processor, Simca was soon grappling with the plastic top to get the thing pulsing. It was a revolutionary innovation back then, and it finally worked. "When you're mixing dough," said Simca, "you can see by the way that the dough comes together in one piece that it is ready to remove. But I think I prefer the old-fashioned mixing bowl." (She soon became an old hand and devotee of this kitchen helper.)

Jeannette wouldn't have any truck with such an object. "You never know when it might bite back," she said, grinning as she ground away at an old-fashioned hand shredder for a zucchini dish.

"Ouch," cried my mother, burning her hand as she took something out of the oven. "Never fear," said Simca. "Here's my truc." She grabbed a potato from the larder, peeled it in a jiffy, and handed my mother a quarter of it. "The starch in that takes the burning sensation out." As indeed it did, Mother concurred.

A whirlwind of energy, Simca was doing pretty well at keeping her eye (if not both her hands) on all the different dishes, as we were already starting pre-preparation for the next day's lesson.

"I need a little strengthenin' medicine," said Winnie Stuart in her soft Southern accent around noon, so we broke out a bottle of chilled white wine and jumped into our first apéritif. The table was elegantly set by the time we sat down to sample our first "Simca's Cuisine," which we thoroughly enjoyed, especially the savory onion-cheese-anchovy Provençal pizza with tomato sauce.

"And," said Simca as we toasted her prowess in the kitchen, "I also elaborated another style of pizza I called 'Venetian,' with mozzarella cheese. Pizza's one of those things you can play around with."

After our monumental lunches, we had to force ourselves not to give in to daily afternoon-long siestas, often going sightseeing instead—mainly to nearby art museums. They are excellent places to bone up on culture and walk off a few ounces, if not pounds.

We lived through a sybaritic week of Simca's wickedly rich chocolate desserts, at least four kinds of soufflé, her extravagant pastry-covered sea bass, which we decided looked positively cute with its little eyes and scales as fashioned by Simca's slim fingers. She has very attractive, expressive hands—ideal for her métier.

"What did you learn?" friends asked when I got back to Paris. What could I say? How to fillet a sole, beat egg whites until they're an artwork of peaks, get a fish suited up in pastry? Simca's lessons are more than that. For one thing, they're fun. For another, they're an inspiration. So I came up with: "I learned that I need a helluva lot of practice."

I've been back several times to attend or help out with classes at La Campanette, but I think no visit there has been more fun than that first one.

My mother, Madeleine Beck

Otherwise satisfying years for me, the seventies were marred by the death of my brother Maurice at age seventy-four, in 1975. Maurice had inherited the Rainfreville property from my mother and lived there until he died, but his children finally had to sell it, since they already had their own houses, and Rainfreville posed problems about getting children to classes at different times in Dieppe. So the old house sadly disappeared from our lives to new owners. It still stands, but I am sorry to see that many of the big and beautiful trees have been razed and the lawns look unkempt, detracting from the charm of our childhood home. I still miss my older brother, but always cheer up with periodic visits from his children—my Beck nephews, Maurice Henri, Jean-Claude, Michel, a sculptor, and Christian, who is still working in the silicate business in Normandy—and their wives.

Besides Michael as my official assistant, I had a wonderful friend, Mary-Helene DeLong, from Anoka, Minnesota, who spent nearly one whole winter assisting me in my kitchen, helping me with my correspondence, teaching me all kinds of things about Americans and their food attitudes. She was frail, cheerful, and gentle, and I was terribly grieved when she died barely middle-aged in 1982.

When Jean and I finally left Neuilly to live at Bramafam, I think Jean, born and raised a "city boy," missed Paris more than I did. I'd had my fill of the increasing concrete blocks going up, the inconveniences of driving along clogged streets, the noise and pollution.

"Relaxing" down at Bramafam, we were leading a more active life than ever. There were always my groups of pupils, as varied in personality as pupils in college classes, though most had a common and sincere interest in food. Some understood cooking principles right away: how you've got to be deftly light-fingered with your puff pastry; how you have to improvise if anything goes wrong; how you have to taste as you add seasonings, rather than slavishly follow a recipe. Other pupils were clearly not very gifted. They would ask rather silly questions, like: "Why do you boil the tomato before you peel it?" (Answer: You don't; you just plunge it in simmering water to loosen the skin.) Or: "How many minutes do you cook the onions to get them to that translucent stage?" (Answer: That all depends.)

Thanks to *Simca's Cuisine,* I was traveling for professional reasons. One of my most exciting trips was to Venice in the fall of 1974 to do a series of demonstrations with Julie Dannenbaum at the Gritti Palace. Michael accompanied me as my asssitant and, with his eye for the beautiful, was just as dazzled as I was by the Gritti's splendor and Venice itself. We found time to sightsee, and we took tea at Florian's, where the tourists were surrounded by pigeons, the Piazza San Marco was covered with pigeon droppings, and the café orchestra manfully belted out "Arrivederci, Roma." But mainly we were very busy organizing our equipment and produce, sharpening our knives daily, laying out the vegetables and fish or meat to prepare, communicating in fractured Italian with kitchen employees.

This was the first of nine wonderful trips to Italy in successive years. Once, we even stayed at Rome's Grand Hotel. Demonstrations there were a trial, because Michael had to rig up a system for cooking on top of the complicated stove, an arcane thing that supposedly could be used to cook eight dishes at different temperatures. But no matter what he did, the whole stove—oven and all—seemed to turn into a mighty, brazier-hot inferno the minute the gas was lit. My legs were usually cooked before lunch was! We were very glad to say *Arrivederci, Roma.*

Seven stints at the Cipriani in Venice were more successful, since the hotel's efficient manager, Natale Rusconi, furnished us with a very big and professional demonstration area above the hotel's restaurant, overlooking the lagoon. Venice has a peculiar smell—a mixture of salt water and pollution—but I happen to like it, because it's unique to that shimmering city. And it never seemed to interfere with the taste of the food there; in fact, both the students and ourselves had good appetites. We were teaching mainly French dishes, but I fully appreciated the world's "other" great cuisine, that of Italy, which is usually so straightforward and honest, both colorful and tasty.

The terrace at Le Mas Vieux.

Un déjeuner élégant au Cipriani à Venise

An Elegant Lunch with Natale Rusconi
at the Cipriani in Venice

✦ *Pizza veneziana*
Venetian pizza

✦ *Terrine de volaille pollo verde Cipriani*
Cipriani-style terrine of chicken baked in the skin

Salade verte mixte

—

Vin rouge léger italien

✦ *Neige de framboises*
Raspberry snow mousse

—

Champagne demi-sec

Pizza veneziana

Venetian Pizza

—

For 6 to 8

Half the recipe for Pizza Dough (see
  following recipe), made the day before

For topping:
6–8 ripe tomatoes
½ cup strong Dijon mustard
4 egg yolks
1 lb. mozzarella or Fontina cheese
1 Tbsp. finely minced garlic

Salt and pepper
Dried herbes de Provence (see page 503)
½ cup grated Parmesan cheese
½ cup tiny Niçoise olives, pitted
Olive oil

Special equipment needed:
A 10″ by 15″ rectangular baking tray,
  lightly greased

Prepare the pizza dough the day before and refrigerate, wrapped in plastic.

Slice the tomatoes ⅜″ thick, lay on paper towels, and sprinkle with salt to remove excess moisture. After a few minutes, pat dry with paper towels and transfer to a baking sheet lined with aluminum foil. Place under the broiler for a few minutes to dry and half cook the tomatoes, then set aside to cool.

Roll out the dough and fit it into the baking tray, pressing with your fingers until it fits the pan exactly. Build up the edges slightly to make a border to contain the filling. Using a pastry brush, paint the dough first with mustard and then with beaten egg yolks. Cover with an even layer of mozzarella slices, overlapping them slightly so the pizza is completely covered. Sprinkle with minced garlic and salt, pepper, and herbs, to taste. Top with cooked tomato slices, and sprinkle with half the Parmesan cheese, and sprinkle with drops of olive oil.

Set in a preheated 400°F oven and bake for 15 minutes. Remove from oven and sprinkle the remaining Parmesan, olives, and a little olive oil over the filling, then return to the oven for 15–20 minutes to finish baking. If possible, let cool completely and reheat several hours later.

Serve tepid, cut in little squares (*bouchées*) for parties, or in a large rectangle for lunch.

Short-Pastry Pizza Dough

—

For 2 pizzas (10 to 12 servings)
Enough dough to make two 10" by 15" pizzas
For 10 to 12 servings

4 cups flour

1 tsp. salt

1 cup plus 4 Tbsp. cold butter, cut into small cubes

1 egg, beaten with 3 Tbsp. ice water or cold white wine

Special equipment needed:

A large mixing bowl

A large fork

*P*repare dough 1 day before serving the pizza. Put flour and salt in a large mixing bowl and stir with a large fork to mix. Add butter cubes, and blend with a large fork until butter is thoroughly incorporated into the dry ingredients. Moisten with the egg and water (or wine), and stir briefly to mix. Shape into a ball, wrap in plastic, and refrigerate overnight.

Terrine de volaille pollo verde cipriani

Cipriani-Style Terrine of Chicken Baked in the Skin

—

For 10 to 12

One 4–5 lb. roasting chicken or turkey

7 oz. prosciutto, in ⅛" slices

2 Tbsp. butter

½ tsp. dried thyme

1 lb. boiled Canadian bacon (which is similar to French ham)

¼ tsp. ground coriander

1 chicken gizzard

2 Tbsp. dried herbes de Provence (see
    Aide-Mémoire, page 503)
6 oz. chicken livers
⅓ cup Cognac or bourbon
3 whole eggs
1 egg yolk
1 cup crème fraîche (page 501) or heavy
    cream
Salt, pepper, and nutmeg
12 pistachios, peeled and halved
1 bay leaf

Optional: If you use turkey instead of
    chicken, increase the Canadian bacon
    by an amount sufficient to line the
    bottom, sides, and top of a 10-cup
    ceramic terrine

Special equipment needed:
A food processor
A 10-cup ceramic terrine with lid
A bain-marie (see page 503)

*U*sing a sharp knife, carefully remove the skin of the chicken in one piece and set aside. It will be used to line the terrine.

Bone the chicken, removing the breast meat and cutting it into strips. Remove the rest of the chicken meat from the carcass and chop roughly in a food processor with half the prosciutto, the Canadian bacon, ground coriander, the butter, and the gizzard. Mix all in a bowl, stirring in the herbes de Provence and the thyme.

Trim the chicken livers and cut each into quarters. Macerate in half the Cognac or bourbon, reserving the rest for the filling.

Lightly beat the eggs and the extra yolk in a bowl, then whisk in the crème fraîche. Add to the ground meat mixture and mix well. Correct the seasoning, adding salt, pepper, or nutmeg, if needed. Stir in the reserved Cognac or bourbon.

Cut the reserved prosciutto slices into thin strips about ⅔″ wide. These will be used to separate the chicken breast strips from the livers. Line the terrine with the reserved chicken skin. Spread ⅓ of the ground chicken mixture evenly in the bottom of the terrine, pressing down on it with moistened hands to remove any air holes. Cover with a layer of prosciutto (3–4 slices), then make an elegant design by placing half the chicken breast strips with some pistachios along the sides and half the chicken livers, well seasoned, in a line down the center. Cover with another third of the ground chicken mixture. Repeat the design with the chicken breast strips, pistachios, and livers, then finish with a layer of ground chicken mixture. Cover all with chicken skin, and put a bay leaf on top. Place the lid on the terrine and seal with flour paste made with 1 cup flour and ¼ cup water.

Bake in a bain-marie (see Aide-Mémoire) in a preheated 375°F oven for 1½–1¾ hours. When done, remove the lid and replace with aluminum foil and a weight to compress the pâté (in a refrigerator) for about 12 hours.

Neige de framboises

Raspberry Snow Mousse

—

For about 10

For snow mousse:
¾ cup sugar
¼ cup cold water
3 large egg whites
Pinch of salt
2 cups heavy cream
½ tsp. vanilla extract

For flavored filling:
1 lb. fresh raspberries or strawberries
  OR
3 Tbsp. Cognac
2 Tbsp. instant coffee
  OR
3½ oz. dark bittersweet chocolate
1 Tbsp. instant coffee granules

2 Tbsp. Cognac
4 Tbsp. water

Special equipment needed:
A small saucepan (preferably copper) for boiling sugar syrup
A copper basin and a whisk for beating egg whites
A 4-cup stainless-steel mixing bowl for whipping cream
A stainless-steel bowl with splayed opening to allow easy unmolding
A food mill
A chilled mixing bowl for mixing filling of snow mousse
A chilled platter

*P*lace sugar and ¼ cup cold water in a copper saucepan, and bring to a boil. Let boil until the syrup thickens and reaches the "thread" stage. Meanwhile, beat the egg whites with a pinch of salt and a drop of water in a copper basin until they are half beaten, then immediately start pouring the boiling syrup in a thin stream into the egg whites, while beating vigorously. Continue to beat until the whites are stiff and shiny, then place the bowl over ice cubes and continue to beat until the meringue is very thick, smooth, and cool.

Pour the heavy cream into a 4-cup stainless-steel bowl set over ice and whip the cream with vanilla extract until it is almost firm. Lightly fold the cooled meringue into the whipped cream, then spoon this mixture into a stainless-steel mixing bowl with a splayed opening and freeze for 2½ hours, or until the mousse has set around the edges to a thickness of about ½″.

While the mousse is freezing, prepare the flavoring for the filling. For a red fruit filling, crush fresh raspberries (or strawberries) in a food mill, saving a few to decorate the mousse, then strain the juice to remove any seeds. Set the juice in the refrigerator to chill until needed. (See variations below for coffee-flavored and chocolate-coffee fillings.)

When the snow mousse has set around the edges 1½″ thick, scoop out the unset center and place in a chilled mixing bowl, leaving the frozen shell. Beat the chilled raspberry juice into the unset mousse, mixing thoroughly, then spoon this mixture back into the center of the set mousse. Tap the bottom of the bowl sharply on the counter to settle the mousse, then level off the top. Return the snow mousse to the freezer for another 2–3 hours. When ready, the center should not be frozen as hard as the edges but remain somewhat creamy in texture.

To serve, unmold onto a chilled serving platter. Decorate the top with fresh raspberries.

Variation I: M O C H A S N O W M O U S S E
Heat the cognac with the instant coffee, and stir until dissolved. Cover and set aside. When the mousse has frozen about 1″ from the side of the bowl, remove from freezer, scoop out the unfrozen center into an iced mixing bowl, and stir in the coffee-brandy mixture. Spoon the coffee-flavored filling into the center, and place in the freezer. Proceed as directed above.

Variation II: C H O C O L A T E - M O C H A C O F F E E S N O W M O U S S E
Melt chocolate with instant coffee, Cognac, and water, stirring until completely dissolved. Cover and set aside until the mousse has frozen about 1″ from sides of bowl, then proceed as above.

DURING THOSE YEARS, I had another wonderful assistant, Akiko, a Japanese-American who was an avid cook as well as a very hard worker. Like so many Japanese, she was, in fact, a perfectionist, which pleased me no end. Her deft hands with a knife turned out many beautifully fashioned vegetables and dishes, which were as beautiful to behold as ikebana flower arrangements.

On the Road

THE SEVENTIES WERE our big travel years, as Jean, with the leisure time his retirement afforded, wanted to see more of the world. Venice was a good embarkation point for Mediterranean cruises, and we took several. I can be a frantic traveler, but Jean always kept his cool, sometimes irking me with his phlegmatic approach.

Once, we were due to board a Greek luxury liner, and Jean was stalling and stalling. By the time "Monsieur" was ready to move, we and the porter reached the harbor and saw the ship pulling away. I was livid. "Look at us now!" I screamed. "What about our holiday?" Jean just sat down on the luggage, winked at me (which drove me crazy), and said, "Don't worry. We'll make it."

Sure enough, another luxury liner in the same Greek line was just mooring. Jean boarded it, recognized the ship's doctor, whom we'd befriended on another cruise, and they had a short chat. "No problem," said the doctor, who consulted with the ship's captain, and our reservations were validated. We were even allotted the most luxurious cabin on the boat—far superior to what we'd had on the one that sailed away. "See, *chérie,*" gloated Jean. "It doesn't pay to worry so; in fact, it pays to miss the boat!" And we had our cruise, with two beautiful weeks in Crete.

A remarkable cruise that I took on my own was to Morocco. It was based (rather oddly) on cheese and wine. But the guest star was Pierre Androuet, an authority known as Monsieur Fromage—or the "big cheese" of cheese—because of the high quality of the products he purveyed in his restaurant in Paris for over fifty years, until it was bought out by Air France just a couple of years ago.

Androuet is an affable, bright man who is built like a barrel but is in fine health and still wheels around France (driving like a madman, I've heard; I'd like to see him beat me!), lecturing and tasting. He was wonderful on that trip, an articulate and incisive lecturer who never bored anybody when he explained just how you recognize truly great cheeses. Camembert, for example, should have a rough and rustic rind with red spots rather than a pretty and smooth white appearance. He also pointed out the best types of wine for each group of cheeses. Androuet is full of advice, but he often trots out the old chestnut that he attributes to Churchill (others insist it's de Gaulle's): "How on earth can you govern a country that makes over 365 kinds of cheese?"

In 1974, I took two trips. One was to the Napa Valley, to give demonstrations at an estate near Rutherford named High Trees for the towering eucalyptuses flanking the road to the house. As organized by Michael, who was running the whole event, it was more fun than work for me.

The other trip was more exotic, to the Far East, with Jean and several friends. If Bali was beautiful, Borneo was an adventure. By now it must be clear that while I'm something of a sport, I'm no girl scout; I like my comforts. Our stay in a so-called long house was unforgettable. I can only be thankful it wasn't our honeymoon. We arrived at the hotel, which consisted of a couple of "long houses" perched about twenty feet off the ground on stilts, and clambered up a ladder, the boys bringing our luggage after us.

"How quaint!" cried my friend Solange, the Comtesse de Ganay. The women were to sleep on mats laid side by side in one long house; the men were similarly bunked in another. This Spartan arrangement was curious enough. But the sanitary facility was even more exiguous: a lone hole, off to one side. This didn't much bother the men, who chortled about it. But it wasn't so funny for the women. I think a few of us suffered silently until an opportune moment during the next day's tour.

Back home, I started work on my next book, *New Menus from Simca's Cuisine*, with Michael as my assistant to help couch everything in idiomatic English. In this book I concentrated on items that were sometimes inspired by American friends, new versions of classic recipes, and so on. Once, Jim Beard had said, "How on earth do you cook carrots?" So I gave a recipe to answer that query: a delicious way to slow-cook carrots and brussels sprouts. There are some exotic new desserts as well, inspired partially by trips to the Far East, though I must say I think our French desserts made with exotic ingredients are more interesting than the sweets of Tahiti. Our publisher was Harcourt Brace Jovanovich, and the book came out in 1979. I toured Arizona and Texas with Michael in 1980 to sell the book, and we also went to New York. While it was grand to stay in the best hotels and be driven around by a chauffeur in a stretch limousine, I wondered if Michael's tastes weren't somewhat grand for my pocketbook.

Jean and I had been doing lots of traveling: to Israel, Crete, Turkey, Dubrovnik, and the Adriatic coast, among other places. The classic Black Sea and Russian cruise was interesting but gave me no gastronomic illumination whatsoever. On the contrary, we saw for ourselves what a truly poor country the USSR was. We could buy vodka and caviar rather cheaply, while the people themselves had to pay much more, even in "dollar shops," for the caviar—when they could procure dollars. Everything, including the much-touted borscht, was pretty tasteless.

I'm sure cuisine was better back in czarist days; after a supposedly gala Russian lunch with other cruise passengers in Odessa, where we were treated to one bottle of vodka per ten people and a miserable slice of hard-boiled egg to accompany tough brown bread and barely a teaspoon of caviar, we were approached by some Russian women, who wanted to buy our hats and gloves. They were so grateful when we took them off and made gifts of them.

Our trip of trips was the world tour we took with Michael in 1979, when the *New Menus* book was completed but not yet out. Credit where it's due: Michael was a perfect travel agent, with all the arrangements in hand to take us to the South Pacific, Australia, and India.

But we had a terrible start. I had fallen and broken my wrist, which was in a cast. And Jean came down with a very high fever just a couple of days before leaving. He said, "I'll make it anyway," deciding we could not miss out on this great adventure. We flew to California, then to Tahiti, though Jean was still very ill and looked at his lowest as we were about to continue on via plane and boat to Bora Bora.

Although just as lush a tropical isle as shown in the brochures, Bora Bora was not up to our hopes and expectations. There was not much to do but gaze at the tropical flowers and limpid water in the coral shoals and eat fresh fish and fruit. However, Jean did start to feel better.

We loved Australia, where I gave cooking demonstrations with a fellow professional, Belgian-born Wivine de Stoop. I had to struggle through, the cast still on my arm. The Australians seem to exist on their barbecues, but I think I prefer just cooking a steak in a big dollop of butter to that charred effect!

The next stop was Bombay, from which we went on to stay in a palace outside Indore with friends of ours, Richard and Sally Holkar. Richard was half American, but he had inherited the title of maharajah and the ancient palace of Manik Bagh from his grandfather, the Maharajah of Maheshwar.

Though sari-clad women drifted by our room at dawn as if out of a dream, they were on their way to prosaic chores—to wash themselves and their clothes. During the day, many of them worked on a silk-weaving loom that Sally had provided, turning out saris they could sell. This was a fine cottage industry for that country, where, like all tourists, I saw too many scrawny sacred cows and sadly under-nourished people to feel totally at ease with all the comforts we were provided with.

Sally served authentic Indian food, elegantly presented by a butler: silver plates with little bowls holding the dishes and spicy sauces—some very hot and piquant, which I liked. India is redolent of the spices that make up *garam masala*—which we lump somewhat vulgarly in the West under a fairly uniform taste and the name of curry. Sally told us that all self-respecting Indian cooks grind up spices to make their own combinations—as her cook did, sitting on the floor in the kitchen.

Our first dinner was a surprise, as we saw that everyone was eating from his or her hands—the Indian custom. The butler assiduously passed bowls of water for rinsing, but Jean and I preferred not to go native and used the forks beside our plates.

We had had a dramatic first night in Bombay. "Come, madame, there's a fire." The 5:00 A.M. summons from a porter in the magnificent Taj Mahal Hotel was urgent, if low in tone. I hesitated at leaving all our things behind, maybe to burn. "*Du calme,* Simca," said Jean, fastening his bathrobe. A young hotel boy promised he'd stand guard outside our room.

Joining all the other mystified half-clad guests in the hotel lobby, many with luggage piled up around them, we learned that there had been a minor conflagration in a hotel nightclub, and the rugs had caught fire. It was nearly extinguished, but the corridors were still filled with noxious smoke.

As a treat to make up for our inconvenience, the maître d'hôtel conducted the whole assemblage of guests to a brunch feast in the dining room, where the whole staff of splendidly garbed waiters was on hand to give us anything we ordered. Some of the guests took this opportunity to order everything on the menu. Jean and I contented ourselves with caviar and Champagne, a few delicate sweets for a dessert. Not bad for a 6:00 A.M. snack! When we came back to our room, I found a magnificent bouquet of roses on my dressing table and a plate of petits fours, along with a letter of apology for the inconvenience.

With Jeannette

Later trips took us to various Far East stops, including China, to me a somewhat overrated travel destination, probably so attractive to tourists because it has been a mystery for so long. Nevertheless, we were impressed by the beautiful monuments in Beijing, by the Great Wall, and by the fantastic life-size heads and bodies of the military statues in Xian, recently unearthed and a prime attraction in that vast country.

Foodwise, I have to say that I was not thrilled with most of these exotic places, especially mainland China. Hong Kong and San Francisco are much better off for Oriental gastronomy.

Japan? Except for the artful food presentation, I simply do not understand their way of eating at all and would never set foot in a Japanese restaurant again. Sushi and sashimi left Jean and me cold; in fact, we wouldn't dream of eating raw fish. But we probably never ate better or more tender beef than Kobe, which everyone knows is the product of very pampered cattle who drink beer and get daily massages.

After all our gastronomic adventures or disasters, we were always glad to make it home to Bramafam in one piece. However, Jean was starting to have recurring health problems, mainly after that infection he had carried through the Far East trip. His blood sugar was too high, and he was supposed to follow a fairly sugar-free diet. But it was torture for him to forgo things like chocolate desserts, and out of sympathy I just had to turn a blind eye when he served himself a large second helping of chocolate cake or mousse.

Our faithful Jeannette was still doing home cooking for us—my favorite simple vegetable potages in the evening, delicious salads and broiled meat or fish at lunch. But she had diabetes, and her eyesight was failing; she would soon "retire," to be replaced by younger cooks.

Jean continued to be active—overseeing our grounds and gardening, taking care of paying the help and filling out the endless social security forms we had to send in as employers, managing our accounts, and seeing that our cars were running smoothly.

I have never smoked, but unfortunately Jean did, though he tried to conceal it from me, knowing I was concerned about his health. When a household of women or too many visitors overwhelmed him, he'd take a walk uphill to our little pond, which doubles as a small swimming pool. There he would sit and meditate—and more often than not enjoy a cigarette.

We had our little spats about smoking but got along fine in the car, as we both loved fast driving. There was no discussion as we would race up to Paris in seven- or eight-hour sprints, stopping only for a picnic snack. However, after Jean suffered a minor stroke in 1976, which caused him to lose most of the sight in one eye, I usually did the driving.

We still kept up with old Paris friends, and I liked entertaining on a rather grand scale. We put on some gala receptions or more informal brunches on our Bramafam terrace—always my favorite place for lunch, dinner, or brunch when the weather was fine.

Un brunch à Bramafam

A Joyous Bramafam Brunch on the Terrace

✦ *Kougelhof aux lardons et aux noix de macadamie*
Kugelhopf with bacon and macadamia nuts

—

Vodka glacé (chilled or on the rocks)

✦ *Fricandeau de veau*
Veal with Mushrooms, Norman style

✦ *Salade composée au riz*
Mixed rice salad Provençale

Salade verte

—

Un bon vin rosé

✦ *Gâteau de fête au chocolat et aux framboises*
Chocolate feast cake with raspberries

—

Vin blanc mousseux (sparkling white wine)

Kougelhof aux lardons et aux noix de macadamie

Kugelhopf with Bacon and Macadamia Nuts

—

For 4 to 6

1½ oz. fresh yeast or 4 packages active
   dry yeast
5 tsp. sugar
6½ Tbsp. sweet butter
½ lb. slightly smoked bacon or smoked
   pork breast
About 10 Tbsp. flour
1 tsp. salt

1–2 eggs, depending on size
1 oz. macadamia nuts (or English
   walnuts), roughly chopped

Special equipment needed:
A special kugelhopf or charlotte mold,
   4″–5″ in diameter and 6″ high

*B*utter the mold and set aside. Dissolve the yeast and sugar in ½ cup tepid water, and set aside. Cut the butter into pieces, and set aside.

If the bacon is very smoky, place in a pan of cold water, bring to the boil, and let boil for 3 minutes. Drain the parboiled bacon, refresh under cold tap water, then drain again and let dry on paper towels. Remove and discard the rind, cut into very small dice, and sauté in a nonstick pan to remove excess fat. Drain on paper towels.

Sift the flour and salt into a large mixing bowl. Make a well in the flour and add the dissolved yeast, the egg(s), and the butter. Working with your hands or an electric mixer with a dough hook, mix vigorously until the dough becomes smooth and elastic and pulls away from the sides of the bowl (about 5–6 minutes).

Turn into a smaller mixing bowl, make a cross on the top with kitchen scissors, sprinkle with flour, and cover loosely with a hot kitchen towel. Let rise over a pan of warm, not hot, water (100°F) until double in bulk, about 45 minutes. Punch down to remove the gas, and work the diced bacon and chopped nuts evenly throughout the dough.

Let rise and deflate again in the same way, then fill the buttered pan, and bake in a preheated 375°F oven for about 40–45 minutes, or until well risen and nicely browned. Let cool, turning the kugelhopf over when it is tepid. When completely cool, cut into wedges and serve.

Fricandeau de veau

Veal with Mushrooms, Norman Style

—

For 6 to 8

4 lb. top round veal roast

4 cups cooled scalded milk

1½ Tbsp. olive oil

½ head garlic, cloves separated but not peeled

Salt and pepper

1 bay leaf

2 Tbsp. Calvados or bourbon

10 oz. white mushrooms, cleaned, sliced, and sprinkled with lemon juice

Special equipment needed:

A heavy-bottomed cast-iron skillet with lid (or Dutch oven)

Parchment paper

*W*hen choosing meat for a milk-based veal stew such as this, the best choice is the tender portion of the top round roast from the leg. Select a piece approximately 2½″ thick, and remove any nerves and gristle. Tie into a neat bundle with kitchen string. Place in the pot and cover with cooled boiled milk, olive oil, garlic cloves, salt, pepper, and bay leaf, and let macerate 1–2 days in the refrigerator.

To cook, place the pot, uncovered, in a cold oven. Heat the oven to 325°F, carefully watching the cooking so the milk does not boil over the sides of the pot. Keeping the milk at a simmer, let cook for 45 minutes to an hour, or until the milk has thickened in consistency and the meat is slightly browned. When done, remove the meat and keep warm, and strain the milk through a food mill to purée the garlic and remove the peels. Return the garlic purée to the cooking liquid and correct the seasoning, adding the Calvados or bourbon. Bring all to the simmer for a few minutes to evaporate the alcohol, then return the meat to the pot, add the sliced mushrooms, and let cook for at least 6–8 minutes. The mushrooms should be a little undercooked.

When ready to serve, reheat if necessary, then cut into thick slices to serve with the mushrooms around the meat.

Vegetable Suggestion: Serve with a side dish of sautéed cucumbers: Peel, seed, and slice the cucumbers in half lengthwise, then dice. Blanch in boiling salted water. Refresh in ice water, drain, and set aside until ready to serve. Just before serving, sauté in butter to heat, then serve sprinkled with minced chives or parsley.

Wine Suggestion: A sparkling cider.

Salade composée au riz

Mixed Rice Salad Provençale

—

For 8 to 12

Coarse salt
2 cups raw long-grain white rice
2 Tbsp. chopped parsley
½ cup well-drained canned sweet corn
½ cup pitted, diced Niçoise olives
½ cup diced canned pimiento
½ cup canned tiny sweet green peas

3–4 canned anchovy fillets, cut in small dice
1½ cups Mock Mayonnaise with herbs (page 474)

Special equipment needed:
A large pot with lid
A colander
A mixing bowl

$\mathscr{P}$lace 3 qt. water and a handful of coarse salt in a large pot. Bring to the boil, then pour raw rice into the water and let simmer, covered, 16–18 minutes, or until tender. Immediately pour into a colander and refresh with cold tap water, letting the water run to stop the cooking and rinse away the salt. If necessary, the rice can be prepared to this point the day before, and held.

Prepare the other ingredients, cutting all the vegetables and the anchovies the same size as the corn kernels. Mix together with the rice and set aside, covered, until just before serving.

Prepare Mock Mayonnaise with herbs and keep aside until ready to serve. (The eggless mayonnaise can be made in large batches; it keeps well in the refrigerator for 1–2 weeks.) Just before serving, stir the green mayonnaise into the rice mixture. When well blended, correct the seasoning, and serve in a salad bowl.

Gâteau de fête au chocolat et aux framboises

Chocolate Feast Cake with Raspberries

—

For 12 to 16

2¼ lb. raspberries
1 cup granulated sugar
14 oz. quality dark unsweetened
   chocolate
4 envelopes unflavored gelatin
2 cups heavy cream
Confectioners' sugar in a shaker

Special equipment needed:
A génoise cake pan (9″ diameter by
   2″ deep)
A food mill fitted with the finest
   disk
An electric beater
Ice cubes

Crush and strain 1¼ lb. of the raspberries through the food mill. At the same time, bring 2 cups water and the sugar to the boil. Continue to boil until the bubbles are large (the "soft ball" stage). Pour the raspberry juice into the syrup, and let boil 2 minutes, stirring.

Melt the chocolate with ½ cup water, stirring until completely smooth, then pour the raspberry syrup into the chocolate and stir all until very smooth. Soften the gelatin in ½ cup raspberry juice (made by pressing a large handful of the remaining berries through the food mill). When softened, stir vigorously into the chocolate–raspberry juice mixture. Continue stirring vigorously until the mixture is quite smooth and the gelatin has completely dissolved. Let cool completely, but do not allow the mixture to set.

Pour the cream into a bowl set over ice, and whip into a soft, not too stiff, Chantilly. Fold the Chantilly into the cool chocolate mixture and continue folding until the mixture is completely homogenous.

Line the bottom of the cake pan with plastic wrap to help in the unmolding, then fill the pan with the chocolate raspberry cream, smoothing the top with a metal spatula dipped in water. Cover with another piece of plastic wrap and place in the refrigerator for several hours, or until set.

When time to serve, slip the cake onto a serving plate and remove the plastic. Garnish the top with the remaining raspberries, placed close together, in rows and standing up. Using a shaker, sprinkle confectioners' sugar over the raspberries, sprinkling on more just before serving.

For a birthday, place candles between the raspberries.

Wine Suggestion: A perfect brut Champagne, such as Bollinger or Perrier-Jouët.

THE CHILDS WERE SOMETIMES in residence next door, but we kept to our private lives fairly scrupulously, as Julia would be working on her latest writing or TV projects and Paul continued painting in acrylic his beautiful landscapes and taking evocative photographs of our beloved Provençal setting—his other great artistic talent.

THE YOUNGER GENERATION

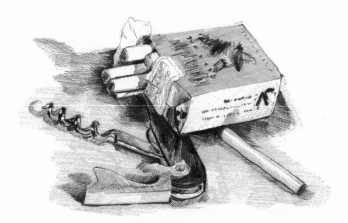

AYOUNGER GROUP IS TAKING OVER the toques now, and if I were to name my many talented friends, it would be a whole new book. But the La Varenne cooking school was a landmark. Julia, who had met English-born Anne Willan in Washington, encouraged her to fulfill her lifelong dream to start a new cooking school in Paris. Up to that point, the Cordon Bleu had had a near monopoly as a serious cooking school there.

When Anne found a good locale for a cooking school on the Rue Saint Dominique, I, along with Julia, Jim Beard, and others, became an investor and "god-parent" to La Varenne. Anne transformed a dilapidated building into gleaming kitchens, and the school was opened in late 1974. While it was considered a curiosity by French amateur cooks, who think they need no lessons, Americans took to it.

As my eightieth birthday rolled around in 1984, La Varenne hosted a surprise reception for me. I had been invited to present diplomas to newly graduated pupils. But the tables were turned, and I turned pink as a shrimp and had to laugh when Anne and Susy Davidson, the current executive head of the school, handed me the

Grand Diplôme. It had taken me nearly three quarters of a century in the kitchen—but I finally "graduated" from a cooking school!

My main birthday celebration was a gorgeous terrace-lawn party at Bramafam, laid on by Susy Davidson and Michael James, who managed to prepare everything in secret, for a sensational last-minute surprise.

Restaurant Friends

JEAN AND I LOVED DISCOVERING and frequenting simple bistros, but we also hit many of the "gastronomic temples" and made friends with the chefs. I love living so near Mougins, which has more than its share of good dining, with Roger Vergé's Moulin de Mougins the area high point, along with his less expensive Amandier. I count silver-haired "Jolly Roger" and his wife, Denise, among my good friends. Together, they exemplify good taste, since his food is matched by her superb bouquets and her eye for antiques and decoration.

Roger is a gracious, even an indulgent, host. So many times he's winked and said, "I've something special for you," then come out with a fabulous version of a new taste sensation in a fish mousse or dessert, or a totally traditional and perfect head cheese.

A word here on nouvelle cuisine, which readers must have gathered that I scorn—or at least what it became, so hackneyed and mediocre that scarcely anyone dares mention it anymore, on either side of the Atlantic. Invention is another matter, and let's hope that the inventive, creative spirit of some of our great chefs keeps on. After all, who wants to eat a coq au vin that always tastes the same?

I have a very soft spot in my heart for Michel Guérard. If one must talk of nouvelle cuisine, then this dynamo deserves the title of king in that domain. He is the only one who really did invent a whole new way of cooking, with his marvelous *cuisine minceur* as well as *gourmande*. All of his sauces are miraculously light and harmonious, even the ones made with zero-percent-fat, low-cal fresh cheese. I growl at foolish women who try to diet for no special health reasons but just want to look like fashion models. But Guérard's diet ideas convert to truly acceptable, well-balanced, and delicious food.

In 1980, the Mondavi winemakers from California were in France, along with a party that included my former assistant Michael James, and they all insisted that

Jean and I go over to Eugénie-les-Bains for a party at Michel's. We were accompanied by Michael James. This is quite a trek, 800 kilometers (480 miles) west of Bramafam. It's easy to go north and south in France. But it's easier to cross the Atlantic than to go from Bramafam west to Eugénie. Although I had classes coming up two days later, I dropped everything, and we took the train to Pau, an all-night trip. Then we drove another forty minutes by taxi over to Eugénie-les-Bains.

"You won't want to come along with us for lunch," Michel said, grinning, when we got there. "I'm taking a busman's holiday to go out with the American crowd for cassoulet." So we and Michael stayed at Michel's for a delicious lunch on our own. I glanced covertly at the dieters; it felt at bit like staring at the handicapped. But they looked pretty satisfied with their artistically presented low-cal dishes, while we went all out for total gourmandise as only Michel's brigade can do it—savoring every morsel of foie gras and rich sauces.

It was a Saturday, and I asked Michel if I could attend an evening Mass in the area. "No problem," he said. "One of our girls will drive you; there's a little chapel just around the corner." I got in the car with the girl, who drove, and drove, seemingly in circles, and to make things worse, in pouring rain. It was soon clear that she was completely lost.

The Mass was just ending when I finally walked into the church, and we didn't get back to the hotel till nearly 9:00 P.M. I was exhausted and unnerved, feeling stupid for insisting on attending Mass, wondering if God has a special place for dunces.

But I pulled myself together for dinner with the Mondavi group and their friends. This was not just any old three-star dinner, though that by itself would have been fine with me. Michel put on a one-man show, complete with orchestra. I had no idea he was such a comic, as he sang and danced, doing a sailor's hornpipe in a striped shirt, ending up in drag as a crazy bride cavorting around in white gown and veil. It was hilarious.

Less funny was taking the early-morning train back to Cannes the next day to greet new pupils—after having tumbled into bed at 2:00 A.M. We got up groggily at 5:00, and the same little car that had finally made it to the chapel the night before sputtered and ran out of gas thirty miles from the Pau train station. It was pouring rain, and our driver was beside himself. Finally, a man who said he was a traveling salesman stopped and offered us a lift. We screeched up to the station just a minute before our train was due to pull out. "Jump on!" said Jean, very sportively hopping up, helping Michael to haul the luggage on board as the train started to move.

Guérard is admirable. But another of our greatest French chefs is Swiss. I mean, of course, Fredy Girardet, whom I met after one of my cures at Bourbonne. Crissier is a dreary little suburb of Lausanne, which is positively radiant with Fredy's good food. It was 1972 when Jean came to the spa to pick me up and take a little tourist detour into Savoie and over to Lausanne, where we'd heard about a great new chef. The former town hall converted to a restaurant didn't look like much, though the inside was attractive in a low-keyed way.

But we knew we'd hit the bull's-eye when the delicate dishes began to appear. There were tiny hearts of green cabbages concealing fresh crayfish in a light cream sauce with Beluga caviar; adorable baby pigeons stuffed with foie gras and truffles, surrounded with a truffled sauce. Then there was a rainbow of exquisite *dégustation* desserts—to taste. This was before nouvelle came into fashion. But Fredy's cuisine really was new. A handsome, polite young man who had taught himself most of his cooking secrets, Fredy was a pioneer. Some of our French chefs were coming to sample his cuisine and learn from it. Fredy is still cooking in Crissier, and how nice that is. Happily, he remains that rarity, a chef who wants nothing better than to turn out good food, as opposed to one of those commercial gadflies who would rather be in front of a TV camera in Tokyo, say, than behind the "piano," or stove, at home.

I think Fredy and Michel Guérard most deserve the terms "inventive," "creative," "genius." That horror nouvelle came up when two ambitious journalists decided to coin the phrase for what was happening to cuisine in the mid-1970s, decreeing that fish should be eaten "pink at the bone," a loathsome idea. Thank heavens, the term as well as the poor cuisine associated with nouvelle has gone out of fashion. And if some hapless cook should happen to serve me crunchy, half-cooked vegetables, I say, "Cook it some more, please. I'm not a rabbit."

Richard the Gourmet-Hearted

I'VE KNOWN RICHARD OLNEY for more than twenty-five years, and he did not appear until now in my memoirs because I feel I must devote a whole section to him. Although he was born in Iowa, he is surely one of the best French cooks I know, in some ways a genius. I was in close contact with him ever since he was a young man in Paris, writing for *Cuisine et vins de France*. During the

1960s and 1970s, Julia and I were able to spend more time with him, since we had all made our main homes in Provence—he'd chosen a lovely hillside spot for himself west of Saint-Tropez at Le Pont de Table, in Solliès-Toucas.

Richard's house, in native stone, is almost a part of the landscape, perched as it is on the green and rocky hillside and surrounded with roses, a trellis of them on his terrace. He grows all kinds of herbs, including the highly scented wild thyme that grows in rocks surrounding his swimming pool, built around a natural hollow in the rocks.

Here he's found inspiration for much of his brilliant food writing. His *Simple French Food* is exemplary in its clarity, and his practical Time-Life series on all aspects of French cooking, from soups to meats and desserts, is a detailed tour de force.

I've often been over to see Richard on my own, just for a breath of fresh air on the cooking scene and to pick his brain. He meets me in hot weather garbed in his favorite outfit—shorts and espadrilles. "Nothing special for you today, Simca," he says, smiling, modest as usual. "We'll just have a little snack." His "little snacks" are nothing less than a lesson in the art of using the best possible ingredients for a perfect dish.

"How about some scrambled eggs?" he said one day as we sipped a refreshing Champagne, which he'd fetched from his cave in the rocks. We sat in the shade, lulled by the pleasant susurrus of cicadas in the grass-tufted rocks. He cooked the eggs in a gleaming copper pan, and I could already whiff the incomparable odor of truffles. To make sure the eggs were cooked to just the right soft texture, he put the pan in another pan of water—a bain-marie—and added an amazing amount of butter, plus nearly a cupful of sliced truffles—a very large amount of the "black diamonds" that are so expensive even in France. Although Richard had purchased his truffles several months before in the winter, when they're in season, they gave off an ineffable, extremely pleasant scent. Richard's secret of saving fresh truffles is simple but effective: He brushes them to remove any trace of dirt, wraps them well in foil, and freezes them. "This keeps them in perfect condition for months," he told me.

The perfect dish of truffled eggs was accompanied by excellent wines. Richard knows that my preferred red is Bordeaux, and he served me something special that day, a magnificent Château Margaux, although we had started out with Provençal hors d'oeuvre and a fresh, fruity local Bandol rosé. Dessert was accompanied by a Sauternes, Château d'Yquem—a pure marvel, as I remember. Richard is reverent about Sauternes and has written a fine book on the subject. *Yquem*, in which he

Richard Olney (left) and James Beard lunching on the terrace at Bramafam

explains the miracle of *la pourriture noble* ("noble rot," the term used to describe what happens to the grapes before sweet Sauternes is made), published by Flammarion in 1985. I think Richard has always served me the best French wines I've ever drunk, and right out of that picturesque little cellar under the rocks.

When Richard heard I was writing my life story with recipes, he sent me a flattering and beautifully written piece, which I must include. I can highly recommend his recipes, as I've enjoyed them just the way he describes them.

A Homage to Simca,
by Richard Olney

To several generations of Americans, Simca is a legend—La Grande Dame de la Cuisine Française—*and the old Provençal mas at Bramafam is a pilgrimage site for the international cultists of gastronomy.*

Beneath the cloak of legend lies a rock bed of la vieille France, *a respect for tradition coupled with a fascination for all that is new, a formal correctness of speech often seasoned with rather astonishing expletives, a fierce loyalty to friends, a determination that knows no bounds and sometimes irrationally refuses to recognize any barriers.*

This last quality was painfully illustrated a number of years ago when Simca slipped on the icy steps leading down from her house and broke a leg. She was found some time later, apparently indifferent to the pain but furious at the inconvenience, trying to pound the splintered and protruding bone back into place with the heel of her shoe so that she could get on with her business.

Twenty-five years or more have passed since "yesterday," when we met; Simca thinks more . . . I have lost track. Each year is punctuated by meals shared and exchanged. When Simca comes to Solliès—an hour and a half's drive—it is always for lunch, often accompanied by one or two of her assistants or devoted fans, to whom she has vaunted the wonders of my hillside retreat.

These are usually summer lunches, served in the dappled shade of the grapevine arbor, although the truffle season sometimes provides the occasion for a winter lunch before the fireplace.

The formula is simple: a first course, a main course, salad, a cheese platter and, sometimes, a light dessert; Champagne for apéritif, a still white wine, two red wines from the same region, and an old Sauternes or another noble rot wine, served either with the dessert or in guise of dessert. Simca's greatest passion amongst wines is Château Margaux, and when I have not chosen a Margaux '53 or '59 to wind up the red-wine service, the cellar usually yields an old vintage from neighboring Saint-Julien or Pauillac. Only once did I serve a suite of glorious Burgundies, and she confided to me later that she had felt a bit tipsy by the time the cheese platter arrived and thought it wiser henceforth to remain loyal to Bordeaux. Lunch dependably lasts four hours or more, and as the day wanes, they take to the road for the return trip.

Because I do not drive and because public transportation to the Alpes-Maritimes is at least as complicated as a trip to Paris or London, my visits to Bramafam are normally two- or three-day affairs. The day before my arrival, Simca will ring up to say, "I thought that you might like to do something with ducks [or guinea fowl . . . or pheasant . . .], so I've bought a couple of fine farm ducks. What else do you need? Truffles? Are you sure not? Foie gras? No?" My answer is invariably, "We'll see what we find." And the day following my arrival, a dinner party will have been organized. ("You have the key to the cellar, Richard. You must choose the wines. The Ducru-Beaucaillou we have been saving for you.") Simca loves a kitchen party, with several people at work, each doing his or her "thing": she is usually at work on a sumptuous dessert, I will have my ducks or whatever, someone will be busy with canapés and someone else with the starter.

Exactly when a casual happening, once or twice repeated, was confirmed as an inviolate tradition, no one quite knows. For many years it had been assumed, by common accord, that I would prepare the pièce de résistance for Jean's birthday dinner each twenty-ninth of October; Simca invariably elaborated one of the wickedly rich chocolate gâteaux that Jean adored and upon which his doctors frowned severely. The meal always opened with something requiring little or no last-minute preparation—smoked salmon, foie gras, a terrine, or a composed salad.

On occasions such as these, I abandon my penchant for simple grills or roasts, daubes, potées, or rapid sautés. The rules of the game require a formal beauty of presentation that will draw the desired oh's and ah's of admiration from the assembled guests (along with the clicking of cameras), an adroit carving and service at table, and a voluptuous play of flavors and textures on the palate.

The preparations are, in spirit if not in detail, inspired by la grande cuisine classique of the past, time-consuming and often expensive, but infinitely amusing when one permits oneself to spend the time on it. Amongst those that I can recall were: Boned and stuffed lamb shoulders, tied into melon forms and braised, accompanied by a white purée of celeriac, turnips, garlic, onions, and potatoes; chickens split down the back, flattened open, stuffed beneath the skin, and baked (to test the possibilities, each chicken was stuffed differently—one stuffing based on eggplant, one on zucchini, and one on truffles); the chickens were accompanied by potato paillassons. There were ducks with a rustic stuffing based on Swiss chard, braised with olives.

Last year, it was a partridge chartreuse—braised boned and cut-up partridge and cabbage (coarsely shredded, blanched, refreshed, and squeezed thoroughly, simmered long and gently in rich stock with carrots, onions, herbs, lean salt pork, and a partially roasted old partridge). Poached in a mold lined with a geometrical arrangement of blanched vegetables and mousseline forcemeat, unmolded and surrounded by pinkly roasted and split young partridges, the dish ended up as a fanciful nineteenth-century extravaganza.

The following is a composite taken from menus I have served Simca, Jean, and our friends over the years. The first time I served the potato and sorrel gratin, Michael James was present— he and Simca were in raptures of ecstasy and returned to Bramafam to prepare it again the next day.

Wines from the northern Rhône Valley will accompany perfectly the main body of the menu: white Hermitage, red Hermitage or a Côte Rôtie, and an older one of either with the cheeses; the same Sauternes that is poured over the peaches or an old Yquem will be sublime.

Un déjeuner pour Simca, par Richard Olney

Lunch for Simca, by Richard Olney

✦ *Marinade de filets de rougets*
Marinated red mullet fillets

—

Hermitage blanc (Rhône Valley white)

✦ *Gigot rôti à l'ail et au vin rouge*
Roast leg of lamb with garlic and red wine

✦ *Boulangère à l'oseille*
Potato and sorrel gratin

Salade verte

Fromages variés

—

Hermitage rouge ou Côte Rôtie

✦ *Pêches au Sauternes*
Peaches in Sauternes

—

Sauternes (perhaps an old Château d'Yquem)

Marinade de filets de rougets

Marinated Red Mullet Fillets

Other fish may be used (eliminate the liver vinaigrette in that case). The important thing is that the fish be very fresh, as they will be served raw. Fillets from larger fish should be thinly sliced.

—

For 5 to 6

2 large red bell peppers
Lemon juice
Salt
Olive oil
6 red mullets, 3–4 oz. each, scaled but
  not gutted
Fish *fumet* (stock) made from the heads,
  bones, and trimmings of the mullets, a
  finely sliced small onion, thyme, bay
  leaf, fragments of parsley, and fennel
  stems, and ½ cup each water and
  white wine

Pepper
Hyssop flowers or tiny fresh basil
  leaves
Hyssop leaves
Basil leaves

Special equipment needed:
A food processor
A large shallow flat-bottomed serving
  dish

Grill the peppers, turning them regularly, until the skin is blistered all over, blackened slightly here and there. (The heat should not be too intense, as the flesh should be cooked.) Lay them on a dish, enclosed in a plastic bag to trap the steam (which loosens the skins), until cool enough to handle. Peel and seed the peppers, saving the juices. Give peppers and juices a couple of whirs in a food processor— just enough to break down the flesh structure without turning them foamy—and pass them through a fine sieve into a bowl. Season to taste with lemon juice, salt, and a bit of olive oil.

To fillet the mullets, use a small, sharply pointed knife, cutting down the length of the back to one side of the bones to remove the first fillet, then cut it off on a bias from high on the head; the other fillet can be removed, after slitting it free from the tail, by gently lifting and pulling at the skeleton while freeing the flesh with the knife tip. Pull out any rib-cage bones remaining in the fillets and trim the edges, if necessary, to remove traces of fin bones. Loosen the fine skin from the flesh at the head end of each fillet and carefully pull it off. Put the livers aside. Lay out the fillets in a dish and sprinkle over enough lemon juice to moisten them well; turn them over a few minutes later.

Reduce the strained fish *fumet* to a syrupy consistency—no more than a couple of tablespoons should remain. In a small pan, with a few drops of olive oil, warm the livers over low heat, turning them, until they firm up; pass them through a fine sieve into a small bowl. Grind pepper over the liver purée, loosen it with a few drops of lemon juice, stir in some *fumet* reduction, add olive oil, and taste for seasoning, adding salt and more lemon juice or *fumet* if necessary.

Choose a large, shallow, flat-bottomed dish; pour in the red pepper purée and spread it evenly over the bottom. The shape of the dish will dictate the pattern in which the fillets are laid out—like the spokes of a wheel for a round platter, or overlapping in well-separated rows for a rectangular dish, for example. They must not be crowded for the beautiful red purée to play its role in the visual effect. Lift each fillet from its dish, lay it for a second on a paper towel to rid it of excess lemon juice, and place it, iridescent outer surface facing up, on the bed of red pepper purée—don't fiddle with your pattern, or you will make a mess. When all of the fillets are in place, pour a ribbon of the liver vinaigrette down the length of each one (serve the remaining sauce separately), sprinkle the length of each with hyssop flowers (or fresh, tiny basil leaves) and the borders of each fillet with finely chopped hyssop leaves; decorate here and there, mainly around the border of the dish, with basil leaves.

Gigot rôti à l'ail et au vin rouge

Roast leg of Lamb with Garlic and Red Wine

—

For 6

1 leg of lamb (about 6 lb.)
Coarse salt
Freshly ground pepper
1 clove of garlic, peeled
1 tsp. dried herbes de Provence (see
   Aide-Mémoire, page 503)
Wine

Olive oil
30–40 firm, unsprouted garlic cloves,
   peeled
Water
Salt
1 cup red-wine reduction (page 284)

*O*rder the leg of lamb whole; the pelvic bone should be removed, but the leg bone should not be sawed through. If you own a *manche à gigot*—a screw handle for the leg bone—have the knuckle or heel joint of the bone sawed off; otherwise it may be left to grip for carving. Remove as much surface fat as possible without cutting into the flesh or its protective membranes.

Put the coarse salt, the pepper, 1 garlic clove, and the herbs into a mortar, and pound to a paste. Add a dash of wine, red or white, to loosen up the paste. With a sharply pointed paring knife, pierce the leg deeply and repeatedly on the bias, each time opening up the vent with your finger and pouring in from a teaspoon some of the paste mixture. Rub any that is left over the surface of the leg; dribble olive oil over the surface and rub it evenly over (this may all be done an hour or two in advance). For pink lamb, neither rare nor well done, count 50 minutes to an hour roasting time and about 15 minutes rest in a warm place. Start in a hot oven (450°F), turn it down to 375°F after 10 minutes, and down again to 325°F some 20 minutes later. If you are not using the oven for something else, it can be turned off after about 45 minutes and the roast left to finish cooking as well as resting; open the door toward the end if the oven remains too hot. (If you have a solid, hermetic professional oven that holds heat for a long time, you can put the roast into the hot oven, turn the oven off, and about 1¼ hours later, it will be ready.)

Meanwhile, put the other garlic cloves to cook in a small saucepan, with a pinch of salt and water to cover; bring to a boil and simmer for about 15 minutes, or until they are tender. Drain them, saving the cooking water. Ten minutes before the roast is ready, put them to simmer gently in the red-wine reduction. Remove the roast to a heated platter, deglaze the pan with the garlic cooking water, and add these juices to the red wine and garlic.

The fleshy side of the leg will be the pinkest, the other, leaner side will be more done, and the shank will be well done but, because of its gelatinous structure, will remain moist and succulent. To carve, hold the leg by the *manche à gigot* or, using a folded tea towel, grasp the leg bone. Carve on a sharp bias, holding the knife almost parallel to the bone, slicing away from your person to remove long slices first from one side, then from the other, and finally from the shank, so that each guest may have all three sections. Any juices that flow during carving can be added to the sauceboat containing the red-wine essence and garlic before it is spooned over the served-out slices.

Aromatic Red-Wine Reduction

—

Prepare a *mirepoix* (see Aide-Mémoire, page 503) by finely dicing a large carrot, an onion, and a small branch of celery, all finely chopped, a healthy pinch of dried herbs, a small bay leaf, crumbled or chopped, and a pinch of salt, sweated in a few drops of olive oil or a bit of butter—only enough to prevent the vegetables from sticking to the pan—for about 30 minutes, stirring regularly, or until softened and yellowed but not browned. Pour a bottle of red wine over the mixture, bring it to the boil, and lower the heat to a simmer; leave it to gently reduce by ⅔ or until there is about 1 cupful of liquid left—the longer it takes, the more flavor will be infused into the reduction (a saucepan of a size to just contain the wine when poured in will provide the smallest surface area for evaporation and should extend the reduction to a good 1½ hours or more). Strain the liquid through a fine sieve, pressing the *mirepoix* with a wooden pestle or the back of a spoon to extract liquid without passing any solids.

Boulangère à l'oseille

Potato and Sorrel Gratin

It is important not to add pepper to this preparation (it turns bitter in cooking), not to rinse or sponge the potatoes after slicing (their surface starch is an essential binding element), and to moisten the potatoes and onions with no more water than is absolutely necessary. When the mixture is poured into the gratin dish and spread out, the thick, starchy liquid should not quite cover the surface.

—

For 6

2 large handfuls sorrel leaves, stems removed, cut into chiffonade (coarsely shredded)
Salt
Butter
1 cup heavy cream
2 lb. potatoes, peeled
2 large onions, thinly sliced

Special equipment needed:
A *mandoline,* if possible, for slicing potatoes
A large gratin dish

Cook the sorrel, salted, in a lump of butter over low heat, stirring occasionally, until it is melted and grayish in color; add part of the cream and leave to reduce gently; stir in the rest of the cream and remove from the heat.

Slice the potatoes lengthwise, as thinly as possible, using a *mandoline* if available. Combine them in a saucepan with the sliced onions, a pinch of salt, and only enough water to barely moisten, and bring to a boil, stirring gently and scraping the bottom of the pan with a wooden spatula to prevent sticking. Pour into a buttered large, shallow gratin dish, and spread out evenly. Pour the creamed sorrel into the dish and spread evenly over the potatoes. Bake in a 375°F oven for about 1 hour, or until an irregular gratin has formed and the liquids are sufficiently reduced to no longer produce a bubbling. If the gratin must be cooked in the same oven as the roast, better put it into the hot oven 15 minutes before the roast and leave until the roast is ready to be served, turning the oven down and off as the meat requires.

Pêches au sauternes

Peaches in Sauternes

—

For 6

2 lb. ripe yellow peaches
Sugar
Old amber Sauternes

*P*eel the peaches (if they resist, dunk them for a second in boiling water and drain immediately), slice them into a glass or crystal bowl, sprinkle with sugar, and pour in Sauternes to cover. Cover with plastic film and chill for 2 hours.

Washington Honors

*B*Y 1986, JEAN'S SERIOUS HEALTH PROBLEMS were keeping him bedridden. But when I received an invitation to Washington to be honored by the International Association of Cooking Professionals, Jean—with his customary generosity and sunny goodwill—said, "Please, Simca, go—if only to please me. It's very important that you make this trip."

So I reluctantly packed my bags and set off, to be greeted in Washington by my onetime pupil and enthusiastic supporter Carol Cutler, who had made most of the arrangements. I was touched by the gala reception and the honors, especially when Peter Kump rose to toast me in front of six hundred guests. But the high point was receiving an album with wonderful personal letters, compiled by Peter.

On that trip I also saw my nephew Jean-François Thibault, Chairman of the Romance Languages Department at George Washington University. A tall and boyish-looking man with a freckled face and sandy hair, he has a great sense of humor. At one point he suggested that his good friend and fellow professor Jean-Max Guieu prepare dinner for me. Jean-Max is a good cook, but apparently his courage if not his sense of humor failed when he started to think of entertaining me. I was charmed by his concern and by the account he wrote of his trial.

I Never Cooked for Simca,
by Jean-Max Guieu

When Jean-François called and asked if I could invite Simca to dinner so that we could have a cozy, informal get-together during her trip, I didn't hesitate. "Of course, I'd be delighted," I replied.

As soon as I hung up, I realized: "Simca? For dinner? Chez moi? My God." I felt I'd have to brush up on fonds de sauce, duxelles, maybe my mirepoix. I might have to live through the whole meal with a pounding heart as I worried about asparagus being al dente, the leg of lamb pink, the pear sherbet just beginning to soften.

The pear sherbet? What pear sherbet? My pear sherbet? I'd won a modest fame for it among friends, but my secret was that it was made from frozen canned pears in heavy syrup, churned in the Cuisinart. A cheap, deceptive dessert like that? Simca deserved better! A chocolate mousse, perhaps? Too déjà vu. A decorated charlotte? But the best one was in her own book. Too risky. Someone else's? Tactless.

How about starters, then? Vichyssoise? No! Oysters? No! Quenelles? Yes. Pike quenelles would show my craftsmanship. Whew. Now for the main course. Beef? Chicken? Lamb? Veal? Why not lobsters?

I tried to remember all the great meals I had had in my life—the elaborate menus my mother would turn out; the scrumptious foods I'd seen in glossy magazines. My mind grew numb, went blank. What a mistake I'd made! I was not a cook. Who ever said I liked to cook? In fact, I hated to cook, always did! Why had I gotten into this? Whom would I dare invite to dine with her?

I'd been forming a prayer, and it was answered. Jean-François called and informed me that Simca had been invited to a semi-official dinner and couldn't make it to my house the following week.

My cloud of speculation lifted, and I was so relieved that I decided to go ahead with a dinner anyway—but this time just for a friend named Michael and his parents, who were coming to town. Then I suggested that Jean-François join us after he had dropped Simca back at her hotel.

But because of my original "Simca challenge," I kept fooling around with new ideas. Of course, I'd have my standby leg of lamb with beans, my "old faithful" zucchini casserole. The crowd-pleasing pear sherbet would be de rigueur, but why not try the quenelles after all? Perhaps something a little out of the ordinary, like using whiting instead of the usual pike. A fish is a fish, after all, so I'd dub it a southern French family recipe, "quenelles de merlan"—et voilà! One week later, Michael's parents probably did not realize that the fish loaf in disguise that I served as a first course had been meant as light, puffy little quenelles, which had gone pitifully mushy on me. I decided not to offer seconds when Michael shot me a quizzical look over the bizarre fishy dish.

By now, I was saved by the aroma of roasting lamb, the appetizing hint of rosemary. As I removed the offending fish, I counted on my gigot, *and sure enough, they loved my Provençal dish, which never fails its native sons (I'm from Marseille).*

Then the doorbell rang twice. Jean-François, no doubt; a bit earlier than expected, but no panic. My lamb was still in good shape.

"I rushed up the stairs to warn you," he gasped. "Simca is here, just getting out of the limousine. The party was cocktails plus a few little morsels, and she's starved! Can we eat?"

Simca? Now? I went into a state of shock, as I frantically added plates and silverware, brought on extra chairs, and welcomed her. Back in the kitchen, I hastily resharpened my carving knife and wondered if I should commit hara-kiri instead of slicing more lamb. I wisely decided to finesse the fish mush.

Simca was charming. All smiles, simple and gracious, eating as if she really enjoyed the food. She asked for seconds, adding, "A perfectly cooked lamb! And this zucchini gratin reminds me of Bramafam." I was beaming, euphoric.

Then she asked me if I had a copy of Simca's Cuisine, *which I proudly brought out, grease stains and all, and she signed it, commenting, "That's what I call a real cookbook. It shows you are using it. Bravo!"*

She had written: "To Jean-Max, excellent cuisinier," *a glorious accolade. As she pulled away in the limousine, I couldn't wipe the smile off my face while I waved goodbye, reflecting that it was really too bad she hadn't had the time to stay on to taste my very own pear sherbet.*

On a visit to France, Jean-Max reminded me about a delicious Provençal bread-cake made with orange-flower water. Called *pompe à l'huile,* it's a Christmas specialty from his part of the Midi, around Marseille, where they make a big and beautiful occasion of the Christmas season. Every family traditionally brings out small clay figurines called *santons,* or little saints, for their crèche, and serves festive food, especially thirteen desserts, including the *pompe à l'huile.*

He says his family has always celebrated Christmas with this wonderful confection, and we tasted it together once at a restaurant. After that I had to try it out on Jean-François and Jean-Max. Surprisingly light, it made a good lead-in to the leg of lamb and Jean-Max's own *sorbet aux poires.* We laughed a lot about what he calls the "sheer idiocy" of the pear recipe—but it really does taste good.

Un dîner pour
Jean-François et Jean-Max

Dinner for Jean-François and Jean-Max

Apéritif: Kir

✦ *La pompe à l'huile et à la fleur
d'oranger provençal de Jean-Max*

Jean-Max's orange blossom brioche, Provence style

✦ *Gigot à la fourchette*

Fork-tender leg of lamb

Salade verte

Fromages variés

—

Bordeaux rouge—Pomerol

✦ *Sorbet aux poires "express"*

Quick pear sherbet

—

Barsac (a sweet dessert wine from southwest France)

La pompe à l'huile et à la fleur d'oranger provençal de Jean-Max

Jean-Max's Orange Blossom Brioche, Provence Style

—

For about 1 lb. of dough
For one 12" brioche and one 8" brioche

4 Tbsp. orange blossom water

⅓ cup sugar

2 packages active dry yeast, or 1½ oz.
  fresh yeast

2½ cups pastry flour

3 medium eggs

½ cup extra-virgin olive oil

½ tsp. salt

1 tsp. anise seeds

1 egg yolk

1 Tbsp. water

Special equipment needed:

A food processor

A heavy-duty mixer, equipped with a
  dough hook (optional)

A 12"-diameter nonstick baking pan

An 8"-diameter nonstick baking pan

Orange blossom water (*l'eau de fleur d'orange*) is what gives this flat brioche its special flavor. The bread is a Provençal specialty, served mainly at Christmastime. I believe the "water," made with the essence of orange flowers, is produced only in France. A friend in Australia once tried to find the ingredient there, and when she couldn't, she substituted orange juice! However, the real thing tastes very different, and I recommend it, for it can probably be found in specialty or import food shops. Served with poached pears, chocolate cream, and vanilla-flavored crème anglaise, it makes a lovely dessert.

Slightly warm the orange blossom water, stir in a pinch of sugar and the yeast, and set aside to dissolve.

Put 2 cups of the flour in a food processor, and pour in the yeast–orange blossom water on one side. Hollow out three little holes in the flour, and place an egg in each one. Add half the oil, pulse for 5–6 seconds, then add the remaining sugar, the salt, and the remaining oil. Pulse again for a few seconds to obtain a loose, doughy texture. Transfer to a pastry marble or board, and sprinkle with a little flour.

Knead the dough well with the hands or in a heavy-duty mixer with a dough hook, working it until it becomes glossy and elastic and is no longer sticky. (If using all-purpose flour, you may need less flour.) The final kneading should not be done in a food processor. Sprinkle the anise seeds over the dough, and knead them in until they are uniformly spread throughout the dough.

Lightly flour a mixing bowl, place the dough in it, and sprinkle a little flour over it. Using scissors, briskly cut a cross on the top of the dough to help it rise, then cover with a warm, slightly moist towel and set in a warm place for 2–3 hours, or until the dough has doubled in bulk.

Flour your hands slightly and punch the dough down, turning the bowl, until the mass is completely deflated. The dough can then be used immediately or, wrapped tightly in a plastic bag to prevent any more rising, placed in the refrigerator until time to be used. Do not keep the dough longer than 1–2 days.

When ready to make the *pompe à l'huile,* remove the dough from the bag, sprinkle with a little flour, and take ⅔ of the dough, reserving ⅓ for later. Roll the piece of dough ⅓″ thick, shaping it into a round as you go, to fit into a 12″-diameter baking pan. Place the dough in the pan and flatten it with floured hands to make it even all over. Poke a hole in the center with your finger, then enlarge the hole with scissors, shaping it like a star. Next, around the central hole, make 4 or 5 similar stars, each of them 1″–1½″ in size. Make the same pattern in the smaller mass of dough, placed in an 8″ pan.

Prepare a glaze by beating the egg yolk with 1 tablespoon of water. Brush it over the dough in both pans, then let rise about 30 minutes, or until double in height. Bake in a preheated 400°F oven until nicely golden brown (about 20–30 minutes).

Gigot à la fourchette

Fork-Tender Leg of Lamb

—

For 10 to 12

5 lb. tender leg of lamb

3 Tbsp. virgin olive oil

10 oz. shallots (preferably the violet
  kind), peeled

⅔ lb. garlic cloves, not peeled

Salt and pepper

Large bouquet garni of celery stalk,
  parsley stems, thyme, and bay leaf

2–3 bottles of good red wine (such as
  Cabernet Sauvignon or Bordeaux)

3–4 cups chicken broth

Minced chives and parsley, for garnish

Special equipment needed:

A covered ovenproof skillet large
  enough to hold the deboned meat

A food mill

Debone the leg of lamb, or ask your butcher to do it for you. Be sure to keep all of the bones. Roll and tie the meat into a neat bundle with kitchen twine, like a roast. Using your hands, rub some olive oil all over the meat. Heat the remaining oil in the skillet. When hot, brown the bones, turning them so they sear on all sides. When nicely browned, remove to a platter and replace with the meat, letting it brown slowly on all sides, then removing to a platter. Add the shallots and garlic, and let sweat for 7–10 minutes, shaking the skillet so they cook evenly. When golden, transfer to a platter. Clean the skillet, if needed, removing the fat and any burned particles.

Add a little olive oil to the skillet, then return the bones, meat, and vegetables, add the bouquet garni, and pour in enough wine so that the meat is ⅔ submerged. Let simmer 5–6 minutes to remove the alcohol taste from the wine, then add broth to barely cover. Place a piece of parchment paper over the skillet contents, and cover with the lid. Bring to the simmer over heat, then bake 3½–4 hours in a preheated 375°F oven. Halfway through cooking, turn the meat, add more broth, and stir the contents, scraping the bottom of the skillet. When the meat is done, it should be easy to pierce with the point of a knife. Transfer to a platter and keep warm if it is to be served warm; otherwise, let cool.

Remove the shallots and garlic with a slotted spoon and drain well. Using a food mill, purée the shallots and garlic, then reserve. (Do not use a food processor, as the garlic skins must be removed.)

Strain and degrease the cooking juices, then reduce over direct heat until 2 cups remain. Taste and correct the seasoning. Add the shallot-garlic purée, and mix well with the cooking juices. If serving the meat warm, reheat it in the reduced cooking juices just before serving. Serve sliced and coated with some of the sauce. Serve the remaining sauce in a sauceboat.

If the meat is to be served cold, cut into slices and glaze each slice with cold sauce. Decorate with a mixture of minced chives and parsley.

This dish is a good one for buffet parties, as only a fork is needed to eat it.

Vegetable Suggestion: If served warm, accompany with a green vegetable purée or chestnut purée (page 40). If cold, serve a salad of tender green beans.

Variation: Any kind of game can be prepared in this same manner, but marinate first for 48 hours in 3 parts red wine to 1 part red-wine vinegar. Haunch of venison or young wild boar is delicious cooked the same way.

Wine Suggestion: Serve with the same red wine.

Sorbet aux poires "express"

Quick Pear Sherbet

—

For 4 to 6

1 pt. canned pears in heavy syrup	*Special equipment needed:*
½ cup Poire William liqueur	A food processor
	A plastic bowl

Quarter the pears and put them in a plastic bowl with ⅔ cup of their syrup. Place in the freezer overnight, or until frozen solid. Defrost by dipping in hot water for 20 seconds. Remove carefully, as the contents will slide out quickly, then try to cut into large pieces.

Put in a food processor and process for about 5 minutes, or until it turns white and creamy. Stir with a spatula, and pulse again for 15 seconds, then stir in Poire William. Serve in cups, using an ice-cream scoop, with more Poire William to drink.

Variation: B A N A N A S H E R B E T
Cut 3 ripe bananas into thick slices. Place in a plastic container, cover, and freeze for 24 hours. Cut up the frozen bananas, place in the flood processor, and purée, as above.

I HAVE ALWAYS FELT that my professional success was largely due to America and its cooks. My friends over there wonder why I've never been known as a cooking star in France. For one thing, the French don't take to being taught cooking. They think they've learned it all at their mothers' knees, which many decidedly have not. Americans are more open to new ideas, more generous and willing to experiment, in food as in everything else.

That does not mean I'm disloyal to France or to my French friends. I would never live anywhere else in the world, and I think we have the number one cuisine. But France is peculiar. We have rock stars and movie stars, sports stars and even chef stars, like Troisgros, Guérard, Vergé, the Haeberlin brothers. But cookbook writers and teachers? I don't think many of the dozens of cookbooks available are terribly valid. Ask a Frenchwoman, and she may mention a famous chef's book or a women's magazine with recipes, but she can rarely come up with the name of a cookbook writer, except perhaps for Escoffier or Pellaprat. Even earnest home cooks nowadays have barely heard of Mme Saint-Ange, our equivalent of the Rombauers (Irma and her daughter Marion, who wrote *The Joy of Cooking*) or the English Mrs. Beeton. Mme de Saint-Ange turned out a classic cookbook, elaborating all the steps in every recipe. Her lengthy, dense texts are tough to struggle through, but they omit nothing. While working on *Mastering,* I must say we got ideas from her descriptions. But my favorites are Richard Olney's *Simple French Food* (Atheneum) and the series he did for Time-Life Books, taking the reader through all phases of every kind of cooking, from fish to pastries.

As for TV cooking, we have had some shows here—mainly by Raymond Oliver (onetime owner of Le Grand Véfour), who was the first cook to make a dish for the TV camera, in 1950. I think he should have gotten the Legion of Honor. And his son, Michel, knows how to put on a very lively act as well. But none of them have had the clout of Julia's shows in the States.

TIME PRESENT

As I was rummaging around in my past to begin this memoir, a real-life figure surged right up to help pull the distant past into focus. He was no other than my younger brother, Bernard, whom I hadn't seen for several decades. Handsome, strapping, a good rider, he was the one who taught me horsemanship back in 1935. Mother's "baby," my junior by ten years, he had never been as close to me as my older brother and mentor, Maurice. After Bernard married Marie-José, we drew further and further apart. With his life and military career based abroad, I had totally lost contact with him.

Then in 1986 I discovered that he was retired and living with Marie-José in the south of France—just a few kilometers away at Cagnes-sur-Mer. This is too silly, I thought, and I rang him up and went to see him. It was an emotional reunion, as I found Bernard full of vitality and just as tall and handsome as ever, albeit older, of course. We reminisced for hours with our various tales of work and travel, and we still get together at intervals, to talk mostly about old times.

The reunion with my brother was a happy moment, but it was overshadowed by Jean's death on June 1, 1986—the major tragedy of my life. He had been diabetic for over ten years, but the mysterious virus that plagued him on our round-the-world tour in 1979 turned out initially to be hepatitis B, which then evolved into cirrhosis.

Jean had never drunk more than very moderately, so getting the "drinker's disease" did not seem fair. He tried all kinds of treatment, but to no avail. His condition deteriorated steadily.

April 30 that year was our forty-ninth anniversary, and it should have been an occasion for rejoicing. But by now, Jean was so weak he could barely walk. He had been bedridden in his downstairs study because it was easier for everybody that way. Early that morning, I heard him struggling upstairs. Quickly patting my hair in place, I greeted him smiling, though my heart was sinking.

He smiled, hugging me and sitting down on my bed. "Simca," he said, "happy anniversary! You look like a girl all over again." He laughed and joked about how we had weathered so many years together, and weren't we a picture now. . . . I wanted to cry but didn't dare show my grief in the face of his courage. I've explained my nickname for him, Sing, which means "strength" in its Indian original. He had given me so much strength and courage in our life together.

"Sing, we're indeed a pair," I said. "We'll toast with a sip of Champagne later." Though we both knew the wine was not good for him, we also knew it would be our last anniversary together.

When Jean died in his own bed on that terrible first of June, I did not know how I would be able to go on. Fortunately, his sister France, other friends, and our curate rallied around, since I was unable to function in my state of disarray.

We celebrated a Mass at Plascassier, and then buried him alongside my Beck ancestors in the peaceful little cemetery up at Rainfreville. My life turned gray, and I sank into a kind of limbo. I could savor neither food nor drink, and even my rose-filled flower beds gave me little consolation.

Julia and Paul came over in September and gently encouraged me to pull myself together and rejoin the human race, in order to pursue my first efforts to set down my story and recipes for this book.

And gradually, with God's changing seasons, I started to find reasons to live. I began to notice the chill in the air, sniff the crackling fire—and occasionally give somebody in the house what-for when the fire wasn't made right or was leaking smoke into the room. Poking my nose out on the stone terrace and looking at that fabulous view over to the crest of the next hill and the glimmer of Grasse lighting

*At Bramafam, I always feel
that the days are worthwhile*

up by nightfall, I felt that the days were worthwhile after all. I had met so many new friends among my pupils at La Campanette, had all those memories of good food shared.

A most stalwart friend and neighbor who helped pull me through is Audrey Billam, a widow who moved here from Australia with her three sons and a daughter over twenty years ago. Now living in Castellaras, she often comes to see me and has been an immeasurable comfort through all my troubled times of Jean's illness and death.

Another person I must mention here, one whom visitors often meet, is Harold Earle Fischbacher. A cousin of Jean's who has often stayed at Bramafam, he supported me during my mourning for Jean and still spends a good deal of time with me, staying in the pocket-size room I call "Darrold's"—his nickname. A quiet, gentle man with white hair, he reminds some of my American friends of M. Hulot, the famous French movie personage, in his white summer sun hat. In fact, Harold is half American. He worked for several years in the film industry in the United States and still speaks excellent English. He now drifts in and out of Bramafam between periods spent up in his art bookshop and publishing firm on the Rue de Seine in Paris.

And then there is Jeannette, that very special person in my life. In a way, we prop each other up like two tenacious old birds, though I run the show, as she can neither drive nor read and, besides, is in desperately bad health, nearly blind from her diabetes, crippled up with arthritis. But what a cook she was—an instinctive cook like our Beck family's Zulma.

Nowadays, her routine is to come up to my living room for tea and a good gossip every afternoon. We usually talk about food, and she has me pegged. "Oh, Madame"—she laughs, discussing me with a visitor, throwing up her hands— "Madame won't tolerate undercooked food, odd combinations, or frilly dishes."

"They" is the word Jeannette uses to discuss chefs, the government, youth, the outside world, about all of which she harbors dark suspicions.

Indeed, for her, "they" haven't got the sense of her exotic gray-and-red Gabonese parrot, who occasionally speaks up to her, saying, *"Bonjour, grosse mé-mère"* ("Hello, you fat old thing"), which tickles her. The salt of the earth, Jeannette is a true *paysanne,* close to everything living—especially her cat, my pets, the doves in their cage behind her house.

My Animal Kingdom—
Top Dogs and Cats

MY FRIENDS AND HELPERS ARE A COMFORT, but here I have to pay tribute to the animals on whom I rely for much of my emotional support. Those I have today are very important, but I'll go back a bit to describe some of the others that have kept me company in the past.

We always had a kennel at Rainfreville, but the dogs were Brittany spaniels for my father's hunt, and thus rather "wild" creatures, not really pets. As a little girl, I played with Bazoo, a pug who was an obedient pet for about fifteen years, or until after World War I.

During my first marriage, I had a small wire-haired brindle terrier named Billy, who was my boon companion and a kind of consolation for having no children. One day I was told the dog should be plucked to make his coat thicker. The only place that did this well was a dog-grooming place at the very end of the Faubourg Saint-Honoré, near Boulevard Haussmann, so I drove Billy over there. The man in charge told me it would take a couple of hours, so I went back home to wait. By the time I'd done an errand or two and arrived home, there was Billy on the doormat. He had fled the dog *coiffeur* because he hated being plucked, and even though he'd never been out in Paris in his life except for short walks on a leash, he made his way all the way up to the Étoile and around, plus several blocks farther to our house on the Rue Lesueur.

Jean and I had lovely dogs—first a magnificent airedale named Peter, who got poisoned by a tick and died young, then a perky brown poodle, Vicky, the one who knew how to hunt instinctively.

We bought our black miniature poodle, Iota, in 1973. Now she's deaf, vague, and opaque-eyed, like a doddering old lady; but she snaps to attention when she wants to yap for scraps at the table, a very enthusiastic cheese fan.

For several years we had a stray who adopted us—Phano, a brindle wire-haired rustic country dog, whom I considered a gentleman at heart. Although he created havoc with his barking when the postman appeared, he never failed to drape himself gracefully in his favorite chair facing us as we watched television during dinner.

We needed a fair-size watchdog, so enter Ursus, our black Labrador, whom we drove some seven hundred–odd miles to pick up in Brittany eight years ago. Our three-month-old "black bear" puppy was obviously a dynamo, but his enthusiasm was soon dampened, as he was carsick all the way back to Bramafam. We stopped at Roanne to see Pierre Troisgros, and when Pierre took the puppy in his arms, he announced that he would like to keep him for himself.

Ursus, who sits here as I write, is exceptionally intelligent, a real canine aristocrat. He got used to cars and is hooked on hopping in whenever anybody will take him—waiting obediently as we do our chores.

One day, I fell in a gutter hidden by leaves behind the house, and Ursus was very concerned, lying down to support me as I got up. When he started to move, I said, "Wait, Ursus, that hurts." He stopped, lay quietly, and seemed to "help me up," even though I had broken my wrist.

Ursus's only vice is girlfriends, and sometimes at night he wanders off to court a neighboring bitch, staying out quite a few hours. That worries me, since people steal pedigreed dogs rather often. When he comes home, it's literally tail between his legs. He slinks upstairs and looks at me with real shame in his eyes, but I understand he can't betray his macho instincts.

I've always been adopted by very nice stray cats, who adopt Julia as well when she's in residence, since she is simply gaga over cats and feeds them unstintingly.

Now we share our lovely black-and-white Poussiquette, or Pussycat, more formally known as Whisky at our house (because she is black and white) and as Minoir at Julia and Paul's. This feline is a star, a character, with a lot of dog in her nature. She usually comes when one calls, and follows Ursus out when it is time to "do his duty." The only animal we've had who actually seems to enjoy watching television, she likes to strike beautiful poses and drinks out of a water glass on our table every evening. She is a dedicated glutton and cozies up to anybody near the kitchen for cat biscuits.

One day when Harold spilled a mountain of the biscuits all over the kitchen floor and called for help, I had a fit of laughter at the sight of Pussycat picking daintily at the bonanza. "Here's your chance—help us clean up," I said to Pussycat, who couldn't believe her luck and drifted away.

She loves most visitors and has been known to scare at least one out of her wits when she leapt on the guest room door handle to let herself in at 2:00 A.M. She also occasionally brings a freshly stalked "gift" mouse into the guest room, delicately removing it after presentation. The day she brought in a bird, it was too much for Harold, who tied a little bell to her collar. She's vain enough to like this tinkling ornament and must wonder why she can't pounce on a bird any longer.

So with my distracting pals, I keep on plugging at my work, getting somewhat nervous and irritable if I can't spend time at my trusty typewriter every day. I love the attention of friends, relatives, and neighbors, but less and less tolerate idle conversation. There is so little time left to waste. . . .

I don't entertain much anymore, just simple meals for friends, perhaps somebody's birthday. And of course, I do my best to make it a treat every time, with one of the cakes in this book.

I've usually found marketing almost as much fun as it is work. We're surrounded with good ingredients down here, though our own limited garden produce is nearly always best. A tomato should be firm and vine-ripened, and smell like a tomato. The ones available in winter are shipped in from other countries, and I have to leave them out of the fridge for a few days to ripen as best they can.

Merchants have always been helpful in solving the mysteries of fruits like melon. "You see, madame, that one is ripe for today; you can almost hear the juiciness inside, you can smell the sweetness." Of course, my years of experience have taught me this; but it's nice to get the personal touch from the fruit vendor. I go to the

Ursus, my black Labrador,
is a real canine aristocrat

Pousiquette—known as Whiskey at my
house and Minoir at Paul and Julia's—
is as vain as she is beautiful

Cooking in the demonstration kitchen at La Campanette with a friend and pupil, Charlotte Ferguson

big nearby supermarket, but it's a madhouse and never as much fun as the outdoor stalls.

Buying fish is always a question of who the best fishmongers are. They point out their day's shipment of sole or sea bass, the fish looking almost more alive than dead, firm to the touch and gleaming, eyes bright and clear, not opaque or "dead."

Nowadays it's usually my gardener, doubling as a chauffeur, who does the shopping for me. But he's helped occasionally by my houseguests and also by my fishmongers and butchers, who know my tastes and select the best cuts. Even at the supermarket, the butcher knows that I prefer my steak not marbled, as it's bad for the health; or he chooses the freshest kidneys and calf liver, with never a hint of anything like ammonia, which would mean it is less than fresh.

While I don't drive to market, I still drive myself to the hairdresser or to Mass, or to see a friend nearby. And I roar along in my customary old style, something of a joke among my friends, who tell me I act like a fighter pilot off on a dangerous mission or a grand prix rally driver.

I've cried wolf for so long about giving up teaching that nobody believes me anymore. And I have enjoyed it, for these past thirty-five years, although my legs sometimes feel like water at the end of a morning's lesson. But it's so rewarding when, after a week, we've all become friends, and celebrate with our farewell lunch.

Un déjeuner pour les élèves à La Campanette

A Farewell Lunch for Students at La Campanette

✦ *Les farcis de la Provence*
Stuffed Provençal vegetables

✦ *Sauté d'agneau aux fruits de la Provence*
Sautéed lamb with honey and olives

Salade

Fromages variés

—

Vin rosé de Provence

✦ *Sabayon au Champagne*
Champagne sabayon

Les farcis de la Provence

Stuffed Provençal Vegetables

—

For 6 to 8 (25 to 30 vegetables)

6 large onions (5–6 oz. each)

6 zucchini

3 small eggplants

6–8 ripe but firm tomatoes

3 small red bell peppers

Salt and pepper

Basil leaf, thyme, parsley

For filling:

1 lb. white mushrooms, cleaned
evaporated milk

¾ cup evaporated milk

1 cup natural white rice
  (Surinam)

5 oz. fresh bread

⅔ cup milk

6 garlic cloves, minced

Parsley stems, bay leaf, thyme, basil
  leaf, minced

1 cup olive or vegetable oil

Salt and pepper

3 eggs

Grated garlic

Fresh bread crumbs

Special equipment needed:

A food processor is useful but not
  essential

Prepare the onions, slicing off the tops and scooping out the insides to form a cuplike shape. Chop the scooped-out pulp and cook in a little oil until tender, stirring to keep from browning. Remove when tender, and drain dry on paper towels. Parboil the onion cups until tender (about 5 minutes), then drain and dry.

Scoop out the pulp from the unpeeled zucchini, leaving a cuplike shell. Chop the pulp and sauté in oil until tender. Drain and set aside with the cooked chopped onion.

Peel the eggplants and cut in half lengthwise. Scoop out the pulp, taking care to leave a shell that can be stuffed later. Chop the pulp and fry in oil until tender, then drain and reserve.

Prepare the tomatoes, turning them upside down to rest on their stem ends, then slicing off the bottoms and removing the pulp. Be sure to leave enough pulp to keep the cuplike shape of the tomato. Fry the pulp, then drain and add to the other cooked vegetables. Treat the red bell peppers in the same manner.

Next, prepare the mushroom filling. Thinly slice the cleaned mushrooms and cook them alone in a nonstick pan, stirring, until their natural juices are first given off, then evaporated. When the pan is quite dry, add the evaporated milk and continue cooking until this mixture is again quite dry. Pulse through the food processor to make a purée.

Cook the rice in boiling salted water until just tender (about 18–20 minutes), then drain dry. Soak the bread in the milk. Mix the cooked vegetable pulp, minced garlic, rice, soaked bread, mushroom purée, and all the minced fresh herbs together in a large mixing bowl. Season highly, then mix in the 3 whole eggs and correct the seasoning. The mixture should be very homogenous.

Fill the vegetable "cups" to their tops and place them, close together, in an oiled baking dish. Sprinkle a little oil and grated garlic over each vegetable, top with some bread crumbs, and bake in a preheated 375°F oven for a good hour. Serve in the same dish. (These stuffed vegetables are even better when reheated.)

Sauté d'agneau aux fruits de la Provence

Sautéed Lamb with Honey and Olives

—

For 8 to 10

1 large (or 2 small) shoulder(s) of lamb (or pork shoulder), boneless and trimmed of fat to yield 5 lb.

4 Tbsp. olive oil

4 medium onions, halved

6 garlic cloves, not peeled

2 cups good beef broth (or water and bouillon cubes)

6–7 Tbsp. thick honey

Salt and freshly ground pepper, to taste

2 Tbsp. dried herbes de Provence (see Aide-Mémoire, page 503)

½ cup pitted Niçoise olives

½ cup orange blossom water (see note)

8 Tbsp. butter, diced
1 Tbsp. minced basil and parsley, mixed,
   for garnish

Special equipment needed:
A large skillet
Parchment paper

*T*rim the meat to remove any fat or gristle, and cut into serving pieces. Heat half the oil in the skillet. When hot, sauté half the meat without crowding, turning the pieces as soon as they have browned. When done, remove, using wooden spatulas, and replace with the rest of the meat.

When all the meat has been browned, empty the skillet of meat and excess oil, leaving only 1 Tbsp. (unless it is burned). Add the remaining oil, and slowly brown the onions and whole garlic cloves. Stir frequently and let stew slowly, without burning, for about 10 minutes, then moisten with half the broth. Let the mixture come to the boil, then stir in the honey, pepper, herbs, pitted olives, and orange blossom water. When the mixture returns to the boil, add all the meat and more broth to half cover. Top with parchment paper, and let come to the boil once again, then place in a preheated 375°F oven for a good hour, turning over the meat halfway through cooking. Check the meat to be sure it is tender before removing from the oven. This dish can be prepared to this point and then reheated, if necessary.

Remove the meat and vegetables by pouring through a strainer. Degrease the juices, and reserve. Clean the skillet, and pour in the degreased juices. Over heat, but without letting the sauce boil, whisk in the butter pieces, a little at a time. Add the meat and let reheat slowly, then taste for seasoning, adding more salt or pepper as needed. Do not bring to the boil, or the sauce will separate.

Serve in a warmed shallow serving dish, sprinkled with minced basil and parsley. The vegetables can be served in a separate serving dish.

Note: If orange blossom water is not available in your area, use sweet white wine in which a dried orange peel has been macerated for 24 hours.

Vegetable Suggestion: Young cabbage leaves or broccoli, parboiled, then sautéed in butter.

Wine Suggestion: A red Bordeaux, or a Cabernet Sauvignon from Provence or California.

Sabayon au Champagne

Champagne Sabayon

—

For 12 to 15

12 egg yolks
1 lb. sugar
3½ cups Champagne
½ cup raspberry juice
Tiny fresh mint leaves, for garnish

Special equipment needed:
A heavy-bottomed 2-qt. saucepan
12–15 individual crystal cups

*T*horoughly beat the egg yolks with the sugar in a saucepan until pale yellow and ribboned. Stir in the Champagne and raspberry juice, a little at a time, still beating until all is added. Place over moderate heat, stirring constantly until creamy, not letting it come to the boil, then remove from heat and beat until cool.

The mixture can be served as is, or placed in the refrigerator for 2 hours. It should not be served frozen like an ice cream. To serve, fill the cups ⅔ full and decorate with a tiny fresh mint leaf.

*W*ITH AGE, ONE LEARNS that nothing is eternal—that we will lose those dear to us, and that no matter how full one's life may be, its temporal phase will end.

My joie de vivre, even my raison d'être, went out of my life when my beloved Jean died. I must slow down, I tell myself. Meanwhile, I keep on. . . . Nothing is ever finished until we draw our last breath. And even then, I personally believe in the life hereafter and meeting up with Jean again, even if I won't be able to cook him a chocolate cake.

Part Two

OTHER

+

FAVORITE

+

DISHES

SOUPS, SALADS, PÂTÉS, HORS D'OEUVRE

Consommé à la royale

A Light Vegetable-Based Consommé

—

For 6 to 7 cups

For consommé:
½ lb. cleaned carrots
½ lb. cleaned leeks
¼ lb. turnips
½ lb. celery stalks
¼ lb. onions, sliced
Bouquet garni of celery, tied together
    with parsley stems, bay leaf, and
    thyme

1 Tbsp. salt
Pepper
½ lb. juicy lean beef, cubed

For 1½ cups royale:
6 egg yolks
Salt
Quatre épices (see page 503)
Optional: Dried tarragon (see note)

A food processor
A 4-qt. stockpot
Cheesecloth
A mixing bowl

A wire whisk
A flat 3-cup mold (6½" square and
   1½" deep)
A bain-marie (see page 503)

*R*oughly chop the vegetables in a food processor, pulsing only 5–6 times. Do not chop the bouquet garni. Place the vegetables, bouquet garni, salt, and pepper in a stockpot and cover with 3 qt. cold water. Let simmer 1 hour, removing the scum; if not, consommé will be cloudy. Correct the seasoning and reduce the liquid until 10 cups (2½ qt.) remain. Strain the vegetable consommé, and set aside.

Wrap the raw meat in cheesecloth and secure with string. Place the strained consommé back over heat and bring to the boil. Remove from heat and shake the bag in the consommé for 6 seconds, then cover the pot and let stand for 15 minutes. Remove the meat and correct the seasoning. The consommé will turn cloudy if the meat remains longer than the time specified. Let cool in the refrigerator while making the *royale*.

Beat the egg yolks with the seasoning in a mixing bowl, then pour in 1⅓ cups of the cooled consommé, beating thoroughly until homogenous. Pour the *royale* into a square mold and set in a pan of hot water. Bake in a preheated 350°F oven until set, about 30–35 minutes. Take care that the water bath does not boil. Let cool and then store in the refrigerator until needed. Then remove the fat.

Before serving, cut the *royale* into dice, leaving the rest of the custard in the mold, as it is quite fragile. Reheat the vegetable consommé, and serve in cups or soup bowls garnished with 4–6 *royale* dice.

Note: If you like the flavor of tarragon, before making the *royale* boil a sprig of it in the consommé for about 10 minutes, then remove from heat and let sit with the tarragon. When cool, remove the tarragon and pour into the egg yolk mixture and proceed as above.

Soupe à la Suraile

Norman Sorrel Soup

—

For 4

½ lb. sorrel

2 Tbsp. butter

2½ Tbsp. flour

4 cups chicken broth (or water and
   bouillon cubes)

1 lb. boiling potatoes, peeled and diced

Salt and pepper

4 Tbsp. crème fraîche (page 501), or ½
   cup milk

Minced parsley, for garnish

Special equipment needed:

A heavy-bottomed skillet

A food mill

Trim the sorrel leaves to remove the stems, then wash and dry. Melt the butter in the skillet, add the sorrel, and stir over low heat until the sorrel is wilted. Sprinkle the flour over the wilted sorrel and stir constantly for 4–5 minutes to cook the flour. The mixture will be a thick paste.

Remove from heat and gradually stir in the broth. Return over heat and bring to the boil, add the potatoes and seasoning, and let simmer for 30 minutes. Taste and correct the seasoning.

Put the mixture through a food mill to purée. If you wish, the recipe can be prepared to this point and allowed to cool. Just before serving, reheat and, when beginning to simmer, stir in the crème fraîche or milk. If the mixture is too thick, add a little more milk. Correct the seasoning and serve, sprinkled with minced parsley.

La crème de cerfeuil aux petits pois (chaude ou froide)

Chervil Cream Soup with Small Spring Peas (Hot or Cold)

—

For 5 to 6

1½ lb. tender spring peas (or fresh green beans or okra)

2½ Tbsp. butter

1 Tbsp. vegetable oil

7 oz. onion, sliced

3 Tbsp. flour

6 cups chicken broth (or water and bouillon cubes)

2 bunches fresh chervil, minced, or 2½ Tbsp. dried chervil

Salt, pepper, and nutmeg

1 cup sour cream

Minced fresh chervil, for garnish

Special equipment needed:

A 5–6 qt. skillet

A food mill

If you are able to find fresh spring garden peas, remove the peas from their pods and discard only the "string" on the pod where the peas are attached, as it will not go through a food mill. If such peas are not available, fresh green beans can be substituted.

Heat the butter and oil in the skillet, add the sliced onions, and let cook very slowly, stirring constantly, until tender but not browned. Add the empty pods and peas (or beans or okra), and continue stirring until they have wilted. Do not let brown. Sprinkle flour over the vegetables, stirring to coat them evenly, and continue cooking a few minutes more to cook the flour. Slowly stir in the broth, then let simmer 25–30 minutes, stirring from time to time. Purée through a food mill, then return over heat and add the minced chervil and seasoning. Let simmer 10 minutes, then add the sour cream and reheat, but do not allow to boil. Taste and correct the seasoning as needed.

Serve the soup in warmed bowls or a tureen, sprinkled with minced fresh chervil. If you prefer, the soup can be prepared the day before and served chilled.

Velouté d'asperges

Asparagus Cream Soup

—

For 5 to 6

7–8 oz. asparagus stalks
1 Tbsp. butter
1 Tbsp. vegetable oil
7 oz. onion, sliced
2½ Tbsp. flour
4 cups chicken broth (or water and
   bouillon cubes)

Salt, pepper, and nutmeg
2 cups heavy cream
Minced parsley, for garnish

Special equipment needed:
A 2½–3 qt. skillet
A food mill

This recipe makes use of the tough ends of asparagus stalks, which are normally thrown away after the tips are removed. Carefully peel off the shiny green skin from the asparagus stalks. Cut the peeled stalks into ½″ lengths, wash, and dry with paper towels.

Heat the butter and oil in the skillet, and slowly cook the sliced onions, stirring, until tender but not browned. Add the diced asparagus, and stir until softened, about 10–15 minutes. Sprinkle with flour, and continue to cook and stir for a few more minutes, until the flour is thoroughly cooked. Gradually stir in the broth, add the seasoning, then let simmer about 30 minutes, or until the vegetables are tender. Put through a food mill to purée, then set aside until serving time.

Just before serving, reheat the purée, stir in the heavy cream, and let simmer 3 minutes. Serve in warmed soup bowls, sprinkled with fresh minced parsley.

Velouté d'asperges II

Asparagus Cream Soup II

—

For 4 to 6

½ lb. asparagus stalks

2½ Tbsp. butter

1½ Tbsp. vegetable oil

7–8 oz. onions, sliced

2½ Tbsp. sifted flour

4 cups chicken broth (or bouillon cubes and water)

Salt and pepper

1 lb. soup potatoes, diced

1⅓ cups crème fraîche (page 501)

1 Tbsp. minced chervil or parsley, for garnish

Special equipment needed:

A thick-bottomed casserole

A food mill

*P*eel off the shiny green skin from the asparagus stalks, reserving the tender tips to garnish the soup (parboiled till tender) or to serve with a nice Hollandaise (page 479) or Gribiche Sauce (page 115). Wash and dry the peeled stalks, then cut into ½″ dice.

Melt the butter and oil in a thick-bottomed casserole, add the sliced onions, and stir over medium heat until tender but not browned. Add the diced asparagus pieces and let stew with the onions for a few minutes, stirring constantly. Using a wooden spoon, stir in the flour, which will form a paste with the vegetables. Continue cooking and stirring for 4–5 minutes more, to cook the flour without browning it.

Remove from heat and moisten with the chicken broth, stirring until the mixture is smooth and all the liquid has been added. Return over heat, add the salt, pepper, and diced potatoes, and bring to the simmer. Let simmer 25–30 minutes, covered, or until the vegetables are tender. Put the mixture through a food mill to purée, then set aside until ready to serve.

Just before serving, return over heat and correct the seasoning. Stir in the crème fraîche and bring just to the simmer. Serve in warmed soup bowls, sprinkled with minced chervil or parsley.

Soupe de légumes et aux noix

Vegetable Soup with Nuts

—

For 8 to 10

3 medium-size tender leeks
3 medium carrots
½ small green cabbage
2 medium boiling potatoes
2 medium onions, each studded with 2 cloves
1 small turnip
3 garlic cloves, not peeled
Bouquet garni of celery stalk, parsley stems, thyme, and bay leaf
5 oz. shelled English walnuts

6 thin slices of stale *pain de mie* (page 495), or homemade-style bread, minus crusts
Salt, pepper, and grated nutmeg
5 oz. Gruyère cheese, grated

Special equipment needed:

A food processor
A large covered skillet
A food mill

*P*eel, wash, and dry the vegetables. Do not peel the garlic. Using a food processor, roughly chop the leeks, carrots, potatoes, and turnip, processing only 3–4 seconds. Remove, and roughly chop the cabbage in the same way. Place in a large skillet with the whole onions and garlic, and cover with 10 cups of tepid water. Add bouquet garni and a teaspoonful of kitchen salt. Bring to the boil, then cover and let boil slowly for a good hour. When done, the onion should be tender.

Meanwhile, roughly chop the shelled walnuts into quarters, and remove the crusts from the sliced bread. Set aside.

When all the vegetables are tender, remove the bouquet garni, and taste and correct the seasoning, adding more salt, pepper, and grated nutmeg as needed. The soup can be served as is, but I prefer to pass it through a food mill to obtain a *soupe velouté*. To serve as is, remove the garlic cloves and onions. Peel and roughly chop the garlic and slice the onions, first discarding the cloves. Return over heat and reduce to 8 cups.

Preheat the oven to 425°F. Toast the bread until golden, then set aside. Ten minutes before serving, fill individual soup bowls, or a large terrine, cover with chopped walnuts, then the slices of toasted bread, and sprinkle grated cheese on top. Gratiné in the hot oven just until the top is nicely browned. Serve immediately.

Wine Suggestion: A tasty white wine from the Jura, *le vin jaune,* or a white Gewürtz-traminer.

Petits melons au porto blanc

Small Melons in White Port Wine

This hors d'oeuvre is an easy one to prepare, and in the summer it is my favorite, but only when the melons are sweet and ripe.

> 1 small ripe melon (under 2 lb.) per
> person
> 3–4 Tbsp. sweet white port wine per
> melon (depending on the size of the
> melons)

*R*emove the top of each melon to make an opening, then scoop out the filaments and seeds, using a small spoon. Place in the refrigerator until needed. Just before serving, pour 3–4 Tbsp. wine inside. Serve with a demitasse spoon.

Variation I: MELONS WITH PROSCIUTTO
Place a very thin slice of prosciutto in the opening of the melon.

Variation II: MELONS WITH FRESH PEPPER
Many people like to sprinkle some freshly ground white pepper into each melon (about ¼ tsp. per melon) as an aid to digestion. Never use salt.

Crudités

For 6

½ lb. small radishes
Small cauliflower
½ lb. white button mushrooms
4 medium carrots
½ lb. celery root

Optional: 6 baby purple Italian artichokes
Optional: ½ lb. cherry tomatoes
15–20 black olives
1–1½ cups Mock Mayonnaise with herbs
  (page 474)

I know that most Americans have their own versions of crudités, as we do. I've seen so many at cocktail parties! Personally, I don't much go for the garlic–cream cheese dip that's so fashionable, but I do like my Mock Mayonnaise, with a selection of vegetables such as those above.

For such an informal lunch starter, the vegetables can all be "finger food," as at a cocktail party, or a few can be eaten by hand, others by fork, depending on the presentation.

The radishes are tastier when medium or small. Prepare them by removing the little tail end of the root, and trim their stalks to about ½″ of the radish, if the greens are attractive and in good condition. Wash thoroughly and dry.

Wash cauliflower and remove flowerets in bite-size pieces, squaring off ends with a paring knife. Parboil in salted water for a minute or two to tenderize, then refresh in ice water and drain.

Trim and clean mushrooms with a dampened paper towel. If small, they can be left whole. Larger mushrooms should be quartered or sliced, if you want to eat them by fork.

Peel and cut carrots into neat sticks, or use a food processor to cut them into julienne if they are to be eaten by fork.

Peel and slice the celery root, then cut into very thin strips—or julienne if you plan to mix them with the Mock Mayonnaise or with a mustard-flavored rémoulade sauce.

Parboil baby artichokes in salted water for 5–6 minutes to tenderize, then refresh in ice water and drain.

Arrange the various crudités around a large serving plate, with a bowl of the

Mock Mayonnaise in the center for dipping. For this kind of informal lunch, just about any vegetable will work, although I would never omit excellent black olives, which add a certain color, taste, and texture that I find indispensable. For a change, you may want to substitute a good vinaigrette for the Mock Mayonnaise, use broccoli flowerets if you like them, add baby pickled onions to the array, and so on.

In any case, crudités make a colorful and healthy appetite-teaser before any lunch or dinner—one that's amusing to prepare and can hardly be ruined!

Salade belge

Belgian Salad with Green Beans and Lardoons

—

For 4 to 5

4 or 5 medium potatoes, boiled with
    their skins, sliced, and still warm

2 lb. young green beans

Salt, pepper, and cayenne

½ cup dry white wine

3½ oz. slightly smoked bacon, in tiny
    dice

4 Tbsp. minced shallots

2½ Tbsp. red-wine vinegar

2 Tbsp. minced parsley

2 Tbsp. minced chives

Special equipment needed:

A bain-marie (see page 503)

A nonstick pan

*P*lace the boiled, sliced potatoes in a salad bowl and keep warm over a bain-marie. Parboil the green beans in salted water until crunchy, not soft. Drain and add to the potatoes. Season with salt, pepper, and a little cayenne, then add the white wine and minced shallots and mix lightly.

Cook the diced bacon in a nonstick pan over medium heat, stirring frequently. When slightly browned, remove and drain over paper towels, and add to the salad mixture. Deglaze the pan with the vinegar, and pour over the salad. Mix again, then top with minced parsley and chives. Just before serving, mix again. Serve slightly warm.

Terrine de filets de poisson "Inferno"

Fish Fillet Terrine "Inferno"

—

For 5 to 6

4 fresh red bell peppers, or one 12-oz. can of cooked red bell peppers
1¼ lb. fish fillets, preferably Dover or lemon sole, trout, or pompano
Salt and pepper
4 Tbsp. butter
1½ Tbsp. vegetable oil
⅔–1¼ cups cold milk
Cayenne or Tabasco
Pinch of saffron
4¼ Tbsp. tapioca, or 2 Tbsp. tapioca starch
4 eggs
10 tiny Niçoise olives, pitted and quartered
2 Tbsp. minced chives and parsley, mixed

For the sauce:
¾ cup heavy cream

¾ cup plain yogurt
1 Tbsp. Dijon mustard
Tabasco, salt, and pepper
Optional: 1–2 garlic cloves, peeled and minced
1 Tbsp. mustard seeds, sautéed in a covered nonstick pan

Minced fresh chives and parsley, branches of watercress, or blanched and refreshed green beans, for garnish

Special equipment needed:
A 4-cup Pyrex loaf pan, lined with buttered parchment paper
A food processor
A nonstick pan
A bain-marie (se page 503)

*P*repare the loaf pan and set in the refrigerator until needed. If you prefer using fresh bell peppers, cut in half and remove stems and seeds. Place under broiler, skin side up, until charred. Immediately seal in a plastic bag and let sit for 10 minutes. Remove and discard skins and ribs. (If using canned peppers, pour off liquid and drain dry on paper towels.) Put in food processor and process until puréed.

Cut the fish fillets in half, then make tiny cuts along the sides to prevent them from shrinking during cooking. Season with salt and pepper, and set aside. Heat 1 Tbsp. butter with the oil, and sauté a few fillets at a time, turning after 2–3 minutes. Drain on a rack and cook the rest the same way, adding more butter when needed.

Bring the milk and seasonings to the boil. Stirring constantly, add the tapioca and 2 Tbsp. butter, and continue stirring until thickened and smooth, not grainy. Add more milk, if necessary. If using tapioca starch, which is easier to use than tapioca, dissolve the starch in a little cold water, add the seasoning and saffron, and mix until well dissolved, then stir all into the boiling milk. Continue stirring until thick and smooth. Add this base to the food processor with the red pepper purée, pulse a few seconds, then add the eggs, one at a time.

Spread about ¼ of the puréed red pepper mixture evenly in the prepared loaf pan, place about ⅓ of the fish fillets over the purée, and sprinkle with olives and minced herbs. Continue building the terrine, alternating layers of purée, fish fillets, olives, and herbs, and ending with the red pepper mixture. Cover with buttered parchment paper, set in a bain-marie or a pan of hot water, and bake in a preheated 375°F oven for 30–40 minutes, or until set. Let cool, then refrigerate until ready to serve. (The terrine should be cold before unmolding.)

Meanwhile, prepare the white sauce. In a food processor, process the cream, yogurt, mustard, and seasonings until thick. Remove to a mixing bowl and stir in the sautéed mustard seeds and minced garlic, if desired. (Do not use the food processor for this step, since the mustard seeds should be kept whole.)

Just before serving, unmold the terrine over a platter and garnish with more minced fresh chives and parsley, branches of watercress, or blanched and refreshed green beans. Serve the sauce in a sauceboat.

Pâté de poisson aux crustaces

Fish Pâté in a Terrine, with Shellfish

—

For 8 to 10

For fish pâté base:

¾ cup milk

¾ cup flour, sifted

4 Tbsp. butter

3 egg yolks

Salt and pepper

1 lb. salmon, pike, or anglerfish (skinned, boned, and trimmed)

2 eggs

1⅔ cups crème fraîche (page 501)

1–2 tsp. dried herbes de Provence (see Aide-Mémoire, page 503)

4 Tbsp. butter, creamed

For mushroom purée:

8 oz. cleaned white mushrooms

6 oz. evaporated milk or heavy cream

Salt and pepper

5 oz. cooked shrimp, or any other shellfish (fresh or canned)

Optional: 2 Tbsp. lemon juice

Tomato Sauce (page 486) or Hollandaise Sauce (page 479)

Special equipment needed:

A food processor

A nonstick saucepan

A rectangular porcelain or Pyrex cake mold, buttered

A bain-marie (see page 503) or a receptacle large enough to hold the mold, along with enough simmering water to come ⅔ up the sides of the mold

First, prepare the base of the fish pâté, which is best when made the day before. Bring the milk to a slow simmer. Meanwhile, put the sifted flour in a heavy-bottomed saucepan and add some of the milk, whisking to make a smooth paste. When all the flour has been incorporated, add the rest of the hot milk and 4 Tbsp. butter, and stir vigorously until the mixture is quite smooth. Cook over moderate heat, stirring constantly until the mixture is a thick paste. Remove from heat, let cool slightly, then stir in the egg yolks, one at a time. Return over heat, stirring, until the paste no longer sticks to the pan. Transfer to a food processor, add the mushroom purée, and pulse until homogenous. Taste and correct the seasoning, then remove from the processor and set aside.

Next, prepare the mushroom purée, which will be mixed into the pâté base. Use a food processor to slice the mushrooms, then let cook slowly, alone, in a nonstick pan, tossing and stirring to keep them from browning. You may find it helpful to cover the mushrooms at first, just until they give off their juices, then uncover and continue cooking until the mushroom juices are completely evaporated. Add the evaporated milk and let simmer slowly, stirring frequently, until a thick mass is obtained and all the milk has been absorbed. Season with salt and pepper, purée in a food processor, and set aside.

Roughly chop (do not purée) the cleaned fish in the empty food processor. Add the mushroom base and whole eggs, then pulse to mix. Add the crème fraîche, and herbs as needed. The mixture must be highly seasoned. Pulse 4–5 times to mix, then add the creamed butter, and lemon juice, if desired. (If the mixture is still warm, add chilled pieces of butter instead.) Pulse again, and check the seasoning.

Clean the cooked shellfish or canned shrimp, drain, and dry. Taste and correct the seasoning. To assemble the pâté, pack ⅓ of the mushroom-fish mixture evenly into the bottom of the mold. Next, place half the shellfish in a smooth layer on top of the mushroom-fish mixture, followed by another layer of the mixture. Top with the remaining shellfish and then the last third of the mixture. Tamp down to remove any air pockets, then cover with a buttered piece of foil or a lid.

Place in a bain-marie or roasting pan with hot water and bake in a preheated 375°F oven for about 30–35 minutes, or until set. Let cool a little before unmolding onto a warmed serving platter.

Serve with a Tomato Sauce, such as the one on page 486, or Hollandaise Sauce (page 479). Coat the fish pâté with a little of the chosen sauce, and serve the rest in a sauceboat.

Wine Suggestion: A dry, flavorful white, such as a Pouilly Fumé from the Loire Valley, a Chablis from Burgundy, or a white wine from Provence.

Le rouleau en mosaïque

Mosaic Cocktail Roll

For 10

1 cylindrical loaf of dense white bread, such as *pain de mie* (page 495), about 10" by 3"

For filling:

5 oz. boiled ham

5 oz. prosciutto

5 oz. mortadella

5 oz. pickled red veal tongue (or use twice the quantity of mortadella)

1¼ cups butter

3 Tbsp. Dijon mustard

5 hard-boiled egg yolks

12 Niçoise olives, pitted

12 pistachios, halved

4 oz. Gruyère cheese, diced

Pepper and Tabasco, to taste

Special equipment needed:

A long, sharp bread knife

Aluminum foil

Using the bread knife, remove the ends of the loaf and set aside. Cut the bread exactly in half crosswise, then hollow out the two halves, leaving a neat ½" layer of bread next to the crust. It is important to make the inside as neat as possible.

With a sharp knife, cut the meats into small dice and reserve. Using a large fork, work the butter until creamy; blend in the mustard, then the hard-boiled egg yolks, olives, pistachios, cheese, pepper, and Tabasco. Mix in the diced meat. The mixture should be creamy.

Tightly pack the mixture into the hollowed-out halves of the loaf, press the two halves together, and replace the reserved ends. Roll the bread in aluminum foil to help the rolls keep their shape. Place in the refrigerator to set the filling until time to serve. If in a hurry, set in the freezer, but turn over every 5 minutes.

To serve, cut into ½" slices. The design of the filling will resemble a mosaic.

La tarte aux trois fromages

Three Cheese Tart

—

For 4 to 6

For pastry:
10 oz. Short Pastry (page 488)

For filling:
2 oz. Roquefort cheese
2 oz. creamy goat cheese
Freshly ground white pepper, to taste
Salt

4 eggs
2 cups heavy cream
2 oz. Gruyère cheese, finely diced

Special equipment needed:
An 8″ round fluted tart pan
A food processor
A slightly smaller round fluted tart pan

Prepare the short pastry ahead of time and chill in the refrigerator until needed. Then roll the pastry ⅛″ thick and fit it into the larger tart mold, making the sides double in thickness. Prick the bottom all over with a fork. Place in the refrigerator to chill while preparing the filling.

Using a food processor, mix the Roquefort with the goat cheese (or any thick white creamy cheese, if you cannot find a goat cheese). When the cheese mixture resembles a smooth paste, add some pepper, a little salt to taste, and the eggs, one by one, pulsing to mix after each addition. Finish by adding the cream, then process until the mixture is thoroughly homogenous (about 1 minute). Transfer to a mixing bowl and stir in the finely diced Gruyère cheese. (The Gruyère should not be added to the food processor, as the pieces should be kept whole.)

Meanwhile, place the smaller tart pan on top of the chilled pastry to keep it flat, and bake in a preheated 400°F oven for 12 minutes. Remove from oven and carefully remove the smaller tart pan. Let cool a little, then pour in the filling and bake about 25 minutes, or until set and nicely browned on top. Let cook and serve, barely warm, cut into triangles.

Wine Suggestion: A red Bandol from Provence.

Croûtes dorées au fromage

Golden Crusts with Cheese

—

For 6

18 slices *pain de mie* (page 495), or homemade-style bread, cut into rounds with a 3½"–4" cookie cutter

8 Tbsp. butter

½ cup freshly crumbled white bread crumbs (use trimmings from above, with crusts removed)

1½ Tbsp. milk, or 1 Tbsp. heavy cream

2–3 egg yolks, depending on size

½ cup grated Gruyère and Parmesan cheeses, mixed

Salt and pepper, to taste

Cayenne or Tabasco

1 Tbsp. dried herbes de Provence (see Aide-Mémoire, page 503)

2–3 egg whites

Peanut oil, for frying

Special equipment needed:

A mixing bowl and a fork

A copper bowl and a whisk

A frying pan

*B*utter the slices of bread, and place under broiler to toast slightly. Set aside.

Using a fork, make a paste with the bread crumbs and milk (or cream), add the egg yolks and grated cheeses, and season highly. Set aside.

Thirty minutes before serving, place a walnut-size portion of the egg-yolk-and-cheese mixture in the center of each round of bread. In a copper basin, beat the egg whites and a pinch of salt with a whisk until soft peaks form. Using a metal spatula, spread the whipped egg whites over each bread round, forming smooth, neat mounds.

Heat the peanut oil. (When oil is hot enough to fry the crusts, bubbles will form immediately around a small cube of stale bread tossed into the oil.) Fry the crusts a few at a time, turning them as soon as they are golden on one side. When done, remove with a skimmer or slotted spoon, to drain over paper towels. When hot, the crusts will be nicely puffed; they will deflate with cooling but still be good.

If you prefer, fry the crusts ahead of time and reheat in a preheated 375°F oven for a few minutes before serving.

Volailles en croûte

Poultry Pâté in a Crust

—

For 6 to 8

1½ lb. Short Pastry (page 488)

For filling:
⅔ lb. white mushrooms
2 egg yolks
Salt and pepper, to taste
1½ lb. whole chicken breasts, skinned,
  boned, and cut into chunks
1½ lb. turkey breast, skinned, boned, and
  cut into chunks
½ lb. prosciutto
2 eggs
½ cup crème fraîche (page 501) or heavy
  cream
½ lb. chicken livers or calf liver, diced

2 Tbsp. butter
Dried herbes de Provence (see Aide-
  Mémoire, page 503), to taste
3 Tbsp. Cognac or bourbon
½ lb. pork lard, melted
Optional: 1½ oz. canned truffle,
  julienned
2 Tbsp. water

Special equipment needed:
A nonstick pan
A food processor
A baking sheet lined with heavy-duty
  aluminum foil, buttered

*P*repare the Short Pastry and place in refrigerator to chill until firm, at least 30 minutes.

Clean and dry the mushrooms, then cut off their stems, which may be saved for making soup. Slice the mushrooms and place in a nonstick skillet to sauté without oil or butter. Continue cooking until the juices given off by the mushrooms have evaporated, then transfer to a food processor and purée.

Return mushroom purée to the skillet, and stir in 1 egg yolk over moderate heat. Continue stirring until thickened, then correct the seasoning, transfer to a mixing bowl, and let cool.

Roughly chop the chicken and turkey breast meat in a food processor, and reserve. Cut the prosciutto into strips, and set aside. Beat the whole eggs together with the crème fraîche, and set aside.

Sauté the diced livers in a nonstick pan with butter for 1 minute, then season with salt, pepper, and herbs to taste. Add Cognac or bourbon to the livers and ignite, shaking the pan. When the flames subside, add to the mushroom purée. Stir in the chopped turkey and chicken, eggs and crème fraîche, melted lard, and optional julienned truffle. Correct the seasoning. If you are using the canned truffle, add the juice to the mixture as well.

Roll out the chilled short pastry in a large oval, then return to the freezer while building the pâté. Place ⅓ of the meat mixture on a foil-lined baking sheet. Spread half the prosciutto over the meat, then cover with another third of the meat mixture, followed by the rest of the prosciutto. Finish with the rest of the meat mixture, and pack all into a neat oval loaf. Reserving some of the pastry for a design, cover the loaf with the chilled pastry, tucking it neatly under the pâté mixture so the meat is completely enclosed. Use fluted pastry cutters to cut the scraps into attractive shapes and make a design on the pastry. Glaze all with the remaining egg yolk beaten with 2 Tbsp. water, then refrigerate until firm before baking.

Bake in a preheated 425°F oven for about 40–45 minutes, or until the pastry is nicely browned all over. Let cool 8 hours before serving.

Wine Suggestion: A Tavel rosé.

Ramequins de foies de volaille

Poultry Livers in Ramekins

—

For 12 ramekins,
about ⅔ cup each, or
20 ramekins, about ½ cup each

⅔ lb. cleaned chicken or duck livers

Pepper

⅓ cup Cognac

Butter, for ramekins

1 cup freshly crumbled white bread
   crumbs

2 cups heavy cream

3 eggs

3 egg yolks

3 Tbsp. tomato paste

Cayenne or Tabasco

Salt and nutmeg

1½ Tbsp. minced chives and parsley,
   mixed

Special equipment needed:

Twelve ⅔-cup ramekins, or twenty
   ½-cup ramekins, or a large charlotte
   mold

Parchment paper

A food processor

A food mill

A bain-marie (see page 503), or
   receptacle large enough to hold the
   mold or ramekins with hot water to
   come halfway up the sides

*C*arefully trim the livers, removing any sinews and discolored portions, and place in a small bowl with pepper to taste and Cognac. Let macerate overnight.

Heavily butter the bottom and sides of the ramekins (or charlotte mold), and line bottoms with buttered parchment paper. Set in refrigerator until needed.

Soak the bread with ½ cup of the cream, then transfer to a food processor and purée. Cut the macerated livers into chunks, put through a food mill to remove any remaining sinews, then transfer to the food processor with the puréed bread crumbs. Add the macerating liquid, eggs, egg yolks, remaining cream, and tomato paste. Season highly with cayenne or Tabasco, salt, nutmeg, and freshly ground pepper. Add the minced fresh herbs and pulse 3–4 times to make a smooth purée. Spoon into the prepared ramekins, filling them ¾ full.

Place several layers of newspaper in the bottom of a roasting pan, add the filled ramekins, and pour in ⅔″ hot water. Bake ramekins in a preheated 375°F oven 15–18 minutes, or until set in the middle. Bake the charlotte mold 25–30 minutes, or until set.

If the ramekins are to be served warm, leave in the hot water until ready to serve. If they will be served tepid, let cool before unmolding.

Wine Suggestion: A good red Bordeaux, or a Cabernet Sauvignon from the Mondavi Winery in Napa Valley, California.

Pâté de foies de volaille, au Cognac, ou au Bourbon whiskey

Fowl Liver Pâté, with Cognac or Bourbon

—

For about 10 to 12

½ lb. duck livers, trimmed

½ lb. chicken livers, trimmed

⅓ cup Cognac or bourbon

Pepper

Enough sheets of pork fat (⅛″ thick) to line bottom, sides, and top of terrine

1 cup freshly crumbled white bread crumbs

2 cups crème fraîche (page 501) or heavy cream

½ lb goose or pork fat

½ lb. lean boiled ham

½ cup minced shallots (4–5 shallots)

2 Tbsp. vegetable oil

3 eggs

3 egg yolks

2½ Tbsp. tomato paste

Salt and Tobasco

1 Tbsp. minced chives

1 Tbsp. minced parsley

1 bay leaf

Fresh salad leaves, for garnish

Special equipment needed:

An 8-cup ceramic pâté terrine with lid

A food processor

A food mill

A nonstick saucepan or skillet

$\mathcal{T}$rim the livers to remove any sinews or discolored portions, then marinate in the refrigerator overnight in the Cognac or bourbon, with some pepper.

Line the bottom and sides of the terrine with sheets of pork fat, reserving enough to cover the top.

Soak the bread crumbs in the crème fraîche, then purée in a food processor. Cut the goose or pork fat into small cubes, and add to the food processor. Roughly chop the boiled ham, and add this to the food processor.

Reserving ¼ of the chicken and duck livers for the design, purée the rest in a food mill to remove any hard particles, then add to the other ingredients in the food processor. Meanwhile, in a nonstick saucepan, cook the minced shallots for a few minutes in the vegetable oil, stirring constantly and letting them stew until tender. Add to the food processor, and pulse until the mixture is completely homogenous.

Drain the livers reserved for the design, add the marinade to the food processor, and pulse to mix. Next, add the eggs, the egg yolks, and the tomato paste, pulsing after each addition. Taste and correct the seasoning, adding more salt and pepper, some Tabasco, and the minced fresh herbs.

Fill the terrine halfway, then bang the bottom on the counter to settle the mixture and remove any air pockets. Place the reserved livers in a strip down the middle, and cover with the rest of the pâté filling, packing it well. Cover with a sheet of pork fat, and place a whole bay leaf in the middle. Put the lid on the terrine, and seal the edges with a thick flour-and-water paste.

Place the terrine in a roasting pan half filled with simmering water, and bake in a preheated 375°F oven for 1½ hours. When done, the fat will rise to the top. Let cool until set in the refrigerator (about half a day or overnight).

For serving, the liver pâté can be unmolded and sliced. If the entire pâté will not be used, leave it in the terrine, keeping it fresh by spreading a layer of fat on the open slice. Garnish the dish with fresh salad leaves.

Queue de boeuf en gélée

Oxtail in Aspic

This beef terrine, with carrots and capers, is easy to make, as it needs no baking and the aspic is not clarified.

—

For 8 to 12

4–4½ lb. oxtail, cut into sections
Salt and pepper
6 large, tender carrots
3 whole onions, each studded with
   3 cloves
3 whole garlic cloves, not peeled
3 leeks
1 fresh hot pepper
Bouquet garni of celery stalk, parsley
   stems, thyme, and bay leaf
3 envelopes unflavored gelatin
¼ cup Cognac or brandy, or ½ cup
   Madeira

⅓ cup drained capers
2 oz. fresh bread, crusts removed, and
   crumbled
⅓ cup heavy cream
½ lb. boiled ham, puréed

Special equipment needed:
A large skillet or stockpot
A 6–7 cup ceramic terrine
A food processor

*P*lace the oxtail segments in a large stockpot or skillet, cover with cold water, and bring to the boil. Remove all scum that forms, adding tablespoons of cold water to the pot to replace liquid lost in the process of skimming. Continue skimming until the liquid is completely free of scum, then add salt, freshly ground pepper, vegetables, and bouquet garni. Let simmer 3 hours, or until the meat is tender and begins to fall from the bones.

Strain the stock, reserving the meat and carrots. Measure the strained liquid, which should be about 8–9 cups, and degrease. (To degrease stock, refrigerate overnight to solidify the fat, then lift off in one piece the next day. If the stock is needed the same day, use a special degreasing cup to separate the fat from the stock.)

Pour 6–7 cups of thoroughly degreased stock into a saucepan, bring to the boil, and let reduce. At the same time, moisten the gelatin with brandy or Madeira. When softened, add to the boiling stock, stirring until well dissolved. Remove from heat, correct the seasoning, add 1 tsp. capers, and let cool. The aspic can be prepared to this point and left, covered, in the refrigerator overnight. To use, warm briefly to liquefy before proceeding.

When ready to assemble the terrine, set aspic over ice, and let cool until syrupy. Meanwhile, slice the carrots crosswise to form "coins," or on the diagonal to make ovals. Pour a layer of aspic into the terrine, and place the sliced carrots and capers on top to form a design. Place in refrigerator or over ice until set, making sure that the terrine is level.

Meanwhile, place bread crumbs and cream in a small saucepan, and let soak. Process boiled ham in a food processor until very finely minced or puréed. Set aside. Remove the oxtail meat from the bones in large chunks, not small pieces, and reserve. Heat the bread crumbs and cream together, add the ham, and stir until well combined. Season highly. Add the meat chunks to this mixture, and let cool.

Spread ⅓ of the cooled meat mixture evenly over the jelled aspic, and top with more aspic. Using a small knife or skewer, poke tiny holes through the meat filling to allow the liquid aspic to run between the aspic layers. Chill until set, then arrange more capers and sliced carrots on top, and cover with aspic. Chill until set. Continue building layers of meat filling, aspic, and vegetables, and end with carrots and the remaining capers covered with a thick layer of aspic. Cover and refrigerate until needed.

Unmold, slice, and serve on a lettuce leaf accompanied by a good mixed green salad with endives and chilled cooked sliced beets. Toss with one of my vinaigrettes from pages 482–83.

Wine Suggestion: A light red wine, such as a Cabernet Sauvignon.

Les escargots à l'alsacienne, accompagnés de petits flans de persil

Alsatian Snails with Parsley Cream, in Ramekins

—

For 4 to 6

4–6 doz. canned snails
2 Tbsp. butter, for ramekins

For marinade:
1½ cups dry Alsatian white wine
3 garlic cloves, not peeled
2 shallots, minced
1 small hot pepper
Ground coriander, to taste
Bay leaf, thyme branch, parsley sprig
Salt and pepper

For parsley custard:
3 bunches of flat-leaf (Italian) parsley
½ cup crème fraîche (page 501)
1 Tbsp. minced shallots
3 whole eggs
2 egg yolks

1 cup milk
½ cup light cream
Salt and pepper

For sauce:
1 cup bottled clam juice
1 cup dry Alsatian white wine
3 shallots, finely minced
4 garlic cloves, minced
1 cup crème fraîche (page 501)
Salt and pepper

Special equipment needed:
A strainer
A thick-bottomed casserole or saucepan
A food processor
6 ceramic ramekins
A bain-marie (see page 503)

A few hours or the day before making this dish, rinse the snails in cold water and a little kitchen salt. Drain dry and let marinate until needed with the white wine, whole garlic cloves, minced shallots, and the other herbs and spices. Heavily butter 6 ramekins, and refrigerate until needed.

Next, prepare the parsley custard. Rinse the parsley, dry well, and remove the stems. Drop the leaves into boiling salted water, and let boil for 5 minutes. Drain and pat dry with paper towels. Cook the crème fraîche with the minced shallots in a thick-bottomed saucepan for 3 minutes, add the cooked parsley, and let simmer for another 3 minutes. Transfer to a food processor and process for 10 seconds, then remove and set aside. (You should have about 1 Tbsp. of parsley cream.)

Heat the oven to 350°F. Place the whole eggs, egg yolks, milk, and light cream, with salt and pepper to taste, in the food processor. Pulse 5 seconds to mix, then add the parsley cream and mix again for 10 seconds. Taste and correct the seasoning, adding more pepper than salt.

Fill the ramekins with the parsley custard, place in a shallow ovenproof dish in ½″ of barely simmering water, and bake in the preheated oven for about 35–40 minutes, or until set. Check to be sure the water does not boil. As soon as the custard is set, remove from the oven. Leave the ramekins in the bain-marie to keep warm, while working with the snails and sauce.

To prepare the sauce, combine the clam juice, wine, minced shallots, and garlic in a thick-bottomed saucepan and let simmer until reduced by half, then add the crème fraîche and let reduce again by half. Strain through a strainer, then taste and correct the seasoning.

Pick out the snails and bring the marinade to a simmer to cook the ingredients. When the garlic is tender, strain the marinade, returning the liquid to the sauce-pan. Peel the garlic cloves and press them through a strainer, adding the garlic purée to the strained liquid in the saucepan. Bring the liquid to the simmer, then add the snails to cook until heated through and tender. Correct the seasoning as needed.

When ready to serve, unmold the ramekins and garnish with the snails. Add the remaining snail cooking liquid to the sauce and let simmer briefly to blend the flavors, then pour over the snails and parsley custard. Serve as soon as possible.

Wine Suggestion: Serve the same Alsatian white wine.

Terrine de poivrons doux Ursus

Sweet Red-Pepper Terrine Ursus

I invented this little dish as the book was practically on its way to the printer, and my darling dog was eyeing me and looking for his favorite snack of cheese. Ursus tasted, and approved, the terrine, just like the dogs in the TV commercials—in spite of the cayenne. Guests liked it too! I first tried it using fresh red bell peppers, blackened in the oven for about 30 minutes, then peeled and chopped. But Ursus looked at me somewhat skeptically for making things harder than I had to. So I shortened the whole process, using peppers from a jar, which worked out very well. He and my guests insisted I include it in this book.

—

For 6, as an hors d'oeuvre,
or 20–25 canapés

1 lb. ricotta cheese
3–4 oz. drained sweet red peppers
    (pimientos), preferably Spanish, from
    jar or tin
3–4 oz. anchovies (2 small tins, drained),
    or 1 medium slice smoked salmon
2 Tbsp. olive oil
2 oz. pitted black olives
2½ Tbsp. tomato paste
1 clove garlic, chopped
2 Tbsp. chopped fresh parsley,
    oregano, and basil, mixed

Cayenne, to taste
Olive oil (if needed)
Whole basil leaves, for garnish

Special equipment needed:
A food processor
A round earthenware terrine or bowl,
    approximately 8″ in diameter by
    3″ high (or the equivalent in a
    rectangular shape)

*B*lend all ingredients in the food processor until they reach a creamy consistency, adding a few drops of olive oil if necessary.

Prepare the earthenware or similar bowl by lining with adhering plastic wrap. On the bottom place a few leaves of basil, if you have them. Fill the terrine with the ricotta-pepper mixture, packing down well. Cover and refrigerate for 2 hours or until set.

To serve: Lift out the plastic, turning over immediately onto a serving plate. The pâté dish makes a good hors d'oeuvre starter for a dinner (served with freshly toasted bread), or it may be used as a spread with toast rounds at a cocktail party.

EGG DISHES, QUICHES, SOUFFLÉS, PIZZAS, PASTAS

Les oeufs brouillés aux truffes Richard Olney

Scrambled Eggs with Truffles à la Richard Olney

—

For 4 to 5

4 Tbsp. sweet butter, slightly softened
2 oz. truffles, thinly sliced
8–10 eggs
Salt and pepper

*S*everal hours before you will serve this dish, butter a saucepan very generously. Cover the butter completely with sliced truffles. Break the eggs on top of the truffles, cover, and allow the ingredients to sit together in a cool, but not refrigerated, place. The eggs will thus "imbibe" the aroma and flavor of the truffles.

Twenty minutes before serving, heat water in a large pan and place the saucepan with the eggs and truffles over it. Immediately begin gently whisking the eggs and mixing them with the truffles. Stir constantly over medium heat, keeping the water barely under a simmer. Season with salt and pepper to taste, and stop cooking just before the eggs begin to set, adding a little butter if needed.

The eggs must be served immediately on warm plates and should still be *creamy,* not set or lumpy as most scrambled eggs are.

Wine Suggestion: This dish is so exquisite that it deserves a good wine, such as a decent vintage Château Margaux. (I had a 1947 at Richard's, but such bottles are extremely rare, nearly nonexistent now!)

Soufflé aux champignons avec truffes

Mushroom Soufflé with Truffles

—

For 6 to 8

4 Tbsp. butter
½ lb. white mushrooms, cleaned and
   sliced
6 oz. evaporated milk
Salt and pepper, to taste
Dried herbes de Provence (see page 503)
½ cup crumbled stale white bread
2 Tbsp. crème fraîche (page 501)

4 egg yolks
1½ oz. canned truffles, julienned
5 egg whites

Special equipment needed:
6–8 individual ramekins
A nonstick pan
A food processor

Preheat oven to 400°F. Butter the ramekins, and refrigerate until needed.

Clean and slice the mushrooms, and place in a nonstick pan. Cook, stirring constantly, until the mushrooms release their liquid. Continue cooking and stirring until the liquid is evaporated. Stir in the evaporated milk, and continue cooking until the mixture is quite dry. Season with salt and pepper, and pulse in a food processor until puréed, using the metal blade. Add the dried herbs.

Meanwhile, soak the bread crumbs in the crème fraîche. When soft, add to the mixture in the processor. Add the egg yolks, one at a time, pulsing after each addition.

Transfer the mixture to a mixing bowl, and add the truffles and their juice. Set aside.

Beat the egg whites with 2 drops of water and a pinch of salt until a whisk leaves traces in the whites. Mix ¼ of the beaten whites into the mushroom mixture to lighten it, then lightly fold the mushroom mixture into the remaining egg whites. Do not overmix.

Fill the ramekins ⅔ full, and bake in a preheated 400°F oven for 12–15 minutes, or until nicely puffed and golden brown.

Serve as is, or with Avocado Sauce (page 358).

Wine Suggestion: Côtes du Rhone.

Soufflé panaché, avec sauce tomate

Unmolded Green-and-White Soufflé, with a Tomato Sauce

—

For about 10

1½ Tbsp. butter

2 Tbsp. dry or stale bread crumbs

1 fresh cauliflower (about 3 lb.), cleaned and quartered

Salt

2–3 bunches of watercress or spinach (about ⅔ lb.), washed and trimmed

For soufflé base:

5 Tbsp. (level) flour

1 cup cold milk

Salt, pepper, and nutmeg

4 egg yolks

⅓ cup grated Swiss cheese

⅓ cup crème fraîche (page 501)

6 egg whites

2½ cups Sauce Crème Aurore (Tomato Cream Sauce, page 480)

A 7–8 cup metal or Pyrex soufflé
   mold

A large 7–8 qt. pot
A food processor
A nonstick or enameled saucepan

*B*utter the soufflé mold, and sprinkle with dry or stale bread crumbs. Place in the refrigerator until needed.

Parboil the cauliflower in a large pot of boiling salted water for about 10 minutes. Drain, refresh in cold water, then drain again and reserve. Fill the pot with fresh water, and parboil the watercress or spinach in the same manner; however, this time add the salt *after* the water has returned to the boil, and let boil for 3 minutes or just until the vegetables are tender. Drain, refresh, then squeeze out all moisture with kitchen towels. Place the cauliflower in a food processor and purée, then add the green vegetable, pulse a few seconds, and transfer all to a mixing bowl.

Next, prepare the soufflé base. Place the flour in a nonstick or enameled saucepan and gradually stir in the cold milk until a smooth paste is obtained. Season highly with salt, pepper, and nutmeg, then set over moderate heat and stir continuously until the mixture is smooth and thick. Remove from the heat and add the egg yolks, one at a time, stirring well after each addition. Next, add the vegetable purée and the cheese, and finish with the crème fraîche. Correct the seasoning, and set aside. (The soufflé must be *highly* seasoned, or it will taste bland.)

Beat the egg whites with a pinch of salt and a few drops of cold water until stiff but still soft, not dry. Fold the vegetable–soufflé base mixture into the egg whites, then pour into the prepared mold, filling it no more than ⅔ full. Run your finger around the side of the soufflé to help it rise, then place in a larger pan containing water just barely under the simmer. Bake in a preheated 375°F oven for 1½ hours to 1 hour 40 minutes, or until it is slightly browned and beginning to pull away from the sides of the pan. The soufflé will not rise more than ½″ above the sides of the mold. While baking, prepare the Sauce Crème Aurore.

When ready to serve, remove the soufflé from the oven and let rest 5–8 minutes before unmolding over a shallow serving dish. It will then unmold easily. Coat with some of the tomato sauce, and serve the remaining sauce in a sauceboat.

Gâteau d'omelettes farcies

Three Stuffed Omelets, Sandwiched and Gratinéed

—

For 4

For omelets:
6 fresh eggs
4½ Tbsp. butter
2 garlic cloves, minced
Salt and pepper

For filling:
6 oz. mozzarella cheese
½ lb. good boiled ham
2 eggs
½ cup tomato paste, or to taste
1 oz. freshly crumbled bread crumbs
½ cup crème fraîche (page 501)
Salt and pepper

3 tsp. dried herbes de Provence (see Aide-Mémoire, page 503)

Optional: 3 cups Tomato Sauce (page 486)

To reheat and gratiner:
3 Tbsp. crème fraîche (page 501)
3 Tbsp. grated Parmesan cheese

Special equipment needed:
A large nonstick omelet pan
A round enameled cast-iron baking dish
A food processor

*M*ake three omelets, using 2 eggs and 1½ Tbsp. butter per omelet. Prepare each omelet separately, beating the eggs together in a small bowl and seasoning highly with minced garlic, salt, and pepper. Cook the first omelet on both sides, leaving it flat, then slide it into a buttered round enameled cast-iron baking dish. Prepare the other omelets in the same way, keeping them warm and wrapped in foil until ready to stuff.

Thinly slice the mozzarella and melt ⅓ of it in a nonstick pan. Transfer the melted cheese onto the omelet in the baking dish. Roughly chop the ham in a food processor, adding the eggs, tomato paste, and bread crumbs soaked in crème fraîche. Taste and correct the seasoning. Transfer to a saucepan, and stir over medium heat until slightly thickened. Spread half the ham mixture over the cheese, sprinkle with half the herbs, and cover with the second omelet. Melt another third of the cheese, arrange over the second omelet, then cover with the rest of the ham mixture sprinkled with the remaining herbs. Place the third omelet over the ham mixture and top with the remaining mozzarella, which should not be melted. Bake in a preheated 425°F oven for 10–15 minutes, or until slightly browned.

Serve in the same baking dish, and cut into quarters. If you like, pour a little Tomato Sauce over it, with more in a sauceboat. If prepared an hour before serving, this dish can be reheated by glazing the top with a mixture of heavy cream and cheese, and placing in a hot oven to brown.

Soufflé au fromage bleu / fromage de chèvre

Blue Cheese / Goat Cheese Soufflé

—

For 4 to 6

1 Tbsp. butter
1 Tbsp. flour
4 oz. soft blue cheese or goat or sheep
   cheese, or any strongly flavored
   cheese
3 Tbsp. crème fraîche (page 501)
2 Tbsp. butter
3 Tbsp. flour
1¼ cups cold milk
Salt, pepper, and nutmeg

3–4 eggs, depending on size, separated
2 egg whites

Special equipment needed:
A 6-cup ceramic soufflé mold
A heavy-bottomed saucepan
A wire whisk
A copper basin
A bain-marie (page 503), or roasting pan
   large enough to hold the soufflé mold

*H*eavily butter a soufflé mold, then lightly sprinkle it with flour and shake out the excess. Refrigerate until needed.

Crush the cheese, or grate it if dry, then mix in the crème fraîche and set aside. Melt the butter in a heavy-bottomed saucepan and stir in the flour, continuing to stir until the mixture comes to a boil. Let boil a few minutes to cook the flour, but do not let brown. Remove from heat and pour in the cold milk all at once, then whisk vigorously over heat until smooth. Once the boiling point is reached, let cook a few minutes more, then add all the seasoning—more pepper than salt, as the cheese contains salt. The sauce will be quite thick and smooth. Add the cheese–crème fraîche mixture, and stir over heat to melt the cheese in the white base. Remove from heat and, stirring constantly, add the egg yolks. When thoroughly combined, set aside while beating the egg whites.

Clean a copper bowl with vinegar and kitchen salt, rinse well with cold water, and dry thoroughly. Put all the egg whites in the bowl with a pinch of salt and a drop of water. Beat slowly at first to break up the egg whites, then increase the speed until soft peaks are formed. Do not overbeat.

Fold the cheese-base mixture lightly into the egg whites until well mixed. Fill the prepared mold with the soufflé mixture, then place in a bain-marie half filled with hot water and bake in a preheated 400°F oven for about 25 minutes. Lower the heat to 375°F after 10–15 minutes. The soufflé is done when puffed and lightly browned. Serve immediately, opening the soufflé by piercing it with two forks placed back to back, so it is not crushed in serving. The sides should be set and the middle a little creamy.

Wine Suggestion: A light red Cabernet Sauvignon.

Quiche au fromage italien et aux poivrons rouges

Italian Cheese Quiche with Red Bell Pepper

—

For 10 to 12 (two 10" quiches)

For crust:
2½ Tbsp. butter, creamed
⅔ cup dry bread crumbs

For filling:
10 oz. Italian cheese (Fontina or
  mozzarella)

8 eggs

5 cups crème fraîche (page 501) or sour cream

2 oz. grated Parmesan cheese

Salt and pepper, to taste

Quatre Épices (see page 503)

2 Tbsp. dried herbes de Provence (see page 503)

For garnish:

1–1½ canned pimientos

2 Tbsp. melted butter

Special equipment needed:

Two 10″ or 11″ ceramic pie plates

A fluted pastry wheel

A pastry brush

*P*repare the two pie plates by smearing creamed butter in a thick layer over the bottoms and sides. Sprinkle on enough bread crumbs to coat the butter, then press them into the butter and refrigerate until needed.

Cut the Italian cheese into thin slices, then into tiny dice, and set aside. In a mixing bowl, or using a food processor, beat the eggs with the crème fraîche, Parmesan cheese, and all the seasonings. The mixture should be highly seasoned with pepper and somewhat less salt. Remove the mixture from the food processor, stir in the diced cheese, and correct the seasoning.

Pour the mixture into the two prepared pie plates and bake in a preheated 400°F oven for about 18–20 minutes, or until set and golden brown on the top.

While the quiches are baking, cut the red pepper into strips ½″ wide, using a fluted pastry wheel. When the quiches are done, remove from oven and decorate with the pepper strips, overlapping and resembling a wheel. Brush with melted butter and return to a 425°F oven for just 5–6 minutes. Let cool 15 minutes, and serve warm or tepid.

Wine Suggestion: A light red Bordeaux or Côtes du Rhone.

Quiche castellaras (aux poireaux, au saumon, et aux tomates)

Crustless Quiche with Leeks, Smoked Salmon, and Tomatoes

—

For 8 to 9

For crust:
2½ Tbsp. butter, creamed
½ cup toasted bread crumbs

For filling:
10–12 oz. trimmed leeks
4 Tbsp. butter
½ cup dry white wine
½ lb. smoked salmon, thinly sliced
¾ lb. tomatoes
2½ cups very fresh heavy cream
4–5 eggs, depending on size

2 Tbsp. minced chives
Salt, freshly ground pepper, and grated
　nutmeg
Cayenne or Tabasco

To reheat:
Sour cream

Special equipment needed:
A 10″ ceramic pie plate
A heavy-bottomed saucepan
A food processor

*H*eavily butter the pie plate with the creamed butter, spreading more on the sides than on the bottom. Cover with toasted bread crumbs, pressing them firmly into the butter. Place in the freezer until well chilled.

Clean the leeks and slice thinly, using the white as well as the tender green parts. You should have about 1½ cups of tightly packed sliced leeks. Parboil for 3 minutes in rapidly boiling salted water, drain in a colander, and refresh under cold water, then drain and dry.

Melt the butter in the heavy-bottomed pan. Add the leeks and let stew slowly for about 10 minutes, then add the wine and cook another 10 minutes, or until the leeks are tender and the wine has evaporated. Season highly and set aside.

Cut the sliced smoked salmon into strips ½″ wide, and reserve. Skin the tomatoes by dropping them, whole, into rapidly boiling water for just 3 seconds. Refresh under cold water and drain, then peel. The skin will now come off easily. When cool, cut into slices ½″ thick, remove the seeds, and dry them for 10 minutes on a sheet of oiled aluminum foil in a preheated 375°F oven. Remove from oven, season, and let drain over paper towels.

Using the food processor, pulse the leeks roughly without puréeing, then add the cream, the eggs (one at at time), the chives, and the seasonings. The mixture should be highly seasoned with pepper. Watch the salt, since the smoked salmon is salty.

Pour a layer of the leek mixture ⅓″ into the prepared pie plate. Cover with the smoked salmon strips in an even layer, followed by another layer of leek mixture, followed by an even layer of sliced tomatoes. Top with the rest of the leek mixture, and bake in a preheated 350°F oven for 30–35 minutes, or until the top is nicely browned.

Serve as is, or prepare the dish ahead of time and reheat it when ready to serve. It is best served tepid, not cold. If done ahead of time, top the quiche with a thin layer of sour cream, and reheat in a 350°F oven for 10 minutes.

Wine suggestion: A good dry white wine or light red Bordeaux.

La pizza Bramafam

Provençal Pizza

—

For one 10″ by 15″ pizza

3½ Tbsp. olive oil

1 lb. onion, sliced

1–2 Tbsp. dried herbes de Provence (see page 503)

Salt and pepper

1 cup *thick* tomato purée, seasoned and reduced till quite thick

Basil leaves

Optional: Dash of saffron

20 Niçoise olives

Optional: 6 anchovy fillets

1 recipe Pizza dough (page 348) or a good short pastry (see Basics, p. 488)

7 oz. roughly grated Fontina or mozzarella cheese, mixed with 1½ oz. roughly grated Parmesan cheese

Special equipment needed:

A 10″ by 15″ baking pan

A skillet

$\mathcal{P}$reheat the oven to 400°F and lightly oil the pan in which the pizza will be baked.

Heat the oil in a skillet, add the onion, and cook over moderate heat, stirring, until the onions are golden but not brown. Remove and let drain on paper towels. Sprinkle with the herbs, salt, and pepper.

The tomato purée should be thick, not runny, and well flavored with the basil. If necessary, add more tomato purée and let reduce to proper consistency. Add freshly ground pepper and a dash of saffron, if you like it.

Pit the olives and cut the anchovy fillets in half. To assemble the pizza, roll out the dough and lightly sprinkle with the mixed cheeses. Follow with all the onions, in an even layer, topped with more of the cheese. Cover with the tomato purée and the remaining cheese. Decorate with anchovy fillets and pitted olives.

Bake in a preheated 400°F oven for 15–18 minutes, or until the crust is evenly browned on the sides. Any leftovers can be reheated at 300°F for about 20 minutes.

Pizza Dough

—

For two 10" by 15" pizzas,
or four 13" round pizzas

1 tsp. active dry yeast, or ¾ oz. fresh
   yeast
¾ cup warm water
3½ cups flour
1 tsp. salt
4 Tbsp. good olive oil
2 medium eggs, beaten

Special equipment needed:
A large mixing bowl and large fork, or a
   food processor

$\mathcal{D}$issolve the yeast in 3 Tbsp. of the warm water, stirring until the yeast is well dissolved, then add the rest of the water. Place flour and salt in a mixing bowl and form a well for the liquid. When the yeast is ready, pour into the dry ingredients and mix with a large fork to blend, then add the oil and beaten eggs, and mix thoroughly. If you prefer, this can be done in a food processor equipped with the plastic blade.

With your hands, pull and stretch the dough for about 6 minutes (about 30 seconds in the food processor). When the dough holds together well and no longer sticks to the sides of the bowl, transfer it to an oiled bowl, turning on all sides to coat with the oil. Cover and let rise in a warm (not hot) place until doubled in volume (about 1 hour). This can be done in a bain-marie (or in a bowl set in a pan of hot water), or in an oven that has been turned on for a few minutes, then turned off. If using the oven method, place the bowl on a pot holder so the bottom does not get too warm.

When the dough has risen, punch down and divide in half, or into 4 pieces. Cover each piece with plastic wrap, and let rest for 30 minutes. Now the dough may be refrigerated overnight or frozen for 3–4 weeks. Refrigerated dough can be used directly from the refrigerator; for frozen dough, wait until it is just pliable.

To use, roll the dough on a cool surface to about ¾ the size of the pan, then stretch it the rest of the way with your hands. Place in oiled ovenproof pans, spread with the topping, and bake in a preheated 475°F oven until the crust is nicely browned (about 15 to 20 minutes).

Les gnocchis en verdure à l'italienne

Green Gnocchi, Italian Style

—

For 4 to 6

2½–3 lb. fresh Swiss chard, or 1 lb. frozen spinach

6½–7 oz. ricotta or mozzarella cheese

2 oz. Parmesan cheese, grated

5 Tbsp. flour

3–4 eggs, depending on size

Salt, pepper, and nutmeg

Dried Herbes de Provence (see page 503)

2 Tbsp. olive oil

Additional flour, for coating gnocchi

12 fresh sage leaves (more if small)

7 Tbsp. butter

2½ oz. prosciutto, julienned

Special equipment needed:

A food processor

$\mathcal{T}$rim the Swiss chard, discarding all but the green portion. Wash thoroughly, then parboil for 8–10 minutes in salted water. Refresh in ice water, and drain over kitchen towels. If using spinach instead, prepare it the same way but parboil for only 4–5 minutes.

Grate the mozzarella or purée the ricotta in a food processor, then transfer to a mixing bowl. Without washing the processor work bowl, purée the green vegetable. Add the cheese to the vegetable, and pulse a few seconds to mix, then add the flour, the eggs (one at a time), Parmesan cheese, and all the seasoning. Taste, and correct the seasoning, then spread on a tray and refrigerate a few hours, or put in the freezer just until firm. The mixture can be made the day before and kept refrigerated in a plastic bag.

Use two large spoons to form the mixture into small, short, thick sausage-like gnocchi. Fill a large saucepan with water, add salt to taste and a little olive oil, and bring to the boil. Put about ¼ cup of flour on a plate for dredging the gnocchi. Roll the gnocchi, a few at a time, in flour, shaking off any excess, then drop into the boiling salted water. Add more flour if necessary. Let simmer slowly for about 8–9 minutes, then remove with a skimmer to drain over paper towels. (If covered, the gnocchi can be held ½ hour.)

When ready to serve, sauté the sage leaves for a few seconds in hot butter, then remove. Add the gnocchi, and let reheat completely. Serve in a warmed serving dish with sautéed sage leaves on top and prosciutto strips placed crosswise over each of the gnocchi.

The gnocchi can also be reheated in a casserole with a tasty tomato sauce, and served decorated with sage leaves (but without the prosciutto).

Wine Suggestion: A good Chianti.

Rouleau de fromage garni de foies de volaille et de purée de champignons

Cheese Roll, Garnished with Poultry Liver Spread and Mushroom Purée

—

For 8 to 10

For mushroom filling:
⅓ lb. fresh white mushrooms, trimmed
5 Tbsp. evaporated milk
Salt, freshly ground pepper, and nutmeg
1 egg yolk
1 Tbsp. crème fraîche (page 501)

For chicken liver filling:
⅓ lb. cleaned chicken livers
Pepper
¼ cup Cognac or brandy
1 Tbsp. vegetable oil
2 Tbsp. butter
Salt, pepper, and dried thyme
2–3 Tbsp. stale bread crumbs
9 Tbsp. butter

For cheese roll:
½ cup sifted flour
2 cups cold milk
4 eggs, separated
Salt, pepper, and grated nutmeg
¼ cup grated imported Swiss cheese

Special equipment needed:
A 9½″ by 13½″ jelly roll pan
A nonstick frying pan
A food processor
A heavy-bottomed saucepan
A copper basin and a whisk, or an electric mixer

Line a jelly roll pan with heavy-duty aluminum foil. Butter generously and sprinkle with flour, shaking to remove any excess. Place in refrigerator to chill until needed.

Wipe the mushrooms with a damp paper towel to clean them, then slice thinly.

Place sliced mushrooms in an empty nonstick frying pan over moderate heat, tossing instead of stirring for a few minutes, until they have rendered their natural juices. Continue cooking and tossing until the liquid has evaporated and the pan is quite dry, then pour in the evaporated milk and seasonings. Stir until all the liquid has once again evaporated and the mixture is thick and creamy.

Meanwhile, beat the egg yolk together with the crème fraîche, and set aside. Purée the cooked mushrooms in a food processor, then add the egg yolk and crème fraîche mixture, and pulse to blend. Transfer this mixture to the nonstick pan and stir, over heat, for a few minutes to cook the egg yolk. Place in the refrigerator until needed.

Place the chicken livers, seasoned with a little pepper, in Cognac or brandy to macerate one hour or so. Remove the livers and let drain on paper towels, then cut in half. Heat the oil and butter. When the foam subsides, sauté the livers for a few minutes on each side, add the seasonings, then stir constantly while pouring in the macerating liquid. Shaking the pan constantly, set over heat and ignite. Remove from heat, stir in the bread crumbs, and purée in a food processor, adding the butter a little at a time. Pulse until homogenous, then correct the seasonings. Set in refrigerator until needed.

To prepare the cheese roll base, put the flour in a heavy-bottomed saucepan and stir in about ¼ cup milk, making a thick paste and avoiding lumps. When all the flour has been incorporated, pour in the remaining milk and stir vigorously to blend. Place over heat and stir constantly with a wooden spoon until smooth and thick. Remove from heat and mix in the egg yolks. Season to taste.

Beat the egg whites with a pinch of salt and a drop of cold water until they begin to hold peaks but are not dry. Fold the still-warm milk-flour base into the egg whites, correct the seasoning, and set aside.

Spread half the grated cheese in the bottom of the prepared jelly roll pan, top with an even layer of the cheese roll base, and finish with the remaining grated cheese. Bake in a preheated 375°F oven for about 18–20 minutes, or until slightly browned. While the cheese roll is baking, dampen a dish towel with warm water and wring out thoroughly. When the cheese base is done, remove from oven and cover with the dampened towel. Quickly invert the baking pan to unmold the cheese base. Peel off the foil and tuck it under one of the long sides of the cheese base. Immediately spread the mushroom purée in an even layer over the base, followed by an even layer of chicken liver spread. Using the towel to help, begin along the opposite side from the foil and roll up, jelly roll fashion. Roll onto the foil and remove the towel, then close the ends to seal the foil and keep the roll warm. Wrapped like this, the cheese roll can easily be reheated.

To serve, remove the foil, place on a warmed serving platter, and cut in large slices.

Wine Suggestion: A good red wine such as a Cabernet Sauvignon or a Beaujolais.

Timbale ou couronne Méli-Mélo, à base de pâtes

Pasta Timbale or Ring, with Mushrooms, Smoked Salmon, and Truffles

—

For 5 to 6

1½ Tbsp. butter (if charlotte mold used)
5–6 oz. smoked salmon
1½ oz. canned truffle
6 oz. egg noodles
7 oz. white mushrooms, cleaned
¾ cup evaporated milk
3 eggs
⅓ cup crème fraîche (page 501)
Salt, pepper, paprika, and Tabasco
1 Tbsp. dried herbes de Provence (see Aide-Mémoire, page 503)
Sauce Aurore (page 480)

Special equipment needed:
A 5-cup charlotte mold or nonstick ring mold
A food processor
A nonstick skillet
A mixing bowl
A bain-marie (see page 503), or roasting pan large enough to hold the mold

*H*eavily butter the charlotte mold and keep in the refrigerator until needed. (If using a nonstick mold, no butter is necessary.) Cut the smoked salmon into large dice and the truffle into julienne. Set aside until needed.

Drop the noodles into boiling salted water. When tender, drain thoroughly, being sure that no water remains. Place in a food processor and pulse 5 or 6 times.

Just before cooking, slice the mushrooms. Place in an empty nonstick skillet over moderate heat. Stir constantly until the mushroom juices have nearly evaporated, then add enough evaporated milk to barely cover the mushrooms. Continue stirring until the mushrooms have absorbed the milk and are dry. Add the cooked mushrooms to the noodles, and process until homogenous.

Beat the eggs with the crème fraîche in a mixing bowl, season highly, then pour into the processor and process for 6–8 seconds. Correct the seasoning, adding more dried herbs if needed. Transfer to a mixing bowl, stir in the diced salmon and julienned truffle, then taste again for seasoning. If needed, add more pepper and/or Tabasco.

Fill the prepared mold, place in a bain-marie or roasting pan with hot water reaching halfway up the sides of the mold, and bake in a preheated 375° oven for about 25–30 minutes, or until set and a little "puffed" on top. Unmold over a warm serving dish and serve with tomato sauce.

Variation: The truffle is not absolutely necessary. If you wish, substitute 2 oz. grated Parmesan cheese. The taste will not be quite as delicate, but the result is very good.

Wine Suggestion: A light red wine from Provence, such as Bandol, or a rosé from Provence.

FISH:
MOUSSES, FILLETS, AND
SHELLFISH RECIPES

Quenelles de poisson,
avec pâte à choux, sauce tomate

Fish Quenelles, with Choux Paste and Tomato Sauce

—

For 6 to 8

Pinch of saffron

10–12 oz. fish fillets (such as lemon sole, halibut, hake, or monkfish)

Salt

2 egg whites

½ cup heavy cream

Express Tomato Sauce (page 486)

For choux paste:

¾ cup water

4 Tbsp. butter, cut in pieces

1 cup sifted flour

Salt, pepper, and nutmeg, to taste

2–3 eggs, depending on size

Special equipment needed:
A food processor
A mixing bowl

A saucepan
Ice cubes

*L*et saffron steep in 2 Tbsp. boiling water until needed. Clean the fish, removing all skin and bones, and cut into pieces. Purée the fish with salt in a food processor, pulsing until you have a very fine purée. Add the egg whites and saffron, and pulse again to mix. Place in a mixing bowl and refrigerate, covered, for about 30 minutes.

Prepare the choux paste by bringing the water, salt, and butter to a boil. The butter should finish melting at the same time the water begins to boil. Immediately remove from the heat and stir in all the flour, working vigorously until a smooth paste is obtained. Return over heat and dry the paste, folding vigorously and slapping the paste against the sides of the pan. When a glaze covers the bottom of the pan, remove from heat and add pepper and nutmeg, to taste. Beating vigorously at first, add the eggs, one at a time, mixing well after each addition. When the paste is well blended, set aside.

Remove the fish purée from the refrigerator, place over ice cubes, and working with a spatula, add the cream by spoonfuls, beating thoroughly until all the cream is absorbed. Next, add the choux paste, working vigorously until the mixture is completely smooth.

Shape the quenelles with two large spoons into oval shapes, or use a pastry bag fitted with a ¾″ nozzle to make sausage-like shapes about 2″ in length. Poach the quenelles in barely simmering salted water until they rise to the surface and roll freely, about 6 minutes. When done, remove from water and drain in a strainer over paper towels. Keep covered until ready to serve.

Reheat the quenelles in the Express Tomato Sauce, and serve in a gratin dish, well covered with the sauce.

Saumon en aspic

Salmon in Aspic

—

For 10 to 12

A court bouillon made 2 days before
  (page 485)

4 lb. trimmed, boned fresh salmon

2 egg whites, beaten lightly with a fork

1 cup good dry white wine

5 envelopes unflavored gelatin (for
  10 cups aspic)

1 Tbsp. dried tarragon

Fresh tarragon leaves

2 Tbsp. capers, well drained

12 small green canned asparagus tips

8–10 small hard-boiled eggs, halved

Green Sauce with Avocados (page 358)

Special equipment needed:

A fish poacher, or large covered skillet
  or pot

A strainer and cheesecloth

2 savarin molds

Boil prepared court bouillon 20 minutes, strain, and let cool.

Put the salmon in a fish poacher or large pot, and cover with cold court bouillon. Add dried tarragon and slowly bring to a bare simmer, then let cook for 10 minutes. Remove from heat and allow to cool, leaving the fish in the bouillon.

When cool enough to handle easily, remove and discard the skin and bones, and set fish aside. Strain the court bouillon and return to the pot. Add the beaten egg whites and half the white wine, and whisk over heat until the pot begins to simmer and scum rises to the surface. Let simmer 2 more minutes, then strain immediately through moistened cheesecloth.

Return clarified court bouillon to heat, and reduce. Meanwhile, place dry gelatin in a small bowl and moisten with the remaining wine. Stir the gelatin-wine mixture into the court bouillon. When the court bouillon has reduced to 10 cups and the gelatin is well dissolved, remove from heat and let cool until tepid.

Divide the aspic between the 2 savarin molds, and place in freezer just until the mixture begins to set on the bottom and sides of the molds. Empty the liquid aspic into a mixing bowl, leaving the film of aspic in the molds, and decorate the bottom with a design composed of fresh tarragon leaves, capers, pieces of salmon, asparagus tips, and halved eggs. Cover all with more liquid aspic, and place again in the freezer to set.

When set, build on the decoration, using the rest of the salmon, more tarragon, asparagus tips, and capers. Cover with aspic, and set in the refrigerator to chill, preferably overnight. Pour remaining aspic into a square mold, let set, then cut into diamonds or chop.

Place a hot, wet kitchen towel around the mold for 10 seconds and unmold onto a shallow serving platter. Decorate with aspic diamonds or chopped aspic, and sprinkle with minced fresh tarragon. Serve with *Sauce verte à l'avocat*.

Wine Suggestion: Serve with the same good dry white wine.

Sauce verte à l'avocat

Green Sauce with Avocados

—

For 10 to 12 (about 2 cups)

3 small avocados
2 limes, juiced
3 shallots, minced
Salt
Dash of Tabasco
Optional: 1 garlic clove

1 cup crème fraîche (page 501)
½ tsp. dried thyme
Pepper, to taste

Special equipment needed:
A food processor

Peel avocados, cut in half, and remove pits. Sprinkle with a little lime juice, and place in food processor. Add shallots, more lime juice, salt, and Tabasco sauce. Meanwhile, parboil a peeled garlic clove, mince, and add to the other ingredients in the food processor. Add crème fraîche and pulse to mix, then taste for seasoning. Add more salt, thyme, and pepper, if needed.

Serve with *Saumon en aspic*. The sauce can be served in a sauceboat or used to decorate the platter with the salmon.

Couronne de filets de sole en verdure

Ring of Fish Mousse with Green Vegetables and a Pink Sauce

—

For 8 to 10

2 lb. fresh lettuce leaves, spinach, or watercress, washed thoroughly and stemmed

8 halibut or monkfish fillets, bones removed, about 1 lb.

5 eggs

1 cup thick sour cream or crème fraîche (page 501)

2 Tbsp. finely minced fresh parsley, chervil, and tarragon, mixed

1½ Tbsp. dried herbes de Provence (see Aide-Mémoire, page 503)

Two ½-lb. soles

1 lemon, juiced

Salt and pepper

Optional: 1 lb. fresh mussels, thoroughly scrubbed and debearded

For pink velouté sauce:

3 Tbsp. butter

4–4½ Tbsp. flour

2 cups good court bouillon (page 485)

1 cup crème fraîche (page 501) or heavy cream

Salt and pepper

2 tsp. double-concentrated tomato paste

Special equipment needed:

A food mill

A food processor

A cast-iron skillet with lid

Cheesecloth

An 8″ savarin mold, heavily buttered and lined with buttered parchment paper

Parchment paper

A bain-marie, or a roasting pan large enough to contain the mold and simmering water

A heavy-bottomed saucepan

*P*arboil the cleaned lettuce, spinach, or watercress until tender (5–10 minutes). Drain and refresh under cold running water, then squeeze dry between several thicknesses of kitchen towels. Purée in a food mill, and reserve.

Chop the halibut or monkfish fillets in a food processor, then put through the finest blade of a food mill. Return to the food processor, add the green purée, and pulse to mix. One by one, add the eggs, sour cream or créme fraîche, and fresh herbs, processing thoroughly after each addition. Season highly with the herbes de Provence, and refrigerate until needed.

Sprinkle fish fillets with fresh lemon juice, salt, and pepper, to taste. If fillets are too long, cut them in half.

Meanwhile, place the mussels by themselves in a cast-iron skillet. Cover the pan and shake over high heat until all mussels are open (about 6 minutes). Remove the mussels and discard shells. Strain mussel juice through several layers of dampened cheesecloth to remove any sand. The mussel juice will form the base of the sauce. Add pepper to taste, but no salt, as the mussels and their cooking juices are already salty.

Distribute the 8 fillets crosswise in the prepared ring mold, with the tips pointing upward and with skin side away from the sides of the mold. Place reserved mussels between the fillets. Fill the mold with the fish purée, then fold the tips of the fillets over the filling. Rap the mold on the counter to settle the mixture and release any air pockets. Cover with a buttered sheet of parchment paper, place in a bain-marie or roasting pan with simmering water two-thirds up the sides of the mold, and bake in a preheated 375°F oven for 25–30 minutes, or until set.

While the mousse is baking, prepare the sauce. Melt butter in a heavy-bottomed saucepan. Stirring continuously, add the flour and let cook for a few minutes. Remove from heat, add 1 cup court bouillon and the mussel juice, and whisk vigorously until smooth. Add more court bouillon, if needed, and crème fraîche, and continue to stir until smooth. If the sauce is too thick, add more court bouillon. Season highly, and add the tomato paste. If not needed immediately, set aside with a piece of buttered parchment paper pressed onto the surface of the sauce to prevent a skin from forming. When ready to serve, stir in a little more court bouillon and reheat.

To serve, unmold the fish mousse over a wire rack to drain off excess cooking juices. Stir the cooking juices into the velouté sauce. Return the mousse to the ring mold and unmold onto a warmed serving dish. Coat with some of the sauce, and serve the rest in a sauceboat.

Filets de poisson farcis aux poivrons rouges, sauce verte

Rolled Fish Fillets Stuffed with Red Bell Peppers, Cold Green Sauce

—

For 6

For red pepper stuffing:

2 red bell peppers, or one 6 oz. can
½ cup milk
1 Tbsp. potato starch, or 2 Tbsp. tapioca, finely granulated
2 egg yolks
1½ Tbsp. butter
Salt, pepper, and Tabasco
6–12 lemon sole or whiting fillets (6 fillets of 7–8 oz., or 12 fillets of 4–5 oz.)
Dried herbes de Provence (see page 503)
Juice of 1 lemon
Dry white wine

For green sauce:

3 Tbsp. butter
1½ Tbsp. vegetable oil
1 shallot, thinly sliced
1 bunch fresh watercress
2 egg yolks
¾ cup crème fraîche (page 501)
Salt, pepper, and chopped fresh dill

Special equipment needed:

A food processor
Toothpicks
A shallow baking dish, such as a gratin dish
Parchment paper

The red pepper stuffing is better if made the day before. Place the peppers under the broiler until they are barely charred. Remove and place in an airtight bag. When cool, the outer charred skin and the seeds can be easily removed. If using canned peppers, strain, dry with paper towels, and remove the skin and seeds (if any). Squeeze dry in a kitchen towel, and purée in a food processor. The purée should be almost dry.

Boil the milk, add the potato starch or finely granulated tapioca, and let simmer slowly, stirring constantly, until very smooth and a thick paste results.

Remove from the heat, add the egg yolks and bell pepper purée, and season highly. Stir over heat just to cook the egg yolks, then remove and let cool.

Spread the fish fillets on a cutting board, and trim as needed. Flatten them as much as possible, and season with salt, pepper, herbs, and a few drops of lemon juice. Roll the fillets, leaving in the center a hole the size of your little finger, in which the stuffing will be packed.

Fill the rolled fillets with the red pepper stuffing and secure with toothpicks. If done ahead, keep in the refrigerator, placed standing up in a shallow baking dish, covered with heavily buttered parchment paper.

To prepare the green sauce, melt the butter in a skillet with the oil. When hot, add the shallot and let stew slowly for a few minutes, stirring. Roughly cut up the watercress leaves, stir into the shallot, and continue cooking for a few minutes more.

Beat the egg yolks with the crème fraîche, and stir into the watercress purée. Cook very slowly until slightly thickened. Correct the seasoning with salt, pepper, and dill, and set aside.

To cook the fish rolls, boil the white wine to evaporate the alcohol, and pour around the fish rolls to a depth half the height of the rolls. Cover with parchment paper, and bring to a simmer over direct heat, then place in a preheated 375°F oven for 12–15 minutes.

Place your hand on the parchment paper to hold the fish rolls in place, and pour the cooking juices into a pan. Reduce these juices until only ½ cup is left, and pour into the green sauce. Adjust the seasoning as necessary. Keep warm until time to serve, then nap the fish rolls. Do not pour sauce on the red stuffing.

Wine Suggestion: Serve with the same white wine.

Sole Normande du Président Coty

Fish Fillets in a Normandy Cream Sauce

—

For 4 to 6

1 lb. Dover sole, salmon, sea bass, or
 halibut fillets
1 lemon, juiced

For fish fumet:
Fish heads and bones
2½ Tbsp. vegetable oil
6 Tbsp. butter
3 shallots, minced
1 bottle dry French cider or dry white
 wine (such as a California Fumé
 Blanc)

Bouquet garni of a celery stalk, parsley
 stems, oregano, and dried thyme
Salt and pepper
½ lb. fresh shrimp
1 lb. live mussels
1 cup heavy cream

Special equipment needed:
A nonstick skillet
A flat enameled cast-iron gratin
 dish
Parchment paper

*L*ay the fillets on a cutting board and trim to neaten, removing any dark skin. If necessary, flatten the fillets with the side of a cleaver, then sprinkle a little lemon juice on each fillet, cover, and set aside while making the *fumet*.

Rinse the fish heads and bones, and dry well on paper towels. Heat the vegetable oil and butter in a nonstick pan, and when hot, add the shallots and let stew slowly for a few minutes, stirring constantly. Add the fish bones, and cook for 5–6 minutes to sear them. Cover with the cider or wine and an equal amount of water. Add the bouquet garni, bring to the boil, and let cook for 20 minutes. Remove from the heat and strain through a colander, discarding bones and shallots. Return the strained cooking liquid to the heat, bring to the simmer, and let reduce until only half the liquid remains. Season with more pepper than salt, add the shrimp, and let boil for 3 minutes. Strain to remove shrimp, and return the *fumet* to the pan. Remove the shrimp from their shells, set aside, and return the empty shells to the *fumet*.

Thoroughly clean the mussels in several changes of water, scrubbing well to remove any "beards." Cook the cleaned mussels in a covered skillet with some freshly ground pepper and no liquid, shaking the skillet frequently. After 5–6 minutes, all the mussels should be wide open. Discard any that do not open. Remove the mussels from their shells, set aside with the shrimp, and keep both warm, then strain the mussel juice, using a strainer lined with cheesecloth to remove any sand. Add the mussel juice to the fish *fumet,* let simmer a few minutes, stirring constantly, then taste and correct the seasoning as needed. Strain to remove shrimp shells, and set aside.

Preheat the oven to 375°F. Place the fish in a well-buttered gratin dish, and pour in enough strained fish *fumet* to cover it completely. Slowly bring to the simmer over direct heat, cover with buttered parchment paper, and finish cooking in the oven (about 20 minutes).

Remove from the oven, and holding the fish in place with your hand on the parchment paper, pour the *fumet* into a saucepan. Add the cream to the *fumet,* and let simmer and reduce until the sauce is nicely thickened.

To serve, place the fish on a shallow serving platter, with the shrimp on one side and the mussels on the other. Pour the cream sauce over the fish to cover, and serve immediately. If desired, the sauce can also be lightly browned under the broiler.

Dorade braisée au cidre ou vin blanc

Braised Sea Bream or Monkfish, in French Cider or White Wine

—

For 6

For fish:
4 lb. trimmed and cleaned sea bream or
   monkfish, tailbone removed

2 Tbsp. virgin olive oil
1–2 lemons, thinly sliced and cut into
   half-moons

3 Tbsp. butter

1½–2 cups dry fermented French cider
   or dry white wine

1½ Tbsp. butter, in tiny dice

For stuffing:

5 Tbsp. stale white bread crumbs

2 Tbsp. French cider or white wine

2 Tbsp. finely minced shallots (about 3
   shallots)

2 Tbsp. finely minced parsley

1 garlic clove, crushed and finely minced

1 Tbsp. dried herbes de Provence (see
   Aide-Mémoire, page 503)

1 tsp. minced fresh dill

Salt and pepper, to taste

Parsley, for garnish

Special equipment needed:

An ovenproof baking dish, large enough
   for the fish

Aluminum foil

*T*he fish should be trimmed for cooking. For the sea bream, remove the scales and part of the tail, but leave the head. If using monkfish, remove the skin and tailbone.

Prepare the stuffing first. Moisten 3 Tbsp. bread crumbs in the cider or wine. Add the diced butter, minced shallots, parsley, garlic, herbs, dill, salt, and pepper, and mix well with a fork to obtain a purée.

Fill the cavity of the sea bream with stuffing. (For the monkfish, pack the stuffing into the cavity formed by the removal of the bone.) Brush the outside surface of the fish with oil, make 4 or 5 deep incisions in the flesh, and insert the half-moons of lemon vertically into the cuts.

Pour the cider or wine around the fish, and slowly bring to the simmer over direct heat, then bake in a preheated 400°F oven for 35–40 minutes, depending on the thickness of the fish. Halfway through the cooking time, remove from the oven and baste with pan juices. Sprinkle with the remaining bread crumbs and the diced butter. Increase the temperature to 425°F, and return the fish to the oven to finish cooking and brown the top. As soon as the fish is done, remove from the oven and cover with aluminum foil to keep warm. Serve in the same dish.

Serve with boiled potatoes: Boil 2 lb. peeled potatoes until tender, then drain. When ready to serve, pour melted butter over and sprinkle with parsley, salt, and pepper. Serve in a warmed serving dish.

Beverage Suggestion: Serve with the same cider or wine.

Moules en mouclade

Shellfish in a Cream Sauce with Curry

—

For 4 to 6

For shellfish:
3 lb. mussels
12 small crayfish or baby scallops, or half of each
2 cups dry white wine (such as French Chablis, Sancerre, or California Fumé Blanc)
Bouquet garni (see page 503)
1 tsp. dried dill
Freshly ground pepper

For vegetable purée:
2 lb. celery root, peeled and thinly sliced
Salt and freshly ground pepper, to taste
8 Tbsp. butter
¼ cup crème fraîche (page 501)

For sauce:
1 Tbsp. butter
2 Tbsp. flour
½ tsp. curry powder
Salt and pepper
1¾ cups crème fraîche (page 501)
2 Tbsp. toasted bread crumbs
1 Tbsp. butter

Special equipment needed:
An oval gratin dish, preferably enameled cast iron
A food processor
A heavy-bottomed skillet
A strainer, lined with cheesecloth
A saucepan

*H*eavily butter the bottom and sides of an oval gratin dish, and refrigerate until needed. Clean and rinse the shellfish, and scrub the mussels thoroughly. Discard any mussels that do not close when tapped. Place the wine in a heavy skillet, bring to the boil, and let reduce until 1 cup remains. Add 1 cup water, the bouquet garni, dill, and freshly ground pepper. Let boil for 10 minutes, then add the shellfish, and cover. Shake the skillet, and cook until steam escapes and the shells are open. Discard any mussels that do not open. Remove the meat from the shells, and pour the cooking juices through a strainer lined with cheesecloth to remove particles of shell and sand. Reduce the shellfish cooking juices until 2 cups remain, and set aside while preparing the celery root.

Place the sliced celery root in a saucepan with salt, freshly ground pepper, and water to cover. Bring to the boil, and then let simmer until tender. Drain and transfer to a food processor, and purée. Season highly, add the butter and crème fraîche, pulse to mix, taste again and correct the seasoning, then set aside until needed.

To make the cream sauce, melt the butter in a saucepan, stir in the flour, and let simmer for a few minutes, stirring constantly, to cook the flour. Remove from the heat, add the shellfish reduction, and bring to the simmer, stirring constantly, until the sauce is quite smooth and nicely thickened. Add the curry powder and pepper, and taste for salt, as the shellfish reduction will be quite salty. Then stir in the crème fraîche and set aside.

To assemble the *mouclade,* place a layer of celery root purée in the bottom of the gratin dish. Distribute the shellfish evenly over the purée, coat with cream sauce, top with bread crumbs, and dot with butter. The dish can be prepared to this point the morning of the day it will be served. Reheat gently over direct heat, then brown in a preheated 425°F oven for about 10 minutes and serve in the same dish.

Wine Suggestion: Serve the same wine used to cook the shellfish.

Gratin de coquillages

Gratinéed Shellfish

—

For about 6

1½ lb. mussels or clams
Freshly ground pepper
18 small crayfish or scallops
2 cups dry white wine
7 Tbsp. butter
1 lb. tender leeks, cleaned and cut in
　　small dice
3½ Tbsp. flour

1½ cups crème fraîche (page 501)
Pinch of saffron
1 Tbsp. dried thyme

Special equipment needed:
A covered skillet
A heavy-bottomed saucepan
A flat oval gratin dish

*O*ther shellfish can be substituted for the mussels and crayfish. Scrub the shellfish thoroughly in cold water. If using mussels, remove the "beards"; rinse in several changes of water. Discard any that do not close when tapped.

Put the mussels (or clams) with some freshly ground pepper in a covered skillet, and cook over direct heat, shaking the pan, until they open (about 5 minutes). Discard any mussels (or claws) that do not open. Remove the meat from the shells, and carefully strain the pan juices through cheesecloth to remove any sand or grit. Cook the other shellfish the same way.

Pour the white wine into a heavy-bottomed saucepan, add the strained shellfish cooking juices, bring to a boil, and let reduce by half. Meanwhile, clean the skillet used for the shellfish, and melt half the butter in it. When hot, add the leeks and let stew, stirring, until tender (about 25–30 minutes).

In another saucepan, prepare a white roux, melting the remaining butter with the flour and letting the roux cook for 3–4 minutes, stirring constantly. Off heat, whisk in the reduced wine–shellfish-cooking liquid and crème fraîche. Return to the heat, stirring, and add the saffron, thyme, more pepper, and salt if needed.

Spread a layer of cooked leeks evenly in the bottom of a gratin dish, then a layer of the shellfish meat, and coat with half the sauce. Ten minutes before serving, place in a preheated hot oven (450°F) for about 10 minutes, to brown slightly. Serve in the same dish, with the rest of the sauce on the side.

Wine Suggestion: A tasty dry white wine, such as a Pouilly Fumé from the Loire Valley, or a French Chablis.

CHICKEN DISHES

Poulet en ratatouille

Chicken in Ratatouille Provençal

—

For 4 to 6

One 4-lb. tender frying chicken
¾–1 cup virgin olive oil
¾ cup dry white wine
2 large onions, minced
⅔ lb. red bell pepper, skin removed, cut in strips
3 whole garlic cloves, peeled
1 8 oz. tin or 4 cups fresh tomato purée
Salt and pepper, to taste
Large bouquet garni of celery stalk, parsley stems, thyme, and oregano

⅔ lb. eggplant, peeled and cut in 1″ cubes
⅔ lb. zucchini, cut in 1″ cubes
Flour
2 Tbsp. minced fresh basil
1 garlic clove, freshly grated

Special equipment needed:
Two large skillets

$\mathcal{C}$ut the chicken into 9–10 pieces. Heat 3 Tbsp. oil in a heavy skillet. When hot, sauté the chicken pieces in one layer, being sure not to crowd them. When nicely browned, remove, and sauté all the other pieces in the same way. Return all the chicken pieces to the skillet, and pour the white wine over them. Let simmer slowly while preparing the vegetables.

In another skillet, heat 2½ Tbsp. olive oil. Add the minced onion, red bell peppers, garlic cloves, tomato purée, and bouquet garni. As soon as the onions are starting to become tender, pour this mixture over the chicken, and continue simmering until the chicken is done (about 25 minutes).

In the same skillet used for the onion mixture, heat ½ cup olive oil. Season the eggplant and zucchini, roll in flour, and fry in the hot oil until nicely browned on the outside and tender inside. Remove from skillet, drain on paper towels, and keep warm.

The chicken stew may be cooked ahead and reheat for serving. Check and adjust seasoning as necessary. Serve the chicken with all the sauce in a shallow serving dish. Arrange eggplant and zucchini as a garnish around the sides of the dish, or serve separately. Sprinkle with minced basil and freshly grated garlic.

Wine Suggestion: A light red wine of Provence, such as a Bandol.

Fricassée de coquelets à la Jeannette

Chicken Fricassee Jeannette

—

For 4 to 6

2 young frying chickens (2½–3 lb. each), cut up
¼ cup flour
1½ Tbsp. vegetable oil or extra-virgin olive oil

2½–3 cups good, tasty red wine (such as a Bandol from Provence or a Cabernet Sauvignon)
2 cups chicken broth (a little more, if needed)

Bouquet garni of celery stalk, parsley
    stems, thyme, and bay leaf
Freshly ground pepper

For mixture "Jeannette":
6 canned anchovy fillets in oil
1½ Tbsp. tomato paste
5 cloves garlic, mashed
3 Tbsp. butter
Freshly ground pepper
1 red pimiento, or Tabasco

For onion garnish:
20 small onions
2½ Tbsp. butter
Parsley, for garnish

Special equipment needed:
A large cast-iron Dutch oven or
    flameproof casserole
A food processor (optional)

*C*ut the chickens into serving pieces without removing the skin. (For such small chickens as these, it is only necessary to cut them into quarters.) Dredge in flour and shake off any excess. Heat the oil in the cast-iron casserole, and brown the chicken pieces in 2 or 3 lots without crowding them, turning them over as soon as one side is nicely browned. Remove the meat to a dish, and deglaze the empty casserole with the red wine, letting it come to the boil and scraping the bottom to remove the sediment. Boil 3 minutes, then replace the chicken, cover with some of the chicken broth, add the bouquet garni and pepper, but no salt, as the "Jeannette mixture" has plenty of salt. Set aside.

Prepare the anchovy paste by mashing together the anchovy fillets, tomato paste, crushed garlic, butter, pepper, and red pimiento or Tabasco. A food processor can be used, but it is easy to do with only a fork. When thoroughly mixed, stir into the chicken cooking liquid and let simmer for about 20–25 minutes. Taste after 15 minutes, and correct the seasoning. The chicken is done when, pricked with a fork, the juices run out looking clear, not rosy.

In the meantime, cook the onions in the remaining broth. When tender, drain them and sauté in butter. When ready to serve, remove chicken with a slotted spoon and degrease the cooking liquid. Return the chicken, correct the seasoning, and reheat. The sauce should be slightly thickened. Serve in a shallow serving dish with all the sauce, the onions around the edge, and sprinkled with minced parsley.

Vegetable Suggestion: Serve with "ball" potatoes made with a melon baller. Boil the potato balls in salted water until tender. Cover with melted butter and sprinkle with minced parsley.

Wine Suggestion: Serve the same red wine.

Filets de volaille aux concombres

Poultry Strips with Cucumbers

—

For 6 to 8

4 lb. small cucumbers

6 chicken breasts, or 3 lb. turkey
   breast

1 lemon, juiced

4 Tbsp. butter

1½ Tbsp. vegetable oil

3–4 shallots, minced

½ cup cider vinegar or dry white wine
   vinegar

1½ cups chicken broth (or water and
   bouillon cubes)

Salt and pepper

Tabasco

½ cup crème fraîche (page 501)

2½ Tbsp. minced basil or tarragon

Special equipment needed:
A nonstick pan

*P*eel the cucumbers, and cut in quarters lengthwise. Remove the seeds, and cut into dice. Parboil for 4 minutes in boiling salted water. Rinse in a colander, drain, and let dry over paper towels. Slice the chicken or turkey breast into thin strips, sprinkle lightly with lemon juice, and set aside while cooking the shallots.

Melt half the butter with the oil in a nonstick pan, add the minced shallots, and stir constantly for a few minutes until tender, not browned. Remove the shallots, add the rest of the butter to the same hot fat, and sauté the chicken strips over medium heat, shaking the pan and stirring until the pieces are slightly browned on all sides.

Return the shallots to the pan with the chicken, and let stew 2–3 minutes, then remove all and keep warm. Deglaze the pan with the vinegar, let boil, then add the chicken broth. Let boil, and add the seasoning. Return the meat to the pan. The dish can be prepared to this point up to one day ahead and refrigerated, with the cucumbers stored separately until just before serving.

When ready to serve, reheat the meat slowly, and finish the cooking. Reheat the cucumbers in the crème fraîche, mixing in the juice from the meat at the last minute. To serve, place the meat in the middle of a warmed shallow platter, with the cucumbers all around. Pour the sauce over the meat, and sprinkle minced basil or tarragon over the dish.

Une poule verte en pâte

A Green Hen in a Crust

—

For 8 to 10

For crust:
3 cups pastry flour
½ tsp. salt
10 Tbsp. butter
2 Tbsp. melted lard
Pinch of saffron
2 eggs
¼–⅓ cup cold water

For chicken filling:
One 3½–4 lb. chicken
3 Tbsp. butter
1½ Tbsp. oil
3 onions, sliced
2 carrots, sliced
2 Tbsp. flour mixed with 2 Tbsp. curry powder

2½ cups chicken broth, or half dry white wine and half broth
3 cloves garlic, not peeled
Bouquet garni of celery stalk, parsley stems, and thyme

For green vegetables and stuffing:
1½ lb. cleaned lettuce, spinach, or Swiss chard
3½ oz. fresh melted pork fat or lard
4 eggs
⅔ cup crème fraîche (page 501) or sour cream
Salt and pepper
Optional: 3 Tbsp. Cognac
¾ lb. unsalted raw smoked ham, cut in dice
1 egg yolk, for glaze

Special equipment needed: A food processor
A heavy cast-iron skillet with lid A large rectangular tin or Pyrex
Parchment paper mold

*P*repare the pastry dough for the crust by mixing all the crust ingredients together, shape into a ball, and let rest 1 hour in the refrigerator.

Cut the chicken in pieces. Heat 1½ Tbsp. butter and all of the oil in a heavy cast-iron skillet until beginning to smoke. Add the dark chicken pieces in 1 layer and let them brown lightly on all sides, turning as needed. Remove and replace with the light chicken pieces, onions, and carrots. When nicely browned, remove all. Strain the cooking butter and return it to the skillet, adding the remaining butter. When hot, sprinkle with the flour-curry mixture, and stir until a light roux results. Pour in the chicken broth (or half wine and half broth) and bring to a boil, stirring constantly with a wire whisk. Add the garlic, salt and pepper, browned chicken pieces, and bouquet garni. When simmering, cover with parchment paper and the skillet lid, and cook 30–35 minutes, turning the chicken pieces after 20 minutes. Alternatively, bake in a 375°F oven for the same time, or until done. Remove chicken pieces, and set aside to cool. Remove the skin and bones from the chicken, and pulse the meat for a few seconds in the food processor, then set aside. The chicken should be chopped, not puréed. Strain the cooking liquid, reduce to ½–¾ cup, and set aside.

Blanch the lettuce or other green vegetable 5–15 minutes, refresh, drain, and squeeze out all excess moisture. Put through the food processor, then sauté slowly in a skillet with rendered fresh pork fat, stirring constantly. Remove from the skillet, stir in 4 eggs beaten with crème fraîche, and the strained, reduced cooking juices from the chicken (½–¾ cup). The mixture should not be runny. Add the diced ham, chopped chicken, and cognac, and mix thoroughly.

Oil the rectangular mold. Roll out ¾ of the pastry in a neat rectangular shape, and fit it inside the mold, leaving an excess of ⅓" at the top for a border. Fill with the meat-vegetable mixture and pack tightly, then cover with the remaining pastry dough, sealing the edges with the excess from the sides. Cut a funnel in the top to allow the steam to escape, and garnish with a little leaf design made with dough trimmings. Glaze the top with beaten egg yolk, and bake for 45 minutes in a preheated 375°–400°F oven, then for 30 minutes at 350°F. When done, juices should be visible at the top of the pâté. Let rest in a cool place until cold, about 6 hours.

Wine Suggestion: A good Cabernet Sauvignon from Bordeaux or California (Mondavi Winery).

Pain de restes de volaille Susy

Chicken or Turkey Loaf for Susy, Made from Leftovers

—

For 10 to 12

1 lb. leftover turkey or chicken

8 oz. boiled ham

Salt, pepper, nutmeg, and *quatre épices* (see Aide-Mémoire, page 503)

Tabasco

1½ Tbsp. butter

2½ Tbsp. flour

2½ cups hot chicken broth (or water and bouillon cubes)

2 oz. fresh white bread

½ cup crème fraîche (page 501) or heavy cream

3 eggs

¼ cup grated Gruyère cheese

Optional: Tomato Sauce (page 486)

Optional: 1½ lb. Short Pastry or Puff Pastry (pages 488 and 489)

2 egg yolks, for crust

Special equipment needed:

Parchment paper, if using loaf pan

A food processor

A nonstick 9″ by 5″ by 2½″ loaf pan, if not using crust

A bain-marie (see Aide-Mémoire, page 503) or roasting pan large enough to hold loaf pan and hot water

A rectangular baking sheet

If a crust will not be used, prepare a loaf pan by lining the bottom and sides with buttered parchment paper. Set in refrigerator until ready to fill.

Remove the bones from the leftover chicken or turkey. Cut boiled ham into chunks. Place the meats in a food processor with the seasonings, and pulse 4–5 times, until roughly chopped. Do not overwork. Transfer the meat mixture to a mixing bowl, and set aside.

Make a roux: Heat the butter in a saucepan, add the flour, and stir over medium heat until the mixture turns golden. Immediately remove from heat, pour in all the hot broth at once, and whisk until the sauce is completely smooth. Return over heat and let simmer 4–5 minutes, stirring constantly, then remove from heat.

In a small mixing bowl, moisten the bread with the crème fraîche and mix with a fork until quite smooth. Add moistened bread to the reserved meat mixture, then add the eggs, stirring until all is thoroughly mixed. Correct the seasoning, adding more pepper and Tabasco as needed. Add the grated cheese, and mix well.

Fill the loaf pan, if using one, and pack well to eliminate any air pockets. Set in a bain-marie or roasting pan with hot water two-thirds up the sides of the loaf pan and bake in a preheated 375°F oven for 35–40 minutes. When done, remove from oven and let cool a few minutes before unmolding. While baking, prepare Tomato Sauce.

If the loaf is to be baked in a crust, you will need 1½ lb. short pastry or puff pastry. Remove ½ lb. of the dough, roll out into an oval, and place in the center of a metal baking sheet. Set aside in a cold place. Roll out the remaining pound of dough. Shape the meat mixture into a loaf on top of the first piece of pastry dough. Lay the second, larger piece of dough over the meat loaf, and tuck it under the first to completely enclose the loaf. Make a hole in the center of the top surface to allow steam to escape during baking. Decorate the loaf with a design made from scraps of pastry cut with a fluted pastry wheel. Glaze with egg yolks beaten with a little water, then refrigerate until firm. Bake in a preheated 400°F oven for 10 minutes, then reduce heat to 375°F and bake for 25 more minutes, or until nicely browned.

Serve on a warmed shallow serving dish. Glaze with some of the sauce, and serve the rest in a sauceboat.

Wine Suggestion: A rosé from Provence or light red Bordeaux, or a Mondavi Cabernet Sauvignon.

Poulet farci au riz, foies, et truffes

Chicken Casserole with White Wine,
Filled with Rice, Chicken Livers,
and Truffles

—

For 6

4½ lb. roasting chicken

For marinade:
2 Tbsp. dry white wine or Madeira
2 Tbsp. Cognac
2 Tbsp. finely minced shallots
Freshly ground pepper

For stuffing:
2½ oz. chicken livers
4 Tbsp. butter
½ cup very finely minced onion
1 cup raw rice
½ cup dry white wine
2 cups chicken broth
Pinch of saffron
Bay leaf, salt, and pepper
1 egg, lightly beaten
Optional: 1 oz. can of truffles, diced,
    with the juice

To poach chickens:
2 Tbsp. butter

1 bottle of the same wine
Bouquet garni of celery stalk, parsley
    stems, thyme, and bay leaf
2½–3 cups chicken broth

For sauce:
3 oz. can red pimiento, well drained
    and dried, cut into small dice
4 Tbsp. sweet butter, creamed
3½–4 Tbsp. flour
Cayenne, Tabasco, and salt
Parsley, in bunches and minced, for
    garnish

Special equipment needed:
A larding needle and kitchen
    string
A flameproof casserole with lid
A large piece of cheesecloth
Parchment paper
A sieve and a rubber spatula
A heavy-bottomed 6-qt. saucepan

*M*ix all ingredients for marinade and set aside. To prepare the chicken, slit the skin down the front, and peel it back from the breast. Remove the meat on each side of the breastbone in two pieces. Cut out the breastbone, which will give you a boat-shaped cavity for stuffing. Slice the breast meat into strips ½″ wide, and place in the marinade. Cover and refrigerate while preparing the stuffing.

For the stuffing, clean and trim the chicken livers and cut into ¼″ dice. Sauté in 2 Tbsp. butter, just until they stiffen slightly. Set aside in the cooking juices. Sauté the minced onion in 2 Tbsp. butter until tender but not browned, then add the raw rice and stir over medium heat until the rice turns milky and begins to brown. Add ½ cup dry white wine, and let boil about 3 minutes to evaporate the alcohol, then add 2 cups chicken broth, the saffron, bay leaf, salt, and pepper. Stir once, cover the pan, and cook for 12 minutes, or until the liquid is entirely absorbed. Discard bay leaf and let cool. The rice should not be quite done, as it will continue to cook inside the chicken. When cool, stir in 1 lightly beaten egg, the chicken livers, and their cooking juices. Correct the seasoning, and set aside.

Salt the cavity of the chicken, then spread on a layer of rice stuffing, then a layer of diced truffles. Repeat the process, molding the rice into a dome at the breast end. Cover the rice with the marinated breast strips and replace the skin over the breast. Sew together, and then truss the chicken. Rub the rest of the butter over the entire chicken, and place it, breast side up, in a casserole. Pour in the wine, bring to a boil to evaporate the alcohol, add the bouquet garni, then pour in broth to reach about halfway up the side of the chicken. Bring to a simmer, cover with the cheesecloth, then parchment paper, then the casserole lid, and poach in a pre-heated 375°F oven for about 1½–1¾ hours.

Meanwhile, prepare the pimiento butter. With a rubber spatula, work the cut-up pimiento and half the creamed butter through a sieve, then stir together until homogenous, making a smooth pimiento paste. Alternatively, this could be done in a food processor. Set aside.

When the chicken is done, remove from the casserole and drain the juice from the vent. Strain the cooking juices and degrease, then reduce until you have 2 cups of liquid. Correct seasoning.

Melt 2 Tbsp. butter in a heavy-bottomed saucepan, add 4 Tbsp. flour, and cook 2–3 minutes, stirring constantly. Do not allow to brown. Remove from heat, and add 1 cup of the cooking juices and additional chicken broth as needed, to equal 2 cups of liquid. Mix with a wire whisk off the heat, beating until quite smooth and thoroughly mixed, then return to the heat. Bring to the boil, stirring constantly until the mixture is quite thick. Add the pimiento butter by spoonfuls, along with the cayenne, Tabasco, and salt as needed.

When ready to serve, remove the trussing strings and place the chicken on a heated platter. Spoon a little of the sauce over the chicken, and garnish with bunches of parsley. Sprinkle minced parsley on top.

Vegetable Suggestion: Very thinly sliced string beans, sautéed in butter, or tiny garden peas, or tender broccoli.

Wine Suggestion: Serve the same as was used to cook the chicken, ideally Chablis.

Poulet en fricassée au curry

Chicken Fricassee with Curry

—

For 4 to 6

For 2½ cups chicken stock:
Neck, wingtips, and giblets from chicken
Bouquet garni of celery stalk, thyme, bay leaf, and parsley
Salt and pepper
1 carrot, quartered
1 whole onion

For fricassee:
2 Tbsp. vegetable oil
3 medium onions, sliced
4 Tbsp. butter
One 4-lb. broiling chicken, cut into serving pieces
1½ Tbsp. flour

1½ Tbsp. curry powder
Bouquet garni, as above
Salt and pepper

For garnish:
1½–2 apples, preferably Granny Smith
1½ Tbsp. butter
1 cup raw rice

Special equipment needed:
A large stockpot
A cast-iron skillet with tight lid
Parchment paper
A nonstick skillet

$\mathcal{P}$repare the chicken stock the day before, placing neck, wingtips, giblets, bouquet garni, salt, and pepper together in a stockpot with 1 qt. water. Bring to the boil and skim off any scum, then reduce to a simmer, add carrot and onion, cover, and let cook for 1½–2 hours. Strain, place in the refrigerator overnight, and degrease by removing the solidified fat the next day.

Using a cast-iron skillet, heat the oil, then add the sliced onions. Stir until all is beginning to brown, then remove and set aside. Add 3 Tbsp. butter to the hot pan, and add the dark meat of the chicken, cooking the pieces in a single layer. Turn the pieces so they brown evenly on all sides (about 6–7 minutes). Remove, add more butter, and brown the rest of the chicken in the same way. Return all the pieces of chicken to the pan, and sprinkle evenly with the flour. Cook the flour on the chicken pieces until slightly browned, then add the curry powder and cook in the same way (about 3 minutes). Each piece of chicken should be evenly coated with flour and curry.

Add enough stock to cover the chicken halfway. Shake the pan and stir to dissolve the flour in the stock, then return the onions to the pan, add the bouquet garni, and bring to the boil. Cover with parchment paper and the skillet lid, and bake in a preheated 350°F oven for about 25–30 minutes, or until done. Halfway through the cooking, turn the meat over and correct the seasoning, adding more salt and pepper, if needed.

While the chicken is cooking, peel, core, and slice the apples. Melt 1 Tbsp. of the butter in a nonstick pan, add the sliced apples, and cook until tender, turning slices when the first side is tender and slightly browned. Remove from heat and set aside.

Bring a large quantity of salted water to the boil, add the rice, and let simmer 16–18 minutes, or until tender. Drain and rinse under cold running water to remove salt, then drain dry. Keep warm until ready to serve, then reheat with the rest of the butter. When the chicken is done, remove to a warmed serving dish. Strain and degrease the cooking juices, and reheat the chicken in the juices, if needed. Serve on the warmed platter surrounded with the apples, and with the rice in another dish.

Wine Suggestion: Slightly chilled good Beaujolais, perhaps Julienas or Brouilly.

Dinde en fricassée à la niçoise, avec riz et tomate

Turkey Casserole Niçoise, with Rice and Tomato Sauce

—

For 10 to 12

2 lb. turkey breast, thickly sliced

2½ Tbsp. olive oil

8 Tbsp. butter

2 dozen pearl onions, carefully peeled

2–3 garlic cloves, crushed

Bouquet garni of celery stalk, thyme, parsley, and bay leaf

1½–2 cups dry white wine

1½–2 cups chicken broth

Pepper and salt

For rice rings:

Salt

2½ cups raw rice (not parboiled, converted rice)

Pinch of saffron

3 Tbsp. butter

Optional: ½ cup frozen tiny green peas, parboiled

1 cup tomato paste

2 garlic cloves, minced

½ cup pitted black Niçoise olives, roughly chopped

Optional: 1 tsp. potato starch dissolved in cold water

Chopped parsley, for garnish

Special equipment needed:

A heavy-bottomed cast-iron pan

Parchment paper

2 nonstick ring molds

2 shallow serving platters

Cut the turkey breast into strips ½″ wide and 2″ long. Heat the oil in the cast-iron pan with 2–3 Tbsp. butter. Add the peeled onions and let cook, shaking the pan, until they are slightly browned on all sides. Remove the onions with a slotted spoon, and drain on paper towels.

If the fat has burned, discard it, clean the pan, and replace with fresh oil and butter. Otherwise, reheat the fat. Add the turkey strips, being sure not to crowd the pieces. As soon as they have browned on all sides, remove, and cook the other turkey strips in the same manner, adding more butter and oil as needed.

Return all the turkey pieces and onions to the pan, add the crushed garlic cloves and the bouquet garni, and pour in the white wine. Slowly bring to the boil, and let simmer 2–3 minutes to evaporate the alcohol, then pour in enough broth to cover all. Add pepper, salt (if the broth is not salted), then cover with parchment paper and the pan lid. Bring to the simmer, then cook slowly in a preheated 350°F oven, or let simmer on the stove, for 20 minutes. Remove from heat, and set aside until ready to serve.

Next, prepare the rice. In a large saucepan, bring 4 qt. water and a handful of salt to the boil. Add the rice and saffron, and stir until the water returns to the boil. Let boil uncovered 16–18 minutes, or until the rice is tender. Drain in a colander, then rinse with cold running water to remove the salt. Drain to dry. Reheat with the butter (and green peas), then pack into the ring molds. Just before serving, heat through in a preheated 375°F oven (about 10 minutes).

Before serving, remove and reserve the turkey and onions, then strain and degrease the sauce. Return the sauce to the pan, and add the tomato paste and minced garlic. Bring to the boil and let reduce to concentrate the flavors until 2 cups remain. Stir in the chopped olives, and correct the seasoning. If the sauce is too thin, thicken it with potato starch well dissolved in a little cold water. Let simmer until thickened, stirring until smooth. Add the turkey and onions to the sauce to reheat, being careful not to break up the turkey pieces.

To serve, unmold the rice rings onto warmed serving platters and arrange the turkey with its sauce in the centers of the rings. Sprinkle with chopped parsley to garnish. Any remaining sauce can be served on the side in a warmed sauceboat.

Wine Suggestion: Serve either a dry white wine or a light Provençal rosé.

Civet de canard aux pruneaux

Duck Stew in Wine, with Prunes

—

For 9 to 10

3 nonfatty ducks, about 3 lb. each
3 carrots, thinly sliced
3 large onions, sliced

1 garlic (about 8 cloves), separated and
   peeled
Peppercorns

2 bouquets garnis of 3 celery stalks,
thyme, a bay leaf, and parsley stems
3 bottles of good-quality strong red
wine, such as Côtes du Rhône
24–30 dried prunes, steeped in hot tea
until softened
2 Tbsp. butter
1½ Tbsp. peanut oil
2 Tbsp. flour

Chicken broth (if needed)
Salt and pepper, to taste

Special equipment needed:
Strainers
A small casserole for cooking the prunes
A large cast-iron casserole with lid
Parchment paper
A food mill

*T*he ducks should be cut up and placed to marinate the day before or the morning of the day the dish will be served.

The ducks should be cleaned and singed, if necessary. Cut off and reserve the wingtips. Remove legs, thighs, wings, and breast, making 8 serving pieces per duck. Chop the carcass, neck, and wingtips. Place all the duck pieces in a large bowl, and cover with the vegetables, whole garlic cloves, and several crushed peppercorns. Stick a bouquet garni in the middle, and pour in enough wine to just cover. Set in a cool place, but do not refrigerate.

Drain the duck pieces, duck bones, and vegetables, using a large strainer. Save everything except the bouquet garni. Drain the prunes, discarding the tea, and cook them for about 8–10 minutes in enough of the remaining wine to barely cover. Drain, and keep the wine.

In the large casserole, heat half the butter with the oil. Carefully dry the duck pieces with paper towels, leaving the vegetables for later. Slowly brown the duck pieces, without crowding, skin side first. When nicely golden brown on both sides, remove, and brown the other pieces the same way.

Using the same fat, brown the duck bones, then remove; add the vegetables, cooking and stirring until they are tender, then remove them. Skim off excess fat, and stir in the remaining butter. When melted, add the flour and stir over moderate heat until the roux is slightly browned. Off heat, pour in the wine that was used to cook the prunes, and whisk until smooth. Add the remaining wine, and let simmer a few minutes, then add the duck pieces, browned bones, and vegetables. If the wine doesn't completely cover everything, add chicken broth to cover. Place a fresh bouquet garni in the middle of the pot, and correct the seasoning, adding more salt and pepper, if needed. Cover with parchment paper and the casserole lid. Bring to the boil, then bake in a preheated 375°F oven for about 45 minutes. The duck is tender when the point of a sharp knife easily pierces the meat. Remove the duck pieces to a warmed dish, and keep warm and covered until needed.

Discard the duck bones, leaving the vegetables in the cooking liquid. Let simmer to reduce until about 3½ cups remain. Strain and discard the vegetables, reserving the garlic cloves. Degrease the cooking juices.

Purée the garlic in a food mill and stir into the sauce. Adjust the seasoning and reduce, if needed, being sure to leave at least 3 cups of sauce.

Ten minutes before serving, return the duck to the sauce just to reheat. Serve immediately, garnished with the reserved prunes.

Wine Suggestion: A Châteauneuf-du-Pape, or the same wine used in the cooking.

Pintades aux pruneaux et au vinaigre de Xérès

Guinea Hen with Prunes and Xérès Vinegar

—

For 6 to 7

4 Tbsp. butter

2 Tbsp. oil

1 lb. sliced onions

10 garlic cloves

2 guinea hens (3½–4 lb. each), or
  4 Cornish hens

Salt and pepper

½ cup Xérès vinegar (also called sherry
  or Jerez vinegar)

2 cups dry white wine

Bouquet garni of celery stalk, thyme, bay
  leaf, and parsley stems

2½ cups chicken broth

¾ lb. dried prunes

Minced chervil or parsley, for garnish

Special equipment needed:

2 skillets (1 ovenproof)

Parchment paper

A food mill

*H*eat half the butter and oil in a skillet. When hot, add the sliced onions, and stir for a few minutes. Add the garlic and 2 Tbsp. water, and let stew, covered, stirring from time to time, for about 30 minutes.

Meanwhile, cut each hen into 6 pieces and season lightly with salt and pepper. Heat the remaining butter and oil in another skillet. When hot, lightly brown the guinea hen pieces in a single layer, beginning with the dark meat, and without crowding the pieces. When slightly browned, remove and place on the bed of stewing onions and garlic.

Deglaze the empty skillet with the vinegar, scraping the bottom with a fork to remove all the sediment, then add the wine and let boil for a few minutes to evaporate the alcohol. Pour this mixture over the hen pieces, place the bouquet garni in the middle, and add chicken broth to half cover the meat. When simmering, cover with parchment paper and the lid, and finish cooking in a preheated 375°F oven for about 25–30 minutes. If using the smaller Cornish hens, the time will be reduced to about 20 minutes. About halfway through the cooking, turn the hen pieces and correct the seasoning.

When done, remove the hen pieces to a warm platter and discard the bouquet garni. Strain and degrease the cooking juices. Purée the onions and garlic through a food mill (not a food processor), and parboil the prunes to plump them.

Return the cooking juices to a skillet, add the remaining chicken broth, and let reduce until 2 cups remain. Add the puréed vegetables and the prunes. Just before serving, reheat the hen pieces very slowly.

To serve, place the hen pieces on a warmed serving platter sprinkled with minced chervil and with the prunes placed around in a ring. Serve the cooking sauce on the side in a sauceboat.

Wine Suggestion: A good light red Bordeaux or Cabernet Sauvignon.

MEAT DISHES: BEEF, LAMB, VEAL, PORK, RABBIT

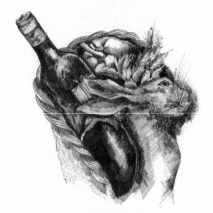

Filet de boeuf ou gigot d'agneau grand veneur

Beef Sirloin or Leg of Lamb with Grand Veneur Sauce

—

For 6 to 8

3 cups strong red wine

½ cup red-wine vinegar

2 Tbsp. extra-virgin olive oil

10 black peppercorns

3 bay leaves

1 onion, sliced

1 carrot, sliced

2–4 garlic cloves, not peeled

4 lb. beef sirloin or trimmed leg of lamb

Olive oil
1 Tbsp. tomato paste
1½ Tbsp. red currant jelly
Optional: ⅓ cup crème fraîche (page 501)

For optional avocado sauce:
5–6 small avocados
Juice of ½ lime

Ketchup
Optional: ⅓ cup crème fraîche (page 501)
Salt and pepper

Special equipment needed:
A ceramic or glass terrine or bowl
A bain-marie (see page 503)
A food processor, for avocado sauce

Combine wine, vinegar, olive oil, peppercorns, bay leaves, onions, carrots, and garlic cloves in a large bowl or terrine. Add the meat to the marinade. If meat is not completely covered, add more wine. Let marinate for 24–36 hours, turning the meat halfway through.

Remove meat from marinade, reserving liquid, and dry carefully with paper towels. Tie with kitchen twine, and rub with olive oil. Roast in a preheated 500°F oven for 20–25 minutes, turning over when one side is done (about 15 minutes). Keep warm until ready to serve.

Meanwhile, prepare the Grand Veneur (or Chevreuil) Sauce: Strain the marinade, and boil until reduced by half. Reduce heat, add tomato paste and red currant jelly, stirring until the jelly has melted. If you wish, fold in 3 oz. crème fraîche over low heat. Keep warm in a roasting pan containing hot water.

To make Avocado Sauce: Halve avocados and remove pits. Scoop flesh into a food processor, reserving the shells, and add lime juice and a dash of ketchup. Process until smooth, then scrape purée into a mixing bowl and set aside. Add crème fraîche to the food processor, and process until thick. Fold whipped crème fraîche into the avocado purée. Taste and correct seasoning, fill reserved avocado shells, and set aside.

Slice the beef or lamb, and serve on a warmed serving platter glazed with some of the Grand Veneur Sauce. Garnish platter with filled avocado shells, and serve remaining Grand Veneur Sauce in a sauceboat.

Wine Suggestion: A red Burgundy or a Beaujolais.

Boeuf à la tzigane

Gypsy-style Meat Stew with a Hungarian Flavor

—

For 8 to 10

3½ lb. beef sirloin

5 Tbsp. mild virgin olive oil

1 lb. medium onions, finely chopped

3–4 Tbsp. flour

2 cups good chicken or beef stock

½ cup very concentrated tomato
   purée

Salt and pepper

Pinch of sugar

2 Tbsp. Dijon mustard

Optional: Worcestershire sauce

Cayenne

1½ cups crème fraîche (page 501)

1 Tbsp. butter

Optional, for sauce or side dish: 1 lb.
   white mushrooms, cleaned and sliced,
   sautéed in butter

Bunch of watercress or parsley sprigs,
   for garnish

Special equipment needed:
A heavy cast-iron saucepan or skillet

Trim the meat of any fat and gristle, and cut into pieces 1″ by 1″ by 2″. The meat should remain rare, so it must be fairly thick.

Heat 2 Tbsp. oil in a cast-iron skillet. When hot but not smoking, sauté the meat in one layer, without crowding. Using a wooden spatula, turn the pieces so they brown slightly on all sides. When all the meat is browned, remove and keep warm.

Clean the pan and add 3 Tbsp. oil. Add the chopped onions and cook until wilted, then sprinkle with flour and stir well to combine. Add the stock and tomato purée, and bring to the boil, stirring constantly and shaking the pan. Reduce heat and let simmer slowly while adding the seasoning: a little salt, more pepper, the mustard, cayenne, sugar, and Worcestershire sauce if you like it. This dish should be highly seasoned. Let the sauce base continue to simmer and reduce until it has thickened slightly, then stir in the crème fraîche and let simmer until 2½ cups remain. The sauce can be prepared to this point the day before.

To serve, heat sauce to just below simmering, add the sautéed meat, and let reheat, without boiling, for 3–4 minutes—no longer, or meat will be overdone. The meat should be quite pink inside. Off heat and just before serving, stir in the butter in little pieces. For a richer dish, add some sautéed sliced mushrooms to the sauce as well. Garnish the serving dish with watercress or parsley.

Vegetable Suggestion: Serve with 2 cups rice, cooked in water, or simple boiled potatoes.

Wine Suggestion: A red wine, such as Châteauneuf-du-Pape, Hermitage rouge, or Côtes de Provence.

Curry de boeuf

Braised Curried Beef

—

For 6 to 8

3–4 lb. beef (brisket, which I prefer, or top round, bottom round, or rump roast)
4–5 ripe tomatoes or 2 Tbsp. tomato paste
4 oz. sultana (golden) raisins
2 large Golden Delicious apples
2–3 bananas, depending on size
3 medium onions
5 garlic cloves
4 Tbsp. olive oil
Optional: 3 oz. pulverized macadamia nuts, pecans, or English walnuts
2½ Tbsp. curry powder

¼ tsp. ground cinnamon
1 pt. plain yogurt
4 cups chicken broth (or water and bouillon cubes)
1 large bouquet garni of celery stalk, thyme, bay leaf, and parsley
Salt and pepper

Special equipment needed:
A large enameled cast-iron saucepan with lid
Parchment paper
A smaller saucepan
A food processor or food mill

$\mathcal{R}$emove the fat and sinews from the meat, and cut into cubes 1½″ square, then set aside. Blanch whole ripe tomatoes in boiling water for 10 seconds, remove and refresh in cold water, then core and peel. Cut in half crosswise, turn over, and squeeze very gently to remove their seeds and excess juices. Cut the drained tomatoes into large dice, and reserve. Parboil the raisins until softened, then drain and set aside. Peel the apples and bananas, cut into large dice, and set aside. Peel and slice the onions, and crush the garlic.

Heat the oil in a large saucepan, then slowly brown the meat on all sides. Remove and let drain on absorbent towels, then add the onions to the same hot fat. When soft and slightly browned, add the apples and bananas, then the tomatoes or paste, and garlic, and let stew slowly. Mix in the raisins (and nuts), and continue to stew until the mixture is homogenous, then stir in the curry powder, cinnamon, and yogurt, which will make a wonderful base in which to cook the meat. Add the meat and 4 cups chicken broth to the saucepan, and slowly bring all to the simmer. Place a large bouquet garni in the center, add pepper and salt to taste (remembering that canned chicken broth or that made with cubes is salted), then place a piece of parchment paper over the meat and cover with a lid. Place in a preheated 375°F oven, and let simmer 1½–1¾ hours.

When the meat is just tender, remove all. Strain and degrease the cooking juices, then place in a saucepan and reduce over high heat to concentrate the flavors, adding pepper if needed.

Purée the vegetables and fruit with the reduced cooking juices in a food processor or food mill, then return over heat and bring to a simmer, stirring constantly. Just before serving, gently reheat the meat in the sauce. Serve in a warmed shallow serving dish, glazing with the sauce.

Vegetable Suggestion: Serve the beef curry with a risotto, which you can make as follows: Slowly stew 1 sliced onion in 4 Tbsp. butter until quite soft but not browned. Add 2½ cups rice and continue to stir over heat until the rice grains become milky, then pour in 5 cups boiling chicken broth or water. Bring to the simmer, stir once, then cover and place in a preheated 375°F oven for 18–20 minutes, or until the rice has absorbed the liquid. Remove from oven and let set, covered, a few minutes, then fluff with a fork and serve.

Wine Suggestion: A good red Beaujolais or Côtes du Rhône.

Aiguillette de boeuf au potiron

Beef Stew with Pumpkin

—

For 4 to 6

2 lb. bottom round of beef or
    brisket
2 medium onions, sliced
3 Tbsp. extra-virgin olive oil
1 tender green cabbage
5–6 garlic cloves, not peeled
1 cup beef broth or water
Peel from an orange, dried

Salt and pepper
Dried herbes de Provence (see page 503)
3 lb. fresh pumpkin

Special equipment needed:
A heavy-bottomed skillet or Dutch oven
    with lid
Parchment paper

*T*rim the beef, removing any fat and gristle, then cut into 1½″ cubes. Peel and slice the onions. Heat the oil in a heavy-bottomed skillet, add the sliced onions, and let stew, stirring, until they are just beginning to be tender. Using a slotted spoon, remove the onions from the pan, and reserve.

Using the same hot oil, brown the beef cubes slowly on all sides. Do not crowd the pieces of beef. If necessary, do this step in batches. Meanwhile, parboil the cabbage for 6 minutes only. Drain, refresh in cold water, drain again, and dry, then cut into strips and reserve.

As soon as all the meat is evenly browned, remove and reserve. Add the whole garlic cloves to give flavor to the drippings, then deglaze the pan with beef broth or water. Return the meat, onions, and cabbage strips to the pot, add the dried orange peel, and salt, pepper, and herbs to taste.

Meanwhile, peel the pumpkin, remove the seeds and fibers, and cut into 1″ cubes. Add to the stew, and mix thoroughly. Bring all to the boil over direct heat, cover with parchment paper and the pan lid, and bake in a preheated 375°F oven for about 2 hours. Halfway through the cooking, stir to ensure that all cooks evenly. When done, the meat should be very tender. Taste and correct the seasoning.

Remove the meat when tender, and strain and degrease the sauce. Discard the orange peel, as it should not be served. Pick out the garlic, purée through a food mill, and add back to the sauce. (If you wish, you can also purée the vegetables to a finer consistency, but it is really necessary only to purée the garlic, to remove its skin.) Combine the meat, vegetables, sauce, and garlic purée to reheat. Taste and correct the seasoning, adding more herbs if necessary. This dish should be highly seasoned.

Serve in a warmed serving dish, the meat mixed with the vegetables.

Wine Suggestion: A good rosé from Provence or a light red Côtes de Provence.

Daube de boeuf Jeannette

Beef Stew Jeannette

—

For 5 to 6

Optional: 8–10 canned anchovy
    fillets

3½ lb. lean stewing beef, preferably top
    round, cut into cubes 1″ square

6 oz. lean bacon, cut into ½″ dice

½ cup olive oil

2 medium onions, sliced

3 garlic cloves, mashed

1 onion, studded with 3 cloves

Peel from an orange, dried

2½ cups red wine from Provence

Beef broth to cover the meat (or water
    and bouillon cubes)

3 Tbsp. tomato paste

Large bouquet garni (see page 503)

Salt and pepper

4 oz. tiny Niçoise olives, pitted

1 Tbsp. minced basil or parsley

Special equipment needed:

A heavy-bottomed skillet with lid

Parchment paper

If you have decided to add the optional anchovy fillets, insert a small piece in each beef cube, using a larding needle or a pointed knife, then set aside. Parboil the bacon 6–7 minutes, refresh, then drain and dry on paper towels.

    Heat half the oil in a heavy-bottomed skillet. When very hot, add the diced bacon and stir until it begins to brown, then remove and let drain on paper towels.

Without crowding the pieces, add the beef cubes to the hot oil. Turn the pieces when nicely browned. When all sides are evenly browned, remove the beef cubes with a slotted spoon, and reserve. Add more oil and the sliced onions, and let stew slowly, stirring, until tender but not browned.

Return the meat and bacon to the skillet, and add the garlic, the orange peel, onion, and the wine. Bring to the boil, then add broth (or water and beef bouillon cubes) to cover, stir in the tomato paste, place a large bouquet garni in the middle, and season with more pepper than salt, as the olives will provide salt.

When the mixture begins to simmer, cover with parchment paper and the lid, and place in a preheated 375°F oven for at least 1½ hours, or until the meat is tender. Turn the beef cubes halfway through cooking. A few minutes before serving, remove the onion, add the olives, taste, and correct the seasoning.

Serve in a warmed shallow serving dish, accompanied by boiled potatoes or rice, sprinkled with minced basil or parsley.

Wine Suggestion: Serve with the same wine.

Sauté d'agneau à la mamounia

Lamb Sauté Mamounia

—

For 10 to 12

2 lamb shoulders, boned (about 5 lb.)
3–4 Tbsp. olive oil
8 Tbsp. butter
1½ Tbsp. vegetable oil
4–5 medium onions, chopped
10 cloves garlic, not peeled
⅓ oz. saffron
Pepper and salt
6–7 Tbsp. honey or maple syrup
1½ cups dry white wine
2 cups beef or lamb broth, or bouillon

Large bouquet garni of celery stalk, parsley stems, and mint
2 Tbsp. dried herbes de Provence (see Aide-Mémoire, page 503)
2 lb. seedless raisins, steeped overnight in orange blossom water or white wine
Minced fresh mint, for garnish

Special equipment needed:
A large ovenproof skillet with lid
Parchment paper

*R*emove the fat and gristle from the lamb, and cut into 3–4 oz. serving pieces. Heat olive oil in a large skillet, and lightly brown the meat on all sides, taking care not to crowd the pieces. When done, remove to paper towels to drain, and brown the rest of the meat in the same way.

Clean the skillet and melt 5 Tbsp. of the butter with the vegetable oil. When hot, add the onions, and stir until softened, then add the garlic, saffron, pepper, and honey (or maple syrup). Stir constantly until the skillet contents are just under the simmer, then stir in the wine. Let boil a few minutes to evaporate the alcohol, then return the meat to the skillet. When boiling once again, pour in enough broth to half cover the meat, and bring to the simmer.

When simmering, place the bouquet garni in the middle, add the herbs, and cover with parchment paper and the lid. Bake in a preheated 350° oven for 20–25 minutes, turning the pieces from time to time to keep them from drying out. Taste and correct the seasoning, then return to the oven for 15–20 minutes more. When done, the meat should be very tender. Taste again to correct the seasoning, adding more salt and pepper as needed.

Remove the meat, cover with foil, and keep warm while preparing the sauce. Strain and degrease the cooking juices. Purée the garlic cloves through a food mill (to remove the tough skin), and stir purée into the cooking liquid. Return over heat, and add raisins and remaining butter. Taste and correct the seasoning.

To serve, arrange the meat on a warmed shallow serving dish, with the raisins all around. Cover with sauce, and serve any extra sauce in a sauceboat. Sprinkle fresh mint over the meat to garnish.

Vegetable Suggestion: Risotto or noodles.

Wine Suggestion: A full-bodied red wine such as a Côtes du Rhône or a Cabernet Sauvignon.

L'agneau braisé aux broccoli

Lamb and Broccoli Casserole

—

Optional: ½ lb. fresh cêpes or large
    white mushrooms
10 oz. broccoli florets
1 lb. lamb, preferably from leg or
    shoulder, with no bones or fat (or
    12 oz. leftover lamb)
Salt and pepper
4 garlic cloves, minced
Dried herbes de Provence (see page 503)
½ cup dried bread crumbs

4 Tbsp. beef or chicken broth
3 large eggs
1½ lb. fresh tomatoes (about 10 small
    tomatoes), cut in half and placed cut
    side down on paper towels to drain
2 Tbsp. olive oil

Special equipment needed:
An enameled cast-iron gratin dish

*W*ipe clean with a damp cloth, and cut off the caps of the cêpes. Discard stems, or save for another use. Place caps on a baking sheet, and bake in a preheated 375°F oven for 10 minutes, then set aside.

Wash and drain broccoli. Remove and discard stalks, then parboil florets for 5 minutes in rapidly boiling salted water. Refresh in cold water, drain dry, and set aside.

Trim the raw meat, removing any gristle or nerves, and cut into chunks. Chop roughly. Transfer to a mixing bowl after chopping. Stir in seasoning, garlic, herbs, bread crumbs moistened in broth, and eggs. Stir well until thoroughly combined. (The food processor cannot be used for this mixing, as it will purée the meat.)

If using cooked lamb, chop roughly, then add garlic, seasoning, herbs, and eggs. Mix, then taste, and correct the seasoning.

If using mushrooms, place the baked caps in a single layer in an oiled gratin dish. Next, place a layer of the meat mixture over the mushrooms, and top with an attractive arrangement of halved tomatoes and broccoli. Sprinkle olive oil over all, and bake in a preheated 375°F oven for about an hour if the meat is raw, 20 minutes if the meat has been cooked.

This dish can be reheated, if needed, and served in the same dish.

Wine Suggestion: A full-bodied red wine from Provence, or a Côtes du Rhône.

Piccata de veau, au jus de citron vert

Veal Slices with Lime Juice

—

For 4 to 6

1½ lb. veal sirloin or top round
6 Tbsp. extra-virgin olive oil
2–3 limes, juiced
Salt and pepper
5 Tbsp. butter
Fresh mint leaves, for garnish

Special equipment needed:
A mallet to pound the meat
A heavy cast-iron skillet

*A*sk your butcher to cut the veal scallops ¼″ thick. Place the scallops between pieces of wax paper and pound each scallop to a thickness of ⅛″. Using a sharp knife, remove any fat and filaments from the meat (if left on, the meat will curl up as it cooks). Place the scallops in a shallow dish with 3 Tbsp. olive oil, the juice of 1–1½ limes, and salt and pepper to taste, and let macerate for about 1½ hours.

Drain the meat, reserving the macerating liquid, and wipe dry with paper towels. Heat the remaining olive oil in the skillet, and sauté the scallops over moderate heat, a few at a time so as not to crowd them while cooking. Turn each scallop when browned. Remove when both sides are done (about 3–5 minutes), and cook the others in the same way.

Deglaze the skillet with the reserved macerating liquid, adding more lime juice to taste, then let reduce over high heat. Remove from heat, and whisk in the butter, 1 Tbsp. at a time, then taste, and correct the seasoning.

Just before serving, reheat the veal scallops in the sauce, not letting it boil, turning them over to be sure they are well coated. Serve on hot plates, garnished with fresh mint leaves and accompanied by Gratinéed Eggplant (page 413).

Mignon de veau en croustade, sauce madère à la moutarde

Veal in a Crust, with Madeira and Mustard Sauce

—

For 4 to 6

For short pastry:
1½ cups pastry flour
8 Tbsp. chilled butter, cut in pieces
1½ Tbsp. vegetable oil or lard
Salt
3–4 Tbsp. cold water

For mousseline filling:
½ lb. turkey or chicken breast meat, skinned
Salt, pepper, and nutmeg
2 eggs
¾ cup crème fraîche (page 501), chilled

For meat:
2 lb. boned veal sirloin roast, about 1½" thick

For glaze (for pastry):
1 egg, beaten

For sauce:
1 Tbsp. vegetable oil
2 Tbsp. butter
2 shallots, minced
¼ lb. cleaned white mushrooms, chopped
1 cup Veal Stock (page 476)
½ cup Madeira
Pinches of salt and pepper
1 tsp. mild mustard with crushed mustard seeds

Special equipment needed:
A food processor
A 16" by 20" baking sheet lined with buttered heavy-duty aluminum foil
A food mill
A strainer

$\mathcal{M}$ake the short pastry in a food processor, according to the method on p. 488 but omitting the egg yolks. Wrap in a plastic bag and refrigerate overnight, or at least 1 hour.

Prepare the mousseline filling: Cut the turkey or chicken into chunks, and purée in a food processor with salt, pepper, and nutmeg, to taste. Add the eggs, one at a time, and process until each is completely incorporated. Remove from the processor, and chill over ice or in the freezer until very firm. Return to the food processor, and add the crème fraîche by tablespoons, pulsing until all is homogenous. Correct the seasoning, and refrigerate until needed.

Rub the veal with oil, and place in a preheated 425°F oven for 10 minutes, turning the meat so that it browns evenly. Remove from oven, season with salt and pepper, and let cool.

Roll out the pastry into an 18″ by 14″ rectangle, and place on a buttered foil-lined baking sheet. Set in the freezer for a few minutes, or until firm again. When firm, spread the mousseline filling in the center of the pastry. Put the meat on the filling and wrap neatly in the pastry, sealing it with beaten egg glaze. Make three slits in the top to allow steam to escape during baking. Decorate the top with pastry "leaves" cut from the scraps, and glaze all with beaten egg. Bake in a preheated 450°F oven for 35–45 minutes, or until nicely browned.

While the veal is baking, prepare the sauce: Heat oil and butter together in a pan. Add the shallots, and let stew until tender. Add the chopped mushrooms, and let stew, stirring, until tender. Stir in the veal base and Madeira, and let simmer until reduced by ⅓. Season highly, then put through a food mill and strain. Return over heat and correct the seasoning, adding the mustard. Keep warm until ready to serve.

To serve, slice the veal in its crust, and serve the sauce in a sauceboat.

Vegetable Suggestion: Serve with parsley custards from *Les escargots L'Alsacienne* (page 335).

Wine Suggestion: A tasty Tavel rosé from the Rhône Valley.

Paupiettes de veau aux aubergines

Veal Paupiettes, Filled with Eggplant

—

For 6

6 thinly sliced veal scallops, 7½"–8"
   by 3"

For stuffing:
2½ lb. eggplant
3 Tbsp. olive oil
7 oz. onions, sliced
3 garlic cloves, minced
3 shallots, minced
1 egg
⅓ cup stale bread crumbs
Salt and pepper
3 chicken or duck livers, cleaned

6 Tbsp. butter
Dried herbes de Provence (see page 503)
1 Tbsp. vegetable oil
3 very small ripe tomatoes, seeded and
   sliced
Fresh basil, minced

Special equipment needed:
A nonstick pan
A food processor
Toothpicks
A large enameled cast-iron gratin
   dish

The veal scallops should be very thinly sliced, as they will be rolled with an eggplant stuffing inside.

Using a sharp knife, remove the eggplant skin in 6 large bands, leaving ⅛" of the flesh attached. Scoop out and discard the seeds from the remaining eggplant flesh, dice, and set aside. Heat 1½ Tbsp. olive oil in a nonstick pan, and cook the eggplant bands very slowly, turning them as soon as one side is tender. Remove and set aside.

Cook the sliced onions, garlic, and shallots in 2 Tbsp. melted butter in the same pan, stirring until tender, not burned. Add the remaining diced eggplant, and continue cooking until tender. Remove and purée in a food processor, adding the egg and bread crumbs. Season highly.

Sauté the diced chicken or duck livers in 1½ Tbsp. oil and 2 Tbsp. butter and little seasoning, tossing to turn them over. Remove the livers as soon as they are done, dice, and set aside. The insides of the livers should be pink. Pour the cooking juices into the food processor with the eggplant mixture, pulse, and correct the seasoning. Transfer to a mixing bowl, stir in the diced livers, and again correct the seasoning, using the herbs.

To assemble paupiettes: Place the scallops on a board, and season. Spread each scallop with a layer of the eggplant mixture, smoothing with a metal spatula to make them neat. Roll up and secure with toothpicks.

Using the same nonstick pan, sauté each rolled paupiette in 2 Tbsp. butter and 1 Tbsp. oil to sear the meat, until slightly browned. Remove toothpicks, roll each paupiette in an eggplant skin, and secure with toothpicks.

Place the paupiettes in a gratin dish, pour a little of the cooking juices over each, and top with the tomato slices (without seeds), a little salt, and pepper. Bake in a preheated 400°F oven for 25–30 minutes. The paupiettes should remain very tender and juicy. Serve in the same dish and garnish with basil.

Wine Suggestion: A good rosé from Provence.

Poitrine de veau belle fermière

Stuffed Breast of Veal

This delicious recipe calls for a highly seasoned green vegetable, eggs, rice, and liver filling.

—

For 10 to 12

One 6-lb. (or two 3½-lb.) boned veal
  breast
Veal bones from above
5 Tbsp. olive oil
Salt and pepper

For filling:
3 Tbsp. olive oil
1 lb. cleaned fresh spinach, chopped, or
  10 oz. frozen spinach, thawed and
  squeezed dry

3 shallots, minced
2 garlic cloves, minced
½ cup stale bread crumbs
2 eggs, beaten with 2 Tbsp. heavy cream
1½ oz. grated Gruyère cheese
2 Tbsp. minced parsley
2 Tbsp. minced basil
Salt and pepper
3 large eggs
½ cup raw white rice
2½ Tbsp. butter
Optional: 5 chicken livers or 5 oz. calf's
  liver, cut in small dice

For braising veal breast:
¼ cup olive oil

2 onions, quartered
2 carrots, quartered
2 cups dry white wine
2½ cups veal stock or chicken broth
Bouquet garni (page 503) with celery
  stalk
2 Tbsp. dried herbes de Provence
  (see Aide-Mémoire, page 503)

Special equipment needed:
A nonstick saucepan
A skillet
A food processor
A larding needle and kitchen string
A large shallow roasting pan, oiled

*H*ave your butcher bone the veal breast for you and make a "pocket" in the meat. Brown the bones slightly in a skillet with 3 Tbsp. of the olive oil. Sprinkle the inside of the meat with salt and pepper, and set aside.

Prepare the filling next. Heat 2 Tbsp. oil in a nonstick pan, and add the chopped and squeezed-dry spinach, the shallots, and garlic; let stew slowly, stirring until all the moisture has evaporated and the spinach has become tender (3–4 minutes). Place the mixture in a food processor and purée, then mix in bread crumbs, eggs beaten with cream, grated cheese, parsley, and basil. Correct the seasoning.

Boil the 3 eggs for 10–12 minutes, refresh in cold water, and peel. Parboil the rice for 8 minutes in boiling salted water, and drain. It should be only half cooked.

If using the liver, heat the butter with 1 Tbsp. oil in the nonstick pan. When hot, sauté the diced chicken livers (or calf liver) for about 3 minutes, turning to cook evenly. Season with salt and pepper.

Mix the green purée together with the rice and optional livers in a large mixing bowl, correct the seasoning, and stir until all is homogenous.

Fill the veal pocket, starting with a layer of green mixture, then placing a hard-boiled egg in the middle, followed by another layer of green and an egg. Repeat until the pocket is filled, then close the opening, using a larding needle and kitchen string. The opening must be tightly closed, as the meat will shrink when cooked.

To cook, place the meat in a shallow oiled roasting pan, and brown slowly on all sides. Add the onions, carrots, and browned veal bones. Deglaze the skillet with a little wine and stock, and pour over the meat. Add the bouquet garni and herbs, and bake in a preheated 375°F oven for 1¾–2 hours, basting every 10–15 minutes and turning over 2 or 3 times.

Reduce the remaining wine and stock to half. When the meat is done, remove and set aside until cool enough to handle. Deglaze the roasting pan with the reduced wine and stock, scraping all the sediment at the bottom of the pan and letting it boil. Strain and degrease, then return to heat. Two cups should remain. Correct the seasoning, and keep warm.

Serve the meat cut into thick slices, with the reduced sauce in a sauceboat on the side. Ideally, the eggs will be cut in half (or pieces), making an attractive design.

Wine Suggestion: Châteauneuf-du-Pape.

Vitello tonnato à la milanese

Veal with Tuna Sauce

—

For 6 to 8

3 Tbsp. extra-virgin olive oil
1 cup chopped onion
1½ lb. veal loin
10 oz. canned tuna, packed in oil
3½ oz. anchovy fillets, packed in salt
½ cup cold milk
2 cups dry white wine
Bouquet garni (see page 503)
Peel from an orange, dried

1½ Tbsp. dried herbes de Provence (see page 503)
2 cups beef broth (or bouillon cubes and water)
Salt and pepper
1½ envelopes unflavored gelatin
2 limes or lemons, juiced (½ cup)
Pickled gherkins and capers, for garnish
Mock Mayonnaise (page 474)

Special equipment needed:
A heavy-bottomed skillet
Parchment paper

A food processor
A 6-cup rectangular loaf pan

*H*eat olive oil in a heavy-bottomed skillet. Stirring constantly, add the chopped onion, and let stew, without browning, until tender. Tie the veal with kitchen twine so that it retains its shape during cooking. When the onion is tender, remove with a slotted spoon and set aside. Add the meat to the hot pan. Let brown slowly on all sides, turning the meat as it browns.

Meanwhile, rinse tuna and let drain on paper towels. Soak the anchovy fillets in milk to remove the salt, then rinse and drain dry on paper towels.

When the meat has browned on all sides, return the onion to the pan, increase heat, and pour in the white wine. As the wine begins to boil, add the tuna, anchovy, bouquet garni, and dried orange peel. Add broth to barely cover, season, and bring to the boil. Cover with parchment paper and the lid, and bake in a preheated 375°F oven for about 1½ hours, stirring halfway through the cooking.

Soften the gelatin in ½ cup lime or lemon juice. When the meat is done, remove from oven and let cool. Strain the cooking liquid to remove the fish, bouquet garni, and orange peel. Degrease, if needed, and discard bouquet garni and orange peel. Purée the fish in a food processor. Return the strained cooking liquid to the pan, add the softened gelatin, and stir over heat until the gelatin is completely dissolved. Correct the seasoning, and let reduce until 3 cups remain. Remove from heat and stir in the fish purée. Let cool to room temperature, then place in freezer until beginning to set.

Line the bottom of a 6-cup loaf pan with parchment paper. Using sliced gherkins and capers, make a design in the bottom of the mold. Slice the meat into thin, even slices. Spread each slice evenly with some of the half-set fish purée, and reassemble the roast, with the slices placed upright in the loaf pan. Top with the remaining fish purée. Rap the bottom of the loaf pan against the counter to settle the mixture and remove any trapped air, then smooth the top, if needed. Refrigerate until well set, at least 3 hours.

To serve, unmold onto a shallow serving dish, with a sauceboat of Mock Mayonnaise (page 474) on the side and a mixed green salad.

Wine Suggestion: Italian dry white wine or Fumé Blanc from California.

Plat principal à base de riz à l'indonésienne

Nasi Goreng (A Rice Dish with Ham, Egg, and Leek)

—

For 4 to 6

1 cup natural long-grain rice
4 Tbsp. butter
1 egg
Salt and freshly ground pepper, to taste
4 oz. good-quality boiled ham
1 medium leek, tender white part only, julienned

Optional: Dried herbes de Provence (see Aide-Mémoire, page 503)

Special equipment needed:
A large covered skillet, preferably enameled cast iron
A nonstick omelet pan

*H*eat 3 qt. water with 2 Tbsp. salt in a large enameled skillet. When boiling, add the rice, stir once, cover, and let simmer 17–18 minutes, or until the rice is tender. Pour into a strainer and rinse with cold tap water to stop the cooking and remove the salt. Drain and dry.

Melt 1 Tbsp. butter in a nonstick pan. Beat the egg with a drop of water and salt, and freshly ground pepper to taste, then pour into the pan without stirring. When golden brown on the bottom, turn to the other side to do the same. Remove to a cutting board and let cool slightly, then cut in narrow strips 1½″ long and ¼″ wide. Cut the ham the same size.

When ready to serve, reheat the rice in the same skillet with the remaining butter, and season with salt and pepper. When hot, stir in the ham, egg, and raw julienned leek. Mix well and serve immediately.

If you wish, season to taste with herbes de Provence.

Wine Suggestion: White or rosé of Provence.

Bouchées frites à la Madras

Curried Meat Patties with Bell Peppers

—

For 4 to 5

1 lb. boned pork

2 medium onions

2 garlic cloves, peeled

1 lb. bell peppers (yellow, green, red, orange)

½ tsp. Madras curry powder

1 clove, crushed

¼ tsp. freshly ground nutmeg

Salt and pepper

Dried herbes de Provence (see Aide-Mémoire, page 503)

1 egg, beaten

½ cup stale bread crumbs

3–4 Tbsp. flour

Vegetable oil

2 cups Express Tomato Sauce (page 486)

Special equipment needed:

A food processor

A large deep frying pan

Trim the meat, removing any gristle or nerves, and cut into large cubes. Place in a food processor and roughly chop; do not purée. Transfer meat to a mixing bowl, and set aside.

Chop the onion and garlic in the food processor. Cut the bell peppers in half, remove stems and seeds, and place under broiler or on a gas burner until the skin has blackened. Immediately place charred peppers in plastic bags. Seal and let cool, then scrape off the charred skin with a paring knife or paper towel. Add the peeled peppers to the processor with the chopped onion and garlic, curry powder, crushed clove, nutmeg, salt, pepper, herbs, beaten egg, and bread crumbs. Process for 3–4 seconds, but do not purée.

Transfer contents of food processor to a mixing bowl with the chopped meat, and mix well. Test for seasoning by poaching a spoonful of the meat mixture and tasting. Correct the seasoning (it should be highly seasoned). If not using immediately, cover with plastic wrap and set in refrigerator.

When ready to use, sprinkle flour over a tray. Using two spoons, shape the meat into egg-size balls and roll in the flour. Shake off any excess flour, and refrigerate until ready to cook.

Heat 2″ vegetable oil in a large frying pan. When hot enough to fry, add a few bouchées and fry 2–3 minutes on each side, turning as each side turns golden brown. Remove with a slotted spoon, and drain over paper towels to remove excess oil.

Meanwhile, prepare the Tomato Sauce. Place the drained bouchées in the sauce to keep warm.

Vegetable Suggestion: Plain rice, or tender string beans sautéed in butter.

Wine Suggestion: A full-bodied red or rosé.

Civet de porcelet, aux raisins de Málaga et au vin rouge

Pork Stew with Málaga Raisins and Red Wine

—

For 10 to 12

1½ Tbsp. lard

10 oz. pork breast, cut into 2″ pieces

2¼ lb. young pork shoulder, cut into 2″ pieces

12 medium onions, halved, or 24 small onions

4 Tbsp. flour

2 bottles strong red wine

3 garlic cloves

Bouquet garni of celery stalk, parsley stems, marjoram, and thyme

Salt, pepper, and cayenne

1 tsp. Allspice

2 cups reduced chicken broth (or water and bouillon cubes)

⅔ cup dry seedless Málaga raisins or pitted prunes, steeped in hot tea, drained

Chopped fresh parsley, for garnish

Special equipment needed:

An ovenproof large skillet with lid

Parchment paper

*M*elt lard in the skillet. When hot, add the pieces of pork breast, turning as soon as each side browns slightly. Add the pieces of pork shoulder, and brown the same way, then remove all to drain on paper towels. Add the onions to the hot fat and cook until softened, then remove with a slotted spoon and set aside with the browned pork.

Strain the fat to remove any burned particles, clean the pan, and return the strained fat to the pan. Add the flour, and stir constantly over medium heat until the roux turns golden brown. Whisking constantly, slowly pour in the wine, and continue whisking until the mixture is smooth in consistency. When all the wine has been incorporated and the roux is boiling, return the meat and onions to the pan. Add the garlic, bouquet garni, all the seasoning, and bring to the simmer. Place a piece of parchment paper over all, cover with the lid, and let simmer for about 30 minutes.

Remove lid and parchment paper, pour in the broth, and correct the seasoning. Place in a preheated 375°F oven for 1½ hours, or until the pork is very tender. Remove meat and onions, then strain and degrease the cooking liquid and return it to the cleaned skillet. If the sauce is too thin, reduce and correct the seasoning. You should have about 3 cups.

Just before serving, heat the sauce and stir in the Málaga raisins. Let simmer 3 minutes, then return the meat and onions to the sauce to reheat. It is not necessary to bring the sauce to the boil.

Serve in a preheated shallow serving dish with the meat in the middle, the onions on one side, and the raisins on the other side, sprinkled with chopped parsley.

Vegetable Suggestion: Serve with boiled rice or steamed potatoes.

Wine Suggestion: The same wine, or a full-bodied red Hermitage or Châteauneuf-du-Pape or Côtes du Rhône.

Curry de porc pili pili

Pork Curry with Pili Pili (Hot Pepper)

—

For 10 to 12

6 lb. boned pork, without fat or gristle

5 Tbsp. oil

Vegetable oil

3–4 medium onions, chopped

3 Tbsp. curry powder

3 medium apples, grated

½ cup concentrated canned tomato purée
 (or fresh, made with 4 lb. tomatoes)

3 bananas, sliced

Bouquet garni of bay leaf and thyme

One pili pili (small dried finger-shaped
 hot pepper), or pasilla pepper, crushed

Optional: 3–4 garlic cloves, chopped

2½ cups chicken broth

Salt and pepper

For saffron rice:

⅓ cup olive oil

3 cups raw long-grain rice

7½ cups chicken broth (or water and
 bouillon cubes)

½ tsp. saffron

1 bay leaf

½ tsp. dried herbes de Provence
 (see Aide-Mémoire, page 503)

4½ Tbsp. butter, cut in pieces

Special equipment needed:

2 large cast-iron skillets or saucepans
 with lids

Parchment paper

Cut the pork into 1″ cubes. Heat 3 Tbsp. of the oil in a cast-iron saucepan or skillet large enough to hold all the meat, and when hot, add the meat. (If your pan is not large enough, divide meat into batches, adding more oil if necessary.) Sauté over moderate heat, stirring occasionally so that all sides become lightly colored but not browned, then remove the meat and reserve. Add the chopped onions to the same pan, with more oil if necessary, and stir until the onions begin to get tender. When quite tender but not browned, remove the onions and the fat, and reserve onions.

Rinse and dry the pan, pour in 2 Tbsp. oil, and when hot, add the meat and onions. Stir in the curry powder, grated apple, and tomato purée, and bring to a simmer, then add the bananas, bouquet garni, and pili pili or pasilla. If garlic will be included, add it now. Pour in the broth, add a little salt and more pepper, and again bring to the boil. Lower the heat to a simmer, and let cook for 10 minutes. Taste and correct the seasoning, cover with parchment paper and the lid, and set in a preheated 375°F oven for about 1 hour. After 30 minutes, stir the mixture thoroughly, taste, and correct the seasoning, then let finish cooking. The meat should be very tender.

Meanwhile, cook the saffron rice: Heat the olive oil in a thick-bottomed saucepan (preferably cast iron), add the rice, and stir over medium heat until the rice grains turn slightly golden. Pour in the broth, add the saffron, bay leaf, and herbs, and bring to the boil. Reduce the heat to a simmer, cover, and let cook for 18–20 minutes, or until all the liquid has evaporated and the rice is fluffy and very tender. Remove from the heat, and stir in the butter. Correct the seasoning. Serve the pork curry in a heated dish, with the rice on the side.

Wine Suggestion: A Tavel rosé, Côtes de Provence, or a Bandol.

Côtes de porc au Muscadet

Pork Chops with Special Dry White Wine

—

For 6

4 Tbsp. butter

4 Tbsp. vegetable oil

10 oz. onions, chopped

1½ Tbsp. flour

3 Tbsp. white-wine vinegar

2 cups dry white wine (such as Anjou Muscadet or Napa Valley Fumé Blanc)

2 cups chicken broth

Salt and pepper

6 pork chops (about 7 oz. each, trimmed and ready to cook)

Bouquet garni of celery stalks, parsley stems, and thyme

2 Tbsp. strong Dijon mustard

3½ oz. gherkins, thinly sliced

Special equipment needed:

2 heavy-bottomed skillets (1 ovenproof)

Parchment paper

A food mill (preferred) or a food processor

Heat half the butter and oil in a heavy-bottomed skillet. When hot, add the chopped onions and 2 Tbsp. water. Let stew slowly, stirring, until the onions begin to turn golden (about 20 minutes). Sprinkle with flour and let cook, stirring constantly, until the onions are coated evenly with the flour, then moisten with the vinegar and cook over low heat until the acidity has disappeared. Add the white wine, and stir vigorously until all is smooth, then pour in the broth and bring to the boil. Lower the heat, and let simmer uncovered until reduced, then taste and correct the seasoning.

In a second skillet, heat the remaining butter and oil, and without crowding them, brown the pork chops in a single layer, turning them over when browned on one side. Remove and brown the other chops the same way, then place in the onion-wine sauce with the bouquet garni, and correct the seasoning. The sauce should nearly cover the meat. Cover with parchment paper and a lid and bake for 20–30 minutes, or until tender, in a preheated 375°F oven.

When done, remove the meat and reserve. Strain the sauce to remove the onion, and degrease thoroughly. Purée the onion in a food mill or food processor, and return to the skillet with the degreased sauce and the meat. If prepared ahead, place in the refrigerator until 30 minutes before serving.

Reheat slowly for 30 minutes before serving, stirring occasionally and adding ½ cup water to thin the sauce. Turn the meat once to help it reheat. When hot, stir in the mustard and gherkins. Serve with sweet green peas or spinach (boiled for 5 minutes and served buttered), or with buttered noodles.

Wine Suggestion: Serve with the same white wine.

Lapin de caloge en ratatouille

Domestic Rabbit or Turkey in a Ratatouille

—

For 4 to 6

One 4-lb. rabbit, or the same weight of turkey

24 tiny onions

1 lb. zucchini, not peeled

10 oz. eggplant, peeled
1½ lb. ripe tomatoes
3½ Tbsp. olive oil
2½–3 cups dry white wine
Optional: 2 Tbsp. cider vinegar
8 garlic cloves, not peeled
Bouquet garni of celery stalks, thyme,
  bay leaf, oregano, and parsley stems
Salt and pepper

1 hot pepper (pasilla or jalapeño)
Optional: 2 Tbsp. tomato paste

Special equipment needed:
A large ovenproof skillet with lid
Parchment paper
A strainer
A food mill

*C*ut the rabbit or turkey into serving pieces. Parboil the onions in salted water for 6 minutes, drain, and reserve. Cut the zucchini in half lengthwise, remove the seeds, if any, and cut into cubes. Cut the peeled eggplant into cubes the same size as the zucchini. Peel and quarter the tomatoes, and remove the seeds.

Heat the oil in the skillet. When hot, brown the meat pieces, turning them as soon as each side becomes nicely colored. When all sides are browned, pour in the wine. If you like additional acidity, add the vinegar as well, then bring to the boil, reduce the heat, and let simmer 5 minutes. Add all the vegetables, except the onions, along with the garlic cloves (peels intact), bouquet garni, salt, pepper, and the hot pepper. If the liquid does not cover the skillet contents, add water. Cover with parchment paper and the skillet lid, and bring to the simmer.

Place in a preheated 375°F oven for 40–45 minutes, or until tender. After 20 minutes, remove from oven and correct the seasoning, adding the tomato paste if you wish to give more flavor to the ratatouille. Add the parboiled onions to the skillet, and finish the cooking time (20–25 more minutes).

When the meat is done, pour all through a strainer. Remove and discard the bouquet garni and separate out the meat and garlic cloves. Purée the garlic cloves with a food mill (not a food processor, as the peels must be removed). Degrease the cooking liquid, stir in the garlic purée, and correct the seasoning. If necessary, let the cooking liquid reduce to concentrate the flavors and thicken slightly.

When ready to serve, reheat the meat and vegetables in the sauce. Serve in a warmed serving dish.

Wine Suggestion: Serve with the same white wine used in the cooking, a white Burgundy or California Fumé Blanc.

VEGETABLES

Tomates farcies à la Provençale

Stuffed Tomatoes with Eggs and Bell Peppers

—

For 10

10 medium-size ripe tomatoes with
  a nice round shape
Salt and pepper
3½ Tbsp. olive oil
3 medium shallots, chopped
4 garlic cloves, minced
½ red bell pepper (canned), diced
Ground coriander
1½ Tbsp. dried herbes de Provence (see
  Aide-Mémoire, page 503)
10 eggs

1½ cups crème fraîche (page 501)
3 Tbsp. tomato paste
3 Tbsp. minced parsley and chives,
  mixed, or chives only

Special equipment needed:
2 heavy-bottomed saucepans
A food processor
An ovenproof baking sheet large enough
  to hold the filled tomatoes

$\mathcal{C}$ore each tomato, then use a small spoon to scoop the pulp from the inside, leaving a neat shell. Do not discard the pulp. Sprinkle a little salt inside and place the tomatoes upside down in a colander to drain. When they have lost most of their water, dry well with paper towels.

Heat 2 Tbsp. of the oil in a saucepan. When hot, add the reserved tomato pulp and cook over low heat, stirring frequently. In another saucepan, cook the shallots and garlic in the remaining olive oil until tender. Stir constantly and do not let burn. Add the diced red bell pepper and continue to stir. When the tomato pulp has reduced to a nice thick consistency, transfer to a food processor and add the cooked shallots, garlic, and red pepper. Purée all, then remove and correct the seasoning, adding more pepper, ground coriander, and the herbs.

Beat the eggs with the crème fraîche, season highly, then stir in the tomato mixture. Add the tomato paste. Place the dry tomato shells on the baking sheet, and fill with the egg mixture. Bake in a preheated 375°F oven for about 20–30 minutes, or until set.

Serve tepid or cold, sprinkled with the minced fresh herbs.

Wine Suggestion: A good rosé from Provence.

Aubergine gratinée aux tomates

Gratinéed Eggplant and Tomatoes

—

For 4 to 6

3 lb. small eggplants
Salt
1½ lb. ripe tomatoes
6 Tbsp. virgin olive oil
½ cup chopped onion
3–4 garlic cloves, minced
Dried herbes de Provence (see page 503)
Pepper

3 oz. Gruyère cheese, freshly grated
1½ oz. Parmesan cheese, grated

Special equipment needed:
Large nonstick saucepan
Oval gratin dish, preferably enameled
   cast iron

*P*eel the eggplants and slice thin. Cut large slices in half crosswise. Sprinkle with salt, and place in a strainer for about 30 minutes to disgorge their natural water. Rinse under cold tap water, and drain dry on a kitchen towel.

Meanwhile, peel the tomatoes, separate into quarters, and press to remove seeds and juice.

In a large nonstick saucepan, heat 1½ Tbsp. oil. When hot, add the tomato, onion, and garlic, and let stew slowly, stirring from time to time until soft. Remove from heat, and set aside.

Heat the remaining oil in a large saucepan or skillet, add the dry eggplants, and let them fry slowly, turning as needed. When tender, remove and drain over paper towels.

Spread a layer of eggplant in the bottom of a gratin dish, sprinkle with herbs (for a nice Provençal flavor), salt and pepper, a layer of tomato mixture, more herbs, followed by a layer of the grated cheeses mixed together. Repeat the layers once more, again ending with the cheese. Ten minutes before serving, *gratiner* under a broiler for 10–15 minutes, or until well reheated and nicely golden brown.

Note: Serve this dish with a lamb or beef stew, or other Provençal dishes.

Wine Suggestion: Bandol de Provence.

Ramequins de petits légumes

Vegetable Flans in Ramekins

—

For 4 to 6 as an entrée
For 8 to 10 as a side dish

3 Tbsp. butter	4 oz. zucchini
4 oz. green beans	Handful of sorrel leaves
4 oz. young carrots	3 Tbsp. vegetable oil
2 oz. peeled eggplant	Pepper

Dried herbes de Provence (see Aide-
  Mémoire, page 503)
1½ cups heavy cream
Salt
3–4 eggs (depending on size), plus 2
  yolks
2 Tbsp. minced chives

Special equipment needed:
Eight to ten 4-oz. ramekins
A large saucepan
A mixing bowl
A bain-marie (see page 503) or a
  roasting pan large enough to hold
  ramekins with simmering water

*B*utter the ramekins, and place in the refrigerator until needed. Save any remaining butter to scatter over the custard before baking.

Cut the green beans into pieces 1″–2″ long, and set aside. Cut ¾ of the carrots into small dice, and slice the rest. The green beans and sliced carrots will be used to decorate the bottoms of the ramekins. Cut the rest of the vegetables into small dice.

Parboil the green beans in boiling salted water until tender. Remove with a slotted spoon, refresh in cold water, drain again, and set aside. Parboil the sliced and diced carrots in the same boiling water, drain, refresh, and drain again. Sauté the eggplant and the zucchini in oil, stirring until tender, then season highly with pepper and herbs, and set aside. Wilt the sorrel leaves with 2 Tbsp. cream, season, and set aside.

Blend together the eggs, egg yolks, sorrel mixture, and remaining cream in a mixing bowl. Dry the vegetables on paper towels, then make pretty designs in the bottoms of the ramekins with the sliced carrots and green beans. Extra green beans and sliced carrots can be diced and mixed in with the custard. Mix the remaining vegetables into the custard, adding more seasoning and the chives.

Fill the ramekins with the custard-and-vegetable mixture, scatter the remaining butter over them, and place in a bain-marie or roasting pan containing an inch of hot water. Bake in a preheated 350°F oven for about 25–35 minutes, or until the custard is set in the middle.

Serve unmolded around a meat dish or as an entrée dish accompanied by a green salad.

Wine Suggestion: A light red wine or Cabernet Sauvignon.

Ratatouille in Timbales or Ramekins

For 20 timbales or ramekins
For a hot hors d'oeuvre quiche, use an 11" pie plate.

For quiche "crust" (optional):
2½ Tbsp. butter, creamed
⅔ cup bread crumbs

For filling:
4 garlic cloves
1 or 2 onions (7 oz.)
1 red bell pepper (7–8 oz.)
1 eggplant, peeled and cut into large
   cubes (7–8 oz.)
10 oz. small zucchini
Salt and pepper
4–5 Tbsp. olive oil
1 Tbsp. dried herbes de Provence
   (see Aide-Mémoire, page 503)
⅔ cup tomato paste

5–6 eggs
¾ cup crème fraîche (page 501)
Optional: Tabasco

To garnish quiche (optional):
1 Tbsp. grated Parmesan cheese
2 Tbsp. butter, cubed

Special equipment needed:
20 timbale molds or small ramekins, or
   an 11" ovenproof pie plate
Parchment paper
A food processor
2 large mixing bowls
A heavy nonstick skillet

*H*eavily butter the molds, line the bottoms with buttered parchment paper, and refrigerate until needed. If preparing the quiche, butter the pie plate heavily, then press the bread crumbs into the butter to form a crust. Refrigerate until chilled and quite firm.

Peel the garlic, mince fine, and set aside. Quarter the onion and chop roughly in the food processor. Peel the bell pepper, remove and discard the seeds, then add to the onion. Pulse 6–7 times, then add the peeled, cubed eggplant. Pulse several times to chop roughly, then transfer to a large bowl.

Meanwhile, slice the zucchini, sprinkle with 1 Tbsp. salt, and let stand for 10 minutes to drain the juices. Rinse well to remove the salt, then dry thoroughly between kitchen towels. Place the zucchini in the food processor, chop roughly using a disk with medium holes, then add to the other chopped vegetables and mix well.

Heat half the oil in the skillet, then stir in the chopped vegetables and minced garlic. Cook over moderate heat, stirring from time to time and adding more oil, if needed. Continue cooking until very tender, about 45 minutes, then season highly with salt, pepper, and herbs.

Transfer to a large bowl, stir in the tomato paste, and add more seasoning if needed. In another bowl, beat the eggs with the crème fraîche; pour this into the cooked vegetables, mix well, then add Tabasco to taste. The recipe can be prepared in advance to this point.

Thirty minutes before serving, fill the prepared timbale molds or ramekins, and bake in a preheated 400°F oven for about 15 minutes. If making the quiche, first sprinkle Parmesan cheese over the top and dot with butter, then bake for 25 minutes, or until the top is shining and nicely browned. Unmold timbales to serve. This dish is best served tepid, rather than hot or cold. It reheats well.

Wine Suggestion: Côtes de Provence.

Little Green Flan

—

For 8 to 10

½ cup minced fresh herbs (chervil-parsley, tarragon-parsley, or basil-parsley, leaves only)
Butter, to grease the ramekins
9 large eggs
2½ cups heavy cream
Salt, pepper, and Tabasco
2 Tbsp. minced fresh herbs, for garnish

Special equipment needed:
A food processor
10 small ramekins
A bain-marie (see page 503) or roasting pan large enough to hold the ramekins and simmering water

*M*ince the green herbs in a food processor. Heavily butter the insides of the ramekins, then coat with the herbs, pressing them into the butter to make them adhere. Refrigerate while preparing the flan mixture. Reserve the excess herbs.

Boil 3 eggs for 12 minutes, refresh for 5 minutes in cold water, then peel. Remove the white and reserve for another use. (See note.) Purée the hard yolks in a food processor. When well puréed, add the remaining herbs, and pulse to mix. Next, add the remaining 6 eggs, and process 10 seconds. Add the cream and seasoning, and pulse again until homogenous.

Fill the ramekins ¾ full, set in a bain-marie, and bake in a preheated 375°F oven for 15–20 minutes, or until they are set. Do not overcook. When just set, remove and let cool.

To serve, unmold the cold ramekins on a tray and decorate with minced herbs. Refrigerate until time to serve.

Note: The hard-boiled egg whites that are not used in this recipe can be pressed through a fine sieve to make a garnish, or mixed with half their weight of Roquefort cheese and put through a food mill, for topping green salads.

Wine Suggestion: A brut Champagne with raspberry wine (1 Tbsp. per glass).

Zucchini Bramafam

Grated Zucchini, Cooked with Cream and Shallots

—

For 5 to 6

1½ lb. small fresh zucchini
4 Tbsp. butter
2 Tbsp. vegetable oil
3 Tbsp. finely chopped shallots or green
    onions
1 garlic clove, crushed
Salt and pepper
2 Tbsp. finely minced chervil or parsley

Optional: 1 Tbsp. Dijon mustard
Optional: 1 cup heavy cream

Special equipment needed:
A food processor equipped with the
    grater disk
A large nonstick skillet

Wash and trim the zucchini, and grate, using a food processor with the grater disk. Remove the excess moisture by sprinkling the grated zucchini with salt and placing in a strainer with a weight on top. Let drain for about 30 minutes, shaking frequently, then rinse with cold tap water to remove the salt. Let dry thoroughly between kitchen towels. (You should have about 3 cups of zucchini at this point.)

Melt the butter and oil in a nonstick skillet, and when hot, add the shallots and crushed garlic clove and stir frequently for about 2 minutes, or until they are beginning to get tender. Adding the grated zucchini, shake the pan and stir with a wooden spatula from time to time, cooking over medium heat for about 10 minutes, or until any liquid evaporates and the zucchini is tender. Season highly and serve as is, sprinkled with the minced herbs.

For a more elaborate dish, stir in the mustard mixed with heavy cream, and cook slowly until the cream has been absorbed by the zucchini. Correct the seasoning and serve, sprinkled with the minced herbs.

La "crique" auvergnate au fromage bleu d'Auvergne

Grated Potatoes with Blue Cheese

—

For 4 to 6

2 lb. boiling potatoes, peeled
⅓–½ cup vegetable oil
½ cup crumbled blue cheese
3 Tbsp. minced chives
Salt and pepper
1 Tbsp. minced parsley, for garnish

Special equipment needed:
A food processor or grater
A nonstick skillet

*R*oughly grate the potatoes, using a food processor or grater. Dry between kitchen towels until all excess moisture has been removed.

Heat half the oil in a nonstick skillet, and when hot, pack with ⅓ of the grated potatoes. Sprinkle with half the cheese, chives, and salt and pepper to taste, remembering that the cheese is salty. Spread another layer of potatoes, followed by the remaining cheese and chives, and more salt and pepper; finish with the rest of the potatoes. Cook over moderate heat, compressing the potatoes with a skimmer, until the bottom is nice and brown, about 10–15 minutes. Using a large spatula, or flipping it, turn the potato pancake to its other side and let brown. The second side will take less time, about 6–8 minutes. When done, the pancake will be nicely browned on both sides and soft in the middle.

Just before serving, slide the potato pancake onto a warmed shallow serving dish and sprinkle with minced parsley.

Gratin de pommes de terre

New Potato Gratin with Cream

—

For 6 to 8

3 lb. small new potatoes, or other boiling
  potatoes
3 cups milk
Salt and white pepper
Freshly grated nutmeg
3 Tbsp. butter
3 garlic cloves, freshly grated

1 cup crème fraîche (page 501) or heavy
  cream
1 Tbsp. minced chervil or parsley

Special equipment needed:
A large nonstick saucepan
An oval baking dish about 12″ by 6″ by 2″

*P*eel and slice the potatoes about ¼″ thick. Pour the milk into a nonstick saucepan, add the sliced potatoes and ½ tsp. salt, and bring slowly to the boil. Add freshly ground white pepper and nutmeg, lower the heat, and simmer 8–10 minutes, or until just tender (not too soft).

While the potatoes are simmering, prepare the baking dish by spreading butter over the bottom and sides, reserving any butter not used. Sprinkle half the garlic over the butter. When the potatoes are done, remove with a strainer and spread half the potatoes in the gratin dish. Sprinkle with the rest of the garlic, and top with the remaining potatoes. Cover with the boiling milk, and bake in a preheated 400°F oven for about 20–25 minutes, or until the potatoes are tender and the milk has been completely absorbed. Immediately remove from the oven and spread the crème fraîche or heavy cream evenly over the potatoes. Dot with the remaining bits of butter, and return to the oven to *gratiner* for about 10 minutes at 425°F, or until slightly browned. Sprinkle with the minced chervil or parsley, and serve immediately in the same dish.

Note: This dish is not as good when reheated, but the potatoes may be half cooked and left to steep in the milk. (Be sure the milk covers the potatoes completely.) When ready to serve, reheat in the milk, and proceed as directed above.

Purée de fenouil verte

Green Fennel Purée with Sweet Peas

—

For 4 to 6

2½ Tbsp. olive oil

6–8 fennel bulbs (about 2½ lb.), trimmed and halved (quartered if large)

3 garlic cloves, not peeled, crushed

1 cup chicken broth (or water and bouillon cubes)

Salt, pepper, and dried herbes de Provence (see page 503)

¼–⅓ lb. peas, drained (canned, frozen and defrosted, or fresh cooked)

7 Tbsp. butter, diced

Special equipment needed:

A heavy-bottomed skillet with lid

A food processor

*H*eat the oil in a heavy-bottomed skillet, and place the fennel bulbs in it in one layer with the garlic cloves. Let cook slowly, turning them so they become golden brown on all sides. Add the chicken broth, season with salt, pepper, and 1 tsp. herbs, and let braise for about 25–30 minutes, or until tender. Drain and discard the cooking liquid. Pick out the garlic cloves and set aside.

Place the fennel bulbs and drained peas in a food processor, and pulse to purée. Add the diced butter, and process until homogenous. Remove the dry skin from the reserved garlic cloves, add the cloves to the food processor, and pulse to mix. Correct the seasoning, adding more sweet green peas if needed. The purée should be highly seasoned, not sweet, and remain a light green color.

Les aubergines de mon ami Costa

Costa's Eggplant Gratiné, Greek Method (with a Cream Sauce)

—

For 6

¾ cup Mornay Sauce (page 480)

For thick tomato purée:
3 lb. ripe tomatoes
2½ Tbsp. olive oil
3 garlic cloves, minced
Salt, pepper, and pinch of sugar

For eggplant:
3 lb. small eggplants

2½ Tbsp. olive oil
Salt and pepper
Dried herbes de Provence (see page 503)
¼ cup grated Gruyère and Parmesan
  cheese

Special equipment needed:
A heavy-bottomed skillet
An enameled cast-iron baking dish
A nonstick skillet

*P*repare the Mornay cream sauce. Set aside, with plastic wrap pressed down onto the surface of the sauce to prevent a "skin" from forming.

Next, prepare the tomato purée. Peel and core the tomatoes, cut in half, and turn upside down, squeezing gently to remove seeds and excess juices. Heat the oil in a heavy-bottomed skillet; add the tomatoes, garlic, salt, a little pepper, and a pinch of sugar. Let stew slowly, stirring occasionally. When the tomatoes have become a well-reduced purée, correct the seasoning and make a layer in the bottom of the baking dish with half the purée.

Wash and dry the eggplants, then remove the stems. Cut lengthwise into slices ⅓″ thick. Place in a colander, sprinkle with salt, and let disgorge for 10 minutes. To remove the salt, toss them in the colander while rinsing under cold running water. Drain and dry thoroughly, pressing out all the moisture between kitchen towels.

Heat the olive oil in a nonstick pan. When hot, slowly fry the eggplant slices, turning them as soon as each side has browned slightly. Drain on paper towels to absorb any excess oil, then place a layer of eggplant slices on top of the tomato purée in the baking dish, using half the eggplant. Sprinkle with salt, pepper, and herbs, cover with the remaining tomato purée, and sprinkle with some of the grated cheese. Follow with a second layer of the remaining eggplant slices, sprinkling them with seasonings, coat with a layer of the prepared Mornay cream sauce, and top with the remaining grated cheese. Prepared to this point, the dish can wait a few hours before baking.

Bake in a preheated 375°F oven for about 25 minutes, or until heated through, then *gratiner* at 425°F for 10 minutes, or until slightly browned. The dish may be reheated.

Carottes et navets à la Vichy

Carrots and Turnips à la Vichy

—

For 4 to 6

1½ lb. tender young carrots
2 lb. small young turnips
12 Tbsp. butter
2½ Tbsp. sugar
Pinch of dried chervil

Salt and pepper
Pinch of grated nutmeg
Minced fresh chervil or parsley, for
  garnish

eel the carrots and turnips. Cut in half lengthwise and then into pieces about 2″ long and ¼″ by ¼″. Place the turnips in a saucepan, with cold water to cover. Bring to the boil and let continue for 2 minutes. Pour into a colander and discard the cooking liquid. Let dry.

Cook the carrots the same way, using another saucepan. Drain, then place both vegetables together in the pan, cover with cold water, and add the butter, sugar, dried chervil, salt, pepper, and nutmeg. Bring slowly to a simmer and let cook, stirring from time to time, until the two vegetables are tender and shiny and the liquid has evaporated. Serve, sprinkled with fresh minced chervil or parsley.

Les effilochés d'endives de Jane

Sautéed Endives

—

For 4

1 lb. fresh Belgian endives, trimmed
6 Tbsp. butter
1 tsp. sugar
Salt and pepper
1½ Tbsp. vegetable oil
1 Tbsp. lemon juice

1 cup heavy cream
Fresh chervil or parsley, minced

Special equipment needed:
A large covered skillet
Parchment paper

ndives are not easy to cook. If the bitter, cone-shaped root is not completely removed from the inside, the endives will taste bitter when cooked. First wash, dry, and trim the endives. Remove the entire root with a sharply pointed vegetable knife, then separate the leaves and cut them into 2″ lengths.

Heat half the butter with the oil in a skillet. When it has become a nutty brown color, add a layer of the cut-up endives. Add the remaining endive leaves with the reserved butter, sugar, salt and pepper to taste, and lemon juice. Turn them with a spatula, so they become slightly browned on both sides, then cover with a piece of buttered parchment paper and the lid. Let cook slowly for about 15 minutes, then remove the lid and add the cream. Cover again with the parchment paper and lid, and let finish cooking, about 10–15 minutes. Taste and correct the seasoning, adding more pepper and lemon juice if required.

Sprinkle with minced chervil or parsley, and serve with white meat, such as veal scallops or steamed chicken.

Gratin de courgettes Amélia

Gratinéed Zucchini Amelia

—

For 8 to 10

Butter for gratin pan
2 lb. small, seedless zucchini
4 shallots, minced
2 Tbsp. butter
1½ Tbsp. vegetable oil
2 eggs
1 cup milk plus 1 cup crème fraîche
    (page 501) or 2 cups whole milk

Salt, pepper, and nutmeg
3 oz. grated Gruyère cheese
⅓ cup raw rice

Special equipment needed:
An enameled cast-iron gratin pan
A sauté pan
A mixing bowl

*H*eavily butter the gratin pan, and refrigerate until needed. Wash the zucchini, but do not peel. If they are a little large, cut them in half lengthwise. If very small, leave them whole. Parboil the zucchini for 6 minutes, then refresh in cold water, drain, and dry on paper towels. Cut into cubes about 1″ in size.

Sauté the minced shallots in the butter and oil. As soon as the shallots are tender, add the zucchini cubes and let cook, without browning, until they have given up all their excess moisture. Remove and let drain over paper towels.

Beat the eggs with the milk and crème fraîche (or the same amount of milk). Season highly with salt, pepper, and nutmeg, then add half of the grated Gruyère cheese, reserving the rest.

Parboil the rice for 6 minutes, then refresh and drain dry. Add the cooked, drained zucchini and rice to the egg-milk mixture, and stir to mix. Pour into the prepared gratin dish, sprinkle with the remaining cheese, and place in a preheated 375°F oven until set (about 20 minutes), then increase the temperature to 400°F for 6–8 minutes to *gratiner* the top. When done, the top should be nicely browned.

Serve in the same dish. If necessary, the gratin can be reheated.

Beignets de navets râpés

Fried Grated Turnips in Bouchées

—

For 6 to 8

½ lb. tender young turnips
5–6 Tbsp. sifted flour
4 oz. yogurt
2 large eggs
1 Tbsp. dried herbes de Provence (see
    Aide-Mémoire, page 503)
Salt, nutmeg, pepper, and cinnamon
Vegetable oil for frying

Special equipment needed:
A mixing bowl
A strainer
A deep skillet

*P*eel and grate the turnips into a mixing bowl. Sprinkle with salt and let sit for 20 minutes to disgorge their water, then put in a strainer and rinse with cold running water to remove excess salt. Squeeze dry between folded kitchen towels. You should have about 3 oz. grated turnips.

Put the flour in a mixing bowl, add the grated turnips, and stir in the yogurt and eggs. Season heavily and let stand for a good hour, beating from time to time.

If the mixture is too thick, stir in a little cold water; however, it should not be runny. Correct the seasoning, adding more pepper if needed. Heat 2–3 Tbsp. of oil in a skillet. When hot, fry 3–4 spoonfuls of the *bouchée* mixture, turning them over when the first side has turned a nice golden brown. Watch carefully, as each side will take only a few seconds to cook. When done, remove with a slotted spoon or skimmer, and let drain over paper towels.

Serve as is, or reheated in a moderate oven with a good tomato sauce.

Wine Suggestion: A good red such as a Cabernet Sauvignon.

DESSERTS: PUDDINGS, TARTS, CAKES, ICE CREAM, ETC.

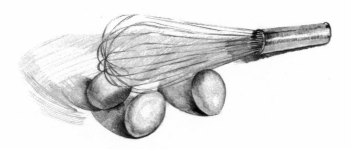

Charlotte de riz à l'orange, meringuée

Orange-flavored Rice Pudding, Meringue Topping

—

For 6 to 8

To caramelize mold:
12 sugar cubes

For charlotte:
1 cup raw long-grain white rice
Salt

4 cups milk
Peel from an orange, dried
4 Tbsp. butter
2 whole eggs plus 3 egg yolks
4 oz. candied orange peel, diced
½ cup sugar

For meringue:

3 egg whites
Pinch of salt
½ cup sugar

For second caramel:

15 sugar cubes
3–4 Tbsp. lemon juice, boiling

Special equipment needed:

A 6-cup metal charlotte mold
Aluminum foil
A large saucepan
A bain-marie (see page 503) or roasting
    pan large enough to contain charlotte
    mold and simmering water

*L*ine the charlotte mold with caramel by placing the 12 sugar cubes in the mold and heating, shaking constantly, until the syrup turns a nice golden brown. Using oven mitts, tilt the pan to evenly coat the bottom and sides, then turn upside down over aluminum foil and let cool.

Drop the rice and a pinch of salt into a large saucepan of boiling water, and parboil for 6 minutes. Immediately drain in a colander, refresh with cold tap water, and let drain dry.

Using the same saucepan, bring the milk to a boil with a pinch of salt, dried orange peel, and butter. Stir in the rice and let simmer slowly for about 25–30 minutes. The rice will be very tender and will have absorbed about ¾ of the milk.

Remove the orange peel and let cool slightly, then stir in 2 whole eggs and 3 egg yolks, reserving the whites for the meringue. Add the diced candied orange peel and sugar, working the mixture to melt the sugar. Pour into the prepared mold and bake in a bain-marie in a preheated 375°F oven for about 30–35 minutes, or until the pudding begins to leave the sides of the mold.

Meanwhile, beat the egg whites for the meringue with a pinch of salt and a teaspoon of water. When they are beginning to turn white and frothy, add ½ cup sugar, a little at a time, and beat vigorously until thick and shiny.

For the second caramel, melt sugar cubes, slightly moistened with water, with 1 Tbsp. lemon juice. As before, shake the pan until the syrup turns a nice golden brown. Immediately stir in 2–3 Tbsp. boiling lemon juice, to prevent the caramel from turning hard and being difficult to pour.

Serve the rice charlotte, warm or cold, unmolded onto a shallow metal serving dish. Top with meringue, using a wet spatula to make a wavy design, and decorate by drizzling caramel over the meringue.

Mousse au chocolat avec Chantilly, seulement au blanc d'oeuf

Chantilly Chocolate Mousse, with Egg Whites Only

—

For about 10

½ lb. semisweet chocolate (German or
    Maillard Eagle)
½ cup very strong coffee, or 1½ Tbsp.
    instant coffee granules dissolved in
    ⅔ cup boiling water
⅓ cup Cointreau or rum
1 cup sugar
5–6 egg whites, depending on size
Pinch of salt
2 cups heavy cream
¾ tsp. vanilla extract

Special equipment needed:
A copper or stainless-steel saucepan
An electric mixer
A copper basin, for beating the egg
    whites
Ice cubes
An elegant glass serving bowl, or
    individual glass bowls, placed in
    refrigerator to chill

Break the chocolate into pieces, and melt very slowly with the coffee, stirring constantly until perfectly smooth and shiny. If necessary, add a little more water. The mixture should remain creamy and not become thick. Remove from heat and keep warm, adding the Cointreau.

In a special copper or stainless-steel saucepan, boil the sugar with ½ cup water. At the same time, beat the egg whites with a pinch of salt in a copper basin until half beaten. As soon as the syrup reaches the "thread" stage, remove from the heat and pour into the egg whites in a thin stream, beating vigorously the entire time. Continue to beat until the whole mass becomes thick and shiny. (This is called an "Italian meringue.")

Fold the chocolate mixture into the egg whites and set aside while making the Chantilly. Whip the cream with the vanilla in a bowl set over ice cubes until the cream has doubled in volume and the beaters leave light traces on the surface. (This is the "soft peaks," or Chantilly, stage.) Fold the whipped cream into the egg-white-and-chocolate mixture. Turn the Chantilly mousse into the chosen serving dish and let freeze for 1 hour. The mousse should be nice and cold, but not frozen.

Le Palais de Glace

Caramel Meringue with Chantilly

—

For 10 to 12

For caramel meringue and Chantilly:

Optional: ½ cup unsalted macadamia nuts
5–6 egg whites, depending on size
Pinch of salt
½ cup water
6½ oz. sugar cubes
2 cups heavy cream
½ tsp. vanilla extract

For vanilla custard cream:

2 cups milk
1 whole vanilla bean, or 1 tsp. vanilla extract
½ cup granulated sugar
5–6 egg yolks, depending on size

Special equipment needed:

An electric mixer (optional)
A copper bowl to beat the egg whites (if not using a mixer)
A heavy-bottomed saucepan or unlined copper sugar-syrup pan
A large bowl (8-cup capacity) with ice
A smaller mixing bowl (4-cup capacity)
1 large, or 2 smaller stainless-steel mixing bowls with splayed sides for easy unmolding (6 cups total capacity)

*I*f you have chosen to use them, toast the macadamia nuts in a 350°F oven until lightly browned. Remove from oven, chop roughly, and set aside to cool at room temperature.

Whisk the egg whites with a pinch of salt in a copper basin until they are half whipped, then set aside while making the caramel, which cannot be delayed once prepared.

Bring ⅓ cup water to the boil. Meanwhile, cook the sugar cubes with a little water, letting the mixture boil until a light-amber caramel is obtained. When the caramel is done, remove from heat and, being careful to avoid the spattering, immediately pour in the boiling water to dissolve the caramel. If necessary, return over heat and scrape the sides and bottom of the pan to collect all the caramel, then pour immediately in a thin stream into the egg whites, beating constantly. Add nuts, if you wish. Set over ice and continue beating until the meringue turns glossy and begins to cool, then set aside and let cool while beating the cream.

Using a small mixing bowl set over ice, beat the cream with the vanilla until it forms soft peaks. Fold this Chantilly into the caramel meringue mixture until all is smooth and homogenous.

This dessert is delicious without the optional garnishes. Fill the mold and let set in the freezer about 3 hours, or until set. Serve unmolded with Crème Anglaise (page 88) poured around the *Palais de glace*.

Timbale d'ananas

Pineapple Timbale with Red Currant Sauce

—

For 4 to 6

For the caramel:
12–15 sugar cubes, moistened with
    water

For the timbale:
6 oz. canned pineapple
Optional: ¼ cup sultana raisins
3 Tbsp. dark rum
½ cup pineapple juice (from above)
½ cup sugar
1 Tbsp. arrowroot, potato starch, or rice
    starch

1 Tbsp. lime juice
4–5 eggs, depending on size

For the sauce:
8 oz. red currant jelly (strained, if needed)
Rum to taste

Special equipment needed:
One 6-cup charlotte mold
Parchment paper
A bain-marie (see page 503)
A heavy saucepan

*P*repare the caramel in the charlotte mold by melting the moistened sugar cubes over low heat, shaking constantly, until the syrup turns a golden brown. Do not let burn. Remove from heat and turn the mold to coat the sides evenly. Let cool, upside down, over wax paper.

Drain the canned pineapple, reserving the juice, then dice or chop roughly in a food processor and set aside. Place the raisins in a small bowl with enough of the rum to cover, and let macerate.

Place ½ cup pineapple juice and 2 Tbsp. sugar in a saucepan and bring to the boil, letting the syrup reduce for a few minutes, then remove from heat and allow to cool. When cool, pour into the starch, add the lime juice, and stir until smooth.

Beat 1 whole egg with the remaining sugar to the "ribbon" stage. Beating vigorously, add the other eggs, the syrup-starch mixture, the rum, diced pineapple, and raisins, if using them. Beat all together.

Fill the caramelized charlotte mold and cover with parchment paper, then place in a bain-marie with hot water, and bake in a preheated 375°F oven for 45 minutes to an hour. Do not let the water in the bain-marie boil. When the timbale is completely set and the custard has begun to pull away from the sides of the mold, remove from the oven and let cool until tepid.

To make the sauce, melt the red currant jelly in 3 Tbsp. water and a little rum, then keep warm until ready to serve.

To serve, unmold the timbale onto a serving dish, glaze with some of the sauce, and serve the rest in a sauceboat.

Timbale aux fruits rouges

Spring Mousse with Red Fruits

—

For 10 to 12

½ lb. small strawberries (*fraises des bois,* if available), cleaned

¼ lb. red currants, if available, for garnish

Lime juice, for the *fraises des bois*

1¾ cups sugar, plus ½ Tbsp. for the *fraises*

½ lb. raspberries, cleaned

5–6 egg yolks, depending on size

1 envelope unflavored gelatin

1½ cups heavy cream

30–36 ladyfingers

Fruit liqueur

Whole raspberries or strawberries, for garnish

Special equipment needed:

A food processor

A strainer

A heavy-bottomed saucepan, preferably copper, for making sugar syrup

An 8-cup charlotte mold, or two 4–5 cup charlotte molds

Parchment paper

*I*f you can find the tiny *fraises des bois,* clean them carefully, sprinkle with a little lime juice and sugar, and refrigerate while making the red fruit mousse. If only large strawberries are available, combine them with the raspberries in the red fruit mousse.

Prepare the fruit coulis first: Purée the red fruit(s) in a food processor with ¼ cup sugar, then strain to remove the seeds, and set aside. Without washing the processor work bowl, add the egg yolks. Meanwhile, boil the remaining sugar with ½ cup water in a heavy-bottomed saucepan, preferably copper, until large bubbles appear (the soft ball stage). Immediately pulse the egg yolks while pouring in the boiling syrup, and continue to pulse until the mixture becomes foamy, like a mousse.

Soften the gelatin in a little of the reserved juice. When softened, add to the egg yolk mousse, pulsing to mix until smooth. Pour in the raspberry juice and pulse about 6 seconds to mix. Let cool, but not long enough to set. When the mousse is cool and about to set, beat the cream to the Chantilly ("soft peaks") stage and fold it into the fruit mousse, working until the mixture is absolutely light and smooth, then let set over ice.

To build the timbale, cut the ladyfingers in half lengthwise and moisten each for no more than a second in a mixture of one part water and one part fruit liqueur, such as Kirsch or Poire William (see note). Line the bottom and sides of the mold with the soaked ladyfingers, placing them like soldiers, with sides touching, around the sides of the mold and in a rose (or star) pattern on the bottom of the mold. Place the cut edges pointing away from the sides and bottom of the mold. Next, add a layer of raspberry mousse sprinkled with the *fraises des bois,* if any. Follow with a layer of ladyfingers, cut in half and nicely soaked as before, and then another layer of *fraises des bois* and raspberry mousse. When filled, cover with foil and let set in the refrigerator.

To serve, unmold and decorate with fresh raspberries or strawberries, and sweetened raspberry juice, simmered to yield a nice syrup and cooled.

Note: If you haven't any fruit liqueur, moisten the ladyfingers with sweetened fresh fruit juice, such as orange juice, and serve the fruit timbale with a syrup made from the same fruit juice.

Soufflé au chocolat

Chocolate Soufflé

—

For 8

Butter, for baking dish
½ cup sifted flour
2 cups milk
7 oz. semisweet or bittersweet chocolate,
   broken into bits
¼ cup water
1 Tbsp. instant coffee granules
6 eggs, separated, plus 3 egg whites

Pinch of salt
¾ cup granulated sugar
Confectioners' sugar in a shaker

Special equipment needed:
A 10–12 cup shallow oval baking dish:
   Pyrex, ceramic, or enameled cast iron
2 medium-size saucepans

$\mathcal{B}$utter the baking dish, and set in refrigerator until needed. Put the sifted flour in a medium-size saucepan, stir in just enough milk to make a smooth paste, then add the rest of the milk, stirring until the mixture is completely smooth. Cook over medium heat, stirring constantly until a thick paste is obtained. Set aside.

Melt the chocolate with the water and instant coffee, stirring until completely smooth, then stir this mixture into the milk-flour paste. When smooth, add the egg yolks, one at a time, and stir vigorously until well blended. This mixture may now wait up to an hour at room temperature.

Thirty minutes before baking the soufflé, beat all the egg whites with a pinch of salt and a drop of water until they form soft peaks. Gradually sprinkle on the granulated sugar and continue to beat until the meringue becomes thick and shiny. Rewarm the soufflé base until it is tepid, then lightly fold the base into the meringue.

Pour the soufflé into the prepared baking dish and place in a bain-marie, or pan of hot water, in a preheated 375°F oven. Bake 25–30 minutes if you like the center of the soufflé to be well set, or just 25 minutes if you prefer a slightly soft center. The soufflé should rise evenly an inch or two above the rim of the dish.

Sprinkle with confectioners' sugar, and serve. Use two forks to keep the soufflé from falling while you are serving it. Put the forks back to back into the soufflé along the line you want to cut.

Couronne de semoule aux poires — Sauce à l'abricot et banane

Semolina Pudding in a Ring Mold with Pears—
Apricot and Banana Sauce

—

For 6 to 8

For pudding:
2½ cups milk
½ cup water
Pinch of salt
4½ oz. wheat or rice semolina
1½ lb. ripe and juicy Comice pears
4 Tbsp. butter
Ground cinnamon
6 Tbsp. Poire William liqueur
1 lemon
3 egg yolks
½ cup sugar
3 eggs
½ cup heavy cream

For sauce:
½ lb. canned pineapple, well
    drained
½ banana, well ripened, sliced
½ lb. apricot preserves
½ cup heavy cream

Special equipment needed:
A heavy-bottomed saucepan
A nonstick sauté pan or skillet
A 6-cup nonstick ring mold
A bain-marie (see page 503)
A food processor

*P*lace the milk, water, and salt in a heavy-bottomed saucepan, and bring to the boil. Stirring constantly, add the semolina, then reduce the heat to a simmer and continue stirring for about 15–20 minutes, or until the mixture has thickened to a smooth paste. Set aside.

Peel, core, and quarter the pears, then cut each quarter into 2 or 3 pieces, depending on size. Cook in a nonstick skillet with half the butter, turning as soon as one side is tender and adding additional butter if needed. While the pears are cooking, sprinkle them with cinnamon to taste. Drain the pears, retaining the cooking juices, and deglaze the pan with Poire William liqueur.

Peel the lemon, taking care not to remove the bitter white pith with the yellow zest, and mince fine. Juice the lemon and set aside. Place the egg yolks in a mixing bowl with the sugar, and whisk until the mixture is pale yellow and forms a ribbon. Beat in the whole eggs and cream, then stir in the semolina paste, blending until homogenous. Add the minced lemon peel, 2 Tbsp. lemon juice, and the deglazed cooking juice.

Fill a ring mold ⅓ high with a layer of the semolina mixture. Place half of the cut-up pears evenly over the semolina, cover with another layer of semolina, then the rest of the pears, and finish with the rest of the semolina.

Place the filled ring mold in a bain-marie or pan containing hot water halfway up the sides of the mold, and bake in a preheated 375°F oven for 35–40 minutes, or until the pudding begins to pull away from the sides of the mold. Let cool a little before unmolding. If cooked ahead, the pudding can be easily reheated over hot water. The pudding is better when served tepid, rather than cold.

Prepare the filling while the pudding is baking. Purée the drained pineapple in a food processor with the banana and apricot marmalade. Whip the cream and add 3–4 Tbsp. Poire William, then fold in the pineapple-banana-apricot purée. Place in the refrigerator until ready to garnish the cooled pudding.

When ready to serve, heap the sauce in the middle of the *cooled* unmolded pudding, and serve any extra in a sauceboat.

Charlotte de riz, à l'orange, avec sauce au chocolat

Orange-flavored Rice Charlotte with Chocolate Sauce

—

For 6 to 8

For caramel:
2 Tbsp. cold water
2 oz. sugar cubes

For charlotte:
5 oz. raw long-grain rice
2 cups milk

Grated peel of 1 orange

1 vanilla bean

3–4 eggs, depending on size, separated

7 Tbsp. butter, diced

Pinch of salt

⅔ cup granulated sugar

2½ oz. diced candied orange peel

For chocolate cream sauce

7 oz. dark bittersweet chocolate

¾ cup boiling water

2 tsp. instant coffee granules

⅔ cup unsweetened evaporated milk

Optional: 3–4 Tbsp. dark rum

Special equipment needed:

A 4–5 cup charlotte mold

A 5–6 qt. saucepan

A large mixing bowl

A large copper basin for whipping the egg whites

A bain-marie (see page 503) or large roasting pan

*C*arefully wash, rinse, and dry the charlotte mold, as any grease will prevent the caramel from coating the mold evenly.

Wearing oven mitts, heat 2 Tbsp. water in the mold, add the sugar cubes, and let boil, shaking the mold all the while, until a nice blond caramel color is obtained. Immediately set the bottom of the mold in cool water to stop the cooking, then place upside down over an oiled baking sheet and let cool.

Bring 3 qt. water to the boil, add the rice, stir once, and let boil again for 3 minutes. Pour into a colander to drain. Place the milk, grated orange peel, and vanilla bean in the same saucepan, and bring to a simmer, then add the drained rice and let simmer slowly until the rice has absorbed the milk but is not dry (about 45 minutes). When done, the rice will be very tender. Transfer to a large mixing bowl, let cool, then stir in the egg yolks followed by the butter, working the mixture with a spatula until homogenous.

Clean a large copper bowl with a mixture of vinegar and salt, rinse well, and dry. Beat the egg whites with a pinch of salt in the copper bowl until half whipped, then add the sugar a little at a time and beat until the meringue is glossy. If you wish, an electric mixer can be used for this step.

Fold the rice mixture into the egg whites, folding lightly so the meringue does not break, then fold in the candied orange peel. Pour the charlotte mixture into the mold, leaving at least ⅔″ at top. Pack the mixture well to eliminate any air pockets. Place in a bain-marie or large pan with hot water 1″ deep and bake in a preheated 375°F oven for about 25–30 minutes, or until set and nicely risen.

Meanwhile, make the chocolate cream sauce. Stirring constantly, melt the chocolate in a heavy-bottomed saucepan with the water and coffee. When smooth and creamy, remove from heat and stir in the evaporated milk, and the rum if you like its taste. Let stand, and the sauce will thicken as it cools.

When the rice pudding is nicely puffed and golden, remove from the oven and let cool before unmolding onto a serving dish. Coat with the chocolate sauce, and serve the remaining sauce in a sauceboat.

Variation: This dessert can be made without using the egg yolks, as they are not necessary to set the pudding. You could use them to make a Crème Anglaise (page 88) instead of the chocolate sauce.

Soufflé léger aux pommes le zephir, avec crème anglaise

"Zephyr" Apple Soufflé with Custard Sauce

—

For 8 to 10

Butter for soufflé molds

For soufflé:
3 large apples (about 2 lb.)
1¼ cups granulated sugar
2 Tbsp. butter
3–4 Tbsp. Poire William liqueur

8 egg yolks
10–12 egg whites

Pinch of salt
Confectioners' sugar in a shaker

For custard sauce (optional):
1¾ cups milk
4 egg yolks
⅔ cup sugar
1 tsp. potato starch
Vanilla extract
Poire William liqueur

Special equipment needed:

Two 6-cup charlotte or fluted soufflé
  molds

A saucepan

A food processor

A small skillet or sauté pan

A clean copper bowl for beating egg
  whites

*H*eavily butter two 6-cup charlotte or soufflé molds, and set aside. Peel, core, and dice the apples. Reserve one apple for sautéing and place the other two in a saucepan with 2 Tbsp. water and 4 Tbsp. sugar. Cook slowly, stirring, until a smooth purée is obtained. Pulse in a food processor, remove, and set aside.

Melt the butter in another pan, add the reserved diced apple, and sauté with 4 Tbsp. sugar. The apple pieces should remain whole, not crushed. Pour the liqueur over the apples and ignite, then set aside.

In a food processor, work the egg yolks with ½ cup sugar until pale and foamy, then add the apple purée, pulse a few more seconds, and transfer all to another bowl. Add vanilla extract and, after mixing, add the diced sautéed apple with the flamed liqueur.

Beat the egg whites with a pinch of salt until they are just beginning to hold their shape, then gradually add the remaining ¼ cup sugar, beating constantly until a thick meringue is obtained. Fold the apple mixture into the meringue with a large rubber spatula, turning the bowl slightly with each stroke, until all is well combined.

Fill the two prepared molds ¾ full, then run your finger around the edge of each soufflé to help it rise. Bake in a preheated 425°F oven for 20–25 minutes, or until the tops are nicely browned. A few minutes before serving, sprinkle the tops with confectioners' sugar and return to a hot oven (450°F) for 2–3 minutes to caramelize. This soufflé may be served as is, or with a custard sauce.

To make the custard sauce, bring the milk to the boiling point. Meanwhile, work the egg yolks with the sugar and starch until the sugar has completely dissolved. Stirring constantly, slowly add the hot milk and mix thoroughly, then pour the mixture back into the saucepan. Return to moderate heat and stir constantly with a wooden spatula until the mixture thickens sufficiently to coat the back of the spatula. Remove from heat and continue to stir until smooth. Add the Poire William liqueur, then let cool and serve in a sauceboat.

Les œufs à la neige

Snow Eggs, or Floating Islands

A very old recipe, yet still appreciated.

—

For 5 to 6

For meringue:
6 large eggs
Pinch of salt
¾ cup confectioners' sugar
3 cups milk
1 tsp. vanilla powder or extract

Special equipment needed:
A clean copper basin and whisk, or an
    electric beater
A colander
A large spoon and a metal spatula
A skimmer
A mixing bowl
A large skillet

Separate the eggs, placing whites in a copper basin and yolks in a mixing bowl. Pour 3–4 qt. water into a large skillet, and slowly bring to the simmer. Meanwhile, beat the egg whites with a pinch of salt until soft peaks form. Beating vigorously, pour half the sugar in a thin stream into the egg whites, and continue beating until thick and shiny.

Using a large spoon, shape ⅓ of the meringue into a large egg, smoothing the top with a metal spatula to remove air pockets, then slide the "egg" into the barely simmering water. Quickly shape two others in the same manner, and slide them into the water as well. These snow eggs take only about 25–30 seconds to cook. When done, remove with a skimmer (or slotted spoon) and place in a colander to drain over kitchen towels. When well drained, transfer to a shallow serving dish, placed in a single layer without crowding.

Beat reserved egg yolks, adding the remaining sugar gradually until the mixture is pale and forms a "ribbon." Meanwhile, bring milk and vanilla to the boil. When boiling, remove from heat and very slowly pour the hot milk into the egg yolks, while beating constantly to keep them from scrambling. When the milk has been incorporated, return all to the saucepan, place again over heat, and stir constantly until the mixture begins to thicken. Immediately remove from heat and, still stirring, set in cold water to stop the cooking. To prevent the custard from overcooking, continue stirring until it has cooled slightly. The custard can be served now, poured around and over the snow eggs, or it can be covered and kept in the refrigerator for a few hours. Press plastic wrap right on the surface of the custard to keep a "skin" from forming.

Petits flans à la purée de fruits

Fruit Purée in a Custard, in Ramekins

This easy dessert can be prepared ahead and kept in the refrigerator until needed. I sometimes use dried fruits, such as bananas, apricots, prunes, pineapples (before using, they must be steeped in warm water until they have softened, about 1–2 hours, depending on dryness).

———

For 6

For fruit purée:
2 bananas
½ lb. Granny Smith apples (1–2 apples)
3 Tbsp. butter
¼ cup sugar
1 lemon

For custard:
2 whole eggs
1½ Tbsp. sugar
1½ Tbsp. ground almonds
2½ Tbsp. crème fraîche (page 501) or
    heavy cream
Optional: 2–3 Tbsp. Kirsch or other fruit
    brandy

1 cup milk
Pinch of salt

For optional red currant sauce:
½ lb. red currant jelly
3 Tbsp. water
2 Tbsp. Kirsch or other fruit brandy

Special equipment needed:
A heavy-bottomed saucepan
A food processor
A bain-marie (see page 503)
Six 6-oz. ceramic ramekins, or one 3-cup
    baking dish

$\mathcal{P}$eel the bananas and cut into thick slices. Peel and dice the apples. Heat the butter in a heavy-bottomed saucepan. Stirring constantly, add the diced apples to the butter. When the apples are beginning to soften, add bananas and continue stirring. The bananas will go soft very quickly. When they appear to be puréed, remove from heat, and add half the sugar and a little lemon juice. Set aside while preparing the custard.

Break the eggs into a food processor, add the remaining sugar, and process until the sugar is almost completely dissolved. Add the ground almonds, crème fraîche, milk, and salt, and pulse until thoroughly blended. Add the fruit and brandy. Process 5–6 seconds, or until homogenous.

Fill the ramekins or baking dish, place in a bain-marie, and bake in a preheated 350°F oven for 18–20 minutes, or until set. Let cool completely before serving.

For a more elaborate presentation, serve custards unmolded and coated with red currant sauce: Heat jelly with water and liqueur, stirring until completely homogenous. Unmold each ramekin over individual dessert plates, and coat with the red currant sauce. If a baking dish was used instead of individual ramekins, do not unmold but spoon out individual servings, then drizzle sauce over the tops.

Tarte à l'orange Pamela avec chocolat

Orange Cream Tart Pamela with Chocolate Glaze

—

For 6 to 8

For pastry dough:
1½ cups pastry flour
⅔ cup butter, softened
Pinch of salt
2 egg yolks, mixed with 3 Tbsp.
 water

For filling:
3 medium-size oranges
2 lemons or limes
8 Tbsp. butter
⅔ cup granulated sugar
4 eggs plus 1 egg yolk

3 oz. almonds, finely ground

3 Tbsp. Cointreau

½ cup heavy cream

Strips of candied orange peel, for garnish

For optional glaze:

4 oz. bittersweet dark chocolate

4 Tbsp. orange juice

Special equipment needed:

A 10″ metal or nonstick tart pan with fluted sides 1½″ high

A food processor

A bain-marie (see page 503)

A metal spatula

*M*ake the pastry dough ahead of time, using the method described in the recipe for warm apple tart on p. 446. Wrap in a plastic bag, and refrigerate. Remove from refrigerator 20 minutes before you plan to roll it out.

Grate the peel of the oranges. Squeeze the juice from the oranges and lemons, and strain. Cream the butter with the grated orange peel, and let the mixture macerate while the tart shell bakes.

Roll out the pastry dough and place in the tart pan, making the sides double in thickness and slightly higher than the sides of the pan. Prick the bottom of the tart shell with a fork to keep the bottom very flat. Place in the refrigerator to chill before baking.

When firm, bake in a preheated 375°F oven for 18–20 minutes. Remove from the oven and increase oven temperature to 400°F. Let the tart shell cool while preparing the filling.

Using a food processor, mix the butter–orange peel mixture with the sugar, then add the eggs and extra egg yolk, and process until the sugar has completely dissolved. Add the ground almonds, Cointreau, fruit juices, and cream, and mix until smooth. Pour into the baked, cooled tart shell and bake at 400°F until set, about 25–30 minutes. As soon as the filling has completely set, remove from the oven and let cool.

This tart is delicious served plain or with the chocolate glaze: Melt the chocolate in a bain-marie or double boiler with the orange juice (or water and Cointreau), stirring until smooth. Keep over hot, not simmering, water until time to glaze the top of the tart.

Allow the tart to cool completely before spreading the chocolate glaze. Use a metal spatula to make the glaze glossy. To decorate, place strips of candied orange peel on the top, radiating outward from the center. Serve cold.

Tarte aux pommes, tiède

Warm Apple Tart

—

For one 9" tart

For pâte brisée:
2 cups pastry flour
Pinch of salt
1 Tbsp. sugar
12 Tbsp. butter
1 egg yolk
3 Tbsp. cold water

For filling:
1½ lb. Golden Delicious apples

1 lemon, juiced
1 cup apricot preserves, strained
2 Tbsp. sugar

Special equipment required:
A food processor
A 9" tart pan
A pastry brush

*P*âte brisée is a very classic "short" pastry, which can be used for quiches or sweet desserts. When using for a savory dish, omit the sugar.

Using the food processor, pulse the flour with the salt for 5 seconds to sift, then add the sugar. Cut the butter into small cubes, add to the mixture, and pulse until the butter is broken into small pieces *but not granular*. Some little pieces of butter should be visible.

Beat the egg with the water, and add to the flour mixture. Pulse 5 or 6 times, or until a ball forms. The consistency of the pastry should be neither dry nor sticky. If necessary, a few drops of water can be added to make a smooth ball. Place on a lightly floured board and knead for about 15 seconds to make the mixture homogenous. Wrap in plastic and chill for 1 hour.

Peel and core the apples, cut in thin slices, sprinkle with lemon juice, and set aside.

Roll the dough to ⅛" thick and fit into the tart pan, making the sides double in thickness. Using a pastry brush, spread a layer of strained apricot preserves on the bottom of the tart shell, then arrange the apple slices, in rows, on top. Sprinkle with the sugar, and glaze with more of the apricot preserves. Bake in a moderately hot oven (400°F) for about 20–25 minutes, or until the apple slices are tender and slightly browned. Glaze the top again to make it shine, and let cool until tepid. Slide onto a serving dish.

Wine Suggestion: A Vouvray or other sweet white wine.

La tarte verte au sucre

Provençal Green Tart for Christmas

This is one of the thirteen traditional desserts served in Provence at Christmas.

For me, frozen spinach is much easier to use than fresh. When mixed with the pastry cream, the taste is not so different than with fresh, since the strongest flavor is the vanilla.

—

For 6 to 8

For short pastry:
2 cups pastry flour
12 Tbsp. butter
1 small egg
1 Tbsp. water
Pinch of salt
1 Tbsp. sugar

For filling:
1 cup milk
1½ tsp. vanilla extract
3 egg yolks
½ cup sugar

1 egg
1 cup flour, sifted
1½ oz. pulverized almonds
½ lb. cooked fresh or thawed frozen
    spinach (squeezed dry with kitchen
    towels)

For glaze:
1 egg yolk, beaten

Special equipment needed:
A 9″ tart pan
A food processor

$\mathcal{P}$repare the short pastry at least an hour ahead and refrigerate (for detailed instructions, see page 488). Roll out the pastry and fit into the tart pan, reserving extra pastry to make a lattice design on the tart. Refrigerate while preparing the filling.

Bring the milk and vanilla to the boil. In a mixing bowl, whisk the egg yolks and sugar until they are pale and make a "ribbon." Mix in the whole egg, flour, and almonds, and whisk until completely smooth. Stirring constantly, gradually pour the boiling milk into the egg-sugar-flour-almond mixture, then pour all into the saucepan. Stir over heat until the mixture comes to the boil. Remove from heat, and continue stirring until the mixture has cooled slightly.

Place the squeezed-dry spinach in a food processor, and pulse briefly. Add the pastry cream to the food processor, and process until thoroughly mixed. Scrape the sides of the work bowl as needed.

Pour the filling into the prepared tart shell, and place a lattice top over the filling. Glaze the crust and lattice top with a beaten egg yolk mixed with a little water. Bake in a preheated 375°F oven for 25 minutes, or until nicely browned. If made ahead, reheat slightly before serving. This tart is better served tepid than cold.

Gâteau au chocolat le Bamboula

Bamboula Chocolate Cake

—

For 6 to 8

For cake:
Butter for pan
7 oz. semisweet chocolate
8 Tbsp. butter
3–4 eggs, depending on size
½ cup sugar
½ cup cake flour
1 oz. almonds, finely ground
1½ tsp. baking powder

Crème Anglaise Sauce (page 88)

Special equipment needed:
An 8½"–9" round cake pan
Parchment paper
A bain-marie (see page 503) or double
    boiler
A food processor
Parchment paper

*H*eavily butter the cake pan and line the bottom with buttered parchment paper. Set in the refrigerator until needed. Melt the chocolate with the butter in a bain-marie or a double boiler, stirring constantly until smooth. Set aside.

Using a food processor, mix the eggs with the sugar. Continue beating until the sugar is well dissolved. Mix in the flour, then the almonds and the baking powder. Pour in the melted chocolate and process a few seconds until homogenous, scraping the sides as needed.

Fill the prepared cake pan, and bake in a preheated 375°F oven for 10 minutes, then reduce the temperature to 350°F and bake 15–20 minutes more. The center should be moist, not dry. Let cool before removing from the pan.

When the cake has cooled, unmold over a serving platter. Serve with Crème Anglaise Sauce.

Galette des rois

Provençal Three Kings Cake

Molded in a ring mold, this moist and tasty tea or luncheon cake is more a pudding with candied fruits than a cake. At Christmastime in Provence, a *Galette des rois* is baked with a little ceramic baby (or a dried bean) hidden inside. Whoever discovers the baby in his slice of cake is crowned "king" with a cardboard crown and must then choose a queen. Whenever the new "king" drinks, the other guests will say, *"Le roi boit! Vive le roi!"* ("The king drinks! Long live the king!")

In Normandy, the *Galettes des rois* are typically made with a short pastry dough, or a puff pastry with almond filling.

—

For 6 to 8

Butter for mold and tray
7 oz. brioche pieces, stale or dried
¼ cup orange blossom water, or dry
    white wine with 1 tsp. grated orange
    peel
2 cups milk
½ cup granulated sugar
1 tsp. vanilla extract
4–5 eggs, depending on size
3 Tbsp. dark rum
3 oz. candied fruits, such as citron or
    cherries

½ lb. apricot preserves, strained
For garnish: white sugar "sprinkles"

Special equipment needed:
A 6-cup nonstick ring mold
Parchment paper
A food processor
A ceramic baby or bean
A bain-marie (see page 503)
A metal tray

*H*eavily butter the ring mold and line with parchment paper. Set aside until ready to fill.

Break the brioches into pieces. If the brioches are not stale, let dry in a slow oven until crusty. Place the brioche pieces in a mixing bowl, moisten the bread with orange blossom water (or grated orange peel macerated in dry white wine). Purée the moistened brioche in a food processor.

At the same time, bring the milk, sugar, and vanilla to the boil. Pour into the food processor and pulse a few seconds to mix, then add the eggs, one by one, and the rum. Transfer to a mixing bowl and add ¾ of the candied fruit, reserving the rest for decorating the galette. Fill the mold and push the ceramic baby or the bean into the mixture. Place in a bain marie, or pan filled with hot water coming halfway up the sides of the mold, and bake in a preheated 375°F oven for 40–45 minutes, or until the custard pulls away from the sides of the ring mold and is dry in the center. Let cool.

When cold, unmold over a buttered metal tray. Paint the top with strained apricot marmalade, and arrange the reserved candied fruit in an attractive design. Return to a hot oven for a few minutes to make the cake glisten, then sprinkle with tiny white sugar "sprinkles." Serve tepid or cold.

Wine Suggestion: A good demi-sec Champagne.

La bûche de Noël

Christmas Log Roll

This dessert may be kept in the refrigerator for about a week and will still be perfect.

—

For 8 to 12

Butter for tray
1 cup sweet butter
1 lb. canned candied chestnuts
⅓ lb. bittersweet chocolate, broken in pieces

1 cup coffee
4–5 Tbsp. dark rum
18 large, or 36 small, ladyfingers
Ground pistachio nuts

Special equipment needed:
An 11″ by 7½″ tray
Aluminum foil

A food processor
A metal spatula

*N*eatly line the tray with aluminum foil. Butter lightly and place in the refrigerator to chill until needed.

Cream the butter. Purée the candied chestnuts in a food processor, then add the butter by spoonfuls and pulse until smooth. Melt the chocolate with ⅔ cup coffee, stirring until very smooth. Add to the food processor, and process until very well blended, then stir in 3–4 Tbsp. rum. Transfer from the processor work bowl to a mixing bowl, and refrigerate until firm.

Meanwhile, prepare the ladyfingers by slicing them in half lengthwise with a serrated knife, and set aside. Mix remaining ⅓ cup coffee and 1 Tbsp. rum in a bowl, and set aside.

When the chestnut mixture is firm, prepare the base of the log by placing 10–12 ladyfingers, first moistened for 2 seconds in the rum-flavored coffee, close together on the foil-lined tray. Neatly spread ⅓ of the chestnut mixture over the ladyfinger base, using a metal spatula, and top with another layer of moistened ladyfingers. Cover with a second layer of the chestnut mixture, and top with another layer of ladyfingers. Cover all with a layer of chestnut cream, and top with 2–3 rolled ladyfingers to simulate a knothole, then spread more of the chestnut cream on top.

Cover all with the remaining chestnut cream to make glossy, then draw lines in the chestnut cream with a fork to imitate bark. Sprinkle with ground pistachios to imitate moss growing on the bark. Place in the refrigerator until nicely set.

Wine Suggestion: A sweet white wine, such as a Sauternes.

Terrine de chocolat

Chocolate Loaf, with Armagnac or Bourbon

This delicious and easily made chocolate terrine requires no baking.

—

For about 8

For terrine:

½ lb. dark bittersweet chocolate

¼ cup water or coffee

4 oz. unsweetened cocoa powder

7–8 egg yolks, depending on size

¾ cup sugar

1 cup sweet butter, softened

2 cups heavy cream

½ tsp. vanilla extract

3 Tbsp. instant coffee granules

⅔ cup boiling water

3 Tbsp. Armagnac or bourbon

24 ladyfingers

Optional: 1½ cups Crème Anglaise
  Sauce (page 88)

Special equipment needed:

A heavy-bottomed saucepan

A mixing bowl and whisk

A 6-cup rectangular loaf pan

Parchment paper

*R*oughly chop the chocolate, place in a heavy-bottomed saucepan, and melt in ¼ cup water (or coffee), stirring over low heat until the chocolate is completely melted and the mixture is smooth. Remove from heat and stir in the cocoa. Return over low heat, stirring constantly until smooth.

Meanwhile, whisk egg yolks in a mixing bowl with the sugar to the "ribbon" stage. Pour into the chocolate mixture, stirring over heat to poach the egg yolks. Stir constantly until the mixture thickens, then remove from heat and set aside. Cream the butter and add to the chocolate mixture, stirring until the mixture is thoroughly blended, then set aside to cool.

Whip the cream with the vanilla to the Chantilly ("soft peaks") stage. Lightly fold the Chantilly into the cool chocolate mixture, and set aside.

Dissolve the instant coffee in ⅔ cup boiling water, stir in Armagnac or bourbon, and set aside.

Slice the ladyfingers in half lengthwise, so that you have two pieces half as thick, but just as wide and as long as the original ladyfinger. Set aside.

To build the terrine: Line bottom and sides of the loaf pan with buttered parchment paper. Moisten the cut side of each ladyfinger for 1 second only in the coffee and Armagnac mixture. Place the moistened ladyfingers tightly together, with rounded sides against the loaf pan, first on the bottom and then upright along the sides of the pan.

Half-fill the prepared pan with the chocolate mixture, and cover with a layer of moistened halved ladyfingers. Cover with the remaining chocolate, and top with another layer of moistened ladyfingers (placed rounded side against the filling). Set in the refrigerator to chill for at least 6 hours.

For a special party, prepare Crème Anglaise Sauce. To serve, unmold onto an attractive serving platter. Partially coat with some of the sauce and serve the remaining sauce in a sauceboat.

Wine Suggestion: A sweet white wine, such as a Vouvray from the Loire Valley, or a sparkling white wine.

Pain de marrons napolitain au chocolat

A Neapolitan Chestnut Loaf with Chocolate

—

For 8 to 10

1½ lb. candied Italian chestnuts, crumbled or roughly chopped
½ cup heavy cream
½ tsp. vanilla extract
3½ oz. dark bittersweet chocolate
¼ cup strong coffee

1 cup sweet butter, softened
¼ cup confectioners' sugar
¼ cup dark rum

For custard sauce:
2 cups milk

⅓ cup granulated sugar
4 egg yolks, plus 1 egg
1 tsp. vanilla extract

Optional garnish:
2 Tbsp. candied violets

Special equipment needed:
A 6-cup rectangular loaf pan
Parchment paper
A food processor
A saucepan

*T*his dessert is quickly and easily made, since it is prepared in the food processor and requires no baking. It is better when prepared a day ahead.

Line the bottom and sides of a 6-cup loaf pan with buttered parchment paper, and set aside until needed. Reserve about ½ cup of the crumbled chestnuts for garnish, and put the rest into a food processor work bowl. Add the cream and vanilla and pulse 5–6 times, then set aside.

Melt the chocolate with the coffee over a bain-marie or very low heat, stirring constantly until the chocolate is quite smooth. Cream the butter with the confectioners' sugar, working over low heat to melt the sugar, then stir in the melted chocolate and the rum. Add this mixture to the food processor, and process until all is puréed and homogenous.

Fill the prepared loaf pan, adding most of the reserved crumbled chestnuts here and there. Bang pan lightly on the table to settle the mixture, then place in the refrigerator to chill for at least 3 hours.

While the chestnut loaf is chilling, prepare a vanilla custard sauce: Bring milk to the boil. At the same time, whisk together the sugar, egg yolks, and whole egg until pale and ribboned. Slowly pour ¾ of the hot milk into the egg mixture, stirring constantly, then pour the tempered egg-milk mixture back into the saucepan. Continue stirring over heat until the custard begins to thicken. Immediately remove from heat, add the vanilla, and beat until cool.

When ready to serve, unmold the chestnut loaf onto a serving dish. Cut into slices and coat with custard sauce. Decorate with a sprinkling of candied violets and chestnut fragments. Serve the rest of the sauce on the side in a sauceboat.

Wine Suggestion: A sweet white wine, such as a Sauternes or a Barsac from Bordeaux.

Marquise au chocolat avec meringue et chantilly

Chocolate Marquise with Meringue and Chantilly

—

For 8 to 10

10 oz. Maillard Eagle or German
    semisweet chocolate
¼ cup strong coffee
4 egg yolks
12 Tbsp. sweet butter

For meringue:
4 egg whites
Pinch of salt
1 tsp. cold water
¼ cup water
⅔ cup sugar cubes

For Chantilly:
1 cup heavy cream
½ tsp. vanilla extract
Optional: Confectioners' sugar

Special equipment needed:
A thick-bottomed saucepan
A copper bowl, if available
An electric mixer
A 2-qt. stainless-steel splayed mixing
    bowl
A tray of ice cubes

*U*sing a thick-bottomed saucepan, melt the chocolate with the coffee, stirring constantly until smooth. Remove from heat, let cool slightly, then stir in the egg yolks, one at a time. When well mixed, place over very low heat and stir until thickened. Do *not* let mixture boil. Remove from heat and stir until slightly cool, then add butter in pieces, stirring until each piece has melted before adding more.

To make the cooked meringue, place the egg whites in a mixing bowl (preferably copper) with a pinch of salt and 1 tsp. water, and beat until white and frothy (about half done). At the same time, boil the water with the sugar to make a syrup. When the syrup reaches the "thread" stage (about 220°–225°F), pour it into the egg whites and beat vigorously with an electric mixer until firm and shiny.

Fold the chocolate mixture into the meringue, transfer to a stainless-steel mixing bowl, and chill in the freezer until set, about 6 hours or overnight.

Ten minutes before unmolding the marquise, beat the cream and vanilla over ice cubes until stiff. Place the Chantilly in a pastry bag equipped with a star tip.

Unmold the marquise by placing the bowl on a hot wet kitchen towel and running a warm wet flexible spatula around the sides to loosen them. Gently turn out onto a serving dish and decorate by piping an attractive design around the sides and top. Serve immediately after unmolding and decorating.

Wine Suggestion: A good brut Champagne.

Charlotte aux pommes, plombières

Flourless Apple Cake with Candied Fruit and Sultana Raisins

—

For 6 to 8

2½ lb. Golden Delicious apples

Juice of 1 lime

Grated peel of 1 lime

10–12 lumps of sugar (for caramelizing the mold)

5 medium eggs

½ cup confectioners' sugar

8 Tbsp. butter, softened

4 oz. pulverized ladyfingers or any stale shortcake

2–3 Tbsp. Kirsch or prune liqueur

2 oz. any candied fruit, diced

2 oz. sultana raisins

Special equipment needed:

A heavy-bottomed casserole

A 4–6 cup charlotte mold

A bain-marie (see page 503) or roasting pan filled with hot water coming halfway up the sides of the mold

*P*eel and quarter the apples, rub with lime juice, and place in a heavy-bottomed casserole with the grated lime peel and any remaining lime juice. Do not add water. Stirring frequently, cook the marmalade until the apples are very tender and the juices have evaporated. Set aside. (It is not necessary to put the apples through a food mill, even if some of the pieces are large.)

While the apples are cooking, caramelize a *very clean* charlotte mold by melting the sugar cubes in it with 1 Tbsp. water. Heat slowly, turning and shaking the mold to mix the contents until the caramel begins to turn golden brown. Do not stir with a spoon. When golden brown, remove from heat and, using cooking mitts, slowly rotate the mold until the caramel covers the entire inside, then place the mold upside down on a piece of foil or a metal baking tray until cool.

Beat the eggs with the confectioners' sugar until well mixed, then set aside. Cream the butter, being careful that it does not separate. Mix the butter into the still-hot apple marmalade, adding the beaten eggs and sugar, pulverized ladyfingers or stale cake, liqueur, candied fruit, and raisins. Mix thoroughly.

Fill the mold, bang it lightly on the counter to settle, and bake uncovered in a bain-marie in a preheated 375°F oven for 50 minutes to 1 hour. Remove when done and allow to cool, then place in the refrigerator until time to serve.

Serve with Crème Anglaise Sauce (page 88) or a raspberry syrup made by cooking puréed fresh raspberries sweetened with confectioners' sugar to taste, or by melting raspberry jam thinned with a little water and Kirsch.

Gâteau d'anniversaire au chocolat à l'orange

Birthday Chocolate Cake with Orange

—

For 8

For génoise cake base:

1½ Tbsp. butter (for buttering cake pan)

12 Tbsp. sweet butter, softened

¾ cup sugar

Grated peel of 1 orange

¾ cup cake flour

1½ tsp. baking powder

4 eggs

Pinch of salt

¼ cup plus 1 tsp. unsweetened cocoa powder

For filling:
½ cup milk
Pinch of vanilla powder or a few drops
    of extract
1 egg yolk
1½ Tbsp. sugar
4 Tbsp. orange liqueur (Cointreau)
10 Tbsp. sweet butter, softened
1 cup heavy cream

8 oz. bitter chocolate
⅓ cup orange juice or water

For garnish:
Candied orange peel

Special equipment needed:
An 8″ by 1½″ round génoise cake pan
Parchment paper

*P*repare the génoise base: Heavily butter the génoise pan, place buttered parchment paper in the bottom, and refrigerate until needed. Preheat oven to 375°F. Cream the butter and ⅔ of the sugar until smooth and pale yellow. Stir the orange peel into the mixture. Sift the flour with the baking powder, and set aside. In another mixing bowl, over hot water, beat the eggs with the rest of the sugar to slightly cook them. Add the flour and baking powder, the salt, and the cocoa powder, and mix. When smooth, turn into the creamed butter-sugar mixture, and beat vigorously to mix. Pour into the cake pan, and bake in the preheated oven for 35–40 minutes. The center should be dry, not moist.

While the cake is baking, prepare the filling. Make a crème anglaise: Boil the milk with a pinch of vanilla powder. While the milk is heating, whisk the egg yolk and sugar in a mixing bowl. Off the heat, pour the hot milk into the egg yolk mixture, and stir until mixed. Return to the heat, and stir until slightly thickened. Remove from the heat, add the orange liqueur and the butter, and stir until all is well incorporated and the mixture is quite smooth.

Beat the heavy cream to the Chantilly ("soft peaks") stage and set aside. Melt the chocolate with the orange juice or water, and stir into the cream filling, then fold lightly into the Chantilly. Place in the refrigerator to firm.

To assemble the cake: With a serrated knife, cut the génoise base into three equal layers and spread each with the butter cream filling. Reassemble the cake, and spread the sides and top with a smooth layer of the butter cream. Decorate with candied orange peel. Place in the refrigerator until time to serve.

Crème brésilienne

Brazilian Mocha Ice Cream

—

For 6

2¼ cups milk
1 Tbsp. instant coffee granules
½ tsp. vanilla powder or extract
2 oz. sugar cubes
3 Tbsp. boiling water
3½ oz. unsweetened chocolate
½ cup sugar
4 egg yolks

Special equipment needed:
A 3-cup ice cream mold with lid

*P*lace the milk, instant coffee, and vanilla in a saucepan, and bring to the simmer.

Moisten sugar cubes with water, and cook slowly in a stainless-steel pan to the caramel stage. Remove from heat, add 3 Tbsp. boiling water to dissolve the caramel, then add small pieces of chocolate and stir over low heat until smooth. Remove from heat and blend in milk mixture.

Beat sugar and egg yolks together in a mixing bowl until pale and thick enough to form a "ribbon." Stir into chocolate mixture and return over heat, stirring constantly, until thickened enough to coat the back of a spoon. Do not overheat, or the eggs will scramble.

Remove from heat, place pan over ice cubes, and whisk constantly until tepid. When cool, fill the ice cream mold and set in freezer for 2 hours to make a soft ice cream, 4 hours for a hard ice cream.

Glace au chocolat

Chocolate Ice Cream

The success of this special chocolate ice cream depends on the freshness of the heavy cream.

—

For 6 to 8

For ice cream:
2 cups heavy cream
1 lb. dark, bittersweet chocolate, grated or finely chopped
4 cups milk
1 vanilla bean
12 egg yolks
¾ cup sugar

For candied orange peel (optional):
2 oranges
¼ cup sugar
5 Tbsp. Campari

Special equipment needed:
2 heavy-bottomed saucepans
An ice-cream freezer or freezerproof mold

Bring the cream to a boil in a heavy-bottomed saucepan, and let simmer a few minutes. Add the grated chocolate to the simmering cream, and stir until the chocolate has melted and the mixture is completely smooth. Set aside and keep warm.

Place the milk, together with a vanilla bean, in another heavy-bottomed saucepan, and bring to the boil. Let simmer for 5 minutes.

Meanwhile, beat the egg yolks and the sugar to the "ribbon" stage. Stir a little of the boiling milk into the egg-sugar mixture to temper it, then pour all into the hot milk, stirring constantly. Cook over very moderate heat, stirring constantly with a wooden spoon to keep the mixture from sticking. When the mixture has thickened sufficiently to coat the back of the spoon, remove it from the heat and, continuing to stir so the eggs do not scramble, place immediately in a cool water bath to stop the cooking.

Pour the chocolate-cream mixture into the custard and beat until cool, then pour into a mold and place in the freezer, or freeze with an ice-cream freezer.

Serve the ice cream by itself in individual glass bowls, or decorated with glazed orange peel made as follows: Wash and dry the oranges. Using a potato peeler, remove the peel from the oranges, taking care not to remove the bitter white pith as well. Cut the peel into very fine strips, and place in a saucepan with cool water. Heat just to the boil and strain immediately, discarding the water. Return the orange peel to the saucepan, cover with the sugar, Campari, and 2 Tbsp. water, and bring to the simmer. Let simmer about 10 minutes, or until the liquid has evaporated and the orange strips are glazed. Let cool.

Sprinkle the strips over the chocolate ice cream to garnish.

Note: The ice cream can also be served garnished with halved cooked pears.

Beignets de pommes

Apples Fried in Batter

—

For 6

For batter:
1 cup flour
½ tsp. plus a pinch of salt
1½ Tbsp. vegetable oil
1 egg yolk
¾ cup milk
2 egg whites

For apples and macerating mixture:
4 crisp apples

3 Tbsp. granulated sugar
3 Tbsp. brandy
½ tsp. cinnamon

For frying:
1½ cups vegetable oil

For garnish:
Confectioners' sugar

Special equipment needed:
A nonstick frying pan

*P*repare the batter 1 hour before you plan to serve the beignets. Beat together the egg yolk and milk. Mix the flour and ½ tsp. salt together in a mixing bowl, then slowly stir in the oil, followed by egg yolk mixture. Continue mixing until you have a very smooth mixture. Let stand in a cool place for a good hour.

Peel and core the apples, then cut in regular slices ⅛″ thick. Let macerate with the sugar, brandy, and cinnamon for about 30 minutes, turning them to be sure they are evenly coated.

Just before serving, lightly beat the egg whites with a pinch of salt until they are the consistency of snow. Beat the batter once more, then fold in the egg whites. Once the egg whites have been incorporated, the batter must be used immediately.

Heat the oil. (Test for proper frying temperature by dropping in a crust of stale bread. When ready, bubbles will rapidly form around the bread. The oil is too hot if the bread browns in just a few seconds.) Dip each apple slice into the well-beaten batter, allow excess batter to drip off, then place 3 or 4 beignets in the pan to fry. Turn once to brown evenly, then remove and let drain on paper towels. Keep warm in a slow oven.

Serve as soon as possible, sprinkled with a little confectioners' sugar.

Note: If using this batter for vegetables or cheeses, ¾ cup beer (or a mixture of half milk and half water) can be substituted for the ¾ cup milk.

The oil used for frying can be reused up to 3 times if well strained each time.

Babas au rhum

Rum Babas

—

For about 12 babas

For baba dough:
1 cake fresh yeast (about ½ oz.), or
  1 Tbsp. active dry yeast
3 Tbsp. tepid water
2 Tbsp. sugar
⅛ tsp. salt
3 large eggs (or 4 medium eggs)
1½–2 cups flour, sifted
4 Tbsp. melted butter

For syrup:
1 cup sugar
2 cups water
⅔ cup dark rum

For glaze:
½ cup apricot preserves, strained
2–3 Tbsp. dark rum
12 candied cherries

Special equipment needed:
12 cylindrical baba molds, 2″ deep by
  2″ diameter

A pastry brush
Paper cupcake liners

*B*lend the yeast and water together with a fork until well dissolved. Add the sugar, the salt, and then the eggs, one after the other.

With your fingers, mix in the flour and the melted butter, kneading the dough by lifting, pulling, and slapping it against the work surface for about 5 minutes. At first the dough will be quite sticky, but it will gradually become elastic and no longer stick to your hands or the work surface. It is ready when you can hold the dough in both hands, slap it vigorously on the work surface, then stretch it to a length of 10″–12″ and give it a full twist without breaking it.

Form the dough into a ball, and place in a large bowl. Cut a 1″-deep cross in the top, and sprinkle with 1 tsp. flour. Cover the bowl with a dampened kitchen towel, and let the dough rise in a warm place (about 100°F) for about 1½–2 hours, or until the dough has doubled in bulk. When the dough is sufficiently risen, gently deflate by gathering it in from the sides of the bowl and toward the center.

Heavily butter the insides of the baba molds. Using both hands, pull off pieces of dough large enough to fill each mold by ⅓. Press the pieces of dough lightly into the bottoms of the cups, but do not bother to even them, as they will smooth out with rising. Place the cups in a warm place, and let the dough rise again, until it is ¼″ above the sides of the cups.

When the dough has risen, immediately place in a preheated 400°F oven for 13–15 minutes, or until nicely browned and risen well above the sides of the cups. Take them out of the oven. Remove from cups and let cool on a rack.

To prepare the syrup for the babas, boil the sugar and water until the sugar has completely dissolved. When cool, stir in the rum.

Arrange the babas in a shallow dish, prick them all over with a fork, then pour the lukewarm syrup over them, letting them stand and absorb the liquid like sponges. Let drain on a rack, then coat the tops with a glaze made of strained apricot preserves and rum. Top each with a candied cherry, and serve in a paper cupcake liner.

BEVERAGES

Champagne Cocktails

The Bellini

*I*n an iced shaker, blend ½ cup fresh peach juice with 1 cup good brut Champagne.

Marie de Ayala Gulbenkian's Mimosa

*I*n an iced shaker, blend ⅓ cup freshly squeezed orange juice with ⅔ cup cold Louis de Ayala Champagne.

Other Favorite Dishes

Crème au chocolat exprès

Easy Chocolate Cream

Made without butter or eggs, this recipe is easily prepared by children.

———

For 5 to 6

7 oz. semisweet or bitter dark
    chocolate
½ cup water
Optional: 1 Tbsp. instant coffee
    granules
6 oz. evaporated milk

Optional:
3 egg whites
½ cup confectioners' sugar

Special equipment needed:
A heavy-bottomed saucepan

*I*n a heavy-bottomed saucepan, melt the chocolate with the water, adding
instant coffee if you wish, and stirring until completely smooth. If using ser
chocolate, you may melt the chocolate over hot water. When melted, remo
heat and pour in the evaporated milk, stirring until homogenous. To give
creamy consistency, pour into a glass bowl and refrigerate for at least 2 h

Variation I: If you have leftover egg whites, you can add a meringue to th
before refrigerating. Beat the egg whites until foamy, then add the confec
sugar, and continue beating until thick and shiny. Lightly fold the mering
the chocolate cream, and refrigerate for 2 hours. Serve as is in the glass b

Variation II: Another possibility is to add a Chantilly to the chocolate cream
of the meringue. Beat ½ cup heavy cream with ¼ tsp. vanilla extract. Whe
beaten, add ⅓ cup confectioners' sugar and continue beating to the Chanti
peaks" stage. Fold the chocolate into the Chantilly, and let set in the refr
Serve as above.

The Champagne Cocktail

*T*o a jar, add ⅓ cup sugar, ½ orange in slices, ¼ lemon in slices, ½ cup cherries (which have been macerated in brandy), and ¼ cup brandy or Cognac. Mix well, and refrigerate for 1 hour. Strain mixture into glasses, add a macerated cherry to each, and pour in chilled brut Champagne, to your taste.

Raspberry Champagne

*P*our 1 Tbsp. raspberry wine from Burgundy (not raspberry liqueur) into a chilled glass. Fill glass with a good brut Champagne.

Other Cocktails

The Sidecar
(my husband's favorite cocktail)

*M*ix together 2 glasses of freshly squeezed orange juice (or half orange and half lemon juice), 2 glasses Cointreau, 2 glasses Cognac (or half gin and half Cognac, if using lemon juice).

The Bronx
(my favorite cocktail in 1930)

*M*ix together 2 cups freshly squeezed orange juice, 1 cup brandy or Cognac, ¼ cup Bénédictine, and ¼ cup French vermouth. Decorate each cocktail with a thin piece of orange peel (zest only).

Sangria
(a summer favorite)

*M*ix together 2 bottles light red wine, ½ cup orange juice, ¼ cup Cognac, ⅔ cup sugar, 1 clove, 2 oranges and one lime, finely sliced. Stir well and let stand several hours or overnight in a cool place. Serve well chilled.

The Tango Cocktail
(1930)

*M*ix together 1⅓ glass dry sherry, ⅓ glass Cointreau, ⅓ glass green Chartreuse, ⅕ glass Grenadine, and a few drops of Angostura bitters.

The Nightcap

*M*ix together 1 cup Cognac, 1 cup Cointreau or Bénédictine, and 1 cup anisette.

Le chocolat mousseux

Frothy Chocolate

A foamy hot-chocolate beverage for children.

This is an old-fashioned beverage that was originally made in a *chocolatière,* which is no longer available. The *chocolatière* was a metal jug fitted with a carved wooden beater that had a narrow, pencil-shaped handle. When the chocolate was prepared, it was poured into the jug, and the beater was moved by rolling the handle between the hands to obtain a foamy mixture. You can get the same results using a food processor fitted with the plastic blade, or a blender.

—

For 4 to 6

3 oz. German sweet dark chocolate
2 cups water
2 cups milk

*B*reak the chocolate into pieces and place in a saucepan with the water. Melt over low heat. When well dissolved, add the milk, stirring constantly. Still stirring, bring to the boil and pour into the food processor. Process for 6–8 seconds, and serve immediately. (If using a blender, do in small batches so it does not spill out the top.)

Serve with small brioche.

Part Three

BASICS

✦

SAUCES & STOCKS

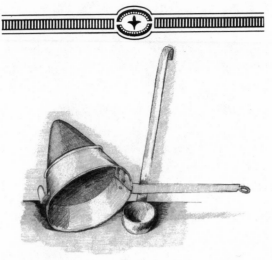

Simca's Beurre Blanc

A butter sauce for fish, eggs, and vegetables.

—

For 2 cups

2½ oz. shallots, finely minced

2 Tbsp. good-quality white-wine vinegar

1 cup dry white wine

2 egg yolks

3 Tbsp. heavy cream

1 to 1¼ cups very cold butter, cut into cubes

Salt and pepper

Special equipment needed:

A heavy-bottomed stainless-steel saucepan

A bain-marie (see Aide-Mémoire, page 503) or a double boiler

*M*ince the shallots fine and place them in a stainless-steel saucepan over *very* moderate heat with the vinegar and white wine. Let simmer until the liquid is reduced to 2 Tbsp. Remove the shallots, if you wish, by pouring the liquid through a fine sieve or damp cheesecloth.

Beat the egg yolks with the cream, and stir into the reduced liquid. Return to the heat, and stir until slightly thickened. As soon as the sauce begins to thicken, remove from the heat and add half the butter, bit by bit, over moderately hot water. Cover and keep warm.

Just before serving, heat the mixture very gently in a bain-marie or in a double boiler, and beat in the remaining butter cubes until a light cream mousse is obtained. Add seasoning to taste.

Serve as soon as possible, with fish mousseline, poached eggs, or tender green asparagus.

Note: This is not the classic method for making beurre blanc. However, made this way, the sauce may be reheated. It is much more difficult to reheat if egg yolks are not used.

Mock Mayonnaise (Simca's Herb Mayonnaise Without Egg)

—

For 1¹/₄ cups

½ Tbsp. strong, creamy Dijon mustard

1 cup vegetable oil

2 Tbsp. evaporated milk, very cold

Ice cube

1 Tbsp. good red-wine vinegar

1 tsp. chopped capers, well drained

12 leaves fresh basil or fresh tarragon, or 1 tsp. dried tarragon

Handful of parsley sprigs, washed, dried, and chopped

¼ tsp. salt

Freshly ground pepper

Optional: Tabasco, to taste

Special equipment needed:

A heavy ceramic mixing bowl, wooden spoon, and wire whisk

Blend the mustard with a little oil in a mixing bowl. Stirring constantly, pour in 3–4 Tbsp. oil in a thin stream. Work constantly while adding the oil, and watch carefully. As soon as the oil is no longer absorbed by the mustard and the mixture looks as if it will begin to "turn," or separate, blend in the cold evaporated milk. The sauce will again become smooth and creamy.

Wedge an ice cube between the wires of a whisk so that it rests securely inside. Whisking constantly, add the remaining oil in a thin stream. The ice will keep the sauce cold and help prevent it from separating. (This is the opposite of the way one makes a classic mayonnaise, for which all ingredients must be tepid.)

Stir in the vinegar, capers, and herbs. Add salt and pepper to taste, and Tabasco if you like. The sauce should be thick and creamy.

Variation: GREEN MAYONNAISE MOUSSELINE
Add ¼ cup whipped cream and more salt, if needed, to make a lighter-textured, more attractive sauce.

Serving Suggestion: Serve this Mock Mayonnaise with a platter of crudités, over cold fish or chicken salad, with an *Assiette anglaise* (cold cuts), with steamed asparagus, or with any cold cooked vegetable. It can also be served over hard-cooked eggs or with a rice salad (page 269).

Beurre d'ail

Garlic Butter

A spread for canapés or a filling for meats, such as lamb.

—

For 1 cup

For canapés:
24 garlic cloves, not peeled
1 cup milk
Salt, pepper, and thyme
1 Tbsp. sugar (approximately)
1 cup crème fraîche (page 501)

Optional: 4 Tbsp. butter, creamed
12 thin slices of rye bread, halved, crust removed

For filling:
1 cup fresh bread crumbs

Special equipment needed:
A food processor

A baking tray lined with oiled aluminum
 foil

*P*arboil the garlic cloves in boiling salted water for 2 minutes. Drain, and pat dry with paper towels. Bring the milk, salt, fresh pepper, and thyme to the boil in the same saucepan. Let boil 5 minutes to reduce, then add the garlic and simmer 6 more minutes. Drain, and reserve the milk if you are making a filling.

Place the garlic cloves on the prepared baking tray, sprinkle with a little sugar, and seal the foil like an envelope. Bake in a preheated 400°F oven for 25–30 minutes. Check occasionally while baking. When done, the garlic should be very soft and slightly browned. Take from oven and let cool. Remove the skins and purée the cloves in a food processor, adding the crème fraîche and seasoning. Add the creamed butter if you have decided to use it.

For canapés, transfer to a bowl and refrigerate until firm enough to spread over triangles of rye bread. If, instead, it will be used as a filling for meats, add 1 cup fresh bread crumbs moistened with the reserved milk to the garlic butter in the food processor. Pulse again until absolutely smooth, then correct the seasoning.

Fond de veau

Veal Stock

—

For about 4 cups

For stock:
⅔ lb. veal knuckle, cut in small
    pieces
2½ lb. veal bones, in small pieces
10 oz. pork rind, with *no* fat

4 onions, not peeled
2 qt. cold water
2 Tbsp. coarse sea salt
Large bouquet garni of celery stalk,
    thyme, bay leaf, and parsley

2 garlic cloves

½ lb. carrots, quartered

For clarifying 4 cups of stock:

2 egg whites, with the broken shells of
the eggs

Bunch of parsley stems, tied together

Salt and pepper

Optional: 3–4 Tbsp. dark port or sherry

Special equipment needed:

A shallow ovenproof tray or roasting
pan

A stockpot, Dutch oven, or similar large
pot

A strainer lined with dampened
cheesecloth

A wire whisk

*P*lace all the meat and bones with the cut-up pork rind in a shallow ovenproof roasting pan, add the whole onions with skins intact, and brown all in a preheated 425°F oven. Turn the pieces frequently so they brown evenly. The pieces should be dark brown, but do not let burn.

Put the browned meat bones and onions in a stockpot or large soup kettle and add 1½ qt. water. Deglaze the roasting pan with the remaining water, scraping up all the sediment with the back of a fork, then pour into the stockpot. Add the salt, bouquet garni, garlic, and carrots. Bring to the simmer, removing any scum as it rises to the surface. When clear, let simmer uncovered for about 3 hours, then correct the seasoning if needed.

Strain to remove the vegetables, bones, and bouquet garni, then place in the refrigerator. When cold, remove the fat. The stock is now ready for use in any kind of brown sauce or tomato sauce.

To clarify: If using the stock for an aspic or in a minestrone, it should first be clarified. To do this, pour all but 1 cup into a large saucepan and slowly bring to the simmer.

Meanwhile, beat the reserved 1 cup stock with the egg whites, shells, and parsley stems. Pour this mixture into the stock *while still tepid,* and beat constantly with a whisk until the mixture reaches the simmer. (A large amount of foam and scum will form.) As soon as the liquid begins to boil, stop beating, and reduce heat. Keep the contents just below simmering for 5 minutes, to cook the scum, which will be removed when all is strained.

Ladle the liquid and the scum through a strainer lined with dampened cheesecloth. Correct the seasoning, adding port or sherry if desired. Let cool, then use as needed.

It keeps in the refrigerator for up to a week, if you boil it up briefly now and then.

Sauce dijonnaise au yogurt

Dijon Mustard Yogurt Sauce with Mustard Seeds

—

For 3 cups

1½ cups heavy cream
2 Tbsp. Dijon mustard
1½ cups plain yogurt
2 garlic cloves, minced fine
Salt, pepper, and Tabasco
2 Tbsp. mustard seeds
Minced chervil, for garnish

Special equipment needed:
A nonstick pan with lid
A food processor

*P*our the cream into the work bowl of a food processor or mixer. Add the mustard and yogurt, and pulse until a Chantilly-like ("soft peaks") mixture is obtained. Add garlic, salt, pepper, and Tabasco, to taste, and pulse briefly to mix.

Using a nonstick pan, lightly sauté the mustard seeds. Keep the cover on the pan, as the seeds jump up when they get hot. Do not brown the seeds, or they will impart a bitter taste to the sauce. Let cool completely.

Transfer the white sauce to a mixing bowl, and stir in the seeds. Do not use a food processor for this step, as the seeds should not be chopped.

Pour into a sauceboat, sprinkle with minced chervil, and serve with cold fish, vegetables, or a salad.

La hollandaise

Hollandaise Sauce

—

For 1 cup (4 servings)

1 lemon plus ½ tsp. white vinegar
4 egg yolks
10 Tbsp. clarified butter, boiling
Salt and pepper

Special equipment needed:
A heavy-bottomed stainless-steel
  saucepan

*P*ut 1 Tbsp. water and 1 Tbsp. lemon juice in a saucepan, beat in the egg yolks, and place over low heat (or a bain-marie), stirring constantly with a wooden spoon until the mixture begins to thicken. Immediately remove from the heat and stir in another Tbsp. lemon juice mixed with 1 Tbsp. water. Stirring vigorously, add the hot butter, pouring in a thin stream. The sauce will thicken. Season to taste with salt and pepper, adding more lemon juice if you prefer more acidity.

To keep the sauce, wrap the container in folded newspaper. Tightly wrapped, the sauce will keep warm for about 30 minutes.

This sauce is excellent with asparagus or any kind of boiled or steamed green vegetable, with steamed fish or fish mousseline, or with egg dishes, such as poached eggs.

Note: You can also use 2–3 Tbsp. orange juice instead of lemon juice (adding just a few drops of vinegar), which gives a delicious, different flavor, especially as an accompaniment to a vegetable, such as broccoli.

The White Sauces: Béchamel and Mornay

BÉCHAMEL

—

For about 1²/₃ cups

1 Tbsp. butter
1½ Tbsp. flour, sifted
1 cup plus 2 Tbsp. cold milk
½ tsp. salt
Freshly ground pepper

Freshly grated nutmeg
Optional: 2–3 Tbsp. heavy cream

Special equipment needed:
A heavy-bottomed saucepan

Melt the butter in a heavy-bottomed saucepan, stir in the flour, and let cook, stirring constantly, until a thick paste, or white roux, is obtained. Do not let the mixture brown. Remove the saucepan from heat and pour in the cold milk all at once, stirring until the roux mixture is dissolved. Return over heat, and stir or whisk vigorously until the sauce is completely smooth. Add the seasoning and let cook, just under the simmer, for a few minutes.

At this point, the sauce may be kept for a while, with a piece of buttered parchment paper pressed onto its surface to prevent a "skin" from forming. To use, reheat while stirring in the cream or additional milk. If using milk, add a tablespoon at a time as required. Correct the seasoning. If the sauce is too thick, thin with a little more milk.

Variation: MORNAY SAUCE Yield: About 2 cups
This sauce may be used with any vegetable you wish to *gratiner,* with gnocchi, over stuffed crêpes, etc.
Use the same ingredients and procedure as for the béchamel, then stir in 4 Tbsp. grated Parmesan cheese, or ½ cup grated Gruyère cheese, a little at a time, and ⅓–½ cup more heavy cream, with additional nutmeg and pepper, to taste.

Variation: AURORE SAUCE (tomato cream sauce)
Stir into the béchamel 2–3 Tbsp. cream and 1–2 Tbsp. tomato paste, according to taste.

Sauce à la crème moutardée

Mustard Cream Sauce

Unlike the béchamel and Mornay sauces, which contain flour, these natural cream sauces are bound by mustard. It is important to use only heavy cream, which is boiled to reduce and thicken.

——

For ³/₄ cup (4–5 servings)

1½ cups heavy cream
½ Tbsp. strong Dijon mustard
Pepper and salt
½ Tbsp. arrowroot dissolved in a little
    cold milk, if needed

Special equipment needed:
A heavy-bottomed saucepan

*P*ut the mustard in a heavy-bottomed saucepan, and stir in 1–2 Tbsp. heavy cream to begin. When dissolved, heat slowly and stir constantly while adding the rest of the heavy cream. Continue to stir, and let simmer slowly until reduced to half the amount, about ¾ cup. If necessary, add pepper and salt, to taste.

If the sauce does not thicken sufficiently, return over heat and reduce further. If it still does not thicken, add ½ Tbsp. arrowroot blended in a little cold milk, and cook a few more minutes.

Variation: SAUCE CRÈME MOUTARDÉE ET TOMATÉE
Prepare the Mustard Cream Sauce exactly as directed above, then stir in 1 Tbsp. tomato paste at the end.

Les différentes vinaigrettes

Classic Vinaigrette Dressings for Salads and Cold-Vegetable Hors d'Oeuvre

—

For 4

2 Tbsp. vegetable oil

1½ Tbsp. olive oil

Salt and pepper

1 Tbsp. minced fresh herbs, such as
   chervil, parsley, chives, or basil

Optional: 1 shallot, minced

1 Tbsp. distilled white vinegar

Special equipment needed:
A small mixing bowl and whisk

*U*sing a whisk, beat the oils together in a small mixing bowl. Add the seasoning, fresh herbs, and optional shallots, and whisk until homogenous, then blend in the vinegar. Although I prefer distilled white vinegar, you can substitute other kinds, such as Xérès (sherry), or red- or white-wine vinegar.

If you wish, make more than you need and refrigerate the extra, stored in a jar, to use when needed. Shake vigorously before using.

Variation I: PROVENÇAL VINAIGRETTE

Parboil 1 garlic clove for 3 minutes; drain, dry, and mash with mortar and pestle. Proceed as above, using only olive oil and minced basil, then blend in mashed garlic.

Variation II: PARISIAN DRESSING

Use the same classic base, stirring 2 Tbsp. Dijon mustard into the oils, before blending in the vinegar. Serve with fresh tomatoes or cooked and chilled green vegetables or potatoes.

NORMAN SALAD DRESSING (for tender lettuces)

Whisk together 2 Tbsp. vegetable oil and 3 Tbsp. cider vinegar or freshly squeezed lemon juice. Mix in 2 Tbsp. heavy cream, 1 Tbsp. minced fresh tarragon, and salt and pepper, to taste.

LORRAINE DRESSING (for tender young dandelion greens)
Although somewhat unusual, this dressing is very popular in the northeastern part of France.

Slowly fry 3 oz. finely diced smoked pork breast in a nonstick pan. When the fat has rendered, deglaze the pan with 3 Tbsp. wine vinegar. Immediately add ½ lb. clean dandelion leaves to the pan, and stir to coat. The greens will be slightly cooked. Correct the seasoning, add 1 Tbsp. minced chives, and serve tepid, with croutons and fresh pepper. (As the smoked pork is salty, no additional salt is needed.)

Beurre de safran

Saffron Butter

For poached or broiled fish.

—

For 4

2 oz. shallots, minced
1½ cups fish *fumet* (page 363)
1½ cups dry white vermouth
½ tsp. powdered saffron
⅔ cup heavy cream
Salt and pepper
Dried herbes de Provence (see Aide-Mémoire, page 503)

⅔ cup butter, very cold, cut into small cubes
Minced basil or parsley, for garnish

Special equipment needed:
A strainer
A whisk
A saucepan

The fish *fumet* should already be well reduced and have good flavor. Cook the minced shallots in the fish *fumet* and vermouth until quite tender, then add the powdered saffron and let reduce slowly until 1 cup remains. Add the heavy cream and seasoning, and let simmer a few minutes to blend the flavors. Strain to remove the shallots, then return over heat and correct the seasoning. Just before serving, whisk in the chilled butter, a little bit at a time. Do not let the mixture come to the boil.

Serve this sauce with any broiled or poached fish or shellfish, and sprinkle with minced basil or parsley to garnish. It will keep a few days in the refrigerator, or frozen for more than 15 days.

Sauce piquante, sans farine

Vinegar Sauce

If you have some leftover roast beef in your refrigerator, an alternative to serving the meat cold with a mayonnaise is to reheat it in this sauce.

—

For about 6–8 slices of beef

¾ cup dry white wine (Burgundy, Alsatian, or Napa Valley Fumé Blanc)
½ cup good white-wine vinegar
2 Tbsp. minced shallots
2½ cups chicken broth
1½ tsp. Dijon mustard
2 hard-boiled egg yolks
1½ Tbsp. minced fresh chives and parsley, mixed

Salt and pepper
Optional: 1½ Tbsp. meat glaze
Sliced gherkins, capers, or pickles, for garnish

Special equipment needed:
A thick-bottomed saucepan
A food mill or food processor

*P*lace the white wine, vinegar, and minced shallots in a saucepan, and let cook until the shallots are tender. Pour in the chicken broth and add mustard, and let simmer slowly until reduced by half, leaving about 2 cups.

Meanwhile, using a food mill or food processor, purée the hard-boiled egg yolks with the minced herbs, making a green mixture. Stir this into the sauce, and bring to the boil. Taste and correct the seasoning. If you have some meat glaze, it can also be added to the sauce, which can be kept in the refrigerator until time to serve.

For serving, reheat, adding more seasoning as needed. Cut the roast beef into even slices and place them, overlapping, in a warmed shallow serving dish. Glaze each slice with the sauce so that the middle stays pink. Never put the meat directly into the boiling sauce, as it will become stiff, brown, and inedible. Garnish the dish with sliced gherkins, capers, or pickles.

Vegetable Suggestion: Chestnut Purée (page 40), or Celery Root with Potatoes Purée (page 41), or Garlic Mashed Potatoes (*Mastering the Art of French Cooking* I, page 520).

Wine Suggestion: Serve either the same wine used in the sauce or a red Beaujolais.

Nage

Court Bouillon

—

To poach 2–3 lobsters or fish

2 lb. broken fish bones
3 qt. cold water
1 qt. dry white wine
1 cup white-wine or Xérès (sherry)
   vinegar
Salt, fresh pepper, to taste
1 onion, sliced
Large bouquet garni of thyme, oregano,
   bay leaf, parsley, and celery stalk

*W*ash and rinse the fish bones, then cut into small pieces and set aside. Place all the other ingredients in a large pot or skillet, slowly bring to the boil, and let simmer 20 minutes. Add the reserved fish bones, and let simmer 20 more minutes. Strain, return to the pot, and reduce by half.

If the court bouillon will not be used the same day, store in the freezer. Use this *nage* as a base for fish soup, or for velouté and butter sauces.

Note: If you lack time to prepare a court bouillon, make a quick fish base with a pound of well-scrubbed mussels or clams. Discard any that do not close when tapped. Simply put the shellfish and some freshly ground pepper in an enameled skillet, cover, and rapidly bring the skillet contents to the boil. Shake the skillet every minute, until all the shellfish are wide open. Discard any that do not open. Remove from heat.

Line a strainer with dampened cheesecloth, and pour the shellfish and their juices into the strainer to remove the sand. Freeze if you will not be using the same day. This shellfish base is especially useful in cream sauces and butter sauces.

Sauce tomate, avec tomate de conserve, en purée

Express Tomato Sauce

—

For about 1½ cups

3 Tbsp. extra-virgin olive oil
1½ Tbsp. minced shallots
1½ celery stalks, minced
1¾ cups chicken broth (or bouillon cubes and water)
½ cup tomato paste
1½ Tbsp. dried herbes de Provence (see Aide-Mémoire, page 503)

1 bay leaf
Salt, pepper, and pinch of sugar

Special equipment needed:
A skillet
A food mill

*H*eat the oil in a skillet. When hot, add the shallots and let stew, stirring, until tender (about 3–4 minutes). Add the minced celery stalks and let cook 2–3 more minutes, stirring constantly. Pour in the chicken broth, and bring to the boil. Add the tomato paste, dried herbs, bay leaf, salt and pepper to taste, and a pinch of sugar, and let simmer 15 minutes. Taste and correct the seasoning, then let simmer a few more minutes if needed. Strain the sauce to remove the shallots, celery, and herbs, then return over heat to reduce, if necessary.

Sauce provençale à la tomate crue

Cold Provençal Tomato Sauce

—

For 4

10–11 oz. fresh tomatoes, absolutely ripe

2 Tbsp. minced parsley
2 garlic cloves, minced
½ cup crème fraîche (page 501)

1 tsp. Dijon mustard
1 Tbsp. wine or Xérès (sherry) vinegar
1 tsp. Worcestershire sauce
Dash of Tabasco
Salt and pepper

*P*repare the tomatoes by peeling them and removing their seeds and excess juices. Dice the pulp and set aside, sprinkled with a little salt to extract excess tomato juice. Let drain on paper towels.

Make a *persillade* of finely minced parsley and garlic. Mix together in a bowl, and set aside.

Place the crème fraîche in a bowl set over ice, and beat until the Chantilly ("soft peaks") stage is reached. Add the mustard, vinegar, Worcestershire and Tabasco sauces, and the *persillade*. Season with salt and pepper, and mix well.

If not used immediately, place in the refrigerator. If serving immediately, mix in the diced tomato, well drained.

Serve with cold fish or vegetables.

PASTRY

Pâte brisée (avec un oeuf)

Short Pastry with an Egg

If using a food processor, follow method given for pâte brisée in Warm Apple Tart recipe on p. 446.

—

For 2 lb. pastry dough

3½ cups all-purpose flour
Salt
1¼ cups butter, diced, or 1 cup butter,
    chilled, plus 4 Tbsp. margarine or
    shortening
1 egg
2–3 Tbsp. cold water

Special equipment needed:
A food processor or large fork
Parchment paper
A rolling pin

*S*ift the flour into a large mixing bowl; add the salt and the butter. Using a large fork or a food processor, work the ingredients until a mixture resembling crumbled meal results.

Beat the egg with 2 Tbsp. cold water, add to the flour mixture, and mix until a single mass is formed. If too dry, add more water as needed. Wrap in parchment paper, or plastic wrap and place in the refrigerator until firm.

Roll out the dough with a rolling pin, and line the chosen pan or pans. Place in the refrigerator to chill until needed.

Paul Grimes's Puff Pastry

—

For 2 lb. puff pastry

2 cups sweet butter, cold

2½ cups pastry flour (or use 1 part cake flour and 2 parts all-purpose flour)

NOTE: Weigh and be sure you have the same weight of flour and butter.

1 tsp. salt

1 cup cold water

1 egg, for glaze

Special equipment needed:
A small saucepan
A rolling pin
A pastry scraper
A cold pastry marble or board

*M*elt 3 Tbsp. of the butter in a small saucepan, and let cool. If you do not have pastry flour, make your own by mixing together cake and all-purpose flours. Reserve ¼ cup of the pastry flour and put the rest in a pile on a large work surface.

Make a well in the center with a pastry scraper, and add the salt and melted butter to the center of the well.

Pour in the cold water, and stir with your fingertips until the salt is dissolved. Continue stirring with your fingers, gradually incorporating flour until the mixture in the well has thickened substantially. When this mixture is so thick it will not run off the work surface, use both hands and fingers to toss the remaining flour into the thickened liquid. Work quickly and thoroughly, as if you were tossing a salad. As soon as you can pull the dough together to form a ball, do so. This is your *détrempe*. Do not knead the *détrempe*, or you will activate the gluten and make the dough elastic. Score the top of the *détrempe* several times with a pastry scraper to help release some of the elasticity, then wrap tightly in plastic and set in the refrigerator for 30 minutes.

While the *détrempe* chills, prepare the *beurrage*. Place the remaining chilled butter on your work surface. Using your fist or a rolling pin, beat the butter to soften it without warming it. Turn the butter over with your pastry scraper after beating each side. When the butter is soft yet still cool to the touch, begin sprinkling the reserved pastry flour over it; the flour will absorb any water that comes to the surface. When all of the flour has been incorporated, you will find that the texture of the *beurrage* resembles that of the *détrempe*. This will make it easier to combine the two mixtures.

Remove the *détrempe* from the refrigerator and place on a lightly floured work surface. Use your rolling pin to form a ½"-thick "tab" at each side of the dough, leaving a 2" mound of dough in the center. Place the *beurrage* in the center of the *détrempe* on the mound, and fold the tabs over to completely enclose it. Seal the edges carefully.

Roll the pastry forward and backward, never sideways, until the pastry is about 10"–12" long. Be careful not to break open the package and let the butter out. Fold the bottom third of the pastry up and the top third down, so that you have three layers of pastry, with an open edge toward you and the fold away from you. Give the pastry a quarter turn to the left so that the folded edge is toward the left and the pastry resembles a book. You have now completed one "turn." Let the dough rest 30 minutes in the refrigerator to "relax" it.

Roll the pastry lengthwise again until its length is approximately 2½ times its width. Fold the pastry into thirds as before, and you will have completed two "turns." Wrap in plastic and let rest in the refrigerator for 30 minutes.

Repeat the rolling and folding process two more times, so that you have four "turns," and chill again for 30 minutes. Give the pastry two final turns, for a total of six turns. Chill thoroughly before rolling and forming. The pastry will work best if you refrigerate it overnight before using.

Working quickly so the dough remains cool, roll dough out to desired (⅛"–¼") thickness. Use a sharp knife or pastry cutter to cut pastry into desired shapes. If at any time the pastry becomes warm or the butter begins to seep out, set in the refrigerator to chill. Once pastry has been formed, refrigerate again before baking, so the dough can relax.

Just before baking, glaze the top with an egg beaten with a teaspoon of water, being careful not to get any of the glaze on the sides of the pastry, or it will not rise evenly. If you wish, use a fork or knife to decorate the top with crosshatching. Bake in a preheated 425°F oven until the pastry is well risen and brown, and the sides are brown and crisp. For large pieces of pastry, reduce oven temperature to 350°F once the pastry has risen and browned, so that the insides are done.

Brioche

—

For 1 loaf

½ oz. fresh yeast, or 1 package active
    dry yeast
2 Tbsp. tepid milk
1 tsp. sugar
1 pinch salt
2 cups (approximately) sifted
    flour
2 eggs

7 Tbsp. butter, chilled
1 egg yolk beaten with 1 tsp. water

Special equipment needed:
A large mixing bowl
A small mixing bowl
A cold pastry marble or board
An 8½" by 3½" loaf pan

*P*ut the yeast, milk, sugar, and salt in a small bowl. Mash and stir with a fork until the mixture forms a wet paste. Put the flour and eggs in a large mixing bowl and work to blend, then pour in the yeast mixture. With the fingers of one hand held together, knead the dough by lifting it, pulling it, and slapping it vigorously on the lightly floured chilled marble or board for about 3 minutes. Set aside while working with the butter.

Place the butter between parchment paper, then beat and work it with a rolling pin until it is the same consistency as the dough. This process is important.

Make an indentation in the dough, add a lump of butter, then knead with your fingers until the butter is thoroughly incorporated. Add another lump, and work it into the dough in the same manner. Continue this procedure until all the butter is absorbed into the dough.

When the butter has been incorporated, knead the dough again, lifting, slapping, and pulling it, for about 5 minutes, then clean your fingers and the sides of the bowl by gathering the dough together with a rubber spatula. Sprinkle the top with a thin layer of flour, cover with a warm wet towel, and set aside to rise at room temperature (68°–77°F) for about 1½ hours. The dough should double in bulk and fill the bowl.

When the dough has doubled, gently deflate by gathering it in from the sides of the bowl and pressing it down in the center with the cupped floured fingers of one hand. Fill the loaf pan, buttered and floured, half full and place in a warm water bath (80°–100°F) for about 30 minutes, or until it has doubled in volume.

When ready to bake, brush the top with beaten egg yolk and place in a preheated 375°–400°F oven for about 25–30 minutes, or until the brioche is nicely puffed and browned.

La brioche d'office

Classic Brioche Dough

For coulibiac, meat, or fish pâté.

—

*For 3½ lb. dough (enough to wrap
2½ lb. fish fillets and filling for
10–12 servings)*

⅔ oz. fresh yeast
3 Tbsp. tepid milk
4½ cups pastry flour
4 eggs
½ tsp. salt
15 Tbsp. butter, melted

Special equipment needed:
A large mixing bowl
A small mixing bowl
A food processor (optional)

*P*lace the yeast in a small bowl, add the tepid milk, and mix with a fork until the yeast completely dissolves. Put the flour, eggs, salt, yeast mixture, and melted butter in a food processor (or in a large mixing bowl), and mix until the ingredients are thoroughly combined and form a single mass. Immediately remove to a lightly floured surface. Knead and throw the dough sharply against this surface for several minutes, until it becomes quite elastic and no longer sticks to your hands or to the work surface.

Turn the dough into a floured bowl, cut a cross on the top with scissors, then sprinkle lightly with flour. Cover with a kitchen towel and place in a warm (90°F) place to rise until doubled in bulk. If you prefer, place the covered bowl in a water bath of the same temperature, but change the water frequently to maintain an even temperature.

When the dough has doubled in size, gently deflate by using floured hands to detach it from the sides of the bowl and gather it together in the center. The dough can now be formed, then allowed to rise again before baking.

If you will not be using the dough immediately, place in the refrigerator or freezer until needed, but I don't recommend the freezer highly, beyond an hour.

Gougère

Choux Paste Method for Gougère

For sweet choux paste and gnocchi,
see variations given below.

—

For about 2½ cups

1 cup water

6 Tbsp. butter

1 tsp. salt

1 cup sifted flour

4 eggs plus 1 egg white

½ cup finely diced Gruyère cheese

¼ cup grated Parmesan cheese

Pepper

Nutmeg

For glaze:

1 egg yolk beaten with 1 Tbsp.
water

Special equipment needed:

A heavy-bottomed saucepan

A heavy metal baking sheet

A pastry brush

*B*ring the water to a boil with the butter and salt. When the butter has melted, remove from heat and add all the flour at once, stirring vigorously until a smooth mass is obtained. Return over direct heat and stir with a spatula, turning the mixture over and beating it against the sides of the pan until a glaze covers the bottom of the saucepan.

Remove from heat and make a well in the paste. Drop 1 egg into the well, and fold it into the mixture, working with the spatula until it is completely absorbed. Fold in the other eggs and extra egg white in the same manner, one by one, being sure that each is thoroughly incorporated before adding the next one.

Stir in the diced Gruyère and grated Parmesan cheeses. Correct the seasoning, adding pepper and nutmeg to taste. If not baked immediately, place a piece of buttered parchment paper directly on the surface of the choux paste to keep it from drying out.

Using 2 large spoons, spoon the paste into a tight ring of large egglike shapes. (Each "egg" should be about 2½″ by 1½″.) Brush the tops with the egg yolk–water glaze, and place in a preheated 400°F oven. After 10 minutes, reduce the heat to 375°F and bake for 15–20 minutes more, or until the crust is quite hard. Serve the *gougère* sliced, preferably slightly warm.

Variation I: SWEET CHOUX PASTE

For sweet choux paste, used to make profiteroles and cream puffs, use the same ingredients and method, omitting the cheese and adding 1 Tbsp. granulated sugar. Shape with spoons or a pastry bag, placing the choux paste on a clean heavy metal baking sheet. Brush with egg yolk glaze, and bake as directed above.

If you wish, cut openings in the sides and fill with sweet frangipane, flavored with coffee or chocolate. Glaze the tops with a fondant of the same flavor.

Variation II: GNOCCHI

The same ingredients and method are used to make gnocchi, except that the cheese is left out. Using a pastry bag and knife to form them, drop the gnocchi into boiling salted water. Let boil for 5 minutes, then drain to dry. Arrange the gnocchi in a baking dish, coated with Mornay Sauce (page 480), sprinkled with grated cheese, and gratinéed.

Pain de mie melba

Bread with Milk

Special bread for melba toast and croutons.

—

For one 1½-lb. loaf

⅔ oz. fresh yeast
1½–1⅔ cups tepid milk
4½ cups pastry flour
1 Tbsp. salt
5 Tbsp. butter, softened (or you may substitute margarine)

Optional: 1 egg beaten with a drop of water, to glaze top

Special equipment needed:
A 2-qt. nonstick loaf pan or oiled cake pan
A pastry brush, to glaze top

*U*sing a small mixing bowl, dilute the yeast in 3 Tbsp. warm (90°F) milk, stirring until completely dissolved. With a food processor or by hand, mix the flour with the yeast, then add the salt and the remaining tepid milk by tablespoons. Do not add all the milk unless it is needed. The dough should be smooth, not runny.

Place the dough on a board or pastry marble and work with your hands, slapping it against the work surface until it becomes elastic. Add the butter by small pieces, kneading until each piece is completely incorporated before adding more butter.

Place the dough in a bowl and allow to rise well in a warm place, taking anywhere from 30 minutes to over an hour. (You can speed this up by placing it in a bain-marie [see Aide-Mémoire, page 503] or pan of warm water). Punch and deflate the dough. Place it in the prepared loaf or cake pan. Make cuts on the top to aid second rising. Sprinkle a very light layer of flour on the top of the dough and allow it to rise until the pan is completely filled. Brush the top with the egg glaze, if you wish. This second rising can take up to 2 more hours.

Bake in a preheated 400°F oven for about 35 minutes. The top and sides should be nicely browned. Let cool on a rack until tepid before using.

Note: To make a lighter bread, let it rise twice, with the first rising in the mixing bowl. Punch down to deflate and slip the dough into the pan, allowing it to rise once more before baking. This process will take 2 more hours.

If you use margarine, the bread will stay fresh longer.

Variation: PAIN DE MIE AUX OLIVES VERTES
Replace the butter with ⅔ cup extra-virgin olive oil. Combine ingredients and knead dough as directed above. When dough is almost ready for rising, add 7 oz. pitted and roughly chopped green olives. (Do not chop olives in a food processor.) Work dough until the olives are well distributed throughout the dough. Let dough rise, and bake as above.

Pâte à crêpes

Crêpe Batter

—

For 20 to 24 crêpes

2 cups cold water
2 cups sifted flour
¼ tsp. salt
4–5 eggs, depending on size
5 Tbsp. butter, melted

Special equipment needed:
A wooden spoon
A wire whisk

Use a wooden spoon and a wire whisk to slowly mix the cold water into the flour and salt, making a paste. Add the eggs, one by one, using the wire whisk to blend until completely smooth. Stir in the melted butter. The batter can be used immediately, or allowed to rest a few hours before using.

To cook, pour the batter into a lightly oiled hot skillet. Quickly tilt the pan in all directions, to cover the bottom of the pan evenly with a thin film of batter. When the bottom of the crêpe has browned, turn the crêpe and cook the other side in the same way.

Fill the crêpes with Salmon Butter (page 230), or with dollops of crème fraîche (page 501) and salmon caviar.

La pâte à frire légère

Light Batter for Deep-Frying

For vegetables, fruits, and cheese canapés

—

For 4 to 6 as an entrée, or for about 24 bite-size canapés

1 cup flour

½ tsp. (large pinch) salt

¾ cup milk or beer—or half beer, half milk

1 egg yolk, beaten

2 beaten egg whites

1½ Tbsp. vegetable oil, plus about 2 cups more for deep-frying

Special equipment needed:

A mixing bowl

A nonstick frying pan

Mix flour and salt in the bowl, then add 1½ Tbsp. vegetable oil; gradually add the liquid and egg yolk, whisking to obtain a very smooth consistency. Cover and set aside for at least 30 minutes.

Just before using the batter, whisk the egg whites until they look like snow. Start heating the frying oil (about 2″–3″ in the pan). Beat the batter again, and fold into whipped egg whites. Before dipping whatever food you will fry into the batter, test the oil for heat by dropping a piece of stale bread crust into the oil. It should bubble nicely but not brown immediately—which would mean the oil is too hot.

Fry your bouchées, coated vegetables, or whatever. As soon as the fried food is golden brown, remove with a skimmer and drain on a paper towel.

Deep-fried food is best eaten immediately, while very crisp. But it may be kept for an hour or two at room temperature and reheated in a moderate oven.

Note: This basic batter (before addition of whipped egg whites) can be stored in the refrigerator for a day or so, well covered with a plastic film. Always add the whipped egg whites at the last minute, for lightness.

WAYS OF COOKING VEGETABLES

Method for Green Vegetables

This method is for green beans, green peas, lettuce, Swiss chard, and spinach, which are all cooked the same way, but for different lengths of time.

Bring a large kettle of water to a rolling boil; gradually add the green beans, keeping the water boiling. When once again at a full rolling boil, add salt and let boil, uncovered, 3–10 minutes, depending on the size of the beans. Check every minute to be sure they do not overcook. When done, immediately pour into a colander and refresh with cold tap water to stabilize their color.

For green peas the timing is similar, but here also it depends on the size of the peas. Swiss chard is cooked in the same manner, but requires 10–12 minutes of cooking before refreshing with cold water. Spinach takes only 5 minutes of cooking, while lettuce (only the green part) requires 6–10 minutes.

Once refreshed, these vegetables can be held until just before serving and then reheated by sautéing in butter. Season with salt and pepper, to taste, and sprinkle with minced parsley.

Methods for Other Types of Vegetables

*F*or vegetables requiring longer cooking, such as dried beans and peas, add 1 tsp. sodium bicarbonate (baking soda) per 3–5 qt. water. It will help the cooking by neutralizing the calcium in the water.

Some vegetables, such as cauliflower, broccoli, and cabbage, take on unpleasant flavors during cooking. A large piece of stale bread added to the pot as the water begins to boil will absorb unpleasant flavors, and reduce unpleasant odors as well.

Vegetables like salsify and artichoke turn black when peeled. To help keep them white, submerge each vegetable immediately after it has been peeled in water that has been acidulated with ½ cup wine vinegar. Cooking these vegetables in the same treated water will also help keep them white. (Similarly, sprinkling lemon juice on fruits, such as apples, is effective in keeping them from darkening.)

Root vegetables, such as carrots and turnips, are best when simply steamed in a covered skillet with a little water. Boiling potatoes that will be sautéed, on the other hand, should be cooked, skins on, in salted water 18–20 minutes, depending on their size. If using the potatoes in a purée, peel them first and then cook in the same manner.

APROPOS OF CREAM AND CRÈME FRAÎCHE

I'M A CREAM FAN. Cream is less fattening than butter—with only half as many calories—and more flavorful than milk. Cream contains a minimum of 60 percent water, whereas butter is denser, nearly totally butterfat, with only 16 percent water. Cream doesn't contain calcium or proteins, as milk does, but it adds a special taste and consistency that milk lacks.

Crème fraîche is cream that has been modified by the addition of specific lactic acids. It has matured until the lactic acids and natural ferments have worked to the point where the cream has thickened and become slightly acidic, giving it a tangy flavor. This process also acts as a natural preservative, preventing the formation of unwanted bacteria in the cream, one principal reason we make crème fraîche in France. Commercially made sour cream is not a substitute; it cannot be boiled without curdling. However, gourmet grocery stores in the United States now offer versions of crème fraîche.

Cream is more fragile than butter, as it contains more water and less butterfat. "Thick" cream in France must contain at least 40 percent butterfat, but without the addition of thickeners, it does not have a viscous consistency. It is preferable not to boil crème fraîche.

In France, we call liquid heavy cream *crème fleurette*. This is what should be used for reductions and for whipping—over ice—in making a Chantilly, meaning whipped to the "soft peaks" stage. The method is to chill your bowl first, then whip over another bowl containing ice, the quickest (indeed, sometimes the only) way to obtain puffy Chantilly. Use a large bowl for whipping, to incorporate air.

To conclude: Thick and slightly acid crème fraîche has a special aroma that adds to the flavor of certain nonsweet dishes, and it should not be cooked much. Liquid heavy cream is used in reductions for thickening sauces, especially with fish; when boiled, it won't curdle. Heavy cream is always used to make whipped cream (adding a little vanilla and sugar for a Chantilly), which can be made ahead and kept chilled for a day.

Crème Fraîche

—

For 1 cup

1½ tsp. buttermilk, or ⅓ cup commercial
    sour cream, or yogurt
1 cup heavy cream

Special equipment needed:
A 2-cup crockery jar

Shake the heavy cream with the buttermilk, sour cream, or yogurt in a crockery jar and keep in a warm place, 60°–85°F, until it has thickened, about 6–8 hours on a hot day, 24–36 hours in cooler weather. When the cream has thickened, shake the jar and store it in the refrigerator.

Use it to enrich velouté (cream) soups or to enhance the flavor of any vegetable soup. Use it also to add flavor to white sauces such as béchamel or Mornay, or for a creamy fish sauce. Crème fraîche doesn't reduce very well; for reductions, use heavy cream instead. A reduction of heavy cream with tarragon gives you a true Norman flavor.

AIDE-MÉMOIRE: FREQUENTLY USED TERMS

I LIKE TO USE my own French terms, since they so well describe the procedures for French cuisine, and most French cooks already understand them. But they may slightly confuse some reader-cooks. So here is a short glossary, an aide-mémoire, in case of necessity.

I have not repeated or gone over the basic ground thoroughly covered in *Mastering the Art of French Cooking*, Parts I and II, and also my own books, *Simca's Cuisine* and *More Recipes from Simca's Cuisine*, which also give detailed descriptions of terms, methods, and ingredients. But I can highly recommend my own books, since I still use them for reference.

Aiguillettes: Thin strips of game bird or poultry breasts.

Bain-marie: Called a "water-bath" by the English. This is basically a method of cooking gently by placing in a pan of hot water. I often use it for cooking soufflés, certain pâtés, custard-based flans, etc., in the oven. The hot water should come half to two-thirds of the way up the sides of whatever mold or dish you are using. As we don't have double boilers in France, or rather, as they're not a usual feature of cooks' equipment, the method of bain-marie is also frequently used for gentler cooking, from soft-scrambled eggs to melting chocolate, and so on—as you'd use a double boiler in the United States.

Ballottine: Classically, a kind of pâté cooked encased in the skin of poultry or a game bird. A cheesecloth may be substituted for the skin.

Bouchées: Bite-sized balls or tidbits.

Bouquet garni: Usually made by tying together one or two small celery stalks with a bunch of parsley sprigs, a few thyme stalks, and a bay leaf. You can also buy ready-made "bouquets garni," or sachets of dried herbs, but I never use them.

Casserole: This is what we call a "false friend" in France. In French, it simply means saucepan. The French equivalent of a casserole dish is *cocotte* (see below). A casserole to eat, like a stew, would be a daube or a ragout, perhaps a gratin.

Chantilly: Whipped cream; heavy cream whipped over ice in a bowl to the "soft peaks" stage, usually flavored with sugar and vanilla.

Charlotte mold: A straight-sided, round, splayed-opening stainless steel container that may be used for chilling and unmolding certain iced or frozen desserts described in this book. I use a French metal mixing bowl of the same "Charlotte" shape; in fact, I find it essential for these chilled desserts, which would be impossible to unmold otherwise.

Choux paste: A dough made with water, butter, flour and eggs and used either mixed with another ingredient (as with fish in *quenelles de poisson*), or as a pastry on its own—for cream puffs or cheese-flavored gougères.

Cocotte: Oven-proof casserole dish with a lid.

Court-bouillon (or "nage"): The "starter" used for cooking fish: seasoned broth of herbs, carrot, onion, with water and/or wine, to which is added fish parts (bones, head, etc.). When reduced and strained, this becomes a *fumet*.

Crème Anglaise: This is a classic custard cited many times in my dessert recipes. You may find varying proportions in ingredients, but basically the procedures for preparation are the same. Here is a typical recipe for crème anglaise:

> 1 cup milk
> ½ tsp. vanilla
> ½ cup granulated sugar
> 4 egg yolks

Heat the milk with the vanilla in a heavy-bottomed saucepan. Beat the egg yolks with sugar until thick, so that a "ribbon" forms when it is poured from a spoon. Beating constantly, gradually pour the hot milk into the egg yolks, then pour all back into the saucepan. Return to the heat and stir constantly until the custard slightly coats the spoon. Do not let the mixture simmer, or it will curdle. Cool before serving.

(*Note:* To keep the mixture from curdling, cook it in a double boiler or over another pan of hot water, following the method known as a "bain-marie.")

Fumet: Reduced and strained fish broth.

Génoise: Classic yellow cake.

Herbes de Provence: This term I use frequently describes a mixture of herbs found so abundantly in Provence. When composing dried herbs, I use my own favorite and highly recommended combination, the acronymic MOTTS. This stands for marjoram, oregano, 2 parts thyme, and savory.

Lardons: Diced or small chunks of bacon, also called lardoons in English.

Marmite: Very large casserole pot (pot roast or pot-au-feu size) with a lid.

Mirepoix: Very finely diced aromatic vegetables.

Quatre épices: This is a commercially available mixture of dried Jamaica pepper, cinnamon, ginger, and bay leaf. You can make it yourself by combining 7 parts pepper with 1 part each of ground cloves, ginger, and nutmeg.

Roux: Basic preparation for many sauces, based on a blending and slow cooking of flour and butter. The few minutes of cooking on low heat gets the floury taste out, before you add milk (for a béchamel), broth, or whatever liquid completes the sauce.

Egg-white tips for soufflés:
The whites whip up best when they're at room temperature. I believe the most efficient way to get those firm white peaks is to beat them with a pinch of salt in a copper bowl (first cleaned by swishing around a bit of vinegar and salt, rubbing and drying). Beat by using a big balloon whisk, and plenty of elbow grease, of course.

Sugar tips:
Sugar syrups are best made in a heavy metal pan (I prefer lined copper).

"Soft ball" stage: reached in making a sugar syrup, when big bubbles form, and a drop of it added to cold water forms a soft ball.

"Thread stage": Later stage than the "soft-ball" as sugar tends to "thread" when spooned up from the saucepan.

"Crack stage": Sugar will turn hard and crunchy when cooled.

An "Italian meringue" is made by incorporating sugar syrup into already whipped egg whites, beating until they become glossy and stand in firm peaks.

INDEX

Page numbers in *italic face* refer to recipes.

bacon *(cont.)*
    kugelhopf with macadamia nuts and, *267–68*
    Paul Troisgros's quiche Lorraine, *221–222*
    poached eggs with red wine and, *71–72*
Baker, Josephine, 76
banana(s):
    and apricot sauce, semolina pudding in a ring mold with pears, *437–38*
    fruit purée in a custard, in ramekins, *443–44*
    sherbet, *294*
Barcelona, 181–82
bass, *see* sea bass
bavarois royale de Mme Lantoine, 178–79
beans, green, Belgian salad with lardoons and, *320*
Beard, James, 197–98, 199, 201, 243–44, 261, 272
James Beard Foundation, 198, 244
béchamel sauce, *480*
Beck, Bernard (brother), 26, 33, 35, 68, 90, 93
    birth of, 28–29
    marriage of, 148, 295
    Simca's reunion with, 295–96
    in World War II, 126, 135, 142–43
Beck, Christian (nephew), 252
Beck, Françoise (sister-in-law), 123, 129, 130
Beck, Jacques (nephew), 130
Beck, Jean-Claude (nephew), 252
Beck, Madeleine Marie Gabrielle Le Grand (mother), 4, 5–11, 18, 26, 28–31, 51, 81, 90, 148, 189
    in Cannes, 7, 58, 67, 80
    dancing lessons and, 45–46
    death of, 243
    diary of, 129, 130, 131, 133–36, 141, 142
    recipes of, 35
    servants and, 7, 11, 129, 133
    Simca's marriages and, 67, 97
    stubbornness and pluck of, 129–33
    in World War II, 123, 126, 129–36
Beck, Marie-José de Francolini (sister-in-law), 148, 295

Beck, Maurice Eric (brother), 4, 5, 8, 26, 28–30, 33–35
    death of, 251–52
    in family business, 30, 91, 148
    Simca and, 18, 25, 27, 33, 295
    in World War II, 122–23, 129, 130, 134, 135
Beck, Maurice Henri (nephew), 135–36, 252
Beck, Maurice-Jules Joseph (father), 4, 5, 7–11, 16, 32–36, 58, 61, 76, 80–81, 92
    appearance of, 10, 28, 33
    dancing of, 45–46
    death of, 33, 80–81, 90
    Jarlauld and, 65, 66–67, 81
    in Saulieu, 51–52
    Simca's driving and, 43, 45
    thirty-sixth birthday of, 18
    in World War I, 28, 31, 32
Beck, Michel (nephew), 247, 252
Beck, Monique (niece), 132
Beck, Simone Suzanne Renée Madeleine (Simca; Nonne; Monette):
    accidents of, 77–78, 245, 246, 262, 278
    allergies of, 33–34
    appearance of, xiv, 31, 65, 66, 67
    astrologer consulted by, 128
    bilingualism of, 4, 10, 46
    birth of, 8
    bookbinding of, 78, 80
    childhood of, xiv, 7–11, 18, 25–28, 214
    cooking lessons of, 3–5, 25, 81–83
    as cooking teacher, xv, 113, 171, 226–228, 243–45, 248–52, 297, 302
    dancing of, 45–46, 94
    driving of, 10, 11, 26, 43, 45, 68, 75, 80, 91, 95, 122–24, 265
    education of, 4, 9, 10, 28–31
    eightieth birthday of, 272–73
    family background of, 5–7, 10, 151
    in family business, 91–92
    first cookbook writing efforts of, 159–61
    forty-ninth anniversary of, 296
    health problems of, 31, 32–33, 128, 132, 217–18
    marriages of, *see* Fischbacher, Jean Victor; Jarlauld, Jacques

canapés:
light batter for deep-frying, *498*
olive spread for, *184*
smoked salmon butter, *230*
canard(s):
en ballottine aux foies de volaille, 156–57
à la Duchambais, 176–77
aux navets et aux olives, 87–88
pâté de foies de volaille, 55
aux pruneaux, civet de, 382–84
au sang, 188–89
Canfield Fisher, Dorothy, 160–61
Cannes, 7, 51, 57–58, 67, 80–81, 122
canoeing, 26, 33–34
caramel, caramelized:
apple charlotte, *224–25*
meringue with Chantilly, *431–32*
mousse, frozen, *241–42*
carottes et navets à la Vichy, 423–24
carrots, 261
and turnips à la Vichy, *423–24*
Cassiot, Aimée, 152, 160
cassoulet, 195
cattle, 9, 16, 69
caul, 242–43
céleri-rave, en purée, avec pommes de terre,
41–42
celery root purée with potatoes, *41–42*
in ramekins, *42*
Cercle des Gourmettes, Le, xiv, 151–59,
163, 171
cerfeuil, la crème de, aux petits pois (chaude ou
froide), 314
Chaliapin, Alexander, 204
Challiol, Marcelle, 205, 214, 215
Champagne:
cocktails, *466–67*
sabayon, *307*
champignons, see mushroom(s)
Chancellor, John, 202
charlottes:
Brazilian mocha, *158–59*
caramelized apple, *244–45*
flourless apple cake with candied fruit
and sultana raisins, *457–58*
Mme Lantoine's royal bavarian, *178–79*

orange-flavored rice, with chocolate
sauce, *438–40*
orange-flavored rice pudding, meringue
topping, *428–29*
raspberry, *188*
strawberry, *187–88*
Charrier (mess cook), 122
Château d'Yquem, 276–77
Château Margaux, 276, 278
cheese, 16, 225, 260–61
blue, grated potatoes with, *419–20*
blue or goat, soufflé, *343–44*
Camembert, Norman soufflé with,
48–49
golden crusts with, *327*
green gnocchi Italian style, *349–50*
Italian, quiche with red bell pepper,
344–45
"little devil" bouchées with, *166*
Provençal pizza, *347–48*
roll, garnished with poultry liver spread
and mushroom purée, *351–53*
sweet red-pepper terrine Ursus, *336–*
337
tarts, individual, Jura style, *108*
three, tart, *326*
three stuffed omelets, sandwiched and
gratinéed, *342–43*
unmolded green-and-white soufflé, with
a tomato sauce, *340–41*
Venetian pizza, *255*
see also Gruyère cheese; Parmesan
cheese
cheesecloth, 242–43
chefs and cooks, 111, 113, 188
in Bourbonne-les-Bains, 218–19
female, 111, 113, 152, 173, 198–202,
205, 245
Indian, 263
military, 80, 122
in Saulieu, 51–52, 79–80
Spanish, 182
as teachers, 82–83, 171, 198, 226–27
see also specific chefs and cooks
chervil cream soup with small spring peas
(hot or cold), *314*

Christmas (*cont.*)
  log roll, *451–52*
  Provençal green tart for, *447–48*
  Provençal three kings cake, *450–51*
Churchill, Sir Winston, 261
Cipriani (Venice), 253, 254
Cipriani-style terrine of chicken baked in
    the skin, *256–58*
clafoutis aux prunes, 147–48
Claiborne, Craig, 197
clam(s):
  gratinéed, *367–68*
  sabayon sauce, *210–11*
Clay (Beard's assistant), 243
Clémenceau, Georges, 80
Club des Cent, 151–52
clubs, gastronomic, xiv, 151–59, 163,
    170
cocktails, *466–68*
coffee:
  chocolate loaf, with Armagnac or bour-
    bon, *453–54*
  Christmas log roll, *451–52*
  ice cream in ramekins, *64–65*
  Mona's divine flourless chocolate cake,
    24–25
  raspberry snow mousse, *258–59*
  see also mocha
confit d'oie, 195
consommé, a light vegetable-based, *311–12*
consommé à la royale, 311–12
convent schools, 29–31
cookbooks, 294
  see also specific cookbooks
Cooking in the Provinces of France (Field and
    Fisher), 227
cooking schools:
  American, 198, 243–44
  French, xiii–xv, 81–82, 171, 226–28,
    243–45, 248–52, 272–73
cooks, *see* chefs and cooks
coq au vin, 138–39
coquillages, gratin de, 367–68
Cordon Bleu, Le, xii–xiv, 81–82, 171, 272
Cornish hen(s):
  in aspic, *231–32*
  with prunes and Xérès vinegar, *384–85*

with tricolored bell peppers and saffron-
    flavored risotto, *222–23*
Côte d'Or (Saulieu), 79–80
courgettes:
  Amélia, gratin de, 425–26
  les farcis de la Provence, 304–5
  oeufs brouillés avec, 145
  sautées, au naturel, 103
  savarin de, 72–73
  zucchini Bramafam, 418–19
  see also ratatouille
court bouillon, *485–86*
Court of the Two Sisters (New Orleans),
    194
Cousins, Ivan, 199
crayfish:
  chicken fricassee with, *167–68*
  in a cream sauce with curry, *366–67*
  gratinéed, *367–68*
cream, 245, *501–2*
cream sauce:
  with curry, shellfish in, *366–67*
  mustard, *481*
  veal cutlets Prince Igor with, *100–101*
  see also tarragon cream sauce; tomato
    cream sauce
crème:
  brésilienne, 460
  au chocolat exprès, 465
crème fraîche, 501, *502*
crème glacée:
  au caramel, 241–42
  à la fraise, 56–57
Creole cooking, 194
crêpes, 227
  batter for, *497*
  filled with almond meringue, *140–41*
cresson, see watercress
croissants, 217–18
croquettes, cheese, *175*
crudités, *319–20*
crustaces, see shellfish
cucumbers:
  poultry strips with, *372–73*
  sautéed, *269*
Curnonsky (Maurice-Edmond Sailland),
    163–70, 180

curry, curried:
    beef, braised, *389–90*
    chicken fricassee with, *379–80*
    meat patties with bell peppers, *405–6*
    pork with pili pili (hot pepper), *408–9*
    shellfish in a cream sauce with, *366–67*
custard(s):
    fruit purée in a, in ramekins, *443–44*
    greengage plum clafoutis, *147–48*
    sauce, "zephyr" apple soufflé with, *440–441*
    see also charlottes; flan(s)
Cutler, Carol, 171, 197, 286

Dannenbaum, Julie, 252
Daudet, Alphonse, 30
Davidson, Susy, 272–73
de Francolini, Marie-José, 148, 295
de Gaulle, Charles, 120, 124, 129, 141, 204, 261
DeLong, Mary-Helene, 252
desserts, 261, *428–69*
    apples fried in batter, *462–63*
    caramel meringue with Chantilly, *431–432*
    Champagne sabayon, *307*
    Christmas log roll, *451–52*
    crêpes filled with almond meringue, *140–41*
    fruit purée in a custard, in ramekins, *443–44*
    greengage plum clafoutis, *147–48*
    Norman flan with apples, *15–16*
    peaches in Sauternes, *286*
    pineapple timbale with red currant sauce, *432–33*
    quick pear sherbet, 287, 288, *293–94*
    rum babas, *463–64*
    semolina pudding in a ring mold with pears—apricot and banana sauce, *437–438*
    snow eggs, or floating islands, *442–43*
    see also cakes; charlottes; chocolate; chocolate cakes; ice cream; mousse; soufflés, dessert; tarts
de Stoop, Wivine, 262
DeVoto, Avis, 188–89, *193–96*

diablotins, les, 166
Dickens, Charles, 45
dinde:
    en fricassée à la niçoise avec riҙ et tomate, 381–82
    au poivre vert sur purée de laitue, filets de, 212–13
    see also turkey
dorade braisée au cidre ou vin blanc, 364–65
Dover sole, *see* sole, sole fillets
Dubosc, Marie-Louise Gabrielle, *see* Le Grand, Marie-Louis Gabrielle Dubosc
duck:
    in aspic, *231–32*
    ballottine with a duck liver stuffing, 152, *156–57*
    in blood sauce, 188–89
    cooked in brown flour, *176–77*
    poultry liver terrine, 55
    stew in wine, with prunes, *382–84*
    with turnips and green olives, *87–88*
duck liver(s):
    in fowl liver pâté with Cognac or bourbon, *331–32*
    in poultry liver terrine, *55–56*
    in ramekins, *330–31*
    stuffing, duck ballottine with a, *156–57*
Dumaine, Alexandre, 79–80
Dussac, Xavier (Du-du), 94

École des Trois Gourmandes, xv, 171, 189, 226–28
écrevisses, see crayfish
eel stew with red wine, 143, *146–47*
egg(s), 338–44
    with bacon and red wine, poached, *71–72*
    a rice dish with ham, leek and, *404*
    short pastry with, *see* short pastry with an egg
    snow eggs, or floating islands, *442–43*
    stuffed tomatoes with bell peppers and, *412–13*
    unmolded zucchini ring with tomato sauce, *72–73*
    whites of, 5, 48, 198
    Zulma's stuffed, *38*

lettuce (*cont.*)
    ring of fish mousse with a pink sauce and, *359–60*
lime:
    juice, veal slices with, *396–97*
    tart, French, *213–14*
Lindbergh, Charles, 76–77
liver, *see* chicken liver(s); duck liver(s)
London, 203
Louise (bistro owner), 130, 133
Lucas, Dionne, 197–202

macadamia nuts, kugelhopf with bacon and, *267–68*
McWilliams, Mr., 200
madeleines de Commercy, les, 122
Mandelieu, 189
Mangelatte, Pierre, xiv
marrons, see chestnut(s)
Martini and Rossi, 6
Mastering the Art of French Cooking, Vol. I (Beck, Bertholle, and Child), xv, 46, 63, 122, 172, 189, 196–204
Mastering the Art of French Cooking, Vol. II (Beck and Child), 59, 204, 207, 216–219, 226, 243–44, 246, 247
mayonnaise, mock (Simca's herb mayonnaise without egg), *474–75*
    beetroot salad with apples and potatoes, *13*
    crudités, *319–20*
    mixed rice salad Provençal, *269–70*
mayonnaise mousseline, green, *475*
meat, *see* beef; beef stews; lamb; lamb, leg of; pork; veal
melons:
    with fresh pepper, *318*
    with prosciutto, *318*
    in white port wine, small, *318*
menus:
    Bramafam, 208, 229, 266, 303
    dinner, 19, 53, 62, 84, 114, 165, 183, 220, 235, 289
    holidays and celebrations, 19, 53, 62, 98, 107
    hunt, 36, 174

lunch, 12, 47, 70, 98, 107, 144, 208, 229, 280, 303
Mère Poulard, La (Mont-Saint-Michel), 111, 113
Michelin tire company, 10
milk, 52, 69
    bread with, *see pain de mie melba*
Mme Lantoine's royal bavarian, 178–79
mocha:
    charlotte, Brazilian, *158–59*
    chocolate coffee snow mousse, *259*
    ice cream, Brazilian, *460*
    snow mousse, *259*
monkfish:
    in French cider or white wine, braised, *364–65*
    mousse, ring of, with green vegetables and a pink sauce, *359–60*
    mousseline, *155*
    quenelles with choux paste and tomato sauce, *355–56*
    stew with red wine, *146–47*
    terrine in aspic, *236–37*
Monseigneur (Paris), 95
"Monsieur le Sous-Prefet aux Champs" (Daudet), 30
Mont-Saint-Michel, 111, 113
Mornay sauce, *480*
Morocco, 260–61
Morue, Berthe, 30
moules:
    avec filets de sole en goujonnettes, sauce crème à l'estragon, 21–22
    en mouclade, 366–67
    see also mussels
Moulin de Mougins (Mougins), 273
mousse:
    chocolate-mocha coffee snow, *259*
    with egg whites only, chocolate Chantilly, *430–31*
    fish, with green vegetables and a pink sauce, ring of, *359–60*
    with fresh fruit, frozen Chantilly, *168–169*
    frozen caramel, *241–42*
    mocha snow, *259*
    orange Cointreau, *50–51*

tomato sauce:
  cold Provençal, *487*
  turkay casserole Niçoise with rice and,
    381–82
  see also tomato cream sauce; tomato
    sauce, express
tomato sauce, express, *486–87*
  chicken or turkey loaf for Susy, made
    from leftovers, *375–76*
  curried meat patties with bell peppers,
    405–6
  fish pâté in a terrine, with shellfish, *323–
    324*
  fish quenelles with choux paste and,
    355–56
  three stuffed omelets, sandwiched and
    gratinéed, *342–43*
  unmolded zucchini ring with, *72–73*
Toulouse, 195
Trenet, Charles, 97
Troisgros, Jean, 219, 248
Troisgros, Paul, 219
  quiche Lorraine of, *221–22*
Troisgros, Pierre, 219, 299
truffles, 276
  chicken casserole with white wine, filled
    with rice, chicken livers and, *377–79*
  mushroom soufflé with, *339–40*
  pasta timbale or ring, with mushrooms,
    smoked salmon and, *353–54*
  Richard Olney's scrambled eggs with,
    338–39
turkey, 202–3
  casserole Niçoise, with rice and tomato
    sauce, *381–82*
  duck ballottine with a duck liver
    stuffing, *156–57*
  fingers with green peppercorns on
    lettuce purée, *212–13*
  loaf for Susy, made from leftovers, *375–
    376*
  poultry pâté in a crust, *328–29*
  in a ratatouille, *410–11*
  strips with cucumbers, *372–73*
  terrine baked in the skin, Cipriani-style,
    256–58

turnips:
  in bouchées, fried grated, *426–27*
  and carrots à la Vichy, *423–24*
  duck with green olives and, *87–88*
Tyree, Lucille, 160, 199, 245–46

United States, Simca in, 46, 122, 189–95,
    242–46, 261–62, 286–94

Valognes, Jean, 135
Varenne, La, 272–73
veal, *396–403*
  in a crust, with Madeira and mustard
    sauce, *397–98*
  cutlets Prince Igor with cream sauce,
    100–101
  with mushrooms, Norman style, *268–69*
  paupiettes, filled with eggplant, *399–400*
  slices with lime juice, *396–97*
  stock, *476–78*
  stuffed breast of, *400–402*
  with tuna sauce, *402*
vegetable(s), 275, *412–27*
  -based consommé, a light, *311–12*
  carrots and turnips à la Vichy, *423–24*
  celery root purée with potatoes, *41–42*
  cold asparagus with gribiche sauce, *115*
  cooking methods for, *499–500*
  Costa's eggplant gratiné, Greek method
    (with a cream sauce), *422–23*
  crudités, *319–20*
  flans in ramekins, *414–15*
  fried grated turnips in bouchées, *426–27*
  grated potatoes with blue cheese, *419–
    420*
  grated zucchini, cooked with cream and
    shallots, *418–19*
  gratinéed eggplant and tomatoes, *413–
    414*
  gratinéed zucchini Amelia, *425–26*
  green, ring of fish mousse with a pink
    sauce and, *359–60*
  green fennel purée with sweet peas,
    421–22
  new potato gratin with cream, *420–21*
  pork stew with beer and, *109–10*